Dialectic

Dialectic

The Pulse of Freedom

ROY BHASKAR

VERSO

London · New York

First published by Verso 1993
© Roy Bhaskar 1993
All rights reserved

Verso
UK: 6 Meard Street, London W1V 3HR
USA: 29 West 35th Street, New York, NY 10001-2291

Verso is the imprint of New Left Books

ISBN 0-86091-368-6
ISBN 0-86091-583-2 (pbk)

British Library Cataloguing in Publication Data
A catalogue record for this book is available from the British Library

Library of Congress Cataloging-in-Publication Data
A catalogue record for this book is available from the Library of Congress

Typeset by MHL Typesetting, Coventry
Printed and bound in Great Britain by
Biddles Ltd, Guildford and King's Lynn

FOR SHEILA

Contents

CONTENTS

CONTENTS

Let this be said, then; and also that, as it seems, whether one is or is not, both itself and the others, both to themselves and to each other, all in every way both are and are not and appear and do not appear. Very true.

PLATO

This struggle [between the infinite and the finite] is a conflict defined not by the indifference of the two sides in their distinction, but by their being bound together in one unity. I am not one of the fighters locked in battle, but both, and I am the struggle itself. I am fire and water ...

HEGEL

In its mystified form, the dialectic became the fashion in Germany because it seemed to transfigure and glorify what exists. In its rational form it is a scandal and abomination to the bourgeoisie and their doctrinaire spokesmen, because it includes in its understanding of what exists a simultaneous recognition of its negative, its inevitable destruction; because it regards every historically developed form as being in a fluid state; in motion, and therefore grasps its transient aspect as well, and because it does not let itself be impressed by anything, being in its very essence critical and revolutionary.

MARX

Preface

This book is the site of an encounter between a dialectically developed critical realism and Hegelian and Hegelian-inspired dialectic in the context of the multiple crises besetting humanity, rationality, the social (and, to an extent, the natural) sciences, Marxism and socialism. While it is, on the whole, a preservative generalization and enrichment of hitherto existing critical realism, it is a non-preservative sublation of Hegelian dialectic. The terms of the critical realist dialectic are non-identity, negativity, totality and transformative praxis or agency, in comparison with the Hegelian trio of identity, negativity and totality. However, my accounts of negativity and of totality are radically different from Hegel's. These four terms correspond to four moments or levels of development of the new system of dialectical critical realism and may, if one likes, be very loosely aligned with the four chapters of the work. *Dialectic* extends and deepens critical realism's characteristic concerns with ontology, existence and causality, science, social science and emancipation into (obviously) the realms of negativity and totality, but also the fields of reference and truth, spatio-temporality, tense and process, the logic of dialectical universalizability and on to the plane of ethics, where I articulate a combination of moral realism and ethical naturalism, which allows me to make the transition from the form of judgements to the content of a freely flourishing society. Moreover, the arguments I employ in this book for a dialecticized transcendental realism and critical naturalism can all be derived from positions which do not already presuppose (although they may entail — in some cases, transformed) scientific practices. *Dialectic* necessarily incorporates an exercise in the problem resolution, critical diagnosis and explanation of causally efficacious irrealist philosophies. For it is my contention that, properly conceived, critical realism and dialectic mutually presuppose one another. In addition to considering dialectic historically and systematically, I have treated it, amongst a variety of other modes, as the logic of argument, the method of immanent critique, the dynamic of conflict, the node of change and the axiology of freedom. All my arguments converge on a position which has very radical implications. Dialectic is essentially to do with the absenting of constraints on absenting absences or ills (which may also be regarded as constraints). This presupposes, inter alia, the critique of ontological monovalence, or a purely positive account of reality, which I show to be totally flawed. Apart from what I have said here, I would make only the rather immodest claim that this is the only system of dialectical philosophy I know to sustain an adequate account of negativity and, a fortiori, since this is the linchpin of all dialectics, I hope of dialectic itself.

I must acknowledge my debt to Sheila Duncan-Bruce, to whom this book is dedicated, and whose tragic loss occurred during its writing. Second, I must thank Colin Robinson, amongst others, at Verso, for his friendship and support during a difficult time, for his patience and the prompt publication of the book. Third, I must yet again express my deep gratitude to Sue Kelly for absolutely invaluable secretarial assistance. I must also acknowledge my appreciation of Justin Dyer's meticulous copy-editing. Next I owe an immense and immeasurable debt to the growing world-wide and interdisciplinary band of critical realists and those interested in it for stimulation, debate and encouragement. Some names picked almost at random must stand in for a comprehensive list that would be impossible to compile: Michael Sprinker, Kurt Bayertz, Joe Urbas, Alan Chalmers, Doreen Massey, Tony Lawson, Gerry Webster, Trevor Pateman, Ed Soja, Margaret FitzSimmons, Terry Eagleton, Chris Norris, Charlie Smith, Peter Manicas, Mario Bunge, Helena Kozakiewicz, Veronique Havalange, Noam Chomsky, Roy Edgley, Tom Bottomore, Charles Taylor, Anita Craig, Sue Clegg, Andrew Sayer, John Lovering, Ülker Seymen, Yilmaz Öner, Jan van Dijk, Tomás Ibáñez, Björn Wittrock, Peter Wagner, Erik Wright, Barry Barnes, Margaret Archer, Terry Lovell, David Will, Guglielmo Carchedi, Bertell Ollman, John Searle, Jeffrey Isaac, Norman Geras, Gregor McLennan, Rom Harré, Gregory Elliott, Rajani Kanth. ... I stress again that this is a sample not a list and I am only too conscious of the contributions of those omitted. The new geographers within this network played a decisive role in the formative process of this book, as did those who persuaded me to take post-structuralism more seriously. The influence of both groups will be felt. Finally I would like to offer my warmest appreciation to those many, many friends whose solidarity has nurtured and sustained me during the writing of this text. Of these I can only specifically mention here a few — Ted

Benton, Andrew Collier, Androulla Karaviotis, Judit Kiss, William
Outhwaite, Kate Soper and, above all, Hilary Wainwright.

ROY BHASKAR
May 1993

Abbreviations

Abbreviations of Works by the Author

RTS2: *A Realist Theory of Science*, 2nd edn, Harvester Press, Brighton 1978 (Harvester-Wheatsheaf, 1989) (1st edn, Leeds Books, Leeds 1975)

PON2: *The Possibility of Naturalism* 2nd edn, Harvester-Wheatsheaf, Hemel Hempstead 1989 (1st edn, Harvester Press, Brighton 1979)

SRHE: *Scientific Realism and Human Emancipation*, Verso, London 1986

RR: *Reclaiming Reality*, Verso, London 1989

PIF: *Philosophy and the Idea of Freedom*, Basil Blackwell, Oxford 1991

N.B.: 'C' stands for Chapter throughout the book.

Abbreviations of Terms

1M   = First Moment
2E   = Second Edge
3L   = Third Level
4D   = Fourth Dimension
EA   = Extrinsic Aspect
IA   = Intrinsic Aspect
ID   = Intransitive Dimension
TD   = Transitive Dimension
TMSA = Transformational Model of Social Activity
T/P   = Theory/Practice

N.B.: These terms, which are used throughout the book, are explained in the text and the Glossary.

Introduction: Critical Realism, Hegelian Dialectic and the Problems of Philosophy — Preliminary Considerations

§ 1 Objectives of the Book

What is developed in this work is neither Hegelian dialectic nor, to my knowledge, any other pre-existing form of dialectic, but a critical realist dialectic. A major point of reference throughout this book will certainly be Hegelian dialectic, and in the course of it I hope to realize Marx's unconsummated desire 'to make accessible to the ordinary human intelligence' — though it will take more than two or three printers' sheets — 'what is *rational* in the method which Hegel discovered and at the same mystified',[1] as well as to clarify the exact relation between Marx's own dialectic and Hegel's one. But I will be discussing a variety of other dialectical (and anti-dialectical) modes, including Aristotelian dialectic, Kantian dialectic and Derridean deconstruction.

A work of this kind — a dialectical critique of purely analytical reason — can claim no more — or less — than dialectical consistency. For the moment this may be exemplified by what I have elsewhere characterized as developmental consistency[2] — the kind of consistency shown by connected theories in an ongoing research programme in science; or in nature by the development of a tadpole into a frog or an acorn into an oak — a consistency redeemable only in the course of, and at the end of, the day. Moreover, this book makes no claim to completeness — and that for immanent dialectical reasons too. Indeed it stands in the closest possible connection to the texts that will immediately follow it: *Hume, Kant, Hegel, Marx* will elaborate the central historical argument of the book and provide a more detailed critical hermeneutics of those four thinkers, *Plato Etcetera* will resume the critical diagnosis and metacritique of the western philosophical tradition sketched in this study, and *Dialectical Social Theory* will engage at a more concrete level with the implications of the book's argument for social theory, geography and history.

This book has as its main objectives:

1. the dialectical enrichment and deepening of critical realism —
   understood as consisting of transcendental realism as a general
   theory of science and critical naturalism as a special theory of
   social science (which includes the emancipatory axiology entailed
   by the theory of explanatory critique);
2. the development of a general theory of dialectic — or better, a
   dialectic — of which the Hegelian one can be seen as an
   important, but limited and highly questionable, special case; and
   one which will moreover be capable of sustaining the development of a general metatheory for the social sciences, on the basis
   of which they will be capable of functioning as agencies of human
   self-emancipation;
3. the outline of the elements of a totalizing critique of western
   philosophy, in its various (including hitherto dialectical) forms,
   including a micro sketch of certain nodal moments in the history
   of dialectical philosophy, capable, inter alia, of casting light on
   the contemporary crisis of socialism.

I shall contend that these objectives are intimately related, and
especially that there are direct and immediate connections between
the critical realist development of dialectical motifs and themes and
the resolution of the problems, sublation of the problematics and
explanation of the problem-fields of contemporary philosophy. To
put this in a nutshell, most philosophical aporiai derive from taking
an insufficiently non-anthropocentric, differentiated, stratified,
dynamic, holistic (concrete) or agentive (practical) view of things.
More generally, philosophy's current anthropomorphizing, actualizing, monovalent and detotalizing ontology acts, I shall argue, as a
block on the development of the social sciences and projects of
human emancipation — for this ontology currently informs much of
their practice. For the transformation of this state of affairs dialectical
critical realism — i.e. the development of dialectic in its critical realist
form — is a necessary but not a sufficient condition. Philosophy, for
its part, being out of joint with reality, is necessarily aporetic. We
shall see in C3 how dialectical critical realism can begin to remedy
this, but I hope the import of these remarks will soon be plain. This
book represents an attempt to synthesize what I take to be the most
fruitful aspects of the dialectical tradition (or traditions), most of
which have come down to us through the mediation of Hegel, with
the contemporary critical realist research programme — to, I think,
their mutual advantage. But the structure of the resulting dialectic is

very different from the Hegelian one. At the beginning, in this new dialectic, there is non-identity — at the end, open unfinished totality. In between, irreducible material structure and heteronomy, deep negativity and emergent spatio-temporality. In this work, I want to show that it is possible to think and act dialectically without necessarily being a Hegelian — or, if you prefer, vice versa.

§ 2 Dialectic: An Initial Orientation

In its most general sense, dialectic has come to signify any more or less intricate process of conceptual or social (and sometimes even natural) conflict, interconnection and change, in which the generation, interpenetration and clash of oppositions, leading to their transcendence in a fuller or more adequate mode of thought or form of life (or being), plays a key role. But, as we shall see, dialectical processes and configurations are not always sublatory (i.e. supersessive), let alone preservative. Nor are they necessarily characterized by opposition or antagonism, rather than mere connection, separation or juxtaposition. Nor, finally, are they invariably, or even typically, triadic in form. To what may such processes, to the extent that they occur, be applied? Obviously to being, in which case we may talk about *ontological dialectics*, or dialectical ontologies which may operate at different levels. Then obviously to our thinking about reality — *epistemological dialectics*; and insofar as knowledge circulates in and/or out of what it is about — *relational dialectics*. Equally obviously to our practice — *practical dialectics*. Clearly, within these generic categories a vast variety of distinctions can be made, specifying more concrete or roughly parallel (e.g. ethical, aesthetic) dialectics. Equally clearly, dialectical processes may occur in our thinking about our thinking about reality, e.g. in the philosophy of science, so that one may talk of a meta-epistemological dialectic, and so on recursively. For critical realism all dialectics, insofar as they occur, are also ontological dialectics, though with respect to any, for example, epistemic investigation we may and perhaps must think of a distinct ontic field (into which the epistemological investigation may itself be reflexively incorporated). Similarly, all social dialectics are also practical dialectics, even though in the case of, say, structural analysis one may and perhaps must abstract from human agency. In respect of science, ontological, epistemological and the class of meta-epistemological dialectics may be mapped onto what I have called the intransitive, transitive and metacritical dimensions.[3] (For critical realism, relational dialectics, however thorough-going, can never abolish the existential intransitivity of the relata.) All these terms have a subject/topic ambiguity. Thus one might hold epistemological dialectics to be engaged with the dialectic of epistemology rather than the dialectic of what it is about, e.g. science. In this book I will be concerned with both kinds of dialectics, the former belonging to what I will style *meta-critical dialectics*, which includes the relations between the two kinds.

Like Hegel, I take dialectic to be a logic of content and not just form. And, like him, I take this to centre on the norms of truth and freedom (mediated in practice by wisdom). That is, I take both to have a certain dynamic to them, a dynamic which I hope to describe. More fully I will show that truth, for example, must be understood as grounded, dynamic, totalizing and context-sensitive, corresponding to the four moments of the critical realist dialectic that I shall shortly outline. But instead of talking immediately of truth and freedom, and respecting the geo-historical specificity of both, I will talk about knowledge as specific kinds of beliefs (of different types) and of emancipation from specific kinds of constraints. To the extent that I abstract from content in the earlier portions of this book, particularly in the exposition of Hegelian dialectic, this is for the sake of didactic clarity alone.

§ 3 Negation

In previous works I have shown how science itself presupposes a critical realist ontology of the world as structured, differentiated and changing. And I have argued that the chief metaphilosophical error in prevailing accounts of science is the analysis, definition or explication of statements about being in terms of statements about our knowledge of being, the reduction of ontology to epistemology which I have termed the *'epistemic fallacy'*.[4] As ontology is in fact irreducible to epistemology, this functions merely to cover the generation of an implicit ontology, on which the domain of the real is reduced to the domain of the actual (actualism) which is then anthroprocentrically identified with or in terms of sense-experience or some other human attribute. Operating hand-in-hand with this overt collapse, engendered or masked by the epistemic fallacy, is its practical counterpart, the ideology of the compulsive determination of knowledge by being — for instance, in the guise of reified facts or hypostatized ideas — in what I have characterized as the 'ontic fallacy'.[5] The epistemic fallacy can be traced back to Parmenides.

But Parmenides also bequeathed another legacy to philosophy: the generation of a purely positive, complementing a purely actual, notion of reality, in what I am going to nominate the doctrine of *ontological monovalence*. In this study I aim to revindicate negativity. Indeed, by the time we are through, I would like the reader to see the positive as a tiny, but important, ripple on the surface of a sea of negativity. In particular, I want to argue for the importance of the concepts of what I am going to call 'real negation', 'transformative negation' and 'radical negation'. Of these the most basic is real negation. Its primary meaning is real determinate absence or non-being (i.e. including non-existence). It may denote an absence, for example, from consciousness (e.g. the unknown, the tacit, the unconscious), and/or of an entity, property or attribute (e.g. the spaces in a text) in some determinate space-time region, e.g. in virtue of distanciation or mediation, death or demise, or simple non-existence. It connotes, inter alia, the hidden, the empty, the outside; desire, lack and need. It is real negation which, as we shall see, drives the Hegelian dialectic on, and it is our *omissive critique* of Hegel — his failure to sustain certain crucial distinctions and categories (including in the end that of absence itself) — that must drive the dialectic past and beyond him. But real negation also connotes a process of mediating, distancing or absenting, i.e. it has a systematic process/product bivalency or homonymy. In fact, as we shall see in the next chapter, it also signifies both process-in-product and product-in-process, so that it has a fourfold polysemy. How could one argue for the importance of real negation in, for example, science? Writings — books, research papers, experimental records — provide striking examples of it. Consider a book in a library. It typically involves an absent (and possibly dead) author, an absent reception necessary for its presence in the library, and absences — spaces inside and in between sequences of marks — necessary for its intelligibility, its readability. Again experimental activity involves a real demediation of nature, preventing or absenting a state of affairs that would otherwise have occurred, so as to enable us to identify a generative mechanism or complex free from outside influence or with such interference held constant. These may, if one likes, be taken as transcendental deductions of the presence of real negation in science, as conditions of its possibility. Real negation — think of empty spaces and absent x's where x stands in principle for any entity or feature. Of course what is absent or void at or from one level, region or perspective may be present at another. This is what I shall refer to as the 'duality of absence'.

Transformative negation refers to the transformation of some thing, property or state of affairs. Such a transformation may be essential or inessential, total or partial, endogenously and/or exogenously effected. Like real negation it has a process/product bipolarity: it can refer to the outcome or the means whereby it is brought about. All cases of transformative negation are also cases of real negation but the converse is not the case. They all involve the cessation or absenting of a pre-existing entity or state. A special, and highly important, case of transformative negation is *radical negation*, which involves the auto-subversion, transformation or overcoming of a being or condition. It is, of course, important in the human domain to distinguish negating processes from self-negating processes and self-negating from self-consciously negating processes. All these species of negation — real, transformative and radical — have a systematic structural/empirical — or better, real/actual — ambiguity which I shall discuss in due course. Transformative negation, especially of the radical kind, is what Hegelians call 'determinate negation', but this is a misnomer — for real ≥ transformative ≥ radical negation may all be more or less determinate — that is, they may be fully determinate (think of the negation of the raw material in a finished automobile) or indeterminate in various degrees; or they may be 'fuzzy', duplicitous or otherwise other than determinate. In Hegelian dialectic real, transformative, radical and determinate negation are all identified, resulting in a linear self-generating process, e.g. of the unfolding of the concept in the *Logics*, but it is important to keep them distinct and see their identification as an important but limiting case.

If real negation is the most all-encompassing concept — extending from non-existence to metacritique — it is in transformative negation that the key to social dialectics lies. Indeed its schema is given by the transformational model of social activity which I have elaborated elsewhere and which will be suitably dialecticized and generalized in C2. Radical negation, for its part, is obviously the pivotal concept in self-emancipation and this connects with 'radical' in a more familiar sense. Moreover, to the extent that we are dealing with a self-contained totality, all transformative negation, that is to say change, will tend to occur as a result of or take the form of radical negation(s), as is arguably the case with global interdependence today.[6] The orthodox Platonic analysis of negation and change in terms of difference not only conflates substantial with formal relations[7] (change is paradigmatically substantial) but also overlooks the fact that differentiation typically presupposes change. This is not to deny that there is equally a case for a category of difference, e.g. established by distinct emergent domains or by sheer alterity or otherness (that is, real determinate other-being), not analysable in terms of change, i.e. without recourse to a unitary origin, a case forcibly prosecuted by Derrida. In rather the same way the implicit supposition behind the doctrine of ontological monovalence is that any instance of real negation can be analysed in purely positive terms. But Pierre's absence from the café doesn't *mean* the same as his presence at home (although the latter entails the former — which is equally entailed by his death) any more than it means the same as Jean's occupying his customary place.*

The chief result of ontological monovalence in mainstream philosophy is to erase the contingency of existential questions and to despatialize and detemporalize (accounts of) being. I shall be concerned with a variety of other modes of negation besides the ones I have already referred to. One may be briefly mentioned here — *subject negation*. This refers primarily to a subject in the process of formation or dissolution (e.g. in Hegelian logic passing over into its 'predicate'). As such it is clearly a variant of transformative negation, but I am going to extend its meaning to cover cases of non-transformative and non-trivially transformative real negation (e.g. non-existence and simple space-time distanciation without any other significant change) and counterpose it polemically to the propositional and predicate negations of standard logic. For it will be vital to my vindication of negativity that one can refer to absence, including non-existence; or, if one prefers to put it this way, that reference is not, contrary to the tradition from Plato to Frege, tied to positive existence. This, I will show in C2. Non-being, within zero-level being, exists and is present everywhere.

---

* In an earlier publication in which I introduced the terms real and radical negation, their definitions were transposed.[8] I now call the notion of absence, including non-existence, 'real negation' because, as I have just argued, it is the primary concept and embraces that of transformative negation including self-negation. Moreover, conceptually, it extends our ontology synchronically, irrespective of over what space-time span the indefinite synchronic is defined, so that it does not depend essentially upon process. I should also mention that in my exposition of what I now call real negation I confused the epistemological question of our criteria for the reality of absence with the ontological question of whether, for example, a thing is, quite independently of us, absent (distanciated or non-existent), not there. I also failed to notice that our criteria for ascribing reality to absences need not be causal, but can be perceptual — as in Sartre's example,[9] where I see Pierre's absence from the café (when I am expecting to meet him), or as in the case of simple non-existential proofs in science, which will be discussed in C2. This was because I was tacitly thinking of non-being (or more generally absence) as *necessarily* involving depth, thus overlooking the simplest species, where it involves merely spatio-temporal distance. Anthony Giddens has given some currency to the term 'distanciation'.[10] However, it seems to me that in his work it sometimes means (a) stretching (and thereby extending presence or embedding) and sometimes simply (b) distancing (and thereby absenting and possibly disembedding). I shall make use of this term, and exploit this duality of meaning to connote the play of absence and presence, e.g. in the conceptual distanciation that occurs in analogical, metaphorial or metonymic work in the transitive process of science, which executes a crucial role in the epistemological dialectic.

I shall also be occupied with negativity and negation in many other senses of the verb to 'negate', including 'deny', 'reject', 'contradict', 'oppose', 'exclude', 'marginalize', 'denigrate', 'erase', 'separate', 'split', 'sunder', 'cancel', 'annul', 'destroy', 'criticize' and 'condemn', and with their interconnections. But my primary emphasis will be on the categories of real, transformative and radical negation of determinate and indeterminate kinds. One other preliminary matter before I pass on. Real determinate negation, absence or non-being, is not equivalent to Hegel's nothing, which entirely lacks determinacy, and any sort of depth. Negativity, although it is the dynamic of Hegel's system and is in fact in the guise of contradiction greatly exaggerated by Hegel, is never developed or even simply retained — it is always cancelled and positivity restored. Seeing this is one of the merits of the young Hegelians. One of the few philosophers to pay serious attention to *categories* of negativity is Sartre, but it should be said straight away that my real negation is not equivalent to Sartrian nothingness but more to his *négatité*; though, as I have defined it, it is not intrinsically related to human activity.

§ 4 Four Degrees of Critical Realism

More generally, in this work, I shall be showing how critical realism, hitherto focusing — in what I shall call its first or prime moment (which I shall abbreviate to 1M) — on the concepts of structure, differentiation, change, alterity (as in the transitive/intransitive distinction — epistemic/ontic non-identity within ontology), trans-factual efficacy, emergence, openness, etc., must be meshed with the characteristically dialectical categories, arguments, themes and pabula expressed in the ideas of negation, negativity, becoming, process, finitude, contradiction, development (which need not be progressive and may just be regarded as directional change including regression, retrogression and decay, in a thing or kind to at the limit fragmentation, chaos and/or collapse), spatiality, temporality, mediation, reciprocity and many more — including such figures as the hiatus, chiasmus and pause — at what I will call a second edge (abbreviated to 2E) of development. 1M suffices for, e.g., an adequate account of science which abstracts from space, time and the process of change, which posits 'principles of difference' or 'metaphysical inertia'. At 2E, which is the narrowly dialectical moment in a four-sided dialectic, the very principles of indifference are called into question and difference, and we have 'metaphysical (neg)entropy'. This is the moment of cosmology, of human geo-history, of personal biography, laborious or routinized work but also of joyful or idle play. At a third level (abbreviated to 3L) of development we have the characteristically totalizing motifs of totality, reflexivity (which is its inwardized form), concrete universality and what I will call 'concrete utopianism', subjectivity and objectivity, autonomy (practico-epistemological duality, consistency and coherence), reason and rationality including phronesis or practical wisdom, and the unity of theory and practice. This is at once the inner truth or pulse of things and the spot from which we must act, the axiological moment and (if there is such) metaphysical alethia. I will postpone thematizing it until after a consideration of the (very different) Hegelian totality. But 3L is not the end of the matter. A fourth dimension (4D) is required — for the critical realist totality is radically open. So we must return to practice. But this is not as a Nietzschean forgetting, but as active and reflexive engagement within the world in which we seek to achieve the unity of theory and practice in *practice*. Each level in this dialectic is preservative. 4D presupposes 3L presupposes 2E presupposes 1M. (This does *not* mean that every category at 2E is instantiated in some employment of a 3L category. Thus one can have dialectical connection without contradiction.) We are left with non-identity, structure, negativity, finitude, essentially transformative change, holistic causality and phronesis at the end — in agency. But agency is, of course, in a sense already there at the outset in the phenomenologicality of science, so we can say, if we like, that the end is implicit in the beginning,* but if we go along with this rather Hegelian way of speaking, we must see the agency as a *radically transformed transformative praxis*, oriented to rationally groundable projects — ultimately flourishing in freedom.

What is the characteristic error at 3L which stands to 2E and 1M as ontological monovalence and actualism respectively do? It consists in ontological extensionalism — or what could also be called ontological partiality or 'externalism', where external is to be taken in the sense

---

* Thus I have previously argued that ontological realism (in the intransitive dimension) is consistent with and necessitated by epistemological relativism (in the transitive, geo-historical process of science), which is in turn consistent with and practically entailed by judgemental rationality (in the axiologically irreducible, intrinsic aspect of, or normative moment in, science).[11] Even more simply, one might cite the ontological arguments of transcendental realism as exemplifying 1M; the meta-sociology of the transformational model of social activity (which is also the logic of the transitive dimension of science) as prefiguring 2E; the naturalistic ethics entailed, or at least facilitated, by the theory of explanatory critique as intimating 3L; and the emancipatory axiology so situated as indicating 4D. But, as we shall see, *this* historical sublation is not entirely preservative insofar as the moments of critical realism are affected by its dialectical deepening which is also a cross-fertilization.

of the denial of internal relationality. A relation aRb is internal if and only if a would not be what it is *essentially* unless it were related to b in the way that it is. Partiality is, of course, closely related to separability, which goes back to Aristotle's definition of substance taken up in crucial respects by Descartes, and in Aristotle derived perhaps ultimately from the Platonic theory of predication. The canonical, and also extreme, version of ontological extensionalism is provided by Hume's famous dictum that things 'seem conjoined but never connected'.* (This is an extreme formulation because it denies even necessary relationships between externally related things.) Besides denying internal relations, other modes of extensionalizing thought and/or practice consist in hypostatizing the moments or aspects of a totality, treating space-time as independent of the system of material things, conceiving morality as independent of the network of social relations (and in particular denying a fact to value and theory to practice link), failing to recognize (and/or being indifferent to) identities-in-differences or unities-in-diversities and/or differences-in-identity or diversities-in-unity, abstracting from specifying differentiations, e.g. by subsuming a particular under a universal without mediation, failing to see the tri-unity of subjectivity, inter-subjectivity and objectivity (e.g. within language or experience) but then equally failing to articulate this tri-unity as formed within an always already existing social world into which we are 'thrown' and as occurring only within an over-reaching material objectivity, of which the social world is a contingent, emergent but cosmically ephemeral outcome. Let us just consider for a moment the thought — reality relationship. A philosophical ontology can be detotalizing or partial in at least four ways: (1) it can objectivize reality, e.g. by extruding thought from it; (2) it can subjectivize reality, e.g. by failing to locate thought within a non-ideational and mediated reality encompassing it; (3) it can split reality, e.g. on eidetic/sensual (Platonic), phenomenal/noumenal (Kantian), or social/physical (hermeneutical) lines; and/or (4) it can adopt some combination of these expedients. Let us take a concrete case — that of Humean empiricism, dominant in mid-twentieth-century philosophical, scientific and social thought and present in that of Kant, Hegel and much post-Nietzschean post-structuralism. We can see its characteristic error at 1M to lie in anthropomorphizing and actualizing reality, at 2E that of positivizing and deprocessualizing (de-spatio-temporalizing) it, at 3L that of subjectivizing it and at 4D, in a characteristic and necessary

---

* 'All events seem entirely loose and separate. One event follows another, but we can never observe any tie between them. They seem conjoined but never connected.'[12]

inversion,[13] reifying and fetishizing that part of it which is the product of human practices. If we write d_r as a domain of the real, d_a as the domain of the actual, d_+ as the domain of the positive, d_s as the domain of the subjective, empiricism can thus be seen to rest on an illicit generalization of the special case $d_r \geq d_a \geq d_+ \geq d_s \geq d_e$ where the latter is identified in terms of human experience, and where human sense-experience is conceived as a product or function of reified facts, i.e. $d_e = d_f$. More generally I shall be arguing that western philosophy, including most dialectical and specifically Hegelian thought, is characterized by a disemancipatory anthropo-centricism/morphism, marked by ontological actualism, mono-valence, extensionalism, subjectivism (in its post-Cartesian period) and de-agentification (a denegation of human agency).

These levels of deepening of critical realism should not be hypostatized. What they specify are co-present and systematically 'intermingle' in reality. Furthermore, although, as in Hegel, it is the second moment — of negativity — that is the narrowly dialectical one, each of the others and the whole are implied in it as a system. Moreover, there are dialectics specific to each level. Thus the dialectics of 1M are typically dialectics of stratification and superstructure-formation or superstructuration, including emerg-ence. The typical dialectical figures here are what I shall call the *dialectical comment*, which I shall write as dc', and *dialectical reason* (dr'), which I shall explicate in relation to Hegelian dialectic. I shall later link these figures to a characteristic pattern of problem-generation, resolution and critique in science and philosophy and to the theme of *theory/practice inconsistency*, which I shall see as essential to dialectic generally and pivotal to the emancipatory spiral of transformist politics and (counter-)ideology. Dialectical reason includes, in metacritical analysis, displaying the common or dialec-tical grounds (dg') of apparently opposed but mutually complicit dialectical counterparts or contraries, as, I shall argue, in the Kantian opposition between knowledge and faith, or more generally between anthroporealism and transcendent — which I shall rigorously differentiate from transcendental — realism, or between empiricism and idealism. This includes the logic of what Derrida has called 'supplementarity',[14] and what Freud called 'compromise formation'. Metacritical dialectical reason also isolates the duplicities and dialectical paralogisms generated by philosophies of identity including Hegel's own. At 2E the dialectics are characteristically dialectics of change, including interchange (reversal), and transition. Determinate transformative negation, though it is present in some guise in all dialectics, comes to the fore here, but the most distinctive figure at 2E is *dialectical process* (dp') — as when, for instance, we are incessantly forced to revise our descriptive, taxonomic and explanatory vocabularies in the light of unexpected, and possibly recursive, epistemic and/or ontic change.

At 3L the characteristic figure is dialectical totality (dt'), as when separated phenomena come to be seen as aspects of a unified (or dis-unified) whole. Hermeneutics provides a good initial heuristic for understanding what it is to think in this dialectical mode. In a painting it is not only that the parts cannot be understood except in relation to the whole and vice versa but — and this is the clue to Hegelian totality — they mutually 'infect' each other — the whole is in the part, as my body is in my writing hand. This is what Althusser meant by 'expressive totality',[15] though he vastly underestimated the extent to which Marx not just in his exploratory work but also in his systematic writings used, in Pareto's graphic image, words 'like bats'.[16] Nor can we say that this was necessarily wrong — it is merely a particular kind of totality. Montage, and pastiche generally, and entities like the British Working Class in February 1992, provide examples of very different sorts of totalities. Let me give a concrete example of a 3L dialectic — the Lefebvrean dialectic of centre and periphery,[17] where this is to be understood partially literally in terms of the globalization of capitalism and culture and partially as a metaphor for the dialectic of power and resource flows between an increasingly integrated and homogenized 'centre' and an increasingly marginalized and fragmented periphery, in the 'south', in the 'north' and in the 'south-in-the-north' — and in the physical, social and psychic peripheralizations therein. At 4D the dominant pivotal figure is dialectical *praxis*, which I shall write as $d\phi$. Relating it to the immediately preceding example, the dialectic here calls for the retotalization of the periphery in the mutual recognitions of identities-in-difference and unity-in-diversity, mediated therefore by mutual recognition of differential (personal, social, local, etc.) identities and involving a degree of recentrification (psychic, social, local and global) in a transformed transformative praxis for the retotalization of the human race. This would involve a non-preservative *dialectical sublation* (ds') of the pre-existing state of affairs.

Sublations, generally, as species of determinate transformative negations, may be totally, essentially or partially preservative. Within and outside these categories further important discriminations may be made, e.g. a transformative negation may preserve what is held to be of value in, even though it is not essential to, the sublated social form. But sublations are not, of course, the only *dialectical result* (dr^0). Results include stand-offs, the mutual undoing of the contending parties, the preservation of the status quo ante, retrogression and many other outcomes besides sublation. Nor does it make sense to talk of an *Aufhebung* in many types of what may be properly called dialectics — e.g. in social life, of *Verstehen* (per se), of structure, process and agency, of presence and absence or of embedding and disembedding in space and time and from space in time and vice versa, or of overlapping, intersecting or disjoint spatio-temporalities. These involve polarities or more complex figures that may figure in sublations or generally outcomes, but, as part of the transcendental parameters of any conceivable social life, are not themselves sublatable, or so it would seem reasonable to suppose. Of course a dialectical outcome or result, of any of these characteristic modes, is only spatio-temporary; the potential starting point for a new round of real transformative negation.

By the end of this chapter the very different topologies of the critical realist and Hegelian dialectics will become apparent. But it should perhaps be said here and now, if it is not already obvious, that, although I will show their connections, my 1M, 2E and 3L do not correspond to the Hegelian moments of understanding, dialectic or negative reason and speculative or positive reason shortly to be discussed. They encompass different types of dialectic, within each of which (dialectical) negativity has a role to play; and the movement or dialectic of critical realism as a whole (which, of course, includes 4D), to be articulated fully in the chapters to come, traverses and envelops all these phases or levels. Nor do the moments of dialectical critical realism match the tetrapolity of analytical, dialectical, totalizing and practical reasoning. For a start, 4D consists not in practical reasoning but in (reasonable) practice — not the same thing at all. Moreover, critical realist dialectical reasoning comprises all these modes of reasoning and practice and their unity. In particular there is a dialectic of dialectical and analytical (or formal) reasoning in the course of which discourse moves in and out of the domain of formal reasoning, be it of a deductive or, for example, inductive type, in which meanings and values remain fixed (or stable in their indeterminacy), which is of great importance in science, philosophy and everyday life. Furthermore, dialectical critical realism is dialogical — discursive, inter-subjective through and through. This will become plain when I discuss the communicative dimension of what I have called the 'social cube' (which is really a space-time cubic stretch or flow) in C2.9. In this way critical realist dialectic incorporates an important range of historical connotations to the word, to be introduced in §6 and thematized in C2, which Hegelian dialectic, rooted in a post-Cartesian monological philosophy of consciousness, however aware of its social matrix, lets slip — a point that Habermas has not been slow to stress.[18]

§ 5 Prima Facie Objections to Critical Realism

There is one other preliminary matter that should be dealt with here before I turn to Hegelian dialectic. It may be contended that critical realism is, or began as, a philosophy of — and *for* — science, even if it is conceded that it is not a scientistic philosophy.[19] How then can I treat of theory generally, or by what right do I identify it as a subset of the domain of the real, or indeed envelop in my critique philosophies — including epistemologies — which do not purport to be about science? Let us consider the last objection first. There is an important grain of truth here. There is indeed a big difference between science and everyday knowledge, which the philosophical tradition has — at least in its post-Lockian period — tended to conflate or otherwise obscure, the significance of which I will bring out anon. But I think, and would like to show, that science provides a hidden 'analogical grammar'[20] for the metacritical analysis of philosophies — at any rate at 1M. (At 2M, 3L and 4D the wider social context is more important, though we should never underestimate the power buried in the human psyche-soma.) Correspondingly, transposing philosophical theses of an epistemological kind into their presuppositions about and implications for science can be extraordinarily illuminating. In particular it affects a *concretization* (itself a dialectical development) of these, which makes it easier to identify exactly what their insights, aporiai, tensions and effects are. A parallel recasting of ethical positions and arguments into social theoretic positions can be equally illuminating. To turn to the first objection now, it is the case that the transcendental arguments used to establish critical realism were in the first instance thrown up by existing reflections on (theories of) science, of which they constituted an immanent critique. But in C3 I intend also to derive (dialectical) transcendental realism both without recourse to science and by taking up the challenge of Heideggerian existential phenomenology. There I will consider science precisely as engaged concernful human activity with *Dasein* exploring its *Umwelt* with its equipment (language, pre-existing, yet not necessarily articulated, knowledge and tools), constituting a 'referential totality' ready-to-hand; that is, I will in effect treat science as an *existential* (employing categories). I will also consider the extent to which dialectical transcendental, more generally critical, realism can be generated by reflection on the presuppositions of the pathology of everyday life.

Finally, I should make it explicit that I do not see science as a supreme or overriding value, but only as one among others to be balanced (in a balance that cannot be wholly judged by science) in ergonic, emancipatory and eudaimonistic activity. Nor do I think the objects of science exhaust reality. On the contrary, they afford only a particular angle or slant on reality, picked out precisely for its explanatory scope and power. Moreover, alongside ethical naturalism I am committed to moral realism and I would also like to envisage an adjacent position in aesthetics, indeed viewing it as a branch of practical philosophy, the art of living well. A last word here. Starting with knowledge as a systematic phenomenon I reject that cognitive triumphalism, the roots of which lie in the epistemic fallacy, which identifies what is (and what is not) with what lies within the bounds of human cognitive competence. Reality is a potentially infinite totality, of which we know something but not how much. This is not the least of my differences with Hegel, who, although a more subtle exponent of cognitive triumphalism, Prometheanism or absolutism, nevertheless is a conduit directly connecting his older contemporary Pierre de Laplace to Lenin and thence diamat and the erstwhile command economies of the omniscient party states. But Hegel was a much more subtle exponent of cognitive triumphalism, as we shall in due course see.

§ 6 On the Sources and General Character of the Hegelian Dialectic

There are two principal inflections of the dialectic in Hegel: (α) as a logical process of reason; and (β), more narrowly, as the dynamo of this process, the method, practice of experience of determinate negation. But to understand both one must go back to the roots of this most complex — and hotly contested — concept in ancient Greek thought. Here I will be dealing briefly with material that I will treat in C2 in more thematic and historical detail.

(α) Derived from the Greek *dialectikē*, meaning roughly the art of conversation or discussion — more literally, reasoning by splitting into two — Aristotle credited Zeno of Elea with its invention, as deployed in his famous paradoxes — most notoriously, of motion. These were designed to vindicate the Eleatic cosmology by drawing intuitively unacceptable conclusions from its rejection. But the term was first generally applied in a recognizably philosophical context to

Socrates' mode of argument, or *elenchus*, which was differentiated from the Sophistic *eristic*, the technique of disputation for the sake of rhetorical success, by the orientation of the Socratic dialogue towards the disinterested pursuit of truth. Plato himself regarded dialectic as the supreme philosophical method and the 'coping-stone' of the sciences — using it to designate both the definition of ideas by genus and species (founding logic) and their interconnection in the light of a single principle, the Form of the Good (instituting metaphysics). At one and the same time dialectic was the means of access and assent to the eternal — the universal-and-necessarily-certain — and such Forms or Ideas were the justification for the practice of dialectic. In this inaugural moment of the western philosophical tradition, funda-mentalism, classical rationalist criteria for knowledge and dialectic were indissolubly linked. Aristotle's opinion of dialectic, which he systematized in his *Topics*, was considerably less exalted.[21] For the most part he regarded it as a mere propaedeutic to the syllogistic reasoning expounded in his *Analytics*, necessary to obtain the assent of one's interlocutors but, being based on merely probabalistic premisses, lacking the certainty of scientific knowledge. This last was, however, dependent on the supplementation of induction by *nous* or that intellectual intuition which allowed us to participate in the divine, i.e. knowledge as Plato had defined it (although Plato had not claimed to achieve it), the true starting points (*archai*) of science. There are places, however, where Aristotle took dialectic, as the method of working from received opinions (*endoxa*) through the discussion and progressive probative augmentation of conflicting views and aporiai, as an *alternative* way of arriving at *archai*.[22] If he had taken this course consistently, Aristotle, however, would never have satisfied Platonic criteria for knowledge (*epistēmē* rather than *doxa*), never have got beyond induction. The first great *achieved* identity theorist was already caught in a vice between Plato and Hume — a vice that was to determine the subsequent trajectory of western philosophy: *historical determination by rationalist epistemology, structural domination by empiricist ontology.*

The sense of conversational interplay and exchange, involving the assertion, contradiction, distinction and qualification of theses, was retained in the practice of medieval disputation. It was this sense that was probably most familiar to Kant, who also took over the Aristotelian conception of dialectic as relying on premisses which were in some measure inadequate as well as the analytical/dialectical contrast. For Kant, dialectic was that part of transcendental logic which showed the mutually contradictory or antinomic state into which the intellect fell when not harnessed to the data of experience.

By a turn to transcendental subjectivity, Kant combined, or seemed to combine, the satisfaction of rationalist demands on knowledge with empiricist criteria for being — but only at the price of leaving things-in-themselves unknowable. Kantian dialectic showed the inherently *limited* nature of human cognitive and moral powers, the resulting inherent impossibilities, as well as the conditions of possibility of human (non-archetypal, non-holy) intelligence and will. For Kant this was enlightenment, but it entrained a systematically sundered world and a whole series of splits, between knowledge and thought, knowledge and faith, phenomena and noumena, the transcendental and the empirical, theory and (practical) reason, duty and inclination, this world and the next (splits which were also interiorized within each term separately), as well as those expressly articulated in the antinomies. These dichotomies were to be only weakly (albeit influentially) repaired in the teleologies of the *Critique of Judgement*.

This spread of connotations of dialectic includes, then, argument and conflict, disputation, struggle and split, dialogue and exchange, but also probative progress, enlightenment, demystification and the critique of illusion.

Hegel synthesized (α) this Eleatic idea of dialectic as *reason* with another ancient strand, (β) the Ionian idea of dialectic as *process* — in (γ) the notion of dialectic as the self-generating, self-differentiating and self-particularizing *process of reason*. This second (Ionian) idea typically assumed a dual form: in an *ascending dialectic*, the existence of a higher reality (e.g. the Forms or God) was demonstrated; and in a *descending dialectic*, its manifestation in the phenomenal world was explained. Prototypes of these two phases are the transcendent dialectic of matter of ancient scepticism, in which the impermanence of the sensate world, or the existence of error, or of evil, is taken as a ground for positing an unchanging or completely true, or perfectly good, realm — logically, of the forms, theologically of God; and the immanent dialectic of spiritual diremption of neo-Platonic and Christian eschatology from Plotinus and Eriugena to Silesius and Böhme, which sought to explain why a perfect and self-sufficient being (God) should disclose itself in the dependent and imperfect sphere of matter. Combination of the ascending and descending phases results in a quasi-spatio-temporal pattern of original unity, loss or division and return or reunification (graphically portrayed in Schiller's influential *Letters on the Aesthetic Education of Mankind*) or a quasi-logical pattern of hypostasis, actualization and redemption. Combination of the Eleatic and Ionian strands yields the Hegelian absolute — a logical process or *dialectic* which actualizes itself by *alienating*, or becoming other than, itself and which restores its self-unity by recognizing this alienation as nothing other than its own free expression or manifestation — a process that is recapitulated and completed in the Hegelian system itself.

The three principal keys to Hegel's philosophy — spiritual monism, realized idealism and immanent teleology — can now be cut. Together they form the pediment to it. The outcome of the first dialectical thread in Kant was a view of human beings as bifurcated, disengaged from nature and inherently limited in both cognitive and moral powers. Hegel's generation, as we shall see in C4, experienced the Kantian splits, dichotomies, disharmonies and fragmentations as calling for the restoration of what Charles Taylor has nicely called an 'expressive unity'[23] — lost since the idealized ancient Greek world — that is, in philosophical terms, for a monism — but one which, unlike Spinoza's, paid due heed to diversity, which would be in effect a *unity-in-diversity*, and to the constitutive role of subjectivity; that is, one which preserved the legacy of Luther, Descartes and the Enlightenment formulated in the great Kantian call to 'have courage to use your own reason'[24] or radical autonomy from 'self-incurred tutelage',[25] and that was firmly predicated on the achievements of the critical philosophy. For Hegel the problem of elaborating a non-reductionist and subject-ive monism gradually became tantamount to the problem, posed by the ascending phase of the second dialectical thread, of developing a complete and self-consistent idealism. Such an idealism would, in fusing the finite in the infinite, retain no dualistic or non-rational residues, thereby finally realizing and vindicating the primordial Parmenidean postulate of the identity of being and thought *in* thought, underpinned by a progressivist view of history. Neither Fichte nor Schelling has been able to accomplish this. In Fichte, the non-ego or otherness of being, although originally posited by mind, remained as a permanent barrier to it; so that the principle of idealism became a more *Sollen* or regulative ideal. Schelling, on the other hand, genuinely transcended dualism in his 'point of indifference' uniting man and nature, but less than fully rationally. For Schelling, this identity was achieved only in intuition, rather than conceptual thought, with the highest manifestation of spirit art rather than philosophy, so that the Parmenidean principle remained unrealized in thought. By contrast, in the Hegelian *Geistodyssey* of infinite, petrified (natural) and finite mind, the principle of idealism, the speculative understanding of reality as (absolute) spirit, is unfolded in the shape of an immanent teleology which shows, in response to the problem of the descending phase, how the world exists (and, at least in the human realm, develops) as a rational totality *precisely* so that (infinite) spirit can come to philosophical self-conciousness in the Hegelian system demonstrating this. Absolute idealism is the articulation and recognition of the identity of being in thought *for* thought.

In this logical process or dialectic the problem of reunification of opposites, transcendence of limitations and reconciliation of differences is carried out in the characteristic figure of what I shall call 'constellational identity'. In this dialectical inscape, which qualifies the monism of Hegelianism, the major, typically idealist, term (thought, the infinite, identity, reason, spirit, etc.) over-reaches, envelops and contains the minor, more 'materialist', term (being, the finite, difference, understanding, matter, etc.) in such a way as to preserve the distinctiveness of the minor term and to show that it, and a fortiori its distinctiveness, are teleologically necessary for the major one. The effect of the Hegelian perspective or *Ansicht* is, on Hegel's own account, 'more than a comfort, it reconciles, it transfigures the actual which seems unjust into the rational'.[26] 'To recognize reason as the rose in the cross of the present and thereby to enjoy the present, this is the rational insight which reconciles us to the actual, the reconciliation which philosophy affords.'[27] 'The dissonances of the world' thus appear, in his friend the poet Hölderlin's words in *Hyperion*, 'like the quarrel of lovers. Reconciliation is in the midst of strife, and everything that is separated finds itself again' — in the movement of self-restoring sameness or self-reinstating identity, which is the life of absolute spirit.

Hegel conducts four principal types of demonstration of this life:

1. the introductory educative dialectics of *The Phenomenology of Spirit* in the medium first of individual experience and then of collective culture;
2. the systematic ascending dialectic of the *Logics* in the abstract sphere of the categories;
3. the systematic descending dialectics of the philosophy of nature and spirit; and
4. the illustrative historical dialectics of Hegel's various lecture series, mainly in the realms of objective and absolute spirit.

(β) The motor of this process is dialectic more narrowly conceived. This is the second, essentially negative, moment in what Hegel calls 'actual thought', which drives the dialectics of (1)–(4) on. It is styled by Hegel as the 'grasping of opposites in their unity or of the positive in the negative'.[28] It is not the case, according to Hegel, that a concept merely excludes its opposite or that the negative of a term (or proposition) simply cancels it. If this were so then Aristotle's criticisms of Platonic *diairesis* and Kant's of pre-critical metaphysics would indeed entrain the anti-speculative implications they themselves drew. Rather, to the contrary, from the vantage point of reason, as distinct from the understanding, a genus always contains, explicitly or proleptically, its own differentiae; and, in a famous inversion of the Spinozan maxim *'omnis determinatio est negatio'*, negation always leads to a new richer determination — this is *transformative negation* — so imparting to categories and forms of life an immanent dynamic and to their conflict an immanent resolution rather than a mutual nullification. Although the principle of the mutual exclusion of opposites, entailing rigid definitions and fixed polarities, is adequate for the finite objects grasped by common sense and the empirical sciences, the infinite totalities of reason (which, of course, constellationally embrace the former) require the dialectical principle of the identity of exclusive opposites. And Hegel's central logical claim is that the identity of opposites is not incompatible with their exclusion, *but rather depends upon it*. For it is the experience of what in non-dialectical terms would be a logical contradiction which at once indicates the need for an expansion of the universe of discourse or thought and at the same time yields a more com- prehensive, richly differentiated or highly mediated conceptual form. It is *this* experience in which dialectic proper consists as the second member of a triad composed of the understanding, dialectic (or negative) and speculative (or positive) reason, representing the principles of identity, negativity and rational totality respectively. I will go into the fine structure of this dynamic shortly. On this interpretation, the dialectical fertility of contradictions depends upon their analytical unacceptability. (Hence any dialectical logic must incorporate an analytical one as a special — and vitally generative — case.) From the achieved vantage point of (positive) reason the mutual exclusivity of opposites passes over into the recognition of their reciprocal interdependence (mutual inclusion): they remain inseparable yet distinct moments in a richer, more total conceptual form-ation (which will in turn generate a new contradiction of its own). It is the constellational identity of understanding and reason within reason which fashions the continually recursively expanding kaleidoscopic tableaux of absolute idealism.

Dialectic, then, in this narrow sense, is a method — or better, experience — of *determinate negation* — which enables the dialectical commentator to observe the process by which the various categories, notions or forms of consciousness arise out of each other to form ever more inclusive totalities until the system of categories, notions or forms as a whole is completed. And in a still narrower sense — in

which it is the second member of the understanding-dialectic-reason
(U-D-R) triad — it is the truth, theory of or comment on (dc' in the
terminology introduced in §4 above) the experience or practice of the
phase (notion, etc.) immediately preceding it, yielding or showing a
contradiction — in effect a *theory/practice inconsistency* — which
speculative reason (dr') will resolve, only, of course, for the
resolution in turn to be susceptible to a further dialectic probe. Now it
is clear enough that if we stay at the level of the understanding we
will not find or recognize contradictions in our concepts or experience
— in general it takes an effort or quantum leap — in what we may call
a *σ transform* — to find the contradiction(s), anomalies or inadequacies
in our conceptualizations or experience — and another quantum leap
— which we may call a *τ transform* — to resolve them. And Hegelian
dialectic is just this method or practice of stretching our concepts to
the limit, forcing from and pressing contradictions on them,
contradictions which are not immediately obvious to the understanding (hence the need for the *σ* transform), and then resolving
them, a resolution which is not immediately obvious either (hence the
need for the *τ* transform). (This is one of the reasons why Hegelian
dialectic is so difficult to *understand*; and a respect in which Hegel's
talk about the self-development of the concept, as if it were automatic
[understanding-like], is at the very least disingenuous.) From this
perspective Kant's great merit is that he advances, at least in the case
of the antinomies, to the level of dc' (he makes the *σ* transform), but
fails to take the further leap into speculative reason, fails to resolve
them (to make the *τ* transform), so falling back as a (transcendental
idealist) philosopher of the understanding. But in fact Hegel does not
think that the U-D-R scheme exhausts the matter. I should hasten to
add that the *σ* and *τ* transforms are my own gloss on Hegel. He thinks
the understanding, which at one point he characterizes as an
'almighty power', is a great advance on the pre-reflective reasonableness of ordinary life which readily tolerates contradictions without
finding anything problematic in them, so there is need for a transition
from pre-reflective thought, what I shall call the *ρ transform*, to the
understanding before we are in a position to engage in ordinary (non-
speculative) science or philosophy. It was, of course, to this pre-
reflective reasonableness that the later Wittgenstein was always
trying, but never quite able, to return. Hegel also thinks that we have
to 'return' to life, but after (dialectical and speculative) philosophy —
in post-philosophical wisdom (in what I will call the *υ transform*). So
we could schematize the whole process as in Figure 1.1.

For Hegel, then, truth is the whole, the whole is a process and this
process is reason (dt' as dp' as dr'). Its result is reconciliation to life

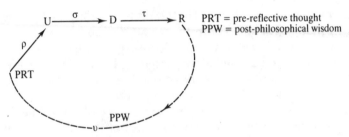

Figure 1.1 The Logic of Hegel's Dialectic

in (Hegelian) freedom. Error lies in one-sidedness, incompleteness and abstraction. Its symptom is the contradictions it generates and its remedy their incorporation into fuller, richer, more concrete, inclusive, englobing and highly mediated conceptual forms. In the course of this process, the famous principle of *dialectical sublation* (ds') or *Aufhebung* is observed: as the dialectic unfolds, no partial insight is ever lost. In fact the Hegelian dialectic progresses in two basic modes: (α) by bringing out what is implicit, but not explicitly articulated, in some notion or social or conceptual form (what I will term 'teleonomic push'); or (β) by repairing some want, lack or inadequacy in it ('teleological pull'). Both are instances of *real negation* in my terms, but only (α) is consistent with a rigorously ex ante, *autogenetic* process/progress of a kind to which, however we interpret him epistemologically (on which in a moment), he is certainly in his dialectics committed. Both may, moreover, be said to involve some theory/practice inconsistency, at least insofar as the notion or form makes, implicitly or explicitly, some claim to completion or adequacy, as the category Being from which the *Logics* start may be said to do. Truth is, however, not only the whole but a norm against which the adequacy of any particular reality to its notion and its stage in the development of the notion or reality (i.e. the idea in its otherness and return to self-consciousness) can be assessed. 'Dialectical', then, in contrast to 'reflective' (or analytical) thought — the thought of the understanding — grasps concepts and forms of life in their systematic interconnections, not just their determinate differences, and considers each development as a product of a previous less developed phase, whose necessary truth or fulfilment it, in some sense and measure, is; so that there is always some tension, latent irony or incipient surprise between any form and what it is in the process of becoming. In short, Hegelian dialectic is the actualized entelechy of the present, comprehended (and so enjoyed) as the end of everything that has led up to it.

§ 7 On the Immanent Critique and Limitations of the Hegelian Dialectic

It is now possible to make some systematic connections between the Hegelian dialectic and the argument we have developed so far, and to comment further upon the former. I shall distinguish (α) Hegel's global dialectics, of the kind discussed in §6(α), from (β) his local dialectics, of the sort schematized by the U-D-R movement of thought and from, within this, the dialectical moment proper (γ). The general character of any U-D-R movement or transition is that of a preservative determinate negation. Now this has the very interesting property of representing a *non-arbitrary principle of stratification*, structuration or superstructure-formation, which I shall explore later. Suffice it to say now that, properly transposed and situated, it forms the kernel to the solution of an important class of philosophical problems (those turning on the absence of an analogue of dr' or dg' at 1M) as well as being an interesting ontological figure in its own right (forming, for instance, an analogue of real material emergence). Within any U-D-R movement, the dialectical moment proper (dc') reports and speculative reason (dr') remedies a *real negation* or absence in the base concept or form at, let us say, level L_1. The dialectical movement to the resolution at L_2 consists in a *transformative negation* of a determinate and preservative type (in consciousness or experience of that at L_1). But I have said in §3 above that all transformative negations are also real negations (though the converse is not the case). In virtue of what is *this* transformative negation a real negation? It absents the absence in L_1. (This is the sense in which determinate negation is the negation of the negation.) It does this by *dialectically bracketing* and retaining or incorporating the base concept, say e; the lack, inadequacy or internal incoherence within e, identified in D; *and* the tension, inconsistency or contradiction between e and what it is meant or trying to be (or implicitly is), identified in the probing comment, and a fortiori the theory/practice inconsistency between the base concept and its comment, in what is in effect a continually unfolding process within a permanent memory store. In this expanding warehouse of reason, each successive operation is in principle bracketed and retained.* Hegelian

---

* Negations do not nullify and contradictions do not spread within this system — because to say of something that is false does not remove it (it has been said) and to say of a pair or more that they are contradictory is not itself contradictory (their contradictoriness is bracketed and negated at a higher level and in this simple way — which bears obvious analogies with the theory of types in standard logic — both the contradictions and their determinate negation are retained).

determinate negation constitutes, then, at once a transformation in the consciousness of the dialectical observer and an expansion of the existing conceptual field. Both are (in principle) additive and cumulative: nothing except absence itself is lost.

The Hegelian totality is constellationally closed, completed. Hegel's, like Aristotle's, is an achieved identity theory, but, unlike Aristotle's, it incorporates the sequence of stages (or conceptual shapes) leading up to it as moments within it and is in fact nothing but this movement of shapes including the finalizing consummating stage, the self-consciousness of spirit as (absolute) spirit in the Hegelian system itself. Speculative philosophy — and its social matrix, rational history — is constellationally finished, at an end. It is at a plateau. There remains a future, of course, but this can be grasped by the understanding — it does not require dialectic or speculative reason. This is the constellational identity of the future within the (Hegelian) present. Now, whatever Hegel says about the autogenetic development of the concept, it is clear as noonday that very few of Hegel's local dialectics take the (α) teleonomic push form, that is, satisfy the requirements of rigorous ex ante progress. It is the failure of concepts and forms to meet the requirement of the posited end — the absolute idea as absolute spirit — this lack and this teleology, that pulls the Hegelian dialectic forwards. It is generally only *retrospectively*, ex post, that a stage can be seen to be deficient. If Hegel's local, and by extension global, dialectics *did* satisfy the ex ante requirement, then the dialectical comment that issues from the σ transform (dc') and the speculative reason issuing from the τ transform that resolves it (dr') could both — and together — be said without qualification to constitute immanent critiques — dc' of the base concept or form (at L_1) and dr' of that and dc'. As it is, we have to qualify this, and to distinguish accordingly between (α') genuinely auto-subversive (ex ante radical and so determinate transformative) *negations* and (β') merely retrospectively situatable (ex post) ones. (In the latter case the critique is really transcendent, not immanent.) And accordingly we might distinguish between good and bad radical negations. Of course, as the Hegelian totality is constellationally closed, all the contradictions, whether teleonomically or teleologically generated, are *internal ones* — and neglect of external contradictions, and more generally constraints, has been a damaging feature of Marxian social theory in the Hegelian mould, one which the foil, say, of Aristotelian dialectics may help to correct. This question of the autogenesis of the dialectical movement is closely bound up with the *linearity* of the Hegelian dialectic. Once again Hegel's theory is at odds with his practice here. His dialectics are not in fact logically, as distinct from textually, linear: they job around all over the place, affecting an incessant variety of *perspectival switches* motivated by Hegel's desire not to just illustrate his dialectics but also to absorb and treat more and more phenomena dialectically in a continuing — and in principle open-ended — process of dialectical suction. Nor is there any reason in principle why dialectics of a Hegelian (or non-Hegelian) type should be linear. They could consist in recursively unfolding matrices, *Gestalten* or any of a variety of topological modes. Surface linearity does, however, seem imposed by the requirements of the textual, especially narrative, form — in what I have elsewhere called 'continuous series'.[29] (Derrida's use, and concept, of spacing is in fact a conscious attempt to overcome this.) These issues of autogeneticity and linearity are related to, but in principle distinct from, the epistemological status of Hegel's dialectics. There are three main interpretations: (a) that they are, or purport to be, totally self-generative and autonomous, dependent on no external subject-matter — the realization of the dream of intellectual intuition from Aristotle to Fichte in a *hyperintuitive*[30] and parthenogenetic process, including — in the transition from Logic to Nature, i.e. in the alienation of the absolute idea — a moment heterocosmic with the creation of the world by God; (b) that they are, or purport to be, the dialectical treatment of various subject-matters, most notably those treated by previous philosophers, which Hegel has thoroughly (and perhaps totally) assimilated and critiqued and is now dialectically expounding — this is the *transformative* or re-appropriative interpretation, most notably formulated as a critique of Hegel's own self-understanding (or representation) of his practice by Trendelenburg; (c) that they are simple phenomenological *descriptions* of a dialectic in the real or at least of the notion as conceptually understood reality — an interpretation that obviously fits the *Phenomenology* and the historical lecture series best and which has been most persuasively and influentially argued by Kojève.[31] I shall return to these issues later.

Corresponding to the distinction just made between good and bad radical negations (and immanent versus transcendent critiques), I want to distinguish between good and bad totalities. *Good totalities* are, though this is not their only characteristic, open; *bad totalities* are, whether constellationally or otherwise, closed. Now this is the exact opposite of Hegel's point of view. For him an open totality would conjure up the spectre of an infinite regress — it would be a 'bad infinite'. But why should an open totality involve an infinite regress? An infinite regress implies *more of the same*, that significant changes (and even the principles of change) might not change, which is just

what the concept of an open totality denies. Later I will show that
totalities in general are and must be open. But for the moment let us
stick with Hegel. Even if it is admitted that there is some kind of
inadequacy or lack in an open totality (tautologically, a lack of
completion), there is no inadequacy or lack in the *thought* of an open
totality, which is what is at stake here. This thought can even, and
perhaps must, be constellationally contained within the present (itself
an indefinite boundary zone between past and future). Of course,
Hegel's realized idealism, his principle of identity, will not allow him
to accept this; there must be no mismatch — rather an identity —
between totality and the thought of totality. But if truth consists in
totality and the conformity of an object to its notion, it is clear that the
concept of an open totality must be more true (complete and
adequate) than the concept of a closed totality, because it is more
comprehensive, englobing and contains the latter as a special case.

As I have described it, the real work of the dialectic is done by the σ
transform which identifies the anomaly or lack in e (at L_1) and the τ
transform which remedies it at L_2. I shall show in §9 how this U-D-R
process can illuminate the epistemological dialectic in science, just as
the non-arbitrary principle of stratification (logically) or superstructure-formation (spatio-temporally) involved in Hegelian preservative
dialectical sublation illustrates analogous principles in nature and
society. I shall also be arguing in C2.6 that although Hegel's global
and crucial local dialectics fail, dialectical arguments are a perfectly
proper species of transcendental argument belonging to the wider
genus of retroductive (ascending)—explanatory (descending) argumentation in science. Dialectical arguments (and, for instance, the
ontological necessities [and contingencies] they can establish) are no
more the privilege of absolute idealism than transcendental
arguments are the prerogative of Kant. I shall further argue that in the
theory/practice inconsistency which the dialectical moment proper
(dc') reports he has identified the most basic form of critique (in
philosophy, science and everyday life): immanent critique.
Unfortunately, locally and globally theory/practice inconsistency
(which I shall sometimes abbreviate to T/P inc.) or incoherence is
always for Hegel resolved in thought, in theory. The practice
therefore remains. Transformative negation is confined to thought.
There is no 4D in Hegel, rather the transfiguration of actuality in the
post-philosophical reconciliation or v transform. Once again Hegel is
untrue to his theory of truth. If reality is out of kilter with the notion
of it, it is reality which should be adjusted, not its truth. The unity (or
coherence) of theory and practice must be achieved in practice.
Otherwise the result is not autonomy, but heteronomy and the re-

appearance of a Kant-like rift. Even the thought of the unity of theory and practice (in theory or practice) must be achieved in practice. Hypostatizing thought not only detotalizes reality, it also detotalizes the *thought* of reality. Here once more the Hegelian totality is revealed as incomplete. This amounts, of course, to an immanent critique of Hegel: his totality is incomplete, his theory inconsistent with his practice and the master concept which drives his dialectics on (for the most part teleologically) — lack or absence (in my terms, real negation) — is not preserved within his system. Positivity and self(-identity), the very characteristics of the understanding, are always restored at the end of reason. Hegelian dialectic is un-Hegelianly-dialectical.

It is also a special case. Within the σ and τ transforms — as at the actual or notional moment D which mediates them — we have moments of *indeterminate* and *underdeterminate negation*. (The same applies mutatis mutandis in the case of the ρ and υ transforms.) Linear radical negation — the production of an outcome as a result of a self-negating process alone — is clearly untypical: as we move in the *Logics* from simple to more complex categories (and the same holds true in Hegel's other textual dialectics), more and more determinations are brought in — and we shall see later that Hegel's doctrine of the speculative proposition, for example, can be heuristically fruitful in social science — but these determinations are always still internal or radical ones, or at the very best constellationally internal. More generally, it is clear that real transformative negations in geo-history are very really of the (even essentially) preservative, i.e. additive (superimpository), type. Indeed, insofar as every notional or social form — including those occurring in the universality of thought — is finite (i.e. insofar as the premisses of Hegel's dialectic of determinate being or 'matter' is true), all space-time beings are 'vanishing mediators'.[32] However, in an Hegelian *Aufhebung*, is not error (partiality, one-sidedness) lost? Hegel will perhaps want to say that the erroneous has been retained as a partial aspect of the truth, but either the error has been cancelled in the coming-to-be or fruition of the end or nothing has been cancelled and *Aufgehoben* loses its threefold meaning — to annul, preserve and sublimate — and the whole Hegelian project is without point or rationale, for, at the very least, a lack of reconciliation to actuality must be lost. In fact in any genuine (materialist) *Aufhebung* it is clear that something has to be lost, even if it is only time ([neg]entropy). On the other hand, it is equally obvious that processes occur in geo-history which are not, at least with respect to some determinate characteristic and within some determinate space-time band, negating but purely accretory, cumulative engrossments or developments. Generally one cannot say a priori whether the geo-historical outcome or result (dr^0) of a process of a Hegelian-dialectical type will

(a) consist of the resolution of the contradiction, inadequacy or lack ($dr^\dagger$);
(b) consist in a rational or reasonable resolution of it (dr');
(c) consist in a rational resolution which conforms to the Hegelian form of radical preservative determinate negation (dr'') — a form which, in its concrete employment, only makes sense if one is prepared to distinguish between essential, significant or valuable characteristics and those which are not
(d) and affords us reconciliation to life (dr'''), let alone
(e) encourages mutual recognition in a free society (dr'''').

Waiving this last for the moment, we can say that Hegelian dialectic identifies what is patently a limiting and special case of a more general schema which can be written as

$$dr^0 \geq dr^\dagger \geq dr' \geq dr'' \geq dr'''.$$

Any general theory of dialectic will have to be able to situate the conditions of possibility and limits of non-resolutary results, non-reasonable resolutions, non-radical-preservative-determinate-negational reasons, and non-reconciliatory radical preservative determinate negations.

§ 8 The Fine Structure of Hegelian Dialectic

A few more preliminary points are called for before we grasp the nettle of 'the positive in the negative' of Hegelian dialectic. I have hitherto advanced two slightly different (but, in the Hegelian scheme itself, mutually implicative) interpretations of (γ), or the dialectical moment proper. On the one hand, I have said it gives, or is, the theory of the practice, experience or form preceding it — i.e. dc' as in effect ($T_1[P_1]$). On the other hand, I have said it reports a theory/ practice inconsistency, or more general lack or inadequacy within it, i.e. dc' as ($-T_1[P_1]$). In the first moment, dc' as D_1, it expresses the theory legitimating the metacritical statement which it articulates in the second, dc' as D_2. D_2, like D_1, is a type of dialectical comment insofar as it isolates at a (notional) meta-level within the transition between L_1 and L_2 what is true of but not contained in L_1, explicitly

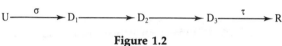

Figure 1.2

articulating an internal rift within L_1 between the practice P_1 and its own self-consciousness or theory as expressed at D_1, viz. T_1. This is the general form of the figure of *practico*-[axio-]*epistemological* inconsistency. But there is also a third inflection to the dc'. This is to see it as expressing an inconsistency between the theory of the practice at L_1 expressed in the dialectical comment and the theory of that practice prior to the comment, i.e. at L_1 itself. And we could write the D_3 form as $T_2 (L_1)/T_1 (L_1)$. It will be important to differentiate these nuances subsequently in differentiated and non-idealist contexts, when the dc' will vary as ideology to ideology-critique (the former taking the $(T_1[P_1])$ form, the latter $(-(-T_1[P_1]))$, for in ideology-critique the *metacritique*, which isolates the absence that drives the dialectic on, constitutes a critique both of the theory and of the theory–practice ensemble — hence the double negation. So we really need to modify the central sector of Figure 1.1 as shown in Figure 1.2.

Second, the actuality to which we return in the v transform is *not* quite the same as the actuality we left in the ρ transform. It is now a (rationally transfigured and comprehended) world in the Hegelian *Ansicht*. (And metacritically — but this is also Hegelian *Nachdenken* [after-thought] — it could be added a world transformed in part by the Hegelian practice itself.) Third, as I have been interpreting it, the ρ, σ and τ transforms (and in critical realist dialectic the ϕ transform in 4D, and even, metacritically in Hegelian dialectic, the v transfiguration) are all determinate negations (with indeterminate and, in principle, multiply-including non-radically and non-linearly determined, fuzzy, duplicitous, polymorphous and indeed a variety of other possible declensions or aspects). But, to reiterate, this terminology is my own, not Hegel's, and the determinate negation of e at L_1 is just dr', including the case where dr' = dc' (in which the notional σ and τ transforms are not distinguishable).

It should also be said that the U-D-R schema, which Hegel himself employs, is an abstract idealization of Hegel's actual practice. In many cases there is no obvious tension or inadequacy in a conceptual form. In some instances (as just mentioned) dc' = dr', i.e. what is resolved is an incoherence within a single concept (the *dyadic* case, on which it is clear that, if Hegelian dialectic is to be both rigorously ex ante and consistently linear, it must ultimately rest or continuously employ); in others, the resolution is between two opposed concepts, coupled in a non-identity relationship (the famous *triadic* paradigm, the classic dr' as ds'); in yet others, the resolution is of an incoherence or partiality within or a contradiction or anomaly between a whole cluster of concepts (the *polyadic* case, which we can subsume under the formula dr' as dt'). In some instances there is an immediate resolution (dc' as dr'), in others the resolution is motivated by a whole sequence of aporetic or antinomial phases (reiterated σ transforms). In some dialectical sequences or rounds the originating element is just the final resolving concept of the preceding round; in others the transition between local dialectics is mediated by more global considerations; in others still there is no very obvious or at best a (e.g. globally mediated) tenuous connection. Where there is no (obvious, or at least immanent/teleonomic) failing in a conceptual or social form, there may just be a perspectival switch (including reversal), a deepening, a concretization, a pun or a joke. No attempt to fit Hegelian dialectics into a unitary mode will work — although the Being-Nothing-Becoming and Unity-Difference—Unity-in-Difference heuristics can illuminate. However, it is noteworthy that the former is radically undermotivated and that the latter is not a local dialectic. Moreover, I agree entirely with Findlay when he remarks that 'whatever Hegel may *say* in regard to the presence of contradictions in thought and reality' (a presence, I hasten to add, which dialectical critical realism will vindicate, though situate), he is in practice concerned with 'the presence of opposed, antithetical *tendencies* ... which work in contrary directions'.[33] In fact we shall see that it requires critical realism (and in particular its non-actualist and non-monovalent ontology) to show the rationale of, and sustain, Hegel's own logical innovations.

Sticking for the moment with Hegelian exegesis it is clear that, irrespective of the three epistemological interpretations outlined in §7, the Hegelian autogenetic moment is *meaning-dependent* and self-particularizing, breaking with the form—concept and concept—instance distinctions of Kantian transcendental analytic. It is also clear that Hegel is committed to the speculative identity of process and totality (dp' as dt') at the point of completion. Now from the consideration that the Hegelian determinate negation is simultaneously both a *transformation* in the observer's consciousness and an *expansion* of the whole conceptual field it follows that the latter can only be held in the mode of '*negative presence*' — what I am going to call, following Kosok's path-breaking study, '*negative referral*'.[34] Now in any determinate negation, whether of the Hegelian conceptual sort or the critical realist metatheoretical (distanciated and transformationalist) gloss on its type, there is and must be both a moment of indeterminacy (prior to the result) and a point of transition (the moment of its becoming). If we say of N that they are not moral, we leave it open whether they are immoral or amoral (or indeed neither). 'Not moral' is the indeterminate negation of 'moral'. Ontologically, indeterminate negation, say at the σ or τ transforms, *precedes* determinate negation, both at each moment in the process and at the end, conceived as the formation of a comment or result. It is a moment of genuine contingency, openness, multi-possibility (and doubt), closed by the ensuing greater determinacy or determination. But epistemologically, in Hegelian dialectic, given the dominance of teleological pull over teleonomic push and the speculative identity of process and product, we can in general abstract a moment of indeterminacy only *retrospectively*, after we know the result. The ontological and epistemic orders are reversed in this in principle four-tiered structure of Hegelian local dialectic. What about the transition point itself? Take a triadic dialectic, where $(-e)$ is the determinate negation of the originating conceptual or social form e, and o is the sublation of (e) and $(-e)$. In principle it seems that we have a choice: either (α) we can say neither (e) nor $(-e)$ apply in the transition state or boundary zone, rejecting the law of excluded middle and/or bivalence, assigning a third value (e.g. ontologically, indeterminate/ underdetermined/fuzzy; epistemologically, undecidable); or (β) we can say that both (e) and $(-e)$ apply, thereby rejecting the law of non-contradiction. In Derridean rejection of 'identity theory' the first option is characteristically taken. In the former case we seem to sacrifice completeness (there is no reference to either determinate element in the boundary zone); in the latter case completeness is achieved (there is reference to both), but we seem to sacrifice consistency. In the Hegelian cumulative memory store, completion must be (constellationally) attained — the Hegelian totality is (allegedly) full — so Hegel must take the second option.

But it is the way in which he takes it that is interesting. The contradiction between the positive contraries (e) and $(-e)$ becomes a *signalling* device for (as well as the purportedly autogenetic mechanism of) the expansion of the conceptual field or universe of discourse. The erstwhile positive contraries are retained, but now in a negative mode (i.e. in the mode of negative presence — that is, as negative sub-contraries), in the formation of o. This is the transition point within the transition zone, the moment of determination which is the negation of the non-identity relationship (e) $\leftrightarrow$ $(-e)$ in which the mutually exclusive elements were coupled, which are thereby both preserved as negative presences. In this way completion (local totality) is attained as a result of contradiction; identity reinstated after non-identity. This last is the constellational identity of identity and non-identity: the envelopment of non-identity by identity for the sake of the preservation/restoration/achievement of identity. This process — of the *transmutation of positive contraries into negative sub-contraries* — explains what I meant earlier when I said that the dialectical fertility of contradictions depends upon their analytical unacceptability and illustrates the 'dialectical bracketing' to which I later referred.

Three consequences follow from this (δ) node within the Hegelian dialectical moment proper, (γ) or D. First, in the expanded field, the erstwhile contraries are reinstated in their full *distinctiveness*, yet they remain *inseparable* moments of the totality which both transcends and encompasses them. Second, such dialectical opposites illustrate *one way* in which the traditional table of oppositions can be completed, for if contraries do not permit both (e) and ($-$e) and sub-contraries neither (e) nor ($-$e) and contradictories do not permit either, dialectical opposites permit both[35] — though, and this remains crucial, *not at the same time*. But there is a simpler way of completing the table of oppositions, and one on which — if Findlay and I are right — Hegel's practice actually depends. In a multiply determined result the exercise of two or more tendencies are invoked to explain the outcome. They are, now simultaneously (but not at the same ontological level), both *really present* (i.e. transfactually efficacious) and *actually absent* (i.e. not manifest or 'realized'); and insofar as they are tendentially opposed or negating they are at once positive contraries and negative sub-contraries (they cannot both be actualized but they can both be present); and, insofar as they have a common causal ground or condition of existence (dg'), they share the dialectical characteristic of being distinct yet inseparable. Critical realism can in this way vindicate, generalize, critically situate and show the limits of (Hegel was an arch expressivist-kinetic-actualist) Hegel's logical insight. The third consequence is the reinstatement of the principle of identity. In general Hegel wants to assert all of the following: 'A is A', 'A is (i.e. passes over into) not A', 'A is B' (the determinate result of the transition) and 'A is A after all'. There are two ways of looking at this last proposition. On the one hand, it is only because A remains self-identical throughout the generative process of the local dialectic (β) that we are able to climb via B to C and thence to C_N. On the other hand, from the perspective of the achieved summit of the global dialectic (α), all the steps that are climbed are explicit — no longer implicit. Their inadequacy and lack is cancelled in the Hegelian retrospective return, though it is not

$$U \xrightarrow{\quad \sigma \quad} D = dc' \xrightarrow{\quad \tau \quad} R = dr'$$

Figure 1.3

forgotten — held in negative presence (but not positive absence — real negation) — in the cumulative memory store of the climb, contained in-and-for-itself at the summit. At this point their logical-rational-spiritual necessity in the chain of things triumphantly shines out: the Eleatic (Parmenidean) face glowing in the Ionian (Heraclitean) fire.

§ 9 Epistemological Dialectic and the Problems of Philosophy

It is now time to redeem my earlier promise and show how dialectic and more especially dialectic of a recognizably Hegelian provenance, albeit one refashioned in critical realist terms, can cast light on central concerns and problems of philosophy. First, let us consider the structure of the U-D-R local dialectic sketched in Figure 1.1 and the non-arbitrary principle of stratification it in principle affords. I want to interpret the schema illustrated in Figure 1.3 as essentially the schema for the epistemological dialectic in the sciences; and the ρ and υ transforms as standing for the relational dialectics in and out of science. Very concretely the ρ transform corresponds to the long training a scientific neophyte must undergo before being able to 'do' science; the U stands for the practice of normal science in something like Kuhnian terms; the σ transform for the gradual or sudden emergence of major anomalies or contradictions in the existing theoretical paradigm, or research tradition or programme. At this point a negative comment — dc' — on the practice of the pre-existing community becomes possible and inevitable, revealing at the very least some lack or inadequacy in it (real negation) and some inconsistency between its own self-understanding and the way it is (T/P or practico-epistemological inconsistency or incoherence). This — D — is the epoch of scientific revolution — with the node within the node (the δ moment) coming from the hint of the restoration of consistency by an expansion of the pre-existing conceptual field, a process only notionally completed at R after the τ transform. In general the epistemological dialectical resolution will involve retroductive-analogical thinking, utilizing paramorphic model-building or other condensations (so that the transformative negation is not an exclusively radical one) and heavily reliant on absented, distanciated and transformed pre-existing knowledge (Bachelard's 'scientific loans'). The determinate result of this labour of transformative negation (in the transitive process of science) will be the identification of a new level of ontological structure, say S_2, described in a new theory T_2 capable of explaining most of the significant phenomena explained by T_1 (at U) plus the anomalies at D, albeit in its own (T_2's own) terms. The phenomena at S_1 identified by T_1 are 'saved' (for the most part) — this is the preservative aspect; theory at T_1 is negated, falsified (the aspect of indeterminate, excluding negation) and transformed into something that could not be predicted and had to be won, fought for, achieved in a labour culminating in the determinate negation and replacement of T_1 by T_2. As science is a social and inter-subjective affair this may involve, besides (and in) work, what is in effect a life-and-death struggle for prestige and recognition, accompanied by reconciliation, at least in the next generation, as the scientific community coalesces around the new paradigm. This now initiates, in principle, the possibility, which may always be circumscribed or practically closed for any number of circumstantial reasons, of a new intra-scientific local dialectic exemplifying my open totality (Hegel's 'infinite regress'). In the meantime there are a variety of interpretations that can be put on the v transform. It can be seen under the aspect of applied science or technology, immediately involving social−natural relations, and/or under the aspect of the (re-)appropriation by the lay community of the skills and knowledge forged in the intra-scientific domain from which the latter is emergent. The ρ transform for its part can be seen not only as scientific training, but also as spanning a whole series of extra-scientific inputs, most notably the social matrix, itself embedded in nature, in which science occurs. More radically, under the sign of the new sociology of science, this whole epistemological dialectic could be interpreted as a 'doxological' dialectic in which the ρ and v transforms were conceived as pervasive in their impact and knowledge/doxa as inextricably coupled to power in the manner of Foucault or alternatively symbolic capital in the style of Bourdieu.

How plausible this will strike the reader I do not know. But Hegel himself would probably have been horrified. Science, for him, was a matter of the understanding — what he meant by 'science' was what we now mean by philosophy, and I would not be unwilling to apply my model there too. But the years separating us from Hegel have seen revolution upon revolution in the sciences and the idea of negatively rational or dialectical (γ) and positively rational or literally *speculative* thought is at least now not at all out of place therein. There *is* something like a logic of scientific discovery,[36] which I am calling the epistemological dialectic here. Of course this will be highly subject-specific and context-sensitive, matters which will occupy us later on.

Before I consider one of the implications of the potentially non-arbitrary principle of stratification or superstructuration implicit in Hegelian dialectics, let me step back a bit to dwell on the notorious problem-field of induction. I should say at the outset that I will treat it only in 1M terms, a 2M treatment will be given in C2. The problem of induction in its simplest form is the problem of what warrant we have for supposing that the course of nature will not change. On the ontology of transcendental realism, the stratification of nature provides each science with its own internal inductive warrant. If there is a *real reason*, located in the nature of the stuff, and independent of the disposition concerned, such as its molecular or atomic structure, then water *must* tend to boil when it is heated. In the epistemological dialectic sketched, this explanatory reason is obtained as a result of the τ transform to dr', when the identification of a new level of structure S_2 is sufficiently confirmed for science — a process in motion — to take this as a starting point — a fact, for a new dialectical round. It is inconsistent with this reason/explanation that water should tend to freeze, blush shyly or turn into a frog. But it remains the case that in an open world any particular prediction may be defeated, so transcendental realism allows us to sustain the transfactuality (universality) of laws in spite of the complexity and differentiation of the world, e.g. so as to enable us to infer the mediated efficacy of tendencies in extra-experimental contexts, thus resolving the metacritically identifiable problem of what I have termed 'transduction'.[37] An ontology of closed systems and atomistic events and a sociology of reified facts and fetishized conjunctions are conditions of the possibility of the traditional problem of induction and conditions of the impossibility of its resolution. Closely connected with this problem are the problems of distinguishing a necessary from an accidental sequence of events, of subjunctive conditionals and of Goodman's and Hempel's paradoxes. All these stem from the absence of a real (non-conventional) reason, located in the nature of things, for predicates to be associated in the way they are. In virtue of his genetic constitution, if Socrates is a man, he must die. Turning too on the absence of a principle of stratification is the traditional problem of universals. If there is something, such as the possession of the same atomic or electronic configuration, which graphite, black carbon and diamonds share, then chemists are rationally justified in classifying them together — the reason is that structure. On the other hand, there is nothing of any deep ontological import that all greengroceries possess in common — in such a

classificatory context a resemblance, rather than a realist, theory
works best (and, of course, critical realism can accommodate and
explain this fact, too). In general, theoretical science is concerned only
with what kinds of things there are, insofar as it illuminates their
ways of acting (the generative mechanisms of nature); and it is
concerned only with what things do, insofar as it illuminates what
kinds there are (the structured entities of nature). This is the dialectic
of explanatory and taxonomic knowledge within the epistemological
dialectic in science.

Also belonging to the same problem-field are the Platonic self-
predicative and, as I shall show in C4, the twentieth-century self-
referential paradoxes. Thus Plato tries to account for some instance of
blueness in terms of its participating in the Form 'blue' as distinct
from, say (as of course *he* could not say), its reflecting light of
wavelength 4400Å, i.e. invoking a new level or order of structure.
This is also the clue to a rational theory of truth, as we shall see in due
course. When we know *why* something is true our assumption *that* it
is true is *grounded*, in a way in which it is not when we are only
subjectively empirically certain of it. The absence of a non-arbitrary
principle of stratification is the critical diagnostic key to many other
philosophical aporiai, or so I shall argue in C4.2. Thus it is easy to find
immediate and direct homologues of the problem of induction — e.g.
Kripke's interpretation and generalization of Wittgenstein's private
language argument;[38] or analogues of it — for instance, the Hobbesian
problem of order as thematized in the history of sociological theory.
To repeat my forewarning, this is only a 1M resolution — at 2E the
course of the deep structure of nature may indeed change, but to this
backgammon is hardly an appropriate response. It should be already
clear that dr', conceived as the outcome of an irreducibly empirical
and heteronomous dialectic in science, involving the transformative
negation of T_1 by T_2 and the identification of a new level of ontological
structure S_2 capable of resolving the aporiai (dc') of T_1, saving,
explaining,   grounding   and   very   probably   redescribing   the
phenomena of the base structure S_1, can at the very least be
illuminating. Once again Hegel would have been horrified by this
result. The rational necessity arrived at is not deployed by *Geist*, it is
not intrinsically related, but contrafactually related, to human
subjectivity, and it remains non-constellationally contingent whether
it is ever actualized. But in this book I am into the business of denying
Hegel exclusive property over his insights. Dialectic neither began nor
ended with Hegel.

I hope I have made a prima facie case for connecting critical realism,
(especially Hegelian) dialectic and essential concerns of philosophy.

These connections will become explicit in the course of *Dialectic*, together with their implications for social theory and practice. In particular my critique of Hegelian dialectic will be systematized in C4 in the course of a sublation of the traditional problem-fields of philosophy. Dialectic will be diffracted *and* retotalized.

Dialectic: The Logic of Absence — Arguments, Themes, Perspectives, Configurations

§ 1 Absence

In C1.3 I argued that real negation > transformative negation > radical negation of a determinate, indeterminate, fuzzy, duplicitous and a mélange of other genres. In C1.6 I claimed that it is real negation or the *absent*, whether in the guise of the inexplicit (as in the case of teleonomic push) or the merely incomplete (teleological pull), that drives the Hegelian dialectic on, and that will drive the dialectic past him. Incidentally the epistemological dialectic sketched in C1.9 can function as the Hegelian dialectic normally operates, by simply overcoming incompleteness — e.g. by augmenting generality or depth without prior anomaly.[1] However, the more typical case here will be that where an inconsistency, caused by a relevant conceptual or empirical lacuna, generates the move to further completeness — in a Gödelian dialectic of:

absence → inconsistency → greater completeness

in principle without end.

Real negation is most simply first considered as the *presence* in some more or less determinate region of space-time (comprising, as a relational property of the system of material things, an objective referential grid) *of an absence* at some specific level or context of being of some more or less determinate entity, thing, power, event, aspect or relation, etc. Consider as a paradigm a stapler missing from a desk drawer, or a tool from a workbench. I want to focus here for ease of exposition on simple determinate non-being within a determinate locale, which, relative to any possible indexicalized observer on any possible world-line, is existentially intransitive, whether or not the absence is positively identified, or even identifiable. But the argument may be easily extended to deal with less determinate kinds. Thus the region may be not only as large or small as is naturally possible but indefinite and/or open. And the entity may be, if it is present, hidden and perhaps necessarily unobservable to creatures like us, whether prosthetically aided or not. The absence may be deep or superficial, real but not actual. The region may be totally empty, constitute a level-specific void or just not contain x. x may be never anywhere (as in simple non-existence), sometimes somewhere else (as in finite or limited existence) or just spatio-temporally distant (as in the 'duality of absence' and, we can add, 'presence', mentioned in C1.3). The absent thus includes, but is not exhausted by, the past and outside. And it may be more or less systematically (e.g. causally) connected to the presence or absence of other determinate beings. At the boundary of the space-time region it may be difficult to say whether x is present or absent or neither or both (or both neither and/or both); and, if 'present' and 'absent' are treated as contraries, we are once more confronted with the spectre of rejecting the principle of non-contradiction or excluded middle or both. Note that the possibility of action/passion at-a-distance and/or across (possibly level-specific) voids — in effect, non-substantial process — provides another ground for regarding real negation (absence) as the more basic category than transformative negation (change). I will postpone treating complications that derive from the fourfold polysemy of real negation, noted in C1.3, viz. (a) as simple absence (our focus here), including nothing; (b) as simple absenting, e.g. through divergent distanciation or substantial or non-substantial process (with or without transformation), (c) as process-in-product, e.g. as in the existential constitution of the nature of an absence by its geo-history; and (d) as product-in-process, e.g. in the iterable or non-iterable exercise of its causal powers. Similarly for those that derive from the phenomena of emergent and/or divergent (or possibly convergent) spatio-temporalities of causally efficacious absent things.

Someone may ask 'what is being negated in real negation?' In the case where x has been absent*ed* from a domain of being, whether by transformation and/or by distanciation, the propriety of this way of speaking may perhaps be granted. But where x is altogether absent from being, as in never anywhere existence, if the reader wishes to substitute 'non-being' for 'real negation' I have no objection. For it is my intention to maintain in this section (1) that we can refer to non-being, (2) that non-being exists, and that (3) not only must it be conceded that non-being has ontological priority over being within zero-level being, (4) but, further, non-being has ontological *priority* over being. In short, negativity wins. My aim in vindicating negativity

in what may seem a prima facie paradoxical way is to foreground the
contingency — both epistemological and ontological — of existential,
not least human existential, questions which the tradition of
ontological monovalence screens. I shall contend that this exercise is
necessary for that emancipation of dialectic for (the dialectic of)
emancipation that is the aim of this work.

My first objective is to argue, against Plato and Frege, that reference
does not presuppose existence; more specifically, that it does not
presuppose either factual existence or positive factual existence. I
want to differentiate within the class of ontics — understood as the
intransitive objects of specific epistemic inquiries — positive
existences or presences, which I shall dub 'onts', from negative
existences or absences, which I shall nominate 'de-onts'. Next I am
going to identify the ontic content, i.e., if you like, the referential
force, weight or charge of a proposition with what Hare has called its
'phrastic', and to make modified use of his further terminology of
'neustics' and 'tropics'.[2] As I shall employ his triptych, tropics —
initially introduced to register mood — demarcate domains of
discourse, e.g. to distinguish the fictional, I, and the factual, F;
neustics convey attitudes such as acceptance, rejection or indecision,
written as √, x and / respectively; while phrastics express the ontic
content of a proposition, the state of affairs it describes or is about,
which may be positive or negative, represented as (e) and (−e). A
(positive or negative) affirmative factual claim typically occurs at the
moment at which (in what I will characterize in C3.2 as the dialectic of
truth) 'referential detachment' — informally the ontological detachment
of the referent from the (inter-subjective/social) referential act
(reference), initially justified by the axiological need to refer to
something other than ourselves — becomes legitimate and necessary.
The argument for referential detachment is the argument for
existential intransitivity and, in science, is the ground for the
argument for the stratified, differentiated and changing ontology
which critical realism has hitherto deployed. And to speak of the
'ontic content' of a proposition is merely to indicate the ontic or
referential aspect of the 'referential−expressive' duality of function
which is a necessary component, or so I shall argue, of an adequate
theory of truth. But I should also hereby give notice that I will be
working with a much more general notion of 'referent' and
'reference' than the ontologically extensionalist mainstream count: -
ances. On my position, one can refer not only to existent (or non-
existent) things, but also to such things characterized in particular
ways. Thus we can refer to laws, powers and tendencies; to totalities,
relations and aspects; to intensions, intentions and actions (or

inactions); and to our discourse about all of them. To refer is just to pick something out for discussion and/or other action, and thus there are no more a priori limits on what we can designate than there are on what we can discuss. This does not abolish the distinction between the activities of reference and predication, but merely enables us to say (predicate) things about everything we normally do and necessarily must.

I have argued elsewhere that we can refer within, as well as (of course) to, fictional discourse. Typically this will presuppose an operation on a tropic. Thus the staging of *Macbeth* will convey the 'conversationally candid' implication, to invoke Grice's convenient expression, that Macbeth did not exist, and in referential and other acts in *Macbeth* we characteristically suspend our belief in that implication. Within the realm of factual discourse, the rejection of a proposition, say to the effect that caloric exists, depends upon an operation on a neustic, denying, in the transitive dimension, the existence, in the intransitive dimension, of caloric or whatever. Let us pass now to real negation. To assert that Pierre is not in the café or that the *Titanic* sank or that Fred's golf balls were lost or that Sara couldn't keep her date with Jemma or that Sophie missed her cue in the matinée presupposes a factual neustic in the transitive dimension, but the ontic content of the proposition — that which we reject or accept and what it is that, in (groundedly) accepting, we referentially detach from our speech acts — is now, unlike the case of caloric, negative. Real negation involves an operation on the phrastic $(-e)$, and the negativity is now explicitly ontological. But patently I can refer to, as I can perceive (or be in a position to infer), Pierre's absence, just as readily as I can refer to the denial of caloric's existence or to Macbeth's fictionality. All three convey negative existential import. But, as I have set up the sequence, they do so in three different ways. The tropic fictional operator 'I' implies, but is not the same as, the neustic rejection of an existential proposition, which in turn implies, but is not the same as, phrastic de-ontification. There are at least three different modes in which things may be said not to be (and I want to assert the logical propriety of fictional and factual, I and F, acceptance and rejection, $\sqrt{}$ and x, and being and non-being ( ) and $(-)$ operators) — although, of course, there is only one sense in which things are not. $F\sqrt{}(-e)$ gives the fine structure of the simple factual positive affirmation of Pierre's death.

Real negativity, understood most simply as absence, or, qua process, absenting, and a fortiori the critique of ontological monovalence, is vital to dialectic. Absenting processes are crucial to dialectic conceived as the logic of *change* — which is absenting.

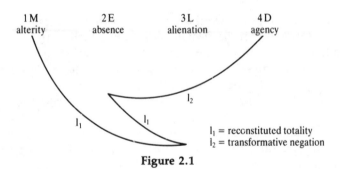

Figure 2.1

Absenting absences, which act as constraints on wants, needs or (more generally) well-being, is essential to dialectics interpreted as the logic of *freedom*. And the whole point of *argument*, on which dialectic has been most traditionally modelled, is to absent mistakes. The absence concerned may be transfactual or actual, in process or static, internally related in a totality or isolated, an inaction or not (cf. 1M–4D).* The dialectical comment (dc') typically isolates an absence (which the resolution repairs), indicating a theory/practice inconsistency or irrelevance, and advising against its dialectical (critical realist) universalizability.** In dialectical critical realism the category of absence is pivotal to 1M–4D links. Thus a 1M non-identity or alterity may generate a 2E absence causing a 3L alienating detotalization or split-off resulting in a fragmented impotent self — *or* to a transformed transformative totalizing praxis absenting the split, or, let us suppose, a reconstituted unity-in-diversity, diagrammatized in Figure 2.1. This is just one example of malign/benign 1M–4D links, in which 2E absence/absenting is the key mediation between 1M non-identity, 3L totality and 4D agency, which has as its prototype the

---

* Statements about transfactualities should not be confused with statements about negativities, although the classes intersect. The d_r/d_a distinction gets its force from the fact that a tendency (which may be positive or negative) may be exercised without being actualized in a (positive or negative) outcome. The d_r/d_+ distinction stems from the consideration that things, their causal powers, their processual and possibly mediated exercise and their results may be absent (negative) as well as present (positive). That said, it should be clear that the concept of a tendency absent from actuality presupposes the critique of ontological monovalence; and that absenting processes are, in open systems, all tendencies, so that the distinctions are interdependent. Indeed the elision of natural necessity, the epistemic fallacy and ontological monovalence I shall declaim as the unholy trinity of irrealism. (The pun is intentional: holes – voids – constitutive absences.)

** For the moment this may be regarded as transfactual, processual-directional-developmental, concrete, agentive (agent-specific or actionable) and transformative — a formula I will later both explain and qualify.

absenting of absence manifest in the satisfaction of desire. More generally, dialectics depends upon the positive identification and transformative elimination of absences. Indeed, it just is, in its essence, the process of *absenting absence*. Moreover, I shall show in C4.2 how the key to the critical diagnosis and rational resolution of the problems of philosophy, generated by 1M destratification or homology, 3L detotalization, 4D de-agentification and 2E positivization, lies in the repair of the absence of the concepts of structure and heterology, concretion, relationality and totality, agentive agency and, above all, absence itself. Reference to absence is quintessential to non-idealistic dialectic. Hence my polemical reference in C1.3 to 'subject', as distinct from traditional predicative and propositional, negation. Later I will connect the concept of, if you like, referential negativity to developmental negation, the critique of the presupposition — which I shall call 'fixism' — of fixed subjects in the traditional subject-predicate propositional form (which presupposes the rigidity, and hence arbitrariness, of definitions), Fischer's notion of necessary as distinct from impossible contradiction (contradictio in *subjecto* rather than in *adjecto*), expressing the idea of a subject in process of formation and the possible uses of the Hegel-derivative 'speculative proposition' in social science.

An extreme case of absence is never anywhere existence. This can be expressed in the form of a non-existential proposition, e.g. in science. Popper holds such propositions to be unfalsifiable, and so 'unscientific'. Despite the fact that counter-examples abound in science (phlogiston, the aether, Vulcan), this is normally taken as gospel. However, in real science, individuals, particulars and universals are always already known under some more or less precise description, tied, when existential questions become pertinent within the specific context of inquiry, to definite demonstrative and recognitive criteria of existence — which they may simply fail to satisfy. Moreover, fallibilism itself depends upon the idea of identifying and remedying mistakes. This entails at the very least (leaving aside the not necessarily trivial sense in which error may be said to consist in the lack of truth) registering the recognition of error in the speech act of denial, which is absentive, and upon comprehending error as paradigmatically *dependent* upon absence; and its correction the repair, that is, the absenting, of the absence. Dialectic is at the heart of every learning process. Furthermore, it is easy to see that in any world in which human agency is to be possible, the human agent must be able to bring about a state of affairs which would not otherwise have prevailed (unless it was over-determined). Sophia acts, and so absents. That is, to put the matter in (anti-)Kantian terms (and so as to show the quiescence and de-agentification implicit in transcendental idealism), the human agent must be able to effect the source of the 'given'. So ontic change (and hence absence) must occur in a world containing human agency. Hence epistemic change must be possible and necessary too. Moreover, both meta-epistemic change (to accommodate change in change about beliefs) and conceptual change (to enable change in definitions) must be possible and necessary also. We begin to envisage dialectic as the great 'loosener', permitting empirical 'open-texture', in the manner of Waismann, and structural fluidity and interconnectedness, in a Marxian-Bakhtinian fashion, alike (and their distinction to boot). Again, unless Sophia sees herself necessarily *acting and so absenting*, she cannot reflexively situate (and hence detotalizes) herself. That is to say, she in practice alienates and reifies, and hence *absents* herself and/or her agency, in a way for which she cannot consistently account. Not to admit absence to our ontology (in that very admission) is to commit *performative contradiction*, the basic form of theory/practice and reflexive inconsistency, and self-referential paradox.

To this it might be argued that there cannot be a complete parity at the transcendental level between the positive and the negative. Fictional disclosure is dependent upon a matrix of factual discourse, in which neustic crosses are cradled by axiologically necessary ticks, in which in turn absences are only identifiable via the network of positive material things. To this objection there are a number of ripostes. First, the identification of a positive existent is a human act. So it involves the absenting of a pre-existent state of affairs, be it only a state of existential doubt. This may be taken as a transcendental deduction of the category of absence, and a transcendental refutation and immanent critique of ontological monovalence. Second, the material world operates as a referential grid for the identification of positive and negative existents, onts and de-onts, only in virtue of their mutual exclusion relations, that is to say, in virtue of their differences in space and changes in time. Only in a state of eternal all-pervasive token monism would the category of absence not be necessary for the deduction of coherent concepts of space and time (which would be really redundant). Such a monism would make all becoming, including acts of identification, impossible. In any event we know it to be false. More important is to note the connection between causality and absence. All causal determination, and hence change, is transformative negation or absenting. All causes are in space-time and effects are negations. Later I shall make much of the point that causality must be grasped as intrinsically tensed spatio-temporalizing process. For the moment we need only record that there is no substance without causality, no material system without its changes. This can also be regarded as a transcendental refutation of monovalence and token monism (which must detotalize the monist). The identification of positive existents depends upon a changing (and therefore at least ontologically bivalent) world.

At this point, having registered the connections between space and difference and time and change, I want to digress slightly to comment upon the difference between change and difference. Both categories are essential (and presuppose absence). But (a) change cannot be analysed in terms of difference, as the analytic tradition from the late Plato has been wont to do, any more than (b) difference can be analysed in terms of change, the converse fallacy of the dialectical tradition from at least Plotinus.

(a) Change cannot be analysed in terms of difference because it presupposes the idea of a continuing thing in a tensed process. If the ontologically monovalent tradition dates from the Parmenidean 'one', mediated by the Platonic exegesis of negation as difference, it is completed by the Kantian error of supposing that one can always replace statements about negativities or their derivatives by ones employing purely positive predicates. But Pierre's absence from the café does not *mean* the same as Genet sitting in his place or Pierre's playing football instead of meeting Sartre. (b) Difference cannot be analysed in terms of change because it includes the idea of two or more non-identical tokens, which cannot be necessarily reduced to a unitary origin (which would have to be the single unique origin of everything to yield the required result). More to the immediate point, to allow at least two (and by an extension of this argument, an indefinite number of) non-identicals is transcendentally necessary for our discourse to achieve referential detachment, that is, to be able to talk about something other than itself or even to talk *about* itself at all. Intransitivity is as transcendentally irreducible as I will later argue tense to be. Of course none of this is to deny that differentiating changes and changing differences occur. (In the meantime the reader should be forewarned that in this chapter [and indeed throughout this book], I will be conducting a side polemic against monism, reductionism and fundamentalism, including the ideas of unique beginnings, rock bottoms and fixed foundations, all of which smack of anthropic cognitive triumphalism, which I will connect to centrism and endism as endemic to irrealist dialectics as well as the bulk of analytics.)

My third response to the objection claiming ontological priority for the positive is to argue that a world without voids (absences), that is,

a 'non-clumpy' material object world, in which, as on the classical
Cartesian-Newtonian paradigm, action is by continuous contiguous
impact — in its canonical atomistic form, of condensely compacting
particles (a conception which Newton never eschewed*) — would be
a world in which nothing could move or occur, as it presupposes an
impossible conjunction of atomicity, rigidity and immediacy. That is
to say, in effect, non-atomicity (and hence constitutive absence) and/
or action-at-a-distance (and hence across voids) are transcendentally
necessary features of an intelligible material object world.**[3] Transmission of energy, like information in inter-personal communication,
is possible only by (substantial or non-substantial) travel across, at the
very least, level-specific gaps. This being granted takes me to my
fourth argument against the ontological dominance of the positive. If
a totally positive material object world — a packed world without
absences — is impossible, there is no a priori reason to exclude the
opposite — namely a total void, literally nothing. Negativity is
constitutively essential to positivity, but the converse does not follow.
Leave aside the Heideggerian question of why there is something
rather than nothing. There could have been nothing rather than
something. Of course this is a counterfactual. Beings exist. But by
transcendental argument, non-being is constitutively essential to
being. Non-being is a condition of possibility of being. No non-being
is a sufficient condition of impossibility of being. But there is no
logical incoherence in totally no being. Dialectical arguments establish
the conditions of possibility (dr') of the conditions of impossibility
(dc') of some initially established result or posit. Now, employing a
strategy of 'dialectical detachment' from our initial premiss — positive
existence — in the metacritical end-game, we can argue that not only
is a total void possible, but if there was a *unique* beginning to
everything it could only be from nothing by an act of radical
autogenesis. So that *if* there was an originating Absolute, nothing
would be its schema or form, constituted at the moment of initiation
by the spontaneous disposition to become something other than
itself. Similarly, if there was a unique ending to everything it would
involve a collapse to actualized nothingness, absolutely nothing. In

---

* The Michelson–Morley experiment was designed to determine the velocity of the
aether relative to the earth.
** This has a philosophical social analogue in what Lovejoy, thinking especially of
Leibniz but equally applicable to Hegel, has called 'the principle of plenitude',[4] but
which could perhaps be more aptly labelled 'the principle of repletion'. Its
inapplicability to a world dominated by scarcity (more precisely the combination of
scarcity and waste), characterized by enormous inequities and subject to absolute
ecological constraints should not need remarking.

sum, complete positivity is impossible, but sheer indeterminate negativity is not.*

Within the world as we know it, non-being is at least on a par with being. Outwith it the negative has ontological primacy. Let us linger within the everyday world. Let me also concede the force of the point that, while the converse is equally the case, without positive being we could not know negative being; and even, recognizing the counter-factuality of the hypothesis explored in the previous paragraph, conceive of non-being as contained within a base or zero-level being. Why, it might be enquired, do I want to talk of non-being in referring to such prosaic facts as Jemma not keeping her date with Jacques? To say that Jemma or Pierre or the rain or food or self-esteem or the aether *is not* (is lacking) in some determinate context of discourse is to designate a real absence at some level, perspective, aspect, context and/or region of space-time. 'Is' and 'real' discharge the burden of ontology; 'not' and 'absent' denote negativity. To admit that real absence exists and real absentings occur is tantamount to conceding that non-beings, i.e. de-onts, are, happen, etc. We thus have the theorem: ontology > ontics > de-onts. In §6 I shall argue that it is inconceivable that 'ontology' does not refer and in C4 I shall examine the origins of the dogma of ontological monovalence and its generative role in the aporiai of irrealist philosophy in its analytical, hitherto dialectical and post-Nietzschean forms. Its effects include, as I have already suggested, the deproblematization of existential questions (as the 1M denial of natural necessity deproblematizes essential ones), securing the transmission of a pre-posited positivity from knowledge to being, dogmatically reinforcing the former as hypostatized ideas or reified facts, disguising the human agency

---

* It is customarily presupposed in cosmological discussion (a) that our cosmos is unique (so to speak, synchronically, diachronically, laterally and transcategorially); therefore (b) that its beginning was *the* unique beginning of everything — and in particular of matter, energy, space and time, the concepts of which therefore cannot be employed for or outside it; (c) that the cause of its beginning cannot be considered without antinomy or vicious regress; or (d) insofar as it can be it must be of a monadic-fissuring type, rather than as is characteristically the case in known intra-cosmic geneses, viz. beginnings of a dyadic/polyadic-fusing kind[5] (e.g. as involving an asymmetric compression of pre-existent forces); and finally (e), worst of all, that if there was a unified theory capable of explaining the physical development of the cosmos, perhaps after the earliest moments of time, this would ipso facto yield a 'GTOE' — Grand Theory of Everything.[6] These assumptions bear the heavy imprint of philosophical anthropocentrism, monism, verificationism, actualism, reductionism and cognitive triumphalism. (b) goes against the Lucretian dictum 'nil ... fieri de nihilo' and the Hobbesian maxim that 'nothing taketh a beginning from itself'. Particular or absolutist monistic ontification is illicit. In respect of (c), note a polyadic-fissuring genesis of a Schillerian dialectic would give it a minimum five-term structure, without allowing for indeterminate or subsequent multiple negation.

involved and absenting (and alienating) scientists and laypersons alike from their products. The transmission of positivity from knowledge to being, covered by the epistemic fallacy and then reflected back in its ontic dual, takes place at a posited or hypothesized point of subject–object identity, abolishing intransitivity in what is in effect a point of categorial duplicity, which is actualistically generalized into eidetic eternity. Eliminating absence, most sharply experienced in contradiction and remedied by greater completeness or totality, eliminates change and error alike. Monovalence is the ideology of categorial (including epistemological) stasis. Once more, precisely the same result is achieved by the absenting of alterity, and thus the difference between change and error too. The epistemic fallacy, ontological monovalence and the actualist collapse of natural necessity (and possibility) are of a piece: the unholy trinity of irrealism.

Conversely, welcoming negativity and later totality and agency alongside 1M non-identity, depth and transfactuality to our ontology situates some very interesting possibilities. What is present from one perspective, at one level, in some region may be absent from, at or in another. Presences and absences may be recursively embedded and systematically intermingled in all sorts of fascinating ways. They may stretch forward temporally, spread outwards spatially, spiral inwards conceptually, mediate, switch or transfigure each other relationally, perspectivally or configurationally, structurally sediment, abstract, concretize, contradict and coalesce themselves. Once we specifically thematize causal efficacy, emergence, tensed spatializing process, totality and sui generis social forms, all sorts of topologies become possible: hidden depths, tangled loops, inverted hierarchies, mediatized, virtual and hyperrealities; holes-within-wholes (and vice versa), binds and blocks, intra- as well as inter-action; juxtaposed, elongated, congealed, overlapping, intersecting, condensed spatio-temporalities; intertwined, dislocated and punctured processes. We shall explore some of these in due course. As it is, consider the crucial impact that the symptomatic silence, the telling pause, the vacuum, the hiatus or the generative separation possess. Or remember the effects of the non-occurrences, the undone or left alone — the letter that didn't arrive, the failed exam, the missed plane, the monsoon that didn't occur, the deforestation of the Amazonian jungle, the holes in the ozone layer, the collapse of 'actually existing socialism', the spaces in the text, the absent authors and readers it presupposes, both the too empty and the too full. Absences, immediately or on reflection, all.* There are intervals, voids and pauses, desire, lack and need within being; and such absences and their tendential and actual absenting are, or so I am arguing, transcendentally and dialectically necessary for any intelligible being at all.

§ 2 Emergence

The official motive force of the Hegelian dialectic is, as we have seen, the contradiction that leads to the expansion of the universe of discourse or conceptual field by the positive identification and elimination of absences, including its former incompleteness in some relevant respect. But before I come to contradiction, I want briefly to broach the topic of emergence. This is a 1M category of non-identity but is (a) specifically ontological while (b) falling within the generic Hegelianesque class of stratificational dialectics. In emergence, generally, new beings (entities, structures, totalities, concepts) are generated out of pre-existing material from which they could have been neither induced nor deduced. There is a quantum leap, or nodal line, of (one feels like saying) the materialized imagination — or even, with Hegel, reason — akin to that occurring in the σ or τ transforms of the rudimentary epistemological dialectic of C1.9. This is matter as creative, as autopoietic. It seems, if it can be vindicated, to yield a genuine ontological analogue of Hegelian preservative determinate negation. It consists in the formation of one or other of two types of superstructure (only the first of which has generally been noted in the Marxist canon), namely, by the superimposition (Model A) or intra-position (Model B) of the emergent level *on* or *within* the pre-existing one — *superstructuration* or *intrastructuration* respectively. There is no reason why the two models should not be used in complementary fashion, say in the concept of the *intrinsic superstructure*. These do not exhaust the formal possibilities, especially once one allows extraneous, contra-punctual and transvoid action, emergent and divergent (and generally detached) spatio-temporalities and disembedding mechanisms, including the disembedding of time from space (as in an aeroplane flight) and the disembedding of space from time (as in telephone reception). But they are the most obvious ones. Emergence presupposes the rejection of the ancient antagonism of (normally physicalistic) reductionism and (typical spiritualistic)

---

* The 'too full' reveals, in the human world, an absence of continence, balance or justice: the jewel of wisdom in the Aristotelian doctrine of the 'mean'.

dualism alike, neither of which can sustain a concept of *agentive agency*, presupposing *intentional* materially embodied and efficacious *causality*; and both of which posit the non-phenomenality of intentionality. It acknowledges irreducible real novelty, while rejecting a transcendent cause for it — what Hegel, with medieval Christendom and Kant (especially) in mind, will pejoratively refer to as a 'beyond' or *Jenseits*.

However, before I praise emergence, I must bury Hegelian versions of it. In the real world, whether we are dealing with conceptual, social (concept-dependent, but not -exhaustive) or entirely natural (extra-conceptual) terrain, ontological dialectical processes are not generally the product of radical negation alone, let alone that of the linear kind to which Hegel leans. For our world is an open-systemic entropic totality, in which results (dr^0 in the symbolism of C1.7) are neither autogenetically produced nor even constellationally closed, but the provisional outcome of a heterogeneous multiplicity of changing mechanisms, agencies and circumstances. Moreover, in real emergence the processes are generally non-teleologically causal, only socio-spherically conceptual; and the higher level (ultimately, in Hegel, absolute spirit or, to borrow Charles Taylor's felicitous expression, 'cosmic Geist'[7]) does not posit, but is rather formed from, the lower level.[8] Furthermore, whether the outcome is, macroscopically, a new type of *structure*, or, microscopically, merely a token, or a *structuratum*, to employ Andrew Collier's useful distinction,*[9] it normally remains heteronomously conditioned and controlled by the lower-order one — onto or into which it has been super- or intra-posed. Again, real emergence has an inverse that does not figure in the entelechy of the Hegelian scheme, viz. *disemergence*, the decay, demise or disjoint detachment of the higher-order level. Further, emergence may involve a substantial degree of non-preservative, rather than simply additive, superstructuration. And the result may be internally complex and differentiated, consisting in a 'laminated' system,[10] whose internal elements are necessarily 'bonded' in a multiplicity of structures (perhaps composed of their own structural hierarchies and sub-totalities). Such systems may be decentred,

---

* The concept of a structuratum, is, however, homonymous, between an ontological instance of a structure *or* a concrete individual or singular, which will normally be the condensate of, or of the effects of, a multiplicity of disjoint, and even contradictory, structures or of their ways of acting (generative mechanisms or causal powers). It will characteristically remain heteronomously conditioned, dependent upon and influenced by the levels out of which it has emerged, even where it is causally efficacious on them, as clearly society is on nature and agency on inanimate and animate matter alike.

asymmetrically weighted, and contextually variable, as in the case of the Dennettian-Joycean self, composing an internal pluriverse (to purloin Della Volpe's redolent term[11]), populated by a plurality of narratives, in internal discordance and even palpable contradiction.[12]

Indeed emergence, which I treat in C3 as an example of the dialectic of the real and the actual, establishes distinct domains of difference qua alterity — real determinate *other-being*. Such domains have to be understood in their own terms before (α) any scientistic synchronic or (β) historicist diachronic explanatory reduction can be contemplated. Thus (α) chemical phenomena had first to be classified, described and explained in a dialectic of sui generis chemical principles before any explanatory reduction to physics became feasible,[13] while (β) the tradition of neo-Platonic-eschatological-Hegelian-vulgar Marxist thought has been plagued by assumptions of originarity, uni-linear directionality and teleological necessity of an empirically and conceptually untenable kind. It is best to take specific cases in this neck of the philosophical woods. To comprehend human agency as a causally and taxonomically irreducible mode of matter is not to posit a distinct substance 'mind' endowed with reasons for acting apart from the causal network, but to credit intentional embodied agency with distinct (emergent) causal powers from the biological matter out of which agents were formed, on which they are capable of reacting back (and must, precisely as materially embodied causally efficacious agents, do so, if they are to act at all), but from which, in an open-systemic totality in which events are not determined before they are caused,[14] neither such beings nor the transformations and havoc they would wreak on the rest of nature could have been predicted ex ante. On such a *synchronic emergent causal powers materialism*, reasons (that are acted on) just are causes. Against dualism, we can say that it is in virtue of our complex biological constitution that human agents have the powers we do; while denying, against reductionism, that a power can be reduced to its material basis or condition of possibility any more than the acceleration of a car is the same as its engine. Contemporary reductionist materialisms both face insoluble aporiai and sneak dualism (of a disembodied linguistified neo-Kantian kind) in by the back door.[15] For instance, the very statement of eliminative materialism appears inconsistent with its project — a self-eliminating act. At the time of its utterance such a statement transforms the material world, yielding a performative contradiction or theory/practice inconsistency again. And in a non-solipsistic (or non-token-monist) world, central state materialism cannot account for the understanding of meaning which mediates two or more neuro-physiologically distinct states in inter-subjective transactions, whether they consist in buying a bunch of bananas or enunciating central state materialism itself.

This is just as well. For accepting the causal efficacy of reasons enables us to make sense of the programme of experimental science. For in an experiment scientists co-determine an empirical result which, but for their intentional causal agency, would not have occurred; yet which at the same time potentially affords us epistemic access to the real, transfactually efficacious, but normally empirically counterfactual[16] *causal structures of the world.*[17] (Transfactual thus underpins counterfactual truth.) This furnishes us with a transcendental deduction of emergence, at least for the human realm, which at the same time functions as an immanent critique of scientistic reductionist materialism. But it is furthermore of philosophical significance in two respects. First, insofar as it is inconsistent with the ontological actualism, regularity determinism and spatio-temporary block universalism (which I shall henceforth shorten to blockism) with which reductionism has normally been associated. Thus, for instance, determinism, as it is normally understood, viz. in the Humean-Laplacean manner, such that knowledge is possible so that 'the future is present to our eyes', can be seen to rest on a naïve actualist ontology of laws (the antinomies of which will in due course be fully exposed), and is posited on supposing that because an event at time t_k was *caused* (say, at t_j) to happen, it was *bound* (e.g. at t_i) to happen before it is caused — a confusion of ontological determination with epistemological predeterminism, unwarranted in an *open system* constituted by irreducible alterities — other-beings, as important to the critique of irrealist dialectics as non-beings are to irrealism generally.* Second, it is significant in that it links 1M causally efficacious determination to 2E transformative negation (and the critique of actualism to that of monovalence). In a moment I am going to connect causal efficacy with what I am going to call a '*rhythmic*' defined as a tensed process in space-time. And just as causal powers are processes-entified-in-products, we could say causality is transformative negation in processual (rhythmic) determination. It could be asked why are the pivotal concepts of change and agency being neglected? They are not. For agency is intentional causality and consists in efficacious absenting. Nor is 3L being left out of the picture. For an absenting alienation, absented alienation, splitting

---

* To those reductionists — tendentially type monists — who would deny the phenomena of emergence, contemporary ecological findings come as an awesome warning. For they show the extent to which industrialized humanity has been intervening in (increasingly socialized) nature, and will suffer from its recoil.

detotalization or split-off can exercise a causal effect, and in §7 I shall systematically discuss the intra-active and mediating holistic causality typical of a totality.

In a multi-determined, multi-levelled, multi-linear, multi-relational, multi-angular, multi-perspectival, multiply determined and open pluriverse, emergence situates the widespread phenomena of dual, multiple, complex and open control. Thus typically, in our zone of being, higher-order agencies set the boundary conditions for the operation of lower-order laws. Thus in contemporary capitalist society it is economic considerations which explain when, where and how the physical principles engaged in engineering are put to use (or held in abeyance). This principle also offers keys to the unravelling of the old Marxian conundrum of the 'superstructures'. On Model A we can readily say that it is the relations of production which determine the boundary conditions for the operation and development of the forces of production, and similarly for the relationship between polity and economy. On Model B, in which we envisage the superstructure as intrastructure, that is, formed within the base level, we can argue that it is the latter which provides the framework principles for, or conditions of possibility of, the 'higher' level which may complexify, be supervenient on or relatively autonomous from the base level or, one could say, the totality or whole in which it is interiorized. Thus, deploying Model B, the politics of the new world disorder or the spread of postmodernist culture can be seen as occurring within the context of global capitalist commodification, both figuratively and literally — and, as already remarked, there is no reason why these models should not be deployed concurrently.

Emergence entails both stratification and change. So far I have concentrated on emergent entities and causal powers. But if, as I have already argued, all changes are spatio-temporal, and space-time is a relational property of the meshwork of material beings, this opens up the phenomena of *emergent spatio-temporalities*. There are two paradigms here, both instantiated in reality: (α) they could be relata of a new (emergent) system of material things and/or (β) they could be new (emergent) relata of a pre-existing system of material things. In either event they establish new 'rhythmics', where a rhythmic is just the spatio-temporal efficacy of the process. (In a Wittgensteinian family circle, process can then be regarded as spatialized tensing, the mode of becoming [as absenting] or [plain] absenting of effects.) A rhythmic may be transfactual or actual, positive or negative (i.e. an inefficacy), intra-active or inter-active, agentive or not (corresponding to 1M – 4D). If a substance is paradigmatically a thing, a rhythmic may be substantial or non-substantial (where the non-substantial is aligned under the class of non-being-mediated). If it is non-substantial, then the causal rhythmic of a process must, and even if it is substantial it may (cf. [β] above), be reckoned to be a sui generis causal power of space-time itself. Space-time thus takes on, potentially, a fivefold character as: (a) a reference grid, (b) a measure, (c) a set of prima facie mutual exclusion relations, (d) a potentially emergent (cf. [α]) property, perhaps with causal powers of its own, and (e) a generally entropic process. Eventually I will want to tie space, time and causality very closely, around the theorem of the reality and irreducibility of (always potentially spatializing) tense and the potential and typical spatio-temporality (and hence processuality) of all causal efficacy in the definition of process as the mode of absenting which is the becoming and begoing of effects.

In the meantime, for those who doubt the propriety of such a close linkage (and emphasis on spatio-temporal process), just ponder the extent to which emergent social things (people, institutions, traditions) not only presuppose (that is to say, are dependent on) but also are *existentially constituted* by (as a crucial part of their essence) or merely *contain* (as part of their proprium or accident, to drop into scholastic vocabulary for a moment) *their geo-histories* (and, qua empowered, possibilities for their spatialized futures). In the same way I will argue, when I come to totality and holistic causality, that emergent social things are existentially constituted by or contain their *relations*, connections and interdependencies with other social (and natural) things.[18] This is 3L territory. For the moment I want to stick with 2E spatio-temporalities. Constitutive geo-history displayed in contemporary rhythmics or in the processual exercise of accumulated causal powers and liabilities is only one of several ways in which in §8 I will consider the phenomena of the presence of the past (and outside). But just ponder the extent to which although we may live *for* the future, we live, quite literally, *in* the past.[19] Generally the phenomenon of emergent spatio-temporalities situates the possibilities of overlapping, intersecting, condensing, elongated, divergent, convergent and even contradictory rhythmics (causal processes) and, by extension, space-time measures (overthrowing, inter alia, the idea of a unitary set of exclusion relations).

In exemplification of this phenomenon let me dwell on intersecting and overlapping spaces and times — see Figure 2.2. The last case in the figure shows how discrepant spatio-temporalities can often, but not always, be coordinated either by reference to some explanatory significant loco-periodization or, as here, by reference to a zero-level or base space-time, established by some conventionally agreed (not necessarily physically basic) dating and locating system. As a final example consider the amazing and putatively contradictory juxta-position or condensation of differentially sedimented rhythmics one can find in a city like Los Angeles[20] or New Delhi, where temples, mosques, traditions, religious rites, weddings, inter-caste conflict, electric cables, motor cars, television sets, rickshaws, scavengers and disposable cans coalesce in a locale.

Indeed specifically *conceptual emergence*, e.g. as in the σ and τ transforms of the epistemological dialectic sketched in C1.9, generally depends upon the exploitation of the past or exterior cognitive resources (once again, Bachelard's 'scientific loans') constituting so much conceptual bricolage. But it may also be effected by means of a perspectival switch, the formation of a new *Gestalt*, level or order of coherence *without* any additional input.[21] Emergence is, of course, also necessary for the intelligibility of the actual working of the Hegelian dialectic, which operates merely by filling in, or absenting the absence of, what is from a higher-order perspective a level-specific void. And although in the end Hegel cannot sustain it, this, as Marx famously remarked but insufficiently explained, does give the basic form or essence of many, if not all, dialectics. Emergent entities are, of course, as already remarked, one kind of totality, constituted by the internal relationality of their aspects. This raises the question of the limits or boundaries of an emergent totality. Is it, for instance, an organism, upon whose 'internal teleology' so much of the plausibility of Hegelian ontology intuitively rests; or is it rather the organism in its *Umwelt* or environment constituted at least in part by the various 'affordances' the environment offers for the organism in question?[22] In general one can resolve the problem of the individuation and articulation of an emergent entity and its various aspects only by reference to the explanatory power of the theory which a particular *découpage* permits. This, in turn, will depend to a degree upon our explanatory purposes. However, this does not subjectivize explanation in science (or everyday existence), for what I will call the '*reality principle*' (invoking its Freudian ancestry) imposes

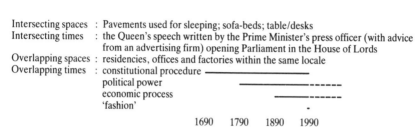

Figure 2.2

its own stratification on science and lay life. Dialectical critical realism
sees totalities within totalities (but studded with blocks, partitions
and distance) recursively. But they are by no means all, or normally,
of the Hegelian, pervasively internally relational, let alone centrist,
expressivist and teleological kind. Rather they are punctuated by
alterities, shot through with spaces, criss-crossed by traces and
connected by all manner of negative, external and contingent as well
as positive, internal and necessary determinations and relationships,
the exact form of which it is up to science to fathom. Similarly, as we
shall now see, not all dialectical connections are contradictory and not
all dialectical contradictions are or depend upon logical contradictions
in the way I have argued Hegel's paradigmatically do.

§ 3 Contradiction I: Hegel and Marx

In C1.9 I isolated the motive force that logical contradiction plays in
Hegelian dialectic (at least in theory) in heralding the expansion of the
existing conceptual field. But by juxtaposing Marx to Hegel I want to
show that logical contradiction is not the same as dialectical
contradiction, although the two classes intersect. Moreover, by no
means all dialectics depend upon contradiction, and even less violate
the logical norms of identity and non-contradiction. First I want to
examine contradiction in its widest compass.

The concept of contradiction may be used as a metaphor (like that
of force in physics) for any kind of dissonance, strain or tension.
However, it first assumes a clear meaning in the case of human
action, which may then be extended to goal-oriented action, and
thence, by a further move, to any action at all. Here it specifies a
situation which permits the satisfaction of one end or more generally
result only at the expense of another: that is, a *bind* or constraint. An
internal contradiction is then a *double-bind* or self-constraint (which may
be multiplied to form a knot). In this case a system, agent or structure,
S, is *blocked* from performing with one system, rule or principle, R,
because it is performing with another, R′; or, a course of action, T,
generates a countervailing, inhibiting, undermining, overriding or
otherwise opposed course of action, T′. R′ and T′ are radically
negating of R and T respectively. As the Hegelian and Marxian
traditions have a propensity for internal as distinct from external
contradictions, it is worth pointing out that external constraints (not
generated by a common causal ground [dg′]) may nevertheless hold
between structures which are internally related, i.e. existentially
presuppose one another.

External contradictions — constraints — would appear to be pervasive — indeed, exemplified by the laws and constraints of nature (such as the speed of light), to be established by the mere fact of determinate spatio-temporal being. But, of course, it does not follow from the condition that every being is constrained, that every particular constraint on a being is absolute or necessary. This should go without saying. Only a blanket actualism would deny it. How about internal contradictions? Their possibility is directly situated by the phenomena of emergent entities (which is why I interposed my discussion of §2), internally related grounded ensembles and totalities generally. However, leaving this aside, it could be argued that for the very fact of change to be possible, even if the source is exogenous, there must be a degree of internal 'complicity' within the thing to the change: that is, in that it must, in virtue of its nature, be 'liable' to the change, so as not to be impervious to its source, and so must possess a counter-conative tendency in respect of the condition changed, which may be more or less essential to the thing's identity. (By definition in such a case — of change, not demise — it must also possess a conative one.) Only unchanging, ultimately eternal, things would lack such a tendency, and such things would seem to have to be or contain everywhere everywhen — a Spinozan monism or Leibnizian monadism. In any case this establishes the most basic kind of *existential contradiction*: finitude. Spatio-temporal location may seem an external constraint, but insofar as it is the fate — condition of being — of such things to perish, i.e. to be limited in extent, it must be reckoned an internal contradiction, even though their extent and duration be entirely contingent. When we turn to human life, existential contradiction may assume the mantle of standing oppositions between mind and body, fact and fancy, desire and desired, power and need, Eros and Thanatos, master and slave, self-determination and subjugation.

Formal logical contradiction is a type of internal contradiction, whose consequence for the subject, unless the terms are redescribed and/or the discursive domain is expanded (as happens in Hegelian dialectic), is *axiological indeterminacy*: 'A and $-A$' leaves the course of action (including belief) indeterminate, or, at least if relevance, contextual, spatio-temporal and normic constraints are imposed, underdetermined; and so subverts the intentionality, and, ceteris paribus, the rationality, of any praxis that would be founded on, or informed by, it. Such axiological indeterminacy in the intrinsic, intentional or normative aspect of social life is quite consistent with a determinate intransitive result, especially if the agent must act — that is to say, if what I have elsewhere described as the 'axiological imperative'[23] applies — for consistency and coherence are not the only generative or causal factors at work in social life (this is the constellational identity of the intrinsic within the extrinsic[24] or, loosely, the rational within the causal). To suppose that they are is to make the epistemic fallacy of logicizing being, into which Hegel falls. The inverse, Kantian, mistake is to extrude thought from, detotalizing, being. Against this, it is important to understand that when logical contradictions are committed, they are real constituents of the *Lebenswelt*. Moreover, they may be consistently described and explained, as the intransitive objects of some epistemic inquiry (say into the state of secondary school mathematics in Essex in 1992). What could be more symptomatic of partial, monovalent (and, if I may say so, complacent) thought than to deny the occurrence of logical contradictions in (social) reality?

Dialectical contradictions are, like logical contradictions, also a type of internal contradiction. They may best be introduced as a species of the more general category of *dialectical connections*. These are connections between entities or aspects of a totality such that they are in principle *distinct* but *inseparable*, in the sense that they are synchronically or conjuncturally internally related,[25] i.e. both (some, all) or one existentially presuppose the other(s). Here we are in the domain of what I have elsewhere called *intra-* rather than *inter-action*,[26] which may take the form of existential *constitution* (cf. p. 54 above), *permeation* (presence within, i.e. 'containment') or just *connection* (causal efficacy) — either in virtue of spatio-temporal contiguity or across a level-specific void. The connection may be absolute, epochal, structurally periodic, conjunctural or momentary. Dialectical connections, including contradictions, may hold between absences and absentings as well as positive instances and processes, and the causal connections and existential dependencies may be transfactual or actual. Real dialectical contradictions possess all these features of dialectical connections. But their elements are also *opposed*, in the sense that (at least) one of their aspects negates (at least) one of the other's, or their common ground or the whole, and perhaps vice versa, so that they are *tendentially mutually exclusive*, and potentially or actually tendentially transformative. Are dialectical contradictions necessarily radical in my terms? This depends upon the — ideally, real — definition of the contradictions. If what is negated is the ground of the negation or the totality then they are necessarily radical; if not, not. The case where one of the poles of a contradiction is the ground itself corresponds to the dyadic mode of the Hegelian dialectic, as the negation is then not only necessarily radical but also linear. But any number of aspects of a totality may be so related (as in the polyadic case of the Hegelian dialectic). Such a radically negating ensemble is thus multi-linear. Both Hegel and Marx were biased towards internal, radical and linear negation — a fact partly explained by the narrative presentational form, or sequential flow or 'continuous series' of the nineteenth-century expository text (as a comparison between *Capital* and Marx's notes and letters bears out).

Dialectical contradictions are not per se logical contradictions. But logical contradictions can also be dialectical contradictions *insofar as they are grounded in a common mistake*, whether the mistake is isolated or not. (The importance of this for the metacritical dialectics of discursively formulated or practically expressed philosophical ideologies will become clear in C4.) Dialectical and logical contradictions, as two species of internal contradiction, intersect but are not coterminous. However, we can describe the logical contradiction as dialectical only when the mistaken ground is isolated, and can do so coherently (without at least a degree of axiological indeterminacy) only when its contradictoriness is removed — which is precisely, on my exegesis, what Hegel intends to do, and sometimes succeeds (brilliantly) in doing.

Dialectical contradictions may be more or less antagonistic, in the sense of expressing or representing or even constituting the opposed interests of (or between) agents or collectivities; and, if antagonistic, they may be partial or latent or rhythmically dislocated, and manifest to a greater or lesser extent in conflict, which in turn can be covert or overt, transfactual or actual, as well as being conducted in a variety of different modes. Of course there are contingent (and within the contingent what should really be distinguished as a distinct class, the accidental) in addition to necessary, and external besides internal, contradictions, thus one has

[1] connections ≥ necessary connections ≥ dialectical connections ≥ dialectical contradictions;

[2] constraints ≥ internal contradictions ≥ dialectical contradictions ≥ logical dialectical contradictions;

and

[3] dialectical contradictions ≥ antagonisms ≥ conflicts ≥ overt struggles;

while of course

[4] real negation ≥ transformative negation ≥ radical negation ≥ linear negation.

[3] is not supposed to rule out non-dialectical, e.g. purely external or contingent, conflicts. On the other hand, it is a mistake to think of conflicts as 'more' empirical than contradictions. The contradiction between contending parties in the law courts may be palpably visible, while deep conflict may never show itself in experience. Hence all the relevant concepts possess a 1M real/actual and 2E real/present contrast. Suppose one distinguishes power$_1$, as the transformative capacity analytic to the concept of agency, from (the transfactual or actual) power$_2$ relations expressed in structures of domination, exploitation, subjugation and control, which I will thematize as *generalized master—slave*(-type) *relations*. The poles of such antagonistic dialectical contradictions, exemplified by the famous contradictions between capitalist and worker or the looker and looked at or master and slave itself, are typically differentially causally charged. One should note, however, that this is seldom completely one-sided and always potentially reversible — as in Foucauldian counter-conduct or strategic reversal. (Power$_1$ includes power$_2$ of course.) In such cases one may talk of a dominant and subordinate pole; and more generally of the primary and secondary (etc.) aspects of a contradiction or contradictions in a totality. Indeed unless, more generally, there were *structural asymmetries* in a multi-angular pluriversal context, it would be difficult to conceive, against inertial drag, causes of change, let alone of directionality, in geo-history. The grounds, structures or mechanisms which generate real dialectical contradictions may themselves form recursively (geo-historically variable componential), hierarchical, power$_2$-dominated, complexes or totalities. Furthermore, any of the figures I have just discussed may induce secondary, tertiary or multiply proliferating elaborations or connections of dialectical or non-dialectical kinds.

In the social world all the figures, from constraint to conflict, will be concept- or meaning-dependent. It is important to stress that this holds for formal logical contradictions too. These are entirely dependent upon (normally tacit) semantic and contextual considerations. We only assume 'A' and '−A' are contradictory because we take for granted that the successive occurrences of the grapheme 'A' are tokens of the same type. But a sceptic could easily deny this, asking what semiotic, hermeneutic or other considerations have prevented the nature of A from changing, and in many cases be right to do so.

'Materialist' dialectical contradictions of the type defined above, such as those identified by Marx in his systematic dialectics, *describe (dialectical), but do not suffer from (logical), contradictions*. The mechanism is not in general teleological, but even when it is, its teleology presupposes causality (a lesser form for Hegel). The practical resolution of the contradiction here is the non-preservative transformative negation of the ground, which is the problem, not the solution. This involves what I am going to call *'transformed transformative totalizing transformist praxis'* ($d\phi'$) in the struggle, presaged upon Marx's analysis of the dialectic processes (dp') of capitalism, for a sublation (ds'), traditionally known as 'socialism', of the replaced social form. Of course Marx's analysis may *contain* logical contradictions — as a line from Böhm-Bawerk to Roemer has contended — but then it is just straightforwardly faulty, a faultiness which may in turn be dialectically explained. The co-presence of absence and presence, that is, the combination of actual absences and real presences (tendential, transfactual) of opposites (at different levels), i.e. of negative sub-contraries and positive contraries, enables the traditional table of oppositions to be satisfied simultaneously prior to, rather than in the switch occurring in, the resolution. Moreover, Marx's dialectical contradictions cannot be said to constitute an identity, but at most a grounded *unity*, of opposites.[27] (One might be tempted to contrast here the Kantian independence, Hegelian identity and Marxian unity of opposites.) Marx's concern is with the *dialectical explanation* and *practical transformation* of capitalism, not with the transfigurative redescription of, and reconciliation to, *Das Bestehende* (the actually existing state of affairs).

None of this is to deny that Marx's systematic ontological and programmatic relational dialectics of the capitalist mode of production presupposes a critical epistemological dialectic of an Hegelian C1.9 kind: that is, an immanent critique of the pre-existing political economy of his day, involving the identification of contradictions, and more generally aporiai, anomalies and absences (such as that of the distinction between labour and labour-power, an absence readily explained by the commodification of the latter), entailing the characterisic nodal (dc') and resolutionary (dr') transforms of a process which, insofar as it inaugurated a research programme, it would be surprising if it did not require further development and deepening.[28] But in terms of C1.8, D_3 — ideology-critique — is now distinguished from D_1 — the ideology or self-understanding of the form or practice in question. This becomes part of Marx's explanandum, as in the case of his identification and description of commodity fetishism. Moreover, once a research programme has been initiated, dialectical detachment from the latter can occur, so that the ongoing metacritique of capitalism, identifying new defence mechanisms and causal tendencies and explaining them, need not be

entirely immanent (radically negating in character*). However, to be
effective, a radical relational dialectic, dependent upon the causal
efficacy and conditioning** of ideas, presupposes a hermeneutic
which takes agents to the point where immanent critique, registering
theory—practice inconsistencies (cf. D_2), is possible. In any event,
there is now an internal rift within the conceptual realm, comprising a
conflict of reasons, mobilized around what I am going to call
hermeneutic hegemonic/counter-hegemonic struggles in the context of
generalized master—slave power$_2$ relations.

Let us accentuate the philosophical contrast between Hegel and
Marx by elaborating the way the logical contradictions of Hegelian
dialectic differ, as species of internal contradiction, from the real
dialectical contradictions of materialist analysis and critique. The
driving force (in principle) of Hegelian dialectic is the transition,
paradigmatically of the elements (e) and (−e), from positive
contraries simultaneously present and actual (thereby continually
violating the principle of non-contradiction, as Hegel both does and
says he does) into negative sub-contraries now simultaneously actual
and absent, but retained as negative presences in a cumulative
memory store, as the dialectical reader's consciousness or the path of
history moves on to a new level of speculative reason. At this stage
they are now retrospectively redescribed as moments of a
transcending totality. Contradiction has cancelled itself. And they are
now, in what we could call Hegel's *analytic reinstatement*, restored to
their positive self-identity. No longer contradictory, they now
illustrate what I have just adumbrated as 'dialectical connection'.
*Hegelian dialectic, when it is contradictory, is logically contradictory but not
dialectically determinate; conversely, when it has become dialectically
determinate, there is nothing contradictory about it at all.* That is to say,
when the elements are contradictory, they are not per se dialectical;
but, when they are dialectical, they are no longer opposed. Hegelian
dialectic is the continual transition from the one state, 'understanding', to the other, 'speculative reason'; it *is* this transition and
everything is always in it. But it is never simultaneously dialectical
and contradictory. The materialist dialectic is. It involves a simultaneity of grounded (transfactual) presence and (actual) absence, of

---

* Thus to use the terminology I introduced in SRHE, pp. 25−6, one can say MC_2
(explanatory critique) > MC_1 (the identification of an absence corresponding to real
negation) > immanent critique.
** It is important to remember this is an axiom of materialist thought, itself bearing
Hegelian credentials (according to which objective spirit formed the humus out of
which absolute spirit grew).

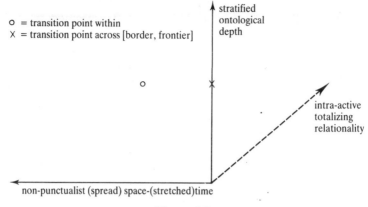

Figure 2.3

practical (existential) inclusion and mutual (tendentially transforma-tive) exclusion. It is this which makes it genuinely dialectically contradictory in a stratified ontology that pre-exists the discourse that describes it.

There is no need, however, to deny Hegel the accolade of articulating dialectical contradictions if we reject, as I shall argue we should, a punctualist view of time. We can then say that what Hegel achieves, i.e. the co-presence of absence and presence, within an (actualist) extended temporal stretch in the mode of succession in time, Marx accomplishes instantaneously within a (transfactually) extended structural depth, in the mode of ontological stratification. Breaking free from both actualism and spatio-temporal punctualism allows for a vastly expanded table or matrix of opposition, as illustrated in Figure 2.3.

Allowing for the embedding of presence and absence, past and present, inside and outside, essence and appearance, transfactual and actual, in a combination of ontological stratification and internally tensed distanciated space-time (or set of such rhythmics) situates the possibility of a new, genuinely multi-dimensional and dynamic logic. Adding the possibilities permitted by 3L intra-active totalizing relationality, enabling the embedding of, for example, containment and separation and 4D transformative praxis, enabling the embed-ding of, for example, agency and power, spreads the canvas even wider. However, reverting to my main point here, and simplifying, while Hegel describes the contradictions of the sundered world at the dawn of the age of modernity (which Kant prefigures) in a non-contradictory and reconciliatory way, Marx attempts to explain the contradictions of that world (giving it a real definition as capitalist) in order eventually to change it. This could be summed up by the formulae:

[5] HD = Logical contradiction → dialectical connection → transfigurative redescription [→ analytic reinstatement].

[6] MD = Dialectical connection → dialectical contradiction → transformist praxis → practical resolution.

Now to complicate matters. Hegel is a deeply ambiguous figure. He is both — Hegel Mark I — the first practitioner of a new socio-geo-historicist mode of thought and expressly interested in change (before 1806), and — Hegel Mark II — the last great metaphysician who (almost) succeeds in realizing the traditional goals of philosophy within an immanent metaphysics of experience (after 1800) and increasingly fearful of change. (Note the discrepant times.) Of Hegel Mark II we could echo Marx on Proudhon: 'Although there has been history . . . there is no longer any.'[29] Indeed this is a potent motif of the philosophical tradition — one which could be provisionally and partially identified as the *normally unconscious and characteristically aporetic normalization of past, and denegation of present and future, change*. Of course Hegel does not believe that the geo-historical process has totally stopped. Hence he refers to Russia and America as lands of the future. But these belong to what I will call the *'demi-actual'*. The future is *demi-present: constellationally closed*. Like Rorty, he believes the 'last conceptual revolution has occurred'[30] — and for Hegel the concept spelled *Begriff* just is 'conceptually understood reality'. It is important to appreciate that Hegel 'Mark I' and 'Mark II' correspond to or designate moments of real history (not just phases of his intellectual career). But this does not prevent Hegel Mark II presenting brilliant diagnoses of real, including non-logical, dialectical contradictions, as witnessed by his remarkable analyses of the contradictions of civil society which he never sublates. Moreover, we have already noticed the normic nature of Hegel's real dialectical practice (see C1.8 — p. 30 above). So Hegel moves closer to Marx. But Marx also steps nearer to Hegel. For his analysis of the capitalist mode of production does not remain at the level of the Hegelian 'understanding' but takes the form of a critique of political economy, engaging σ and τ transforms of the latter, identifying conceptualized forms (value, commodity, money) as diagnostic clues to the inner workings of his intransitive object of inquiry. So a fairer representation of the true nature of Hegel's and Marx's real dialectical

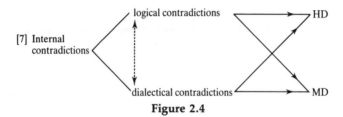

Figure 2.4

practice might be as suggested by the schema in Figure 2.4. It should perhaps be stressed here what is implicit in [5] and [6] above, viz. that the sequential orders of the Marxian and Hegelian dialectics typically differ, viz.:

[8] HD: Logical contradiction – transition – dialectical connection – reconciliatory theoretical result.

[9] MD: Dialectical connection – dialectical contradition – dialectic praxis – transformative negation – resolutionary practical result.

Hegel's resolution is in theory. Marx's is in practice. But this must not be misunderstood. The resolution of all contradictions, including logical contradictions, is practical both in the sense (a) that they consist in the transformative negation of the pre-existing (contradictory) state of affairs and (b) that, qua actions, they are moments of social practices (e.g. typesetting, mathematics). The further senses in which there are differences at stake between Hegel and Marx depend (c) upon some social schematization or theory — a practice, of course — differentiating, for instance, manual from mental labour and/or (d) the different orientations of theoretical and practical reason — with the former concerned to adjust our beliefs to the world and the latter to adjust the world to our will. Following Hegel we can distinguish theoretical reason (dr_t'), practical reason (dr_p') and absolute reason, that is, their unity, coherence or consistency (dr_a'), which is to be achieved for dialectical critical realism in the Cartesian product of senses (a) and (d), viz. practically oriented transformative negation $(d\phi')$, rather than recapitulative redescription — a concept which, in the end, Hegel cannot sustain, in virtue of his constellational closure of dialectical praxis and reason alike.

Theory/practice inconsistency, which is entailed by, though it does not entail, a dialectical comment (dc'), is of special interest for a number of reasons. First, because of its immediately *auto-subversive,* self-deconstructive, performative and radically negational *character*. Second, when set in the context of hermeneutic-hegemonic struggles over power$_2$ or the practical *transfinity* of generalized master–slave relations, because of its significance as a form of immanent (and so necessarily non-arbitrary or ad hominem) critique, insofar as it turns on an agent or community rejecting in its practice what it affirms in its theory and/or expressing in its practice what it denies in its theory. Third, because a cumulative series of theory/practice inconsistencies, in which each phase brings out, precisely, as the *scotoma* or blind spot of the previous phase, the point of its greatest ex ante strength as in fact its greatest weakness (the dc_k' as the dr_j' of the dc_i' [of the $dr_i'_{-1}$]) constitutes what may be called an *Achilles' Heel critique* (as in the sequential parthogenetic process of Hegelian dialectic phenomen-ology), which is of the greatest moment in the history of philosophy and science alike.* Fourth, because insofar as a theory or practice violates an *axiological necessity*, it immediately generates a most interesting kind of *compromise form*, to be explicated in §7. Fifth, because it shows the subject involved to be internally riven, alienated and/or *untrue to itself*. Sixth, because of its *lack of dialectical universalizability*, again to be treated subsequently.

I now want to insist on the practical nature of all theory and the quasi-propositionality of all practice, insofar as it is dependent upon, but not exhausted by, its conceptual, and thus belief-expressive aspects ('actions speak louder than words').** This immediately generates the theorem of *the duality of theory and practice*, in that by means of a transcendental perspectival switch, each can be seen under the aspect of the other. Consequences of this are that a theory or practice may be immediately, or more normally mediately, theory/practice inconsistent; and that theory/theory inconsistencies or logical contradictions proper may be seen under the aspect of theory/practice or practice/practice contradictions, which I will call *quasi-logical contradictions* and *axiological inconsistencies*. Moreover, it follows from the quasi-propositionality of practice that practical or theory/practice inconsistencies will yield at least axiological underdetermination; and from the practical character of theory that insofar as theory/theory contradictions violate axiological necessities they will entrain the compromise form referred to in the previous paragraph, which may be provisionally regarded as necessitated by what I earlier called the

---

* So we can extend the theorem on p. 62 above: $MC_2 > MC_1 >$ immanent critique > AH critique.

** Of course the best conceptualization will often be a hotly contested matter, especially in the context of power$_2$ relations.

reality principle. Note that this does not abolish either (α) the intransitivity of, or (β) the characteristic difference in orientation or 'direction of fit' (sense [d] above) between, theory and practice — generating the important dialectical figure of the non-identity, alterity or *hiatus-in-the-duality* — or (γ) their respective locations in some social schematism (sense [c]). It follows from this that, even if dialectical connections, as defined above, are regarded as necessary for a configuration to be said to be 'dialectical',

1. there is no a priori reason why all dialectics should be social, and hence conceptualized;
2. neither is there any reason why all social dialectics should involve contradictions, whether dialectical, logical or both;
3. there is no necessary reason for believing that all dialectical contradictions involve quasi-logical contradictions or axiological inconsistencies, although there are good grounds for supposing that they will be frequently ideologically mediated by such;
4. only a sub-class of dialectical contradictions involve logical contradictions;
5. all these types may be described and potentially explained (in the intrinsic aspect of science) without contradiction; and finally
6. only epistemological dialectics necessarily breach, at certain critical moments, the formal principles of identity and non-contradiction.

In short most, if not all, dialectics are consistent with adherence to the norms of formal logic (as illustrated in Figures 2.5 and 2.6). This result will be qualified subsequently by consideration of the interconnection between epistemological and other dialectics and the effects of the illicit epistemo-logicization of reality in §10 but it is important to insist on it now. Dialectical critical realism will situate, but not just negate, 'logic'.*

Insofar as theory is practical, it will depend (analytically) upon some prior piece of practical reasoning, e.g. about the efficacy of the practice in arriving at an adequate description of the world. But this depends upon theory, which incorporates theoretical and practical reasoning alike. And insofar as practice is quasi-propositional, it will depend (analytically) upon some anterior theoretical reasoning, e.g.

---

* This is perhaps the point to remark that in characterizing dialectic as 'the logic of absence' in the title of this chapter, I am exploiting a more generic sense of 'logic' than that captured by commitment to the principles of identity and non-contradiction — the sense employed in this passage.

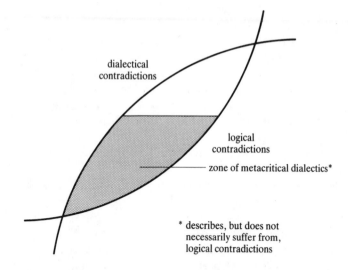

Figure 2.5 Dialectical and Logical Contradictions Intersect
But Are Not Coterminous

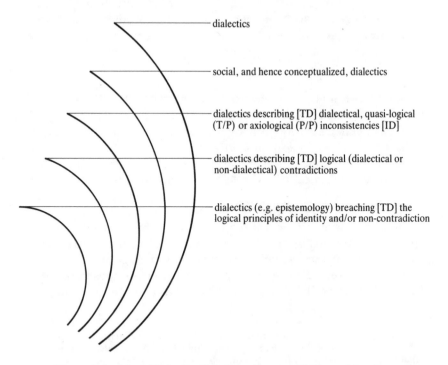

Figure 2.6 Most Dialectics Are Consistent with Formal Logic

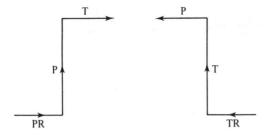

Figure 2.7 Theory, Practice and Reason

about the nature of the world that the practice is designed to change. But this depends upon practice, which also encompasses both theoretical and practical reasoning. And so we have the lemma of the *duality of theoretical and practical reasoning*, mediated by the transformative character of theory and the conceptuality of practice. Once again this does not annul their distinction. The upshot of theory is belief about the world; that of practice, action on it. That theory will express our will and depend upon our wants, and practices will express our (concrete axiological[31]) judgements and depend upon our beliefs. Figure 2.7 is designed to illustrate this. (These two aspects, expression or manifestation and dependency, are different. In the former case theory manifests, qua practice, the upshot of practical reason; and practice manifests, qua quasi-propositional, the outcome of theoretical reason. In the latter case, theory merely existentially presupposes, but is not also, the practical reason upon which it depends; and similarly for practice.)

In the Marxist tradition dialectical contradiction has been most frequently characterized in contrast to either (α) exclusive or so-called 'real' opposition or conflict (Kantian *Realrepugnanz*[32]) on the grounds that their terms mutually presuppose each other, so that they comprise an (existentially) inclusive (as well as tendentially exclusive) opposition; and/or (β) formal logical opposition on the basis that their relations are *meaning*-(or content-)dependent, not purely formal, so that the negation of A does not lead to its annulment, but to its transformative replacement by a new, richer form B. Associated with the first contrast is the theme of the 'unity of opposites', the trademark of Marxist ontological dialectics from Engels on. At the level of social theory this motif most often reduces to internal relationality of antagonists in a structure of domination (with conflicting, mutually exclusive, interests — ultimately one in the preservation, the other in the abolition, of that structure). Associated with the second contrast is the conception of immanent critique as central to the project of radical negation, which is the hallmark of Marxist relational dialectics from Lukács on, with the emphasis on the causal efficacy (as distinct from mere material-infrastructural conditioning) of ideas. In both traditions dialectical contradictions are held to be characteristically 'concrete', in comparison with their 'abstract' analytic contrasts, a distinction I examine in §7.

In Marx's works the terms 'contradiction' (*Widerspruch*), 'antagonism' (*Gegensatz*) and 'conflict' (*Konflikt*), which I have differentiated above, are often used interchangeably. But if some conceptual consistency is imposed, it can be said that in Marx's mature economic writings the concept of contradiction is deployed to denote inter alia: (a) *logical inconsistencies* or other intra-discursive theoretical anomalies, which are related to or can be perhaps reduced to the concept of logical contradiction; (b) extra-discursive (although, of course, generally conceptually mediated) *non-dialectical oppositions*, e.g. supply and demand as comprising forces of relatively independent origins interacting in such a way that their effects tend to cancel one another in notional, momentary or enduring equilibria, which approximate to the Kantian *Realrepugnanz*; (c) *structural* or synchronic or local-period-ized *dialectical contradictions* intrinsic to a particular social form; (d) *geo-historically specific dialectical contradictions* that bring into being a social form and/or crises in the course of its development which are then resolved in the process of transformation which they help to cause. Contradictions of type (d) involve forces of non-independent origins operating so that a force F itself tends to produce or is itself the product of conditions stemming from a ground, namely social form S which simultaneously or subsequently produces a countervailing force F', tending to frustrate, subvert, overcome or otherwise transform F and/or the social form that grounds it, that is, to radically negate them. Such geo-historically specific contradictions are exemplified by those which arise between the relations and forces of production, and particularly between the increasingly socialized nature of the relations and the definitionally private character of the forces. These rhythmic contradictions are grounded for Marx in structural ones of type (c), such as between wage-labour and capital or between the use value and the exchange value of the commodity, which provide ab initio the formal conditions of their possibility. Such (c)-type contradictions are then in turn geo-historically explained (so that we have a meta-ontological dialectic of [c] and [d] types) in terms of (e) an original *generative separation*, split or alienation of the immediate producers from the means and materials of their production. This generates an alienation from their labour and from the planes of their material transactions with nature, their social interactions with each other, the network of social relations in which they produce, and ultimately themselves. The prototype of dialectical generative separation is the Hegelian *'Beautiful Soul'* alienated from her community, but it is given a specific dialectical meaning in Marx. (c)−(e) contradictions are all real dialectical ones.

The identification of (a)s, corresponding to the moment of dc' in the critique of political economy, is of course a part of the real (non-preservative) transformative negation of it, at the level of dr_t' (b)s are simple external contradictions, although it is always possible that a more totalizing analysis at what I have called the 'intensive' and 'extensive' margins of inquiry[33] (and will rehearse in §7) may always reveal them to be internally related. In respect of the thematization of the concept within Marxism it should be noted that dialectical contradictions of types (c)−(e) both constitute real inclusive oppositions, in that their terms existentially presuppose one another (cf. α), and are systematically and intrinsically related to mystifying forms of appearance, such as the value or wage forms (cf. β). These dialectical contradictions neither violate the principle of non-contradiction — for, as already stressed, they may be *consistently described*; nor are they scientifically absurd in any fashion — for the notion of a real *inverted*, or otherwise mystifying, conception of a real object, perhaps the result of the ensemble or ground containing the very phenomena mystified, may be readily accommodated within a critical realist stratified, non-monovalent, totalizing ontology of the sort to which Marx is committed in his mature work, though never able fully to develop. Yet there is a long line of criticism in Marxist, as well as non-Marxist, thought (which begins with Bernstein and reaches its apogee with Colletti) which claims that the notion of dialectical contradictions in reality is incompatible with one or more of formal logic, coherent discourse, scientific practice or materialism. This is not so. For dialectical, as other species of, contradictions, whether simply within being (cf. α') or between being and thought within being (cf. β'), may be straightforwardly consistently described and scientifically explained. It is only if logical, which may sometimes also be dialectical, contradictions are *committed*, as distinct from described, that the norm of non-contradiction is infringed, and provided logic is included within reality, not detotalized, exteriorized, split off or hypostatized (in Platonic-Cartesian-Kantian manner), its fetishistic or otherwise categorically mystifying character betrays no absurdity in the critical discourse in contrast to the conceptualized reality described. It is thus quite incorrect to argue, as Colletti does,[34] that any scientifically legitimate concept of contradiction must reduce to Kantian *Realrepugnanz* or non-dialectical, merely external, opposition. This is the legacy of Colletti's Humean-Kantian empirical realism. Hegel's conceptual realist gloss merely embellishes it and, as we shall see, leaves its structure intact. In particular lacking the concepts of non-logical natural necessity, non-self-cancelling contradiction and an open totality, real negativity and (post-Hegelian Mark II) transformative change disappear from Hegel's own theoretical horizons. Hegel loses not absence, but the concept of absence, and with that the essence of the dialectic itself.

§ 4 Contradiction II: Misunderstandings

In this section I wish to fasten upon the *dialectical fertility* of logical (and other) contradictions. The most creative response to contradiction is to *redescribe the alternatives* in the context of a *transformed* (and in general more complete or totalizing) *problematic* or practical ensemble. In the course of the argument I want to explain why Hegel regards contradiction as ubiquitous, and the sense in which he is right and wrong to do so; and to criticize in turn the unreflected use of the principle of non-contradiction as a *definiens* for reality. *Logic does not determine the nature of being, but at best establishes what the world must be like if we are to perform certain operations successfully.* I shall be considering species of contradiction as *problematic axiological choice situations*, and the latter as belonging to the wider class of *nodal*, turning, connecting, branching *points*, limits and situations; and I shall be looking at a variety of types of response to them. I shall be arguing, inter alia, that it is wrong to confuse *axiological under-determination* — a function of structure in an open totality — with *axiological indeterminacy*. The former includes freedom of choice, which is presupposed by the concept of autonomy as self-determination; whereas the latter implies a situation in which there is *a complete absence of grounds for choice*, and hence of the possibility of rational agency. I will reconnect these issues to the essential themes of dialectic, and, eventually, to the metacritique of the western philosophical irrealist tradition.

There are seven main philosophical errors conjugating around contradiction, and especially logical contradiction, which I will summarily list before commenting on each in turn. They are:

(a) to logicize being — by using the principle of non-contradiction as a criterion — or, in Hegel's case, contradiction as a postulate — for defining reality;

(b) to detotalize being — by refusing to admit the existence of contradictions (logical ones included) in reality;

(c) to belittle or otherwise obtund the significance of contradictions — either as bases for criticism and/or as harbingers, indeed dynamos, of change;

(d) to acquiesce to, rather than try to resolve (or more generally seek an appropriate response to), contradictions;

(e) to imagine triumphalistically that such resolutions are always possible, even if only in principle;

(f) to assume that once a system contains a contradiction, contradictions must spread universally and inexorably throughout it; and

(g) to be intimidated by, or fight shy, of them.

These errors, though not consistent, are not unconnected: they form a dialectical ensemble.

(a) It is both idealist and anthropomorphic, and readily explained in terms of the epistemic fallacy, to use non-contradiction as axiomatic of reality. It is at most an intrinsic norm of thought, whose dominion, in describing the rough epistemological dialectic of C1.9, I have already implicitly contested, a line which will be further pursued in §10. However, a novelty of my exegesis of Hegel is that it is a norm that he covertly accepts, while seeing it ubiquitously violated as the mechanism that powers his dialectic to its final glaceating repose. Both Aristotle and Hegel pan-logicize being. But while Aristotle* comprehends it as necessarily non-contradictory, Hegel comprehends contradiction as the geo-historical motor (Mark I) and the mechanism of the *replication* of the constellational closure of geo-history (Mark II), which I have already referred to as his '*analytic reinstatement*' — for which reason is merely a nominal disguise, and which betrays Hegel as the supreme *non-dialectical dialectician*; so that we could say that not only does Hegel cloak his rational kernel in a mystical shell, but he also drained his rational insight of its dialectical rationality, depositing an analytical skeleton in a dialectically empty cupboard sheening a mirror reflecting a transfigured self-portrait for the observer's admiring gaze.

---

* This is to leave aside the aporiai of matter and accident — the return of the unformless or unactual, that is, of the open systemic repressed, which Hegel will constellationally close in his notion of (in my terms) the 'demi-actual' — that is, the irrational = unactual existent — Krug's pen, the number of species of parrot (in short, whatever his system cannot rationally transfigure/explain).

What Aristotle and Hegel share is the epistemic fallacy (the primordial failing of western philosophy), the hypostatization of thought, a commitment to the principle of (subject–object) identity (which in Hegel transmits the flux in thought to things), a kinetic actualism, a pervasive teleology, an all-encompassing absolute and, ultimately (at least for Hegel Mark II), an *onto-logic of stasis*, of congealment, accompanied by the more or less complacent eternalization of the power$_2$-saturated status quo. However, whereas Aristotle displays a stable hierarchy of forms, in the knowledge of which we can, in some unreciprocated way, participate in the self-thinking thought of God, Hegel unfolds a dynamic totality in which the absolute overcomes its self-diremption in the human medium of his philosophy, for which God is a mere *Vorstellung*, or picture-image. In the totalizing process of reason every momentarily stable structuratum is continuously dissolved and immediately replaced structurally in the 'Bacchanalian revel' which is the infinite life of cosmic spirit. It too is a *causa ens sui*, an unmoved mover, self-identical-and-eternal, but only realized in its unfolding expressive embodiment in the course of geo-history (and its petrified pre-supposition, nature), finally recognized and completed in the constellational closure of absolute idealism. In this system *Geist* manifests itself as process — at first (Mark I) directional, but now (Mark II) completed — and the necessity of the process in the generation and overcoming of (logical) contradictions at transition points or moments. However, as everything existing is continually in process — at first (Mark I) uphill, but now (Mark II) on a plateau — and process is continuous, every moment is a transition point, both itself and not-itself, in the self-becoming (Mark I) or self-replication (Mark II) of its teleologically propelled end. And so logical contradiction is ubiquitous, everywhere and everywhen, expressing logically spiritualized (or spiritually logicized) necessity. The flip side of this is the incessant self-cancellation of contradiction, so that of this continuous play of actualized spiritualized necessity we could say *'plus ça change, plus c'est la même chose'*. This is Hegel's analytical reinstatement masked as dialectical connection; and manifest as cognitive triumphalism, expressivist centrism, rationalizing finalism and coagulating endism. It is worth emphasizing that this was both his express intention (to achieve reconciliation with actuality and so avoid the alienated fate of the 'Beautiful Soul' he himself experienced in the 1790s) and, as we shall see, its subsequent historical impact in the post-Hegelian eclipse of reason.

At this point I am going to 'tack' from my main line in (a) to ask to what extent an immanent despiritualized Hegelianism Mark I might provide a coherent world view? The case for such a (let us say) Xegel is this. Unless things were in contradiction, that is, subject to contradictory forces and processes, nothing would change. But we know change is pervasive. Hence contradiction must be, too. It is there when an animal feels hungry, fights and assimilates its prey. It occurs when it breathes and when it dies. It is present as constraint, as what I called 'inner complicity' and the variety of other types I have described. The case against Xegel is triplex. First, even if contradiction is pervasive, it by no means follows that logical contradiction is. It is, contra (a), quite as wrong to treat some regulative principle of thought as a constitutive definiens of being, whether that be done in Aristotelian, Leibnizian or Hegelian style, as it is to make the converse mistake of (b) of absenting, splitting off, alienating or distanciating thought from (the rest of) being, whether this strategy be pursued in Platonic, Cartesian or Kantian manner.

This ushers in my second point. For two limits can be transcendentally established. (1) There must be sufficient stability of kinds and individuals, of structures and structurata, of mechanisms and their instances for intelligible praxis, sense-perception or identifiable (presupposing re-identifiable) entities to occur. The world must be such that it can be to a degree consistently described and acted upon (at least within our zone of being). (2) But by the same token there must be sufficient differentiation and transformative change for the same phenomena — and, in particular, the negating (absenting) agency presupposed by scientific practice — to be, or have become, possible. The world must be such that it cannot always be consistently described and acted upon for problematic axiological choice situations, nodal points and indeterminate negations, as well as less abstract entities such as emergence and structural change, to occur. Thus at the transition point of the identity of a particular or kind (and such transition points must occur, for, for instance, a token-reflexive statement reporting a change in beliefs, or for emergence or for spatio-temporal divergence to be possible) we have 2E *occurrences* of the problem of induction (in which we have to think the coincidence of identity and change), the 1M resolution of which was sketched in C1.9. *Metacritically we are situated within limits.* There must be sufficient constancy in, for instance, trans-cosmic laws and fundamental constants, such as the speed of light, for change — from dialectical development to entropic dissipation — to be identifiable. And there must be sufficient change, such as radical transformative negation in science, for such constants to become to be known. Neither Parmenidean nor Heraclitean caricatures can apply. Similar considerations apply in the 3L domain of totality. A scientific experiment presupposes a continuous causal nexus but consists in the real demediation of nature. All this means that we may have to accept the co-existence of 'universalist' postulates, such as 'cosmic time', 'Machian inertia' and perhaps the butterfly effect and 'relativist' postulates, such as rapidly diverging world-lines, and a changing (both in the large and in the small) domain of the knowable as well as radical epistemic relativity (including in philosophy). If contradiction is conceived merely as constraint then of course it is ubiquitous. But contradiction conceived as constraint and as radically negating transformative tendency, respectively, instantiates two different kinds of concept.

The third point against Xegel is this. Science in general is concerned only with explanatory and/or taxonomically significant changes, paradigmatically structural changes. And it will seek the cause of such changes in terms of explanatory and taxonomic, more basic and enduring mechanisms and kinds. Of course there may be change too at this level and we are faced with a putative regress in depth. However, it is neither (α) epistemologically nor (β) ontologically vicious. (α) We are always 'thrown' into an epistemological dialectic — as we are 'thrown', at every level, into life, establishing at once our material embodiment, our spatio-temporal being and our perspectival relativity — which precedes us, at some specific point, with established facts, determinate problems, a preset agenda and research programme, into which we in turn will project or throw ourselves. We never start from scratch (the mistake of fundamental-ism — be it the Cartesian cogito, the conventionalist cogitamus or the pragmatic facimus) or finish with nothing (non-constellationally significant) to do (the mistake of endism). The epistemological regress is resolved in practice by the fact that science is a *pre-existing, ongoing social* affair. (β) Insofar as we come up against an ontological limit, beyond which it seems that we cannot advance, so that all that we can get in our 'referential totality', in particular our sense-extending equipment, is for it to be affected (perhaps contextually, holistically and/or stochastically) in certain more or less determinate ways, then it is mandatory on science to posit a deeper level of reality, if we are to avoid invoking miracles as the causes of the changeable detectable effects in our experiential *Umwelt*. The most ontically basic level for us would just consist in the *constellational identity* of a thing's nature with its causal powers, including its tendencies to manifest itself to us in the ways it does (where its nature 'overreaches' those powers). But suppose it is field-like and merely just consists *in* its powers, whether manifest or not, then the ultimate entities would have to be said to consist in the *dispositional* (rather than constellational) (self-)*identity* of their natures with their powers, and a realistic interpretation would still be saved.[35]

But the argument of this chapter is that, within the metacritical limits situated above, (1) change is irreducible and (2) the causal efficacy of a process constitutes, or rather manifests itself as, its spatio-temporal rhythmic. From (2) follows the *constellational identity of causality*, whether substantial, exercised or not, *and space-time* (in potential process). But we know that our universe is an entropically expanding emergent one so that change must be occurring. Some of the ultimata must consist in (a) the *dispositional identity of things with their changing causal powers*, so that in a dialectical kinetic pluriverse *to be* is not only just to be able to do, but *to be able to become*; and (b) their causal powers must be exercised, so that the constellational identity of (embodying the distinctions between) structures, mechanisms and spatio-temporal processes manifests itself in the *rhythmic identity of those changing causal powers with their spatio-temporal exercise*. In short, for at least some ultimata, *being is becoming*, whether manifest or not. These identities do not abolish the categorical differentiations between the concepts. Nor is it at odds with the argument for the ontological priority of the negative in §1. In the first place, for change at the level of the ultimata to occur there must be at least one radically negating kind or two or more kinds. In either case two or more principles are involved (so Parmenidean purely positive token monism is ruled out); if the 'inner complicity' argument holds, then even ordinary multiple determination presupposes internal contradiction; and, tautologically, change as transformative negation involves absence/absenting. In the second place, were we to embark on a horizontal regress back to a unique beginning of everything this could only be, as a non-monistic case of creation ex nihilo, by an act of *spontaneous radical autogenesis* out of nothing, retrospectively endowed with the capacity to produce something out of itself (i.e. *dispositional autogenesis*), involving the paradox of backwards causation* (with which Hegel's system may indeed be fairly charged**) and the self-contradiction of being something with a disposition to the transformative negation of nothing at all. There are no such prima facie problems with absolute edges (or spatial envelopes or endings without temporal posteriors). Note, finally, that I am not claiming

---

* If e_{t2} caused e_{t1} then e_{t1} would have to be endowed with the liability to be produced by et_2 when at t_1 it could not have possessed it (as it was only brought into being at t_2).[36]

** Cf. 'how can there be a conceptual recollection of the manifestation of the absolute, if this manifestation is a *consequence* of its conceptual recollection? In sum, *Hegel claims that the actual is brought into being by discourse that can only occur after the actual presents itself*. So far as I am aware this is a contradiction *which has no Aufhebung*.'[37]

that our ultimata are *the* ultimata (or *ur-stuff*), or that we can know them or that if we did we would be able to explain, less predict, much else.*

So much for Xegel, who epistemologizes being, exaggerates the extent while diminishing the depth of change (and contradiction) and posits an impossible heterocosmic affinity[38] between a self-creating god and a radically closed autogenetics, most obviously in his *Science of Logic*. Back to Hegel. It is a (deep but) contingent fact that the world reveals ontological stratification — of many layers of depth, in many different dimensions (a fact more obvious to us today than in Hegel's time, but which was even then just as transcendentally necessary for science, whether that of Newton or Goethe, Kant or Laplace). Now Hegel is not just a Humean empiricist. He has a concept of necessity which he is prepared to apply to changes and their connections and interrelations. But his ontology is only two-tiered (just as his presentational dialectic tends to be linear and dyadic), not multi-tiered and multi-angular. More importantly, the necessity it endows is spiritual-logical, not natural, a necessity which further manifests itself actualistically and in essential relation to human subjectivity. It is a necessity which manifests itself in the evanescence and transitoriness of being and the bad *Aufhebung* of the self-mediation-cancellation or -transcendence of contradiction, viz. in his analytic reinstatement. The lack of a concept of natural necessity reflects what I am going to call the 'primal squeeze' within irrealism of the missing moments of scientific theory (TD) and natural necessity (ID), squashed between the realms of metaphysics (reason, the a priori, intellectual intuition or [religious] faith) and commonsense

* It is worth stepping aside for a spot of critical realist scholasticism. The concept of dispositional identity is a linear descendant of that introduced at RTS2, pp. 182 and passim. There I also distinguish my normal concept of tendency$_1$, a power whose exercise was normically qualified (or, to put it more affirmatively, one whose exercise was transfactually efficacious) from a tendency$_2$, a power whose intrinsic enabling conditions were satisfied, i.e. a power *ready* to be exercised. But if one includes extrinsic enabling conditions and the distinction between intrinsic and extrinsic releasing and between releasing and stimulating conditions, then we can compose a matrix of possible concepts of tendencies — from the satisfaction of intrinsic and extrinsic enabling conditions (a tendency$_3$ *prone* to be exercised) to that plus the satisfaction of intrinsic stimulating or releasing conditions (a *motivated* tendency$_4$) or the satisfaction of extrinsic but not intrinsic releasing conditions (a *lapsed*, lagged or late tendency$_5$). Corresponding to the *four* moments of the concrete universal I shall analyse in §7 we can also distinguish further concepts of tendency. Thus we might want to distinguish a tendency$_a$ as transfactually efficacious from tendency$_b$ which qualifies the *directionality* of the process (including a process of argument, where we might want to employ the concept of contradiction) and tendency$_c$ which designates the *mediation* of a determination and a generic tendency$_d$ which includes the effects of the others plus conjunctural influences. All these must be differentiated from the concepts of a tendency which is realized in all *normal* circumstances — tendency$_e$.

(experience, the a posteriori, induction or [once again but now conventional] faith). I return to Hegel in §5.

There are two more problems to discuss under (a). First, there is the important consideration that there is no way of getting at — in the sense of grasping — reality independently of thought. So, it might be claimed, we cannot help but logicize being. However, I shall be arguing to §8 that, granting this, there is no case for putting intransitivity under erasure. Negatively, by parity of argument, the erasure, which is an existentially intransitive operation, must erase itself. Positively, a *meta-reflexively totalizing situation* of what may be called the post-Kantian predicament, involving a stratified conception of the self and a distanciated concept of space-time in ontology, particularly when supported by a materialist sociology, allows us to think about being without logicizing it. Second, there is the Leibnizian point that the principle of non-contradiction is necessary for the derivation of coherent concepts of space and time. However neat Leibnizian derivations (which presuppose the prior concepts of alterity and change) may be, once we allow emergent totalities or divergent world-lines, then we must budget for differential space-times, which require for their consistent description (and measure) only a zero-level or base space-time. And it is a contingent fact (1) if we can get this, and (2) whether the differential spatio-temporalities are or are not contradictory. This immediately undermines the palpably antiquated Kantian postulate of a necessarily unitary time-consciousness. Moreover, it is important to reiterate that rejection of actualism and its blockist dual allows for the co-occurrence of absence and presence within a distanciated temporal stretch and/or spatial spread, making possible, within the dialectics of co-presence of absence and presence, such phenomena as an existentially constitutive past within a tensed present, an intrinsic outside and an intra-active relationality within that distanciated stretch/spread.

(b) I do not intend to consume much space on the inverse mistake of detotalizing being by refusing to concede the existence of contradictions in reality, including logical contradictions in social reality (where else could they be?) — the error for which Hegel criticized Kant as being 'too tender for things'. Rather I will turn to (c) the mistake of underestimating the significance of contradictions and (d) that of merely succumbing to them altogether. It will be convenient to illustrate my discussion by taking logical contradictions but, mediated by the theorem of the duality of theoretical and practical reason, much of what I have to say may be extended to quasi-logical, performative and axiological (theory/practice and practice/practice) contradictions.

The result of logical contradiction is, as I have noted, axiological indeterminacy, lack of dialectical universalizability and the absence of grounds for rational autonomy of action. Because many bases of criticism can be reduced to contradiction, it is important to notice that there are others which cannot, such as (1) incompleteness (simple absence), (2) irrelevance (absence of a connection), (3) vicious infinite regress (absence of non-homologous resolution) and (4) reductio ad absurdum (which may be defined as the absence of coherence). The most general criterion in epistemological dialectics is the absence or lack of progressive import, in what may be thought of as a roughly Lakatosian sense.[39] The latter may serve as a template for evaluating processes in general. Now it is important to see that although the complete axiological indeterminacy that flows from formal logical contradiction places the agent in a potentially *dilemmatic situation*, all agency involves both a moment of indeterminate negation and a context of axiological underdetermination. There is nothing wrong with openness per se; it is a necessary feature of the world in which we must act. The world is not algorithmic. In general, we are situated, once again, within metacritical limits, with neither unconstrained (contrary to the paradoxes of material implication) nor predetermined choice. Epistemological openness is precisely necessary for that *dialectical suspension* of analytical reason essential to the σ and τ transforms in science. Such 'suspension' includes the 'bracketing' kind, which, I argued in C1.8, is how the Hegelian dialectic normally works, as distinct from the 'transcendence' that Hegel proclaims. There are a variety of species of 'indeterminate negation' from that which is a necessary moment of rational agency to that which occurs in intrinsically antinomial situations. What we have in science is a *dialectic of dialectical and analytical reasoning* (with 'overreaching' my alternative to Hegelian 'transcendence'). What is needed is a criterion for distinguishing 'good' from 'bad' dialectics. One may call a dialectic a *'bad'* one when one can *explain it* as based on *transcendent-ally*, dialectically (to which I will come in §6) or scientifically refuted *categorial errors*, typically constituting the *common ground* of duals, complements, inversions, ad hoceries and other counterparts, and depending upon such measures as illicit fusion or exchange of non-equivalents or illicit fission or non-parity of equivalents, revealing duplicity and equivocation, generating multiple opportunities for ideological pliability (so that, for instance, the same ensemble can legitimate almost any action). A 'fruitless' *dialectic* is just one, like a Lakatosian degenerating research programme, which is getting nowhere. A *'good'* dialectic is one which is grounded and progressive, in a sense which I will explicate in due course. My main aim here, however, is not to provide criteria for evaluating dialectics, but to home in on a class of *problematic axiological choice situations*, where we do not know what to say or do; and to situate these within the class of *nodal, switch, or limit situations*, such as critical geo-historical turning points or crises. We are here looking at dialectic as *process*, both becoming and consisting in transformative negation, absenting or *change* as both *co-presence and transition*, boundary or intra-active frontier. The dialectic of co-presence of absence and presence is itself an affront to the pretensions of purely analytical reason — a theme which I shall resume in §10. But for the moment it is on the traditional paradigm of dialectic as involving contradiction and transition that I wish to latch. In focusing on problematic axiological choice situations I am in no way subjectivizing process or transition or restricting nodal episodes or moments (less indeterminate negation generally) to the human sphere. It is rather a consequence of not illogicizing being that makes it incumbent on me to consider what we should do in or say about such situations.

Examples of problematic axiological choice situations are (or are yielded by) (1) contradictions, (2) transitions, boundaries and frontiers, (3) nodal points and limit situations generally (e.g. junctions, branches), (4) 2E occurrences of the problem of induction (when there is a switch or transition in the causal powers constitutive of a thing), (5) the duration of the/a/some present,* or more generally that of some period or synchronic or locale or region of space-time, (6) the extent and degree of the dialectical suspension of analytical reason in a potentially promising, but highly anomalous, research programme, and (7) the satisficing or optimizing character or the wisdom or rationality of a particular description, action, way of life or social system.

There are a number of generic responses to problematic axiological choice situations. Custom, tradition or routine is neither a good, nor a relevant, answer. For, whatever the virtues of routine (and routine is in general necessary for the cultivation of virtues), unless it is both accountable and accounted for, it is always liable to the Sartrian charge of 'bad faith'. Moreover, it is not relevant because a

---

* I talk of a or some present for two reasons. First, because it is in principle indefinite in extent. Second, because it, like the concept of real negation, qua absence, applies for any space-time region for any observer or any world-line from any reference frame; that is to say, it is not anthropocentric, although naturally any use of it will be relativistic, as with the concept of the past (or future) or elsewhere. (Insofar as determinate being, whether positive or negative, is spatio-temporal, this feature applies in principle to all our discourse. And the concept of the world-line may be used as a metaphor to illuminate phenomena of epistemic or ethical relativity generally.)

problematic axiological choice situation is just one where we do not know how to go on or what to do. Of course agents may, by access to the resources of a privileged elite, evade the 'axiological imperative', and thereby the problem. But let us leave this 'response' aside. One must, of course, always bear in mind Aristotle's advice 'to seek in each enquiry, the sort of precision the nature of the subject-matter permits'.[40] This is different from the Rortian injunction to 'change the subject'. In practice, principles of balance, compromise, maxi-minimization, as well as relevance or chance[41] may all play a part, which contemporary decision theory (in a chaotic world) has helped to clarify.

In the case of an apparent or real contradiction the agent may do anything from repress it to exploit the opportunities it affords in a self-interested or neo-Machiavellian way. Or she may adopt the Zen (μ) practice of 'unasking the question'.[42] This is different from the Socratic (π) response of 'problematizing it', that is, of seeking the ground(s) of apparently mutually exclusive alternatives which, if and when found, can then be redescribed in the context of a transformed theoretico-practical context, in a non-contradictory way. This is undoubtedly the most progressive response to contradiction: resolution by revolution, i.e. abolition. But what if this strategy fails? And what do we say of the nodal moment of change? Or of the point of transition between two alternative correct descriptions of an entity or from one description to a more accurate one? One seems yet again faced with the options of accepting both the alternatives ('it is raining and it is not raining'), i.e. denying non-contradiction, or rejecting both ('it is neither raining nor not raining'), i.e. denying excluded middle. But there is also the ploy adopted by the late Plato in the concluding remarks of the Parmenides,* where he seems to want to affirm all combinations of (mutually exclusive) possibilities — in a meta-denial of non-contradiction; a position which Derrida often seems to want to invert by rejecting them all — in a meta-denial of excluded middle. (Hegel, wedded to the principle of preservative sublation, and under the influence of Lessing's doctrine of the cumulative character of wisdom as well as Leibnizian optimizing plenitude, tends to Platonism in this respect.) Then there is the ordinary language returned to pre-philosophical 'reasonableness'.

The position I wish to argue for is ontological (and logical) polyvalence, including 'non-valence'. Non-valence may be regarded as a propaedeutic to the Socratic strategy. Both seek to question whether it is a problematic axiological choice situation after all. The non-valent

---

* See the epigraphs at the beginning of the book.

response is to say, quite simply: 'this is the moment' of change. The point of transition. The boundary. This is what needs explaining. *Here is our explanandum*.* The non-valent-Socratic strategy is grounded philosophically in a conception of formal logic (and more generally analytical reason) as an invaluable, but also *dialectically dependent*, moment in the process of scientific thought. Thus to show the deducibility of a transfactually efficacious tendency from a description of deep structure is to satisfy the strongest possible criteria for both necessity and truth. But what we are concerned with is a *dialectic*, understood as dependent upon the practice of real transformative negation in the transitive process of science, not an analytic, *of dialectical and analytical reasoning*.** And the non-valent-Socratic response is grounded sociologically in the conception of the use of analytical choice operators such as $\sqrt{}$, x or / and the degree of freedom or, if you like, reality of choice as dependent on materialized social practices in the context of ideologically discursively moralized power$_2$ relations in the heyday of consumer capitalism.

The central category of dialectic is absence and absenting: for example, in the absenting of mistakes in dialectic conceived as argument,*** and of the absenting of constraints in dialectic conceived as the drive for freedom. Absentings are transformative and/or distanciating (mediating) negations, including disemergence and divergence. Dialectic can thus easily be seen as an onto-logic of change, as analytics is of stasis, and, ineluctably (I will argue), of reification. Now if time is, as classically conceived, the dimension of change,**** then it is clear why the issues of dialectic and space-time are so closely intertwined; and why both are central to axiology, understood as concerned precisely with the absenting of absences, e.g. in desire satisfied, but more generally in the theory of agentive as

---

* And in the case of ultimata 'this is rhythmic identity'.

** 'We have the idea of a super-mechanism when we talk of logical necessity . . . we say that people condemn a man to death and then we say that the Law condemns him to death. "Although the Jury can pardon him, the Law can't" . . . the idea of something super-strict, something stricter than any Judge can be, super-rigidity . . . cf. a lever-fulcrum, the idea of a super-hardness. "The geometrical lever is harder than any lever can be. It can't bend." Here we have a case of logical necessity. "Logic is a mechanism made of infinitely hard material. Logic cannot bend". . . . This is the way we arrive at a super-something.'[43]

*** Argument provides a good antidote to Hegelian-derived conceptions of dialectics. Thus the contradictions one gets in, say, a grounded exchange combine elements of externality and internality, logicality and dialecticality proper. It will be discussed in its own right in §8.

**** This notion needs to be generalized by grasping four-dimensional space-time (in an expanding universe) and emergent spatio-temporalities as equally dimensions of change, entailing the tri-unity of space, time and causality in a tensed, divergent and emergent processual multi-componential, multi-perspectival pluriverse.

distinct from dummy (reductionist) or disembodied (dualist) agency. Now within the dialectic of dialectical and analytical reasoning necessary for science (and the education of desire for freedom) one can locate a distinctive dialectic of inconsistency and incompleteness. In this dialectic, absences generate relevant incompletenesses, which yield inconsistencies, necessitating completer totalities. However, since this world is open, not even constellationally closed, change is always liable (α) mediately to generate a further incompleteness, some relevant absence, at the cost of another inconsistency; or (β) to do so immediately by the transformative negation of some pre-existent, necessitating, mutatis mutandis, further completion or totality (enabling potentially greater rational autonomy of action). In an open world neither inconsistency nor incompleteness are ineliminable; and the possibility of both are transcendentally necessary conditions for science.

I will deal only briefly with the other three mistakes about contradiction I listed at the beginning of this section. In respect of (d) I have argued that the most rational response to contradiction is to resolve it (in a process that may require the non-valent/Socratic π problematization of the disjuncts), whether in the field of theoretical or practical reasoning. But, turning to (e), it may not always be possible to do this. It is a fantasy to suppose triumphalistically that all contradictions can always be resolved, even if only in principle. Some dialectical contradictions may have no *Aufhebung*. Equally the existential contradictions imposed by the sheer facts of finitude, or the constraints imposed by the laws of nature, ecological limits or scarcity in the context of a just distribution of resources in relation to experienced need, or the potential development of powers, may be effectively absolute in any space-time context. All human praxis is naturally, socially and psychologically constrained. If, as I have argued, constraint is a species of contradiction, then universal constants, such as the speed of light, impose absolute contradictions (limits on action, potential binds). One might say, in a Nietzschean way, that contradictions are among the conditions of life. Some of these may indeed be by no means absolute, but may require for their resolution conditions (either theoretical or practical or both) as yet not ripe, or even foreseeable. Other personal (intra-psychic) contradictions may just have to be come to terms with, either by ego-syntonic defence mechanisms or by the consciously elucidated experience of them.[44]

The sixth major error (f) is to suppose that contraditions, once they occur or are tolerated within a system, spread within it viciously and fatally. There is no doubt that contradictions of many types do have a proliferating tendency, but in real life, including that part of it which is logic, they can be isolated and contained by a whole number of 1M−4D type manoeuvres. Perhaps the simplest is to detotalize, sequester or compartmentalize them, or their source; and/or to isolate them, regarding them as tedious, time-consuming or distracting anomalies in an otherwise progressive process which may eventually be able readily to accommodate them. This is the lesson of the history of science, which has never been free from contradictions. The exploitation of Anderson and Belnap's 'relevance logic'[45] by R. and V. Routley, Meyer and others can also be seen as an application of this strategy. This can be partially ontologically vindicated by the consideration that the world does indeed contain *compartmentalized* sub-systems within systems, wholes with holes, themselves possible wholes (with holes, boundaries, frontiers and other limits). The classic case is that of those emergent totalities called persons. Logical techniques such as contraposition or disjunction are quite properly prohibited from stopping the discovery of a white shoe counting in favour of the proposition that all ravens are black — Hempel's paradox. Similarly one cannot deduce anything — or everything — from the co-inclusion within a discourse of the contraries that it is raining and that it is not raining — for instance, that microchips are ginger, upon the truth or falsity of which the question of whether or not it is raining has no conceivable bearing. (It is no accident that Hegel was an enthusiast for the disjunctive syllogism.) In practice, then, contradictions are *sequestered* by relevance, bracketing, distancing, type-levelling, erasing, palimpsesting, procrastinating, repressing or any other of a whole number of compartmentalizing, branching, inoculating or evading devices — as well as by simply refusing to employ contradiction-spreading procedures. The coherence of a piece of formal logical reason is, as I have argued, entirely meaning- and so ultimately action-dependent; and, in the context of the dialectic of dialectical and analytical reasoning which I am in the course of motivating, the best way to look at logic is to regard it as an important, but by no means the only, moment in the process of scientific, and more generally, rational thought and practice.

The final fallacy (g) is to take fright at contradiction, including logical contradication. Contradictions are indeed bearers of change, including intellectual change, and it is Hegel's great merit to stress this. To discover a contradiction, for example, along the σ transform is as worthy as to resolve one along the τ transform. Contradictions may be productive as well as destructive, and under the sign of transformation negation they are necessarily simultaneously both.

They need not be antagonistic, i.e. involve conflict of interest. In general contradictions demand, and in some cases prepare the ground for, their resolution, though only at the limit will they be of the distinctively Hegelian preservative sublatory type. But in or after their resolution we *may* come to a more rational, wiser, deeper, more comprehensive, enlightening, sensitive, empowering or fulfilling way of being.

§ 5 On the Materialist Diffraction of Dialectic

The first step in the direction of a more general dialectic can be taken by considering the nature of Marx's (and more generally 'materialist') criticisms of Hegelian dialectic. As we shall see, this permits the multiple diffraction of dialectic as dialectics to accord with the complexities, angularities and nuances of our pluriversal world. In C4.7–8 the nature of Marx's own positive debt to Hegel and some of its more negative consequences will be shown.

The most significant phases in the development of Marx's thinking on Hegelian dialectic can be divided into three. In the first (c. 1843–44), there is a brilliant analysis of its 'mystified' logic, most especially in his *Critique of Hegel's Philosophy of the State*, which is resumed in the final manuscript of the *Economic and Philosophical Manuscripts*, where Hegel's idealist concept of labour attracts the spotlight. In the immediately subsequent works of the 1840s such as *The Holy Family*, *The German Ideology* and *The Poverty of Philosophy* his reception of Hegel tends to be assimilated to, or at least subsumed under, a virulent polemical assault on philosophy per se. However, from the time of the *Grundrisse* (1857–58) on there is a definite positive re-evaluation of Hegel, well documented in his letters to Engels and others. However, the extent, nature and reasons for this re-evaluation (which I will comment on in C4) remain matters of continuing controversy. But two propositions seem undeniable. Marx remained critical of Hegel's dialectic as such. Yet he believed himself to be employing a dialectic *related* to Hegel's. Thus he writes à propos of Dühring: 'He knows very well that my method of development is *not* Hegelian, since I am a materialist and Hegel is an idealist. Hegel's dialectics is the basic form of all dialectics, but only *after* [NB] it has been stripped of its mystified form and it is precisely this which distinguishes my method.'[46] And in the famous 1873 'Afterword' to the second edition of *Capital* he declares: 'the mystifications which the dialectic suffers in Hegel's hands by no means prevents him from being the first to present its *general forms of motion* in a comprehensive manner. With him it is standing on its head. It must be inverted to discover the rational kernel within the mystical shell' (my italics). These two metaphors — of the inversion and the kernel — have engaged quasi-theological speculation. The kernel image seems to indicate that Marx thought it possible to extract, after a materialist inversion, a *part*, viz. its essence, *but not all*, of the Hegelian dialectic — against, on the one hand, positivistically minded critics such as Bernstein; and, on the other, the neo-Fichtean Young Hegelians and Engels. Unfortunately Marx never consummated his somewhat whimsical wish — 'to make accessible to the ordinary human intelligence, in two or three printers' sheets, what is *rational* in the method which Hegel discovered and at the same time mystified'.[47]

In C4 I shall argue that Marx's debt to Hegel turns largely, but not completely, on the notion of the *dialectical explanation* of contradictory forces in terms of a structured common ground. Be that as it may, there is a remarkable consistency in his criticism of Hegel, with which I shall be concerned here, from 1843 to 1873. (a) *Formally*, there are three chief targets — Hegel's principle of identity, his logical mysticism and his triple *inversions* (which I shall connect to the other two and his substantive critique). Each will be related to three principal motifs of Hegel's philosophy — realized idealism, spiritual (constellational) monism and (preservative) dialectical sublation — and Marx's criticism of them will be related to the three main forms of *philosophical*, viz. epistemological, ontological and practical, material-ism to which Marx is, or at least ought to be, committed (and later I will show how they are connected to his substantive [geo-]historical materialism). Further, Hegel's failure to sustain these will be linked to the centrism, triumphalism and endism of which I have already indicted him. (b) *Substantively*, Marx once more pinpoints three principal failings — Hegel's inability to sustain the autonomy of nature, his cognitivism and his failure to uphold the (geo-)historicity of social forms. Here again I will relate these three critical substantive shafts to the dominant thematics of absolute idealism, the characteristic orientations of Marx's philosophical materialism and to the three aspects of Marx's formal critique. I shall argue that Marx's critique of Hegel can be organized in dialectical critical realist terms as entailing critiques of (α) the epistemic fallacy, i.e. the analysis, definition or reduction of statements about being in terms of or to statements about knowledge; (β) the speculative illusion, viz. the sublimation of social life, and, in particular, irreducibly empirically controlled scientific theory, into philosophy; and (γ) ontological monovalence, viz. a purely positive account of being. As (β) involves the 'primal squeeze' of the mediating term of natural necessity, I will thus be essentially organizing Marx's critique around what I have dubbed the 'unholy trinity' of irrealism. In all this I am going far beyond the letter of Marx's texts — at least in terms of conceptualization and systematicity — the better to demonstrate their rationale. This is no more than I attempted to do for Hegel in C1.8. But it should be said before I commence my exposition that, in endorsing (for the most part) Marx's critique of Hegel, I do not think the dialectic stopped with Marx, any more than I think it will end with dialectical critical realism. There is (ontological) stratification and process in philosophy too.

1. Marx's critique of Hegel's philosophy of identity, namely the identity of being and thought in thought (which I am subsuming under the epistemic fallacy), which is at one with Hegel's claim to have realized the goal of philosophy, idealism,* and generates his expressivist-centrism, is twofold. In his *exoteric* critique, he follows the line of Feuerbach's 'transformative method' showing how the empirical world appears as a *consequence* of Hegel's hypostatization of thought. However, in his *esoteric* critique, Marx contends that the empirical world (the world-as-experienced) is really its secret *condition*. Thus Marx notes how Hegel presents his own thinking (or the process of thought generally as mediated by Hegel, the embodied philosopher) transformed into an independent subject (the absolute idea) as the demiurge of being. He then claims that the content of the speculative philosopher's thought really consists in uncritically received empirical data, essentially the conceptualized (epistemic and social) actually existing order of things, which is in this way reified (and spiritualistically) eternalized. Figure 2.8 represents the gravamen of Marx's charge.

This illustrates what will become a familiar dialectical figure, namely the *tacit complicity* of (apparent) *dialectical antagonists*, which, upon metacritical analysis, can be seen as really mutually pre-supposing *dialectical counterparts* or complements necessary for each other, grounded in a common erroneous (here irrealist) problematic. The counterparts in this case are objective (including absolute) idealism and subjective empiricism. Thus we have seen how, epistemologically, the subjective sense-certainty claimed by classical or positivistic empiricism must be presupposed by idealism in the shape of unreflected data. But, ontologically, the hypostatized ideas of objective idealism assume (as ontic entities) the guise of the reified facts of empiricism. Let us investigate the converse operation. Here

---

* 'Every philosophy is essentially an idealism, or at least has idealism for its principle; and the question then is only how far this principle is actually carried out.'[48]

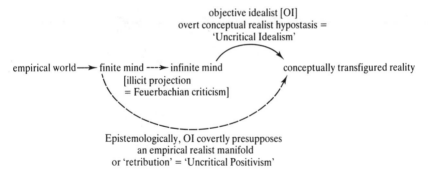

Figure 2.8   Marx's Critique of Hegel's Principle of Identity

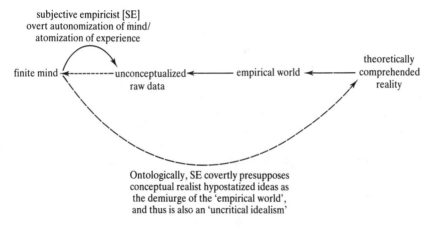

Figure 2.9   The Converse Operation at Work in Classical Empiricism

the overt claim is that finite mind tacitly receives raw (unconceptualized) sense-data. The esoteric critique consists in showing how the reified facts of empiricist ontology covertly presuppose a tacitly transfigured reality, the Feuerbachian projection or alienated product of the positivist scientist's (or layperson's) own mind, facts and their (presumed constant) conjunctions which are, in this way, here again reified and (this time naturalistically) eternalized, as is illustrated by Figure 2.9.[49]

Concepts such as the notion (conceptually understood reality) and the empirical world (which I have used for hermeneutic accuracy in expounding Marx's critique*) embody the epistemic fallacy which co-acts in duplicitous equilibration with its dual, the ontic fallacy, the explication of, or presupposition of the determination of, knowledge by being. The key moves in both cases consist in inverses of each other: the positivistic and speculative illusions, both typically involving the operation I have dubbed 'primal squeeze', the elimination of the middle term of scientific theory or, more importantly, its intransitive object and ontological counterpart, natural necessity. The reduction of philosophy and theory, inter alia, i.e. the positivistic illusion, to a presumed, naturalistically given sense-experience and the reduction of science and social life, inter alia, in the speculative illusion, to a presumed, parthogenetically self-generating philosophy both substitute for empirically controlled critical scientific theory. This presupposes a real world capable of being differentially, changeably and better described, classified and explained. Instead: an ideologically saturated mediation of social (including epistemic) reality, viz. *Das Bestehende* and its existing power$_2$ (master−slave), discursive and legitimating relations (which is the real condition of possibility of positivistic experience and speculative philosophy alike). This social reality itself embodies the interlinked epistemic and ontic fallacies that the transcendental deductions of the intransitive/transitive, philosophy/science and ontological/ontic distinctions (and the necessity of both terms) expose. We are always 'thrown' (as if into an already moving vehicle, so I shall sometimes refer to this as our 'vehicular thrownness') into an already preconceptualized being, whether in life generally or in science in particular. Figure 2.10 depicts the duality of the positivistic and speculative illusions.

As Hegelian 'uncritical idealism' presupposes a converse 'uncritical empiricism', the reverse may equally be seen to be the case for Humean empiricism. At this juncture it is worth noting that there are at least four aspects in virtue of which Hegel may be said to be the supreme *'logical positivist', avant la lettre*. (1) The dialectic is a logical process of reason, in which being is pan-logicized and the process encapsulated in the system expounded in the *Encyclopaedia* flows (or is supposed to) from the *Logics*, as the alienation and self-recognition of the absolute idea in absolute spirit. (2) As I have already argued, negativity is lost in a pacific sea of positivity. Supposedly replete/complete (void-less), the polysemic concept of absence is annulled and contradiction cancelled in Hegel's 'analytic reinstatement'. (3)

---

* Only a tiny fraction of being is 'empirical', and our knowledge of that fraction is dependent on non-empirical, but transfactually efficacious, laws.

The senses in which (a) on a transformative interpretation he explicitly presupposes the findings of the sciences of his day (or those findings which he favours), (b) on any epistemological interpretation, his dialectic tacitly presupposes positivistic empiricism (represented in Figure 2.8) and (c) empiricism must be accepted for the denizens of the demi-actual and the future, that is, for the non-Fichtean endless ending to which he is committed. (4) Insofar as Hegel is committed to the eternalization of the status quo, most explicitly manifest in his constellational closure of the future, he may be said to have reconciled himself to positivity, i.e. authority, in the specifically (early) Hegelian sense.

In what sense is Marx's critique materialist? It depends upon *epistemological materialism*, asserting the existential intransitivity and transfactual efficacy of the objects of scientific thought. This is in effect my transcendental realist interpretation of Marx (which I shall commend in C4). Hegel's position in contrast posits subject−object identity and, its generalized form, actualism, scouting alterity and difference, structure and transfactuality, absence and change, reflexivity and open totality, transformative agency and metacritique. (It is the *realization* of idealism in Hegel Mark II that accomplishes these effects.) In its subjective guise and empirical realist presupposition it is anthro-ethno-ego-present-centric, atomist, punctualist, extensionalist and individualist. In its objective presentation it is *Geist*-eidetically-centrist (which by Feuerbachian critique means, in effect, anthropomorphic), expressivist-holist, blockist, intensionalist

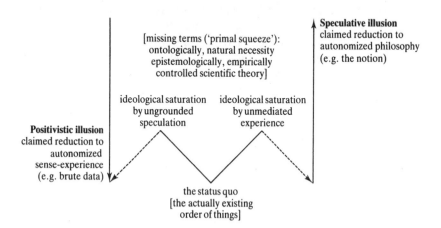

Figure 2.10 The Complementarity of the Speculative and Positivistic Illusions

and collectivist. I shall argue in C4 that these seeming antagonists, mediated by actualism, presuppose a common scientifically, transcendentally and dialectically refutable problematic. Marx's epistemological materialism meshes with the first aspect of Marx's substantive critique, launched in the *1844 Paris Manuscripts*, the 'Introduction' to the *Grundrisse* and countless other places, namely his incapacity to sustain the objectivity of nature and being generally, conceived as radically other to thought, as independently real and as neither teleologically dependent upon, causally necessitated by, nor conceptually reducible to alienations of spirit, thought or any kind of mind. These all amount to a critique of Hegel's *irrealisms* and his claim to have realized the primordial Parmenidean telos of philosophy.

Marx's analysis also has three other important implications. First, conservatism or apologetic is intrinsic to the Hegelian method, not (or at least not only) a result of some personal weakness or compromise. Second, that Hegel's logical theory is inconsistent with his gnoseological practice, in that his dialectical pirouettes and cartwheels turn out to be motivated by non-dialectical, more or less crudely empirical considerations. This theory/practice inconsistency enables us to secure a dialectical comment on/against him, showing that lack of 'seriousness' with which he never tired of taxing Kant. Third, critique of the principle of identity opens up the diffraction this section is about. Thus we can consider ontological and epistemo-logical dialectics and their relations apart from one another, so potentially turning up very different dialectical structures. More generally the critique of a monistic dialectic which is centrist, expressivist, actualized and closed broadens the diffraction into a multiplicity of topological modes, including systematically inter-mingled and embedded ones. This I will come to in a moment.

2. Marx's critique of Hegel's 'logical mysticism' and the parthogenetic play of concepts and the ideological conjuring tricks it legitimates pivots on the notion of the autonomy, or final self-sufficiency of philosophy (and ideas generally). In his essential thrust Marx, as I am interpreting him, wants to affirm the *heteronomy* of philosophy, furnish (as we have already seen) an immanent critique of the speculative illusion, envisage philosophy as only a moment in a practical ensemble or totality and conceive any dialectic in philosophy to be jagged and non-linear and in science to be of a subject-specific kind. But now I am probably being too kind to Marx. For in his critique of Hegel's constellational spiritual monism, and the speculative illusion it depends on, it is not clear (leaving aside his youthful talk about 'the realization of philosophy') whether (α) Marx is wanting the complete abandonment of philosophy or its

supersession by science (in effect the inverse mistake of the 'positivistic illusion'), as is suggested by the polemics of the *German Ideology* period; or (β) he is advocating a transformed transformatively oriented practice in philosophy as dependent upon, and interwoven with, science and other social practices, but retaining relatively autonomous prerogatives of its own to exercise, as is more in tune with his post-1857 dicta and his support for Engels's own philosophical interventions. At a substantive level his critique of the speculative illusion turns on Hegel's cognitivism/theoreticism — for whom 'the only labour ... *is abstract mental labour*',[50] and is in turn based on the second form of philosophical materialism to which Marx is, except for a few early passages, committed, namely ontological materialism, asserting the unilateral independence of social upon biological (and more generally physical) being, and the emergence of the latter from the former. Constellationality, as used by Hegel, is tied to theoretical triumphalism (and thence to endism).* This mediates Marx's first and third lines of critique. Although it is clear that Marx is firmly committed to empirical inquiry and that both his critical and systematic/expository/presentational epistemological dialectics are, unlike both Hegel's and Engels's (which he nevertheless supported), in principle subject-specific (viz. to political economy), it is not so evident that he can be acquitted of the (different, but not unrelated) charges of (a) class/power$_2$ one-dimensionality; (b) presentational linearity; (c) proleptic endism, mediated through the residues of (d) a technologically derived functionalism; (e) Prometheanistically dis-placed triumphalism; (f) a tendentially negentropic convergently centristic unfolding evolutionism; and (g), although he never dis-guised complexity, differentiation and multi-angularity in his theoretical works, a programmatic practical-expressivism.**

3. Hegel is guilty, according to Marx, of a triple inversion of 'subject' and 'predicate'. In each respect Marx describes Hegel's position as an inversion (of the real situation) and his own position as an inversion of Hegel's — the inversion of the inversion. Thus Marx comes to counterpose to Hegel's absolute idealist ontology, specula-tive rationalist epistemology and substantive idealist sociology, a conception of universals as properties of particular things (a reversal of the axis of domination in the concrete universal, one might say), knowledge as irreducibly empirical, and civil society (later, modes of

---

* Conceptually centrism entails triumphalism entails endism — though the converse is not the case.

** That said, corresponding to each charge, one can find contrary evidence in his oeuvre.

production) as the foundation of the state. But here again it is unclear whether Marx is merely affirming the contrary of Hegel's position or rather transforming its problematic. In fact, he is normally doing the latter. Marx conceives infinite mind as illusory projections of alienated finite beings, in Feuerbachian fashion, and nature as transcendentally real, or so I would argue.[51] Moreover, he replaces Hegel's *immanent spiritual teleology* of infinite, petrified and finite mind, which is the real dynamic of his principle of *preservative dialectical sublation* (as manifest in his actual transitions), with a methodological commitment to the empirically controlled investigation of the causal relations within and between (geo-)historically emergent, developing humanity and intransitively real, but modifiable nature. But Marx, following Hegel here, does not clearly differentiate ontology, epistemology and sociology, and so, a fortiori, the different inversions at stake, as I have done. Their distinctiveness is, however, entailed by Marx's first and second lines of attack, which I have interpreted as hinging on the critiques of the epistemic fallacy (the reduction of being to knowledge) and of the speculative illusion (that of science to philosophy).

It is his criticism of the third inversion that I want to associate with (i) the most distinctively Marxian species of philosophical materialism, (ii) the main animus of his substantive criticisms, (iii) my critique of ontological monovalence and finally (iv) with his lancing of Hegel's teleological gnoseo-onto-logical Odyssey.

(i) The most characteristically Marxian form of philosophical materialism is practical materialism, asserting the constitutive role of human transformative agency, based on a double freedom — *from* instinctual determination and *to* produce in a planned, premeditated way — in the reproduction and transformation of socio-spatio-temporal being. It is, or is close to, the conception I have elaborated as the transformational model of social activity and will further develop in §9, where we shall observe the crucial role which the dialectical figure of the hiatus plays in the dislocated duality and dialectics of structure and agency. Historical materialism presupposes epistemological, is rooted in ontological, but *consists* in a substantive elaboration of practical materialism (perhaps most succinctly, certainly most forcibly, expressed in the *Theses on Feuerbach*).

(ii) It was Lukács who first pointed out (in *The Young Hegel*) that the hub of Marx's critique of Hegel's *Phenomenology* was the absence of the distinction between *objectification* and *alienation*. For in identifying the terms, Hegel had rationally transfigured the present geo-historically specific alienated forms of human objectification in the reflection of the alienation of an absolute subject, thus pre-empting the possibility of more truly human, non-alienated modes of human objectification. The rational transfiguration of the present accompanied by the constellational closure of geo-history once again links cognitive and socio-geo-historical triumphalism and endism back to expressivist-centrism and actualism. Moving on to Marx's own critique of Hegel's concept of labour, he insists that this always both (1) presupposes 'a material substratum ... furnished without the help of man'[52] and (2) involves real transformation, entailing at once (a) irredeemable loss and finitude, yet also (b) the possibility of genuine novelty and change — that is, of non-preservative transformative negation, including sublation. (1) ties in with Marx's arrows aimed at Hegel's idealism and spiritual monism; (2) with those directed at his presupposition of (additive) preservative sublation and immanent teleology; and both with his attack on Hegel's constellational closure. In any event it is patent that any Marxian dialectic, if it is to accord with Marx's own critique of Hegel's, must be objectively circumscribed, absolutely finitist and prospectively open, i.e. unfinished.

(iii) Hegel's elimination of the possibilities of non-preservative transformative negation and post-Mark II sublation, his absenting of the notion of absence, checks genuine change, betrays the positivity of absolute idealism and renders Hegel vulnerable to the charge of my critique of *ontological monovalence*. The very most a Hegelian could say is that he is only constellationally monovalent. But as Hegel is not concerned with the demi-actual, the demi-present (or i.e. the future), etc., this is a very weak response indeed.

(iv) As already intimated, it is by no means obvious that there is not a strain of teleology in Marx's work, but in his major theoretical and applied conjunctual analyses Marx's emphasis is on causal, not conceptual, necessity, and teleology is limited to its proper place in the intrinsic aspect of human agency, which presupposes intentional causality, and its appearance elsewhere is, as he writes, as an avowed admirer of Darwin, 'rationally explained'.[53] We can summarize this part of the discussion by saying that, whatever he took over from Hegel, in its most philosophically significant respects Marx's ontology is, or at least has become by the time of *Capital* (which has, or so I shall argue in C4, scientific realism as its explicably unreflected, non-articulated, methodological fulcrum), as much at variance with Hegel's as it is with that of the atomistic empiricism which, in his youthful critique, he shows absolute idealism tacitly presupposes. This would in any event have to be the case for anyone attempting to inaugurate a concrete *science* of *human geo-history*, where the 1M−4D conceptions of ontological depth, structural change, intra-active (organic and) open totality and transformative agency are indispensable. The first two may be said to find analogues in Hegel's notions of necessity and becoming, but they are no sooner in place than they are instantly dissolved* into actuality (and thus closure) and infinity (and thus into logico-divine eidetic eternity), and thence into the self-explanatory and completed field of the notion. This unites for a final time here the three aspects of Marx's critique, which I am proleptically interpreting here in my terms as evolving critiques of the epistemic fallacy (irrealism), ontological monovalence (positivity) and the speculative illusion (philosophical triumphalism, presupposing achieved identity and entailing endist closure).

Marx's epistemological materialism presupposes a *differentiated world*. Thus one consequence of it is that it may be wrong to talk as if 'dialectic' specified a unitary phenomenon. Rather it may designate a number of different topics and configurations. Moreover, breaking into the monistic circuit theoretically enforced by the Hegelian scheme permits us to call upon in the remainder of the chapter (and book) a galaxy of topologies, choreographies and genealogies — for instance, from those resuming the original sense of dialectic as dialogue (whose leading contemporary exponent is Habermas) to those deconstructing it as palimpsesting writing (above all Derrida) or those pursuing the materialist line of negation as essentially involved in the ambit of discursively moralized power$_2$ relations.

Let us illustrate the possibilities opened up by the diffraction of the *extension* of dialectic. It may refer to patterns or processes or relations in philosophy, science or the world; being, thought or their relation (ontological, epistemological and relational dialectics); nature or society, theory or practice. It may be structural, synchronic, locationally periodized or geo-historically dynamic, diachronic, processually spatio-temporalized, tensed or tenseless, generic or subject-specific, abstract or concrete, universal, mediated or singularized. It may utilize any network or rhythmic of 1M–4D figures, theses and themes. And within any such categorization further divisions may be of significance. Thus any epistemological dialectic may be metaconceptual, methodological (critical, exploratory, activating; systematic, expository, presentational), heuristic or imaginary, descriptive and/or explanatory. A dialectic can be totally, partially or non-conceptual; and a conceptual or conceptualized dialectic may be philosophical (and if philosophical, metacritical or aporetic, autonomous or heteronomous, transcendent or immanent, phen-

---

* The flip side of conservative sublation is that one cannot isolate a concept from its future in Hegel.

omenological or not), hermeneutic or action-oriented. A social dialectic may focus on the condensation of rhythmics, of structurally sedimented institutions, the network of social relations between positioned practices, the mutability (or stasis) of inter-subjective inter-/intra-actions, the nature of their material transactions with nature or the kinetics of the intra-subjective sphere, the communicative, moral or power$_2$ relationality of the social fabric. It may be totalizing or compartmentalizing; tendentially$_b$ directional and/or chaotic, dialectically or analytically universalizable, uniformal, differentiated or pluralistic, centrifying or localizing, grounded or not; anthropic or naturalistic; reificatory, voluntaristic or agentive; as we have seen, both empiricist and idealist; consequentialist or de-ontological; a priori or empirically controlled; established by dialectical, transcendental or scientific retroductive-explanatory arguments. To take the case of Marxism again. Marx's emphasis in his use of the term 'dialectic' (where, especially later, it often acts as a synonym for 'scientific') is primarily epistemological (though he is committed to a subject-specific ontological, relational, geo-historical reflexive and evaluatively and practically oriented dialectics too). Engels's is clearly ontological, while Lukács's is relational, setting the tone for the traditions of Marxian social science, dialectical materialism and western Marxism respectively. But a relational dialectic may be conceived primarily as an ontological process, as in Lukács, or as an epistemological critique, as with Marcuse. To take the vexed issue of the Marx−Hegel relation, it is worth noting that such different dialectical modes may be related by (a) a common ancestry and (b) their systematic interconnections within Marxism *without* being related by (1) their possession of a common essence, kernel or core, still less (2) one that can be read back unchanged into Hegel. Marx may still have been positively indebted to Hegel, even if in his work or the programmes he inaugurated it is, or were to have been, totally *transformed* (so that neither kernel nor inversion metaphor would apply) and/or *developed* in a variety of different ways.

Epistemological dialectics involve conceptual distanciation and transformation between at once the constitutive geo-history and intra-active relationality and the trace structure of signs and scientists alike, in the dialectic of inconsistency and incompleteness within the dialectic of dialectical and analytical reasoning in science, particularly in the search for greater depth and/or totality, that we will come, when referential detachment at a level or degree (of totality) is justified, to see as the reason, explanation, ground or truth of being at the next level or degree down. The class of ontological dialectics may vary from: (a) the dialectics of superstructuration or intrastructuration, emergence or disemergence, providing for the dialectician a non-arbitrary principle of stratification, so avoiding the homology or vicious regress or resort to (religious or social) fideism endemic to standard resolutions of the aporiai of philosophy; through (b) the dialectics of absence that will provide my key to the retotalization of a multiply diffracted dialectics; (c) the rhythmic mediation of tensed causally (transfactually) efficacious spatializing process which is the determination of transformative (or perhaps just distanciated) negation, expressed in the social world in the poiesis of praxis, the *making of doing*, including the recursive remaking or undoing of the structured transcendental conditions of any intentional doing at all; to (d) the existential contradiction expressed in the spatio-temporal finitude of human being in a multiple, de-anthropocentric metacritically Copernican-Darwinian-Marxian-Freudian-quasi-Nietzschean world dominated by the logic of commodification in the global village of late/ postmodernity and consumer capitalism: a totalizing movement of extreme (inequitous) diversity in a structured ground. Relational dialectics typically express the Janus-faced nature of the causal efficacy and material conditioning of ideas. Ethical dialectics will take us, via ethical naturalism and moral realism, from the primal scream induced by the absent parent(s) through (to use slightly archaic language) the education imposed on desire by the reality principle or axiological necessity, in a dialectic of truth and freedom, mediated by wisdom to universal human emancipation in a society in which the free flourishing of each is the condition of the free flourishing of all. Absolute reason or dialectical rationality, alethia, theory/practice consistency and dialectical universalizability impose a tendential directionality to this rhythmic absenting of constraints on wellbeing and possibilities. But it is contingent upon a transformed transformative totalizing transformist praxis (which will revolve in large part around hermeneutic hegemonic/counter-hegemonic struggles in the context of discursively moralized power$_2$ relations), itself dependent upon the rationality of agents *and* the contingency of accidents in a contradiction-riven but open systemic world whether freedom or rational autonomy of action will be. What is certain is that, so long as humanity survives, there will always be a conatus for freedom to become.

Having given some examples of the broadening of the extension of the concept enabled, even empowered, by the materialist diffraction of dialectic, let us take a look at that opened by a corresponding diffraction of its *intension* or connotation. A nominal definition of 'dialectic', for preliminary orientational purposes, was given in C1.2. This could be widened even further to subsume any kind of interplay between differentiated but related elements. In §3, in expounding the concept of dialectical connection, I showed that dialectic per se does not necessarily involve any kind of opposition or contradiction. It might be added here, in view of Hegel's obsession with 'the problem of opposites', that neither does opposition, qua alterity or sheer determinate other-being, entrain any sort of contradiction. Even more to the point, we observed that dialectical contradictions, whether described (as, sympathetically interpreted, by Marx) in the transitive dimension or suffered (as, described by Marx, by capitalism) in the intransitive dimension, do not, per se, violate the logical norm of non-contradiction. Dialectical and logical contradictions are intersecting (viz. when grounded in a common mistake) but non-equivalent sets. It is only epistemological dialectics, which may indeed be pre-supposed by other kinds of dialectics, that typically do so. And breaking with the epistemic fallacy means we need no longer go along with Hegel's epistemo-logicization of all dialectic. A map, chiasmus or question mark does not threaten logic any more than cooking an omelette or building a snowperson, although all may be related to or depend on reasoning processes of various types. Even here there are relevant distinctions: between (a) what logic prohibits or demands, (b) what it permits (both of which require the suspension of analytical reason in science) and (c) what it does not speak of. All this is to imagine, in an era of the flourishing of modal, relevance, tense (cf. ontological stratification, differentiation and contradiction, and change), many-valued and other non-standard or deviant logics, that it makes sense to talk of logic in the singular.[54] I suppose one might take formulations of the principle of identity and non-contradiction as essential. But I shall be arguing for the conceptual and causal dependence of identity upon non-identity and non-contradiction on transformative negation or change. One might further want to distinguish between what a non-logical, dialectical heuristic of some specific kind (d) enables, (e) suggests, (f) encourages (supposing enablement implies empowerment in this case). I refer the reader back to Figures 2.5 and 2.6 on p. 68 above.

None of this means, as the reader will be able to discover in §10, that I am going to be 'soft' on analytical reason. Rather I will be arguing for its dialectical-dependency; and championing the idea of the *constellational unity of analytical and dialectical reason within dialectical reason for the sake of absolute reason*. And in my metacritical dialectics of irrealism I will be arguing that, despite his philosophical innovations (the most 'dialectically crucial' of which he was unable to sustain), Hegel acted as the chief mediating replicator of what I am going to call the (typically empirical realist) 'analytic problematic' up to its contemporary Humean, neo-Kantian and post-Nietzschean forms. Indeed I shall show the constellational unity and tacit complicity of analytical and dialectical irrealism under the dominance of the analytical wing. There is a common misapprehension that dialectics is all about contradictions and that all contradictions are logical. I hope by now I have spiked this. Slightly deeper is the misapprehension that dialectics is the study just of change and/or changes and interactions. It is indeed critical of the reifying and disconnecting ontology of analytics, and insists on transformative praxis and intra-active totality. But it is also concerned, as we have seen in some detail, in the case of the *dialectics of co-presence* (i.e. the co-presence of presence and absence in §3) and of the *existential constitution* of products by the processes of their formation and internal relationality (in §2), with alterity in the non-identity theory I am going to develop, depth and transfactuality, argument, hermeneutics and metacritique, sheer absence and meta-totalizing reflexivity, connection and tense, as well as with transition, limit and the other nodal situations examined in §4. No dialectic can ever leave form unmediated by content, however heteronomous its aspirations; or leave untouched concepts such as substance, form, being or activity, or fail to re-examine the connections between space-time and causality or structure, mechanism, process, mediation and result. In short, dialectic will reconceptualize reality and, in reconceptualizing it, help to change it too.

It may be apposite to close this section, as I have credited Marx with a proleptic critique of the epistemic fallacy, so enabling the diffraction of the concept at least tendentially uniformalized by Hegel, by tracing other genealogical lines, threading basic strands of meaning of 'dialectic', each of which Marx or Marxism was radically to transform and each of which, as I shall show in *Dialectical Social Theory*, remains of contemporary relevance for critical social science.

1. From Heraclitus, *dialectical contradictions*. These comprise internally related, mutually exclusive forces of non-independent origins. They are not Newtonian, Kantian or Walrasian equilibria; and they are identified by Marx as generative, essentially constitutive and tendentially transformative of capitalism.

2. From Socrates, *dialectical arguments*. Systematized but also subsequently modified by Aristotle, they remain differentiated from Sophistic 'eristic' by their orientation to the pursuit of groundable ideals. In Marxism the elenchus, on the one hand, (α) is transformed under the sign of the class struggle; and, on the other, (β) sometimes continues to function as, under 'ideal conditions' (e.g. in Gramsci, a

communist society; in Habermas, an unconstrained consensus), a norm of truth. It is worth elaborating somewhat on (α). Arguments depend at once (a) on the mutual recognition of participants, which may involve a struggle, as Hegel famously recognized,* and (b) on some genuine attempt at understanding, as in the dialogical fusion of 'horizons' (Gadamer). Hence my concept of hermeneutic hegemonic/ counter-hegemonic struggles around structures of domination, exploitation and control, and more generally discursively moralized power$_2$ relations of a potentially indefinite number of types (which does not warrant overlooking the more obvious ones — of sex, gender, ethnicity, nationality, class, occupation, age, ability, etc., or failing to seek the causal inter-/intra-relations of each and their grounds).

3. From Plato, *dialectical reason*. This encompasses a spread of connotations, ranging from (a) that conceptually daring, creative, open-textured (Waismann) and flexible thinking processually essential to the epistemological dialectic in science, typically depending on the past or outside, often taking forms such as metaphor, metonymy, paleonymy or consisting in multiply displaced and recondensed paramorphs, constituting operations *on* as well as *with* meanings;[55] (b) enlightenment and demystification as in the Baconian, Kantian and Nietzschean critiques of illusion, but also with a purchase that includes such radical liberals as J.S. Mill (in *On Liberty*), Dewey and Bobbio[56] to (c) the depth rationality of what in C3 I will show can be alethically grounded and materialistically mediated practices of collective self-emancipation.

4. From Aristotle, *dialectical propaedeutics*. I discuss this in some detail in §8. In its broadest aspect it derives from Socratic dialectical argument and overlaps with Platonic reason. In the way I shall interpret it, it sets the boundary conditions for that continual circulation in and out of the sphere of formal reasoning, in which meanings and (e.g. truth) values remain fixed and determinate (or stable in their indeterminacy), characteristic of all (meaningful) discourse in science and ordinary life alike. Conceived in this way, Aristotelian dialectic should constellationally overreach an Aristotelian analytic (though it is worth stressing this is not the position he held).

5. From Plotinus and Schiller, a specific type of *dialectical process*. This normally postulates an original undifferentiated unity, geo-

---

* I cannot refrain here from pointing out that the struggle embodied in the argument may be about more than mutual recognition, just as it may be about more (or other) than absenting class relations.

historical diremption or diaspora and an eventual return to a non-alienated but differentiated self or unity-in-diversity; and it constitutes a deep rooted theme in Judaic/Christian/neo-Platonic thought. In Marxism it remains (α) as the counterfactual limits or poles implied by the systematic dialectics of the commodity form, (β) a postulate in the form of the generative separation between the immediate producers and the conditions of their production, while (γ) acting as a spur in the struggle for a society involving the abolition of all systemic forms of exploitation, subjugation and repression.

6. From Hegel, *dialectical intelligibility*. In Hegel this depends upon the teleologically generated presentation, comment on (i.e. immanent critique of) and preservative supercession of conceptual and socio-cultural forms. In Marx it is transformed to comprise the explanatory critique of the causally generated production of social phenomena — from crises to categories — in terms of their underlying causal grounds.

7. From Marx, *dialectical praxis*. This is the unity of theory and praxis ('absolute reason') in practice (not, as Hegel, in theory) in the non-preservative transformative negation of oppressive social forms, most notably, in Marx's case, the capitalist mode of production.

8. From Kant, Hegel, Marx and dialectical critical realism, *dialectical freedom*. Dependent upon the achievement of absolute reason in dialectical praxis and the transformation of dialectical intelligibility (6) and reason (3), this encompasses the absenting of constraints, including ills generally, which comprise lack of freedoms. This includes the Hegelian dialectic of reciprocal recognition and the Marxian dialectic of real de-alienation, but generalizes, extends and radicalizes these dialectics (cf. C4.5) to aspire to the achievement of a naturalistically grounded social humanity in a trans-specific pluralistic global order subject to the material conditioning imposed by natural constraints, oriented to the self-realization of the concrete singularity of all — a true democratic socialist humanism. What it presupposes and what it implies will be documented in C3.

§ 6 Dialectical Arguments and the Unholy Trinity

Dialectic has the closest possible etymological, historical and thematic links with argument. In this section I want to bracket off (α) the Socratic-Aristotelian tradition of dialectic *as* argument just mentioned, which I will discuss in §8, from (β) the respect in which commentators on the Kant-Hegel-Marx critical tradition might want to talk of characteristically *dialectical*, as distinct from other types of, *arguments.** However, straight away, following the diffraction, we must distinguish (a) wide from (b) more rigorous senses of 'dialectical argument'. The former (a) embraces anything from the expansive sense of interplay mentioned above, through any systematic interconnection that unites a body of thought, such as absolute idealism, Marxism or dialectical critical realism of a 1M−4D kind, which has any claim to be called 'dialectical', to my §3 definition of 3L dialectical connection as between *distinct but inseparable* elements. The latter (b) includes only arguments which turn in an essential way upon 2E notions of real negativity or contradiction, that is, which involve absence or mutual exclusivity (in addition to internal relationality). What distinguishes them ([β] [b]) is that, if sound, they establish *false necessities*, or at the very least significantly conditioned, limited or partial necessities. That is to say, dialectical arguments proper legitimate conclusions which are paradigmatically at once both false and necessary (or at least limited), contradictory, *incoherent* or incomplete in some relevant way, *yet* inexorable or *indispensable*. To put this in a quasi-Kantian manner, they establish *the conditions of impossibility* — in Hegel dr_k', in Marx the dialectically contradictory causal ground (dg') — of the *conditions of possibility* — in Hegel dr_j', in Marx, say, of capitalist accumulation — of *some* more or less transcendentally or otherwise *significant* result or *phenomena* (dr_i') which has already been established or can in any event be taken for granted. Moreover, they establish *ontological conclusions*; and they license *negative evaluative* or practical implications. They may be regarded as a species of the genus of transcendental arguments, provided the latter are interpreted sufficiently broadly (as in effect *categorially* significant forms of *retroductive-explanatory argument*) and so as to allow what I will refer to as '*dialectical detachment*'. *Dialectical necessities* are species of *transcendental necessities* and genera of *natural necessities*, each of which include, but only when epistemically mediated are co-extensive with, *axiological necessities*. But as *false*, or if merely limited *outside* their conditions of validity, they will generate a range of *compromise formations*, ad hoceries, equivocations, duplicities, pliabilities, etc. of metacritical-explanatory import.

It is time to expound and elucidate. An immediate difference between Marx and Hegel, readily explicable on my earlier analysis of §3, must be mentioned. In a Marxian dialectical explanation an explanandum can be shown simultaneously to be both necessary and false (e.g. the wage form) or limited (e.g. the value form), but in

---

* There may, of course, be dialectical arguments about argument as well as arguments about dialectical arguments.

Hegelian dialectic when a conceptual or social form is shown to be necessary it requires an additional demonstrative step for it to be seen as incoherent, i.e. the characteristic combination of necessity and falsity requires distanciated time. In Hegelian dialectic the speculative result (dr') corresponds exactly to retroductive-explanatory arguments in science under which, I have argued elsewhere, once freed from their idealism, Kantian transcendental arguments can correctly be aligned.[57] Does the Hegelian nodal moment proper (dc') correspond to the Kantian dialectical limit (dl')? No. For two main reasons. The Kantian dialectical limit is not surpassable, whereas, of course, the Hegelian dialectical comment precisely is. Then, for all Kant's architectonic encumbrances, the Kantian dialectical limit is characteristically separately established case-by-case, with an irreducible element of heteronomy. On the other hand, any Hegelian dialectical comment is part of a continuous parthogenetic process, systematically, globally, regionally and locally circular, in which each phase is shown to be untrue of or to itself (heterological), its notion or, as Taylor has glossed it, its criterial properties, in a self-propelling sequence of immanent critiques until the totality is completed. Next, the disanalogies with Kantian analytic should be registered. The categories do not apply to things-in-themselves, but only to our mode of apprehending them, whereas, in this respect, Hegel is, like Marx, very much a realist.[58] Secondly, and consistently, Kantian transcendental arguments are designed to establish the conditions of possibility of experience. This may be broadened to social activity as conceptualized in experience, and to social practices or forms of a determinate kind, but must, to stay Kantian in spirit, retain some essential relation to human subjectivity. In this respect, Hegel remains true to his illustrious forebear. But for dialectical critical realism there are dialectical necessities (connections and contradictions), if there are such (and I am arguing that there are), just as there are natural necessities, quite intransitive and independently of our knowing them or any necessary relation to human subjectivity. This 'detachment' from our (subjective) premises is what I will call 'transcendental' detachment.

Another sense in which dialectical critical realism licenses what I am going to call specifically 'dialectical' detachment is that once a phase is overcome in the history of philosophy or social life, such as the epistemic fallacy or the fear of death, we can discard it as an outmoded way of belief or being. We have seen how the magnificence of Hegelian dialectic stems from its being in effect a sequence of Achilles' Heel critiques, attacking a position at precisely its strongest point, showing it in effect to be its weakest. But we have no need to accept Lessing's principle enshrined in the figure of preservative sublation. The history of science, philosophy or humankind could be usefully written as a history of débâcles. As I am using the concept of 'detachment' in four different contexts in this book, it might be helpful if I comment on them. If 'referential detachment' (see §1) is ultimately *for* the sake of axiological need, '*transcendental detachment*' is precisely *from* the same. If transcendental detachment is from our premisses, '*dialectical detachment*' is from sublated conclusions. The '*logical detachment*' (to be discussed in §8) critical realism permits, in contrast to Aristotelian dialectic, is for fully (alethically) adequately grounded conclusions of scientific arguments, enabling reference to the structural and transfactual reasons for, or truth of, phenomena.

It would not be true to say that Aristotelian dialectic has no connection with the critical realist concept I am developing. For typical of Aristotelian dialectic is, as we shall see, the dialectical remark or *distinction* (dd') — the comment on the (or a) preceding remark that it has a degree of truth, but also a degree of falsity, that is, that it is true in one respect but not in another. Is there a connection between dialectical arguments and *narratives*? Yes, for a (progressive) narrative will often take the form of a reflexively monitored episode or life, consisting of a sequence of phases in which each successive moment constitutes a quasi-propositional comment on the alterology or untrue-to-self-or-situation character of the preceding one. A *dialectical life* would be a kind of sequence of immanent critiques, comprising self-reflective overcoming or non-preservative sublation of a concretely singular self (containing an existentially constitutive geo-history and intra-active relationality), dispositionally identical with its changing (developing and waxing and waning) causal powers and tendencies, naturally interconnected with a changing fabric of contingencies, accidents, mediations, rhythmics and contradictions. Generally the beings of social continuants reveal dialectically contradictory, radically self-negating aspects, overladen with super- or intra-structural layers, deposits and residues and the effects of complex, plural, combined and uneven development, radical disjuncts 'striving' to overcome themselves. In C1.3 I referred to the fourfold polysemy of real negation. It is worth going over this again. (1) Simple absence, including nothing. (2) Absenting, including the possibilities of simple divergent distanciation and non-substantial process. (3) Absence as process-in-product, exemplified by existentially constitutive geo-history or intra-active relationality. (4) Absence as product-in-process, exemplified by ongoing social activity, whether reproductive or transformative, spatio-temporal spreading-stretching — for instance, in transfactually causally efficacious (1M)

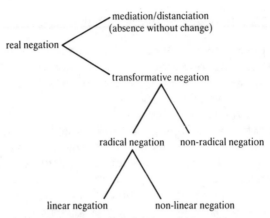

Figure 2.11 Modalities of Negation

tensed rhythmic process (2E) of a reflexively self-monitoring (3L) competent agent in transformative praxis (including the possibility of sheer inaction) (4D). But in addition to sharing this tetrapolity, radical or self-negation has a fourfold polysemy of its own. It can connote (a) auto-subversion (encompassing anything from a counter-conative tendency to self-destruction, e.g. suicide); (b) self-transformation (in some or other respect, which may be more or less total, essential, valuable and/or consequential); (c) self-realization in the sense of the fulfilment of one's needs and potentials, including one's needs and potentials for potential fulfilment; and (d) self-overcoming, either in the Nietzschean sense, or as self-transcendence, or as what we might call auto-emergence. Figure 2.11 maps the four kinds of real negation with which I have been concerned. Whether absenting processes are substantial or non-substantial (as in action-at-a-distance), spatializing or non-spatializing (as in the abstractions involved in conceptual dialectics), they are always causally efficacious, irreducibly tensed. Moreover, every rhythmic presupposes causal efficacy and all causal efficacy presupposes depth, alterity and absence — which the unholy (voidless, replete) trinity of irrealism cannot, as we shall see shortly, sustain.

It is now time to address the issue of ontology directly. At the outset two prevalent misunderstandings must be cleared up. The sense in which (α) everything is ontological, i.e. falls within being (including the epistemic, non-being, etc.), must be distinguished from the sense (β) in which we may want to specify the ontological (as the domain of the existentially intransitive objects or ontics of some transitive or relational process of inquiry or field of action) in contrast to the epistemological, ethical, aesthetic, etc. Second, God has given ontological arguments a bad press. A simple unobjectionable onto-logical argument might go as follows. If (admittedly this is a condition) there is a word or concept or idea,* then there is at least something. Moreover, by Feuerbachian projective criticism, there must be an idealizer, and so at least one human being exists. Further, deploying Marx's critique of contemplative materialism,[60] Wittgenstein's private language argument, Strawson's line in *Individuals*, Vygotskian linguistics, Kleinian object-relations theory, developmental psychology generally or the argument I advanced earlier against token monism, at the human level, more than one human being must exist. So the term 'ontology' must refer, and at least one ontological argument is valid.

I have characterized dialectical arguments as species of transcen-dental arguments establishing, inter alia, ontological conclusions. But there is, especially once the materialist diffraction of dialectic is granted, no reason why this pattern of argumentation should not be used outside the sphere which would normally be called 'transcendental' and/or the categorial condition broadened in the manner of Ryle or Sommers (if one does not want to waive it completely), to designate the establishment of natural (by which I include social) false necessities generally. There are three terms at stake here: 'ontology', 'dialectical' and 'transcendental'. Let us take them in that order. In respect of 'ontology' one might distinguish three senses of the concept specifying differences of level, degree or order, of abstraction, generality and detail. The first concept might demarcate *philosophical* from *scientific ontologies* — the former delineating the *general categorial form* of the world presupposed by the nature of scientific (or other) activities, the latter articulating the *specific contents* of the world, characterized as the intransitive ontic objects of specific epistemics or research inquiries.[61] From this purview, which is the one I have hitherto adopted, philosophy does not exist apart from the sciences and other social practices (and arguably vice versa), and there dawns the vista of a dialectic of philosophy and science, ontology and ontics, etc. A second line pursues a gradation between degrees of distraction and licenses, within a unified concept of ontology, distinctions between global, continental, regional, domain-specific and local ontologies,

---

* For instance, Descartes's project of radical doubt or Hegelian autogenetics (which has been styled nicely a self-perficient scepticism).[59] I only start here because I am engaging in the strategy of immanent critique (in this case, of characteristically irrealist anti-ontological scepticism). The anti-ontologist must at least write something.

figuratively and/or literally, setting up dialectics between the abstract and the concrete, the centre and the periphery, etc. Here again, on the configuration of the concrete universal to be explored in the following section, philosophy is concrete-dependent. A third line would be precisely to take some specific dialectical figure, such as the concrete universal, immanent critique, the hiatus, split or gulf, constellationality, unity-in-diversity or master−slave relations, and apply it across disciplinary boundaries. I do not see why these three strategies, and the distinctions upon which they depend, should be mutually exclusive. Thus one might want to talk of a dialectical ontology, not necessarily established by a dialectical argument in the strict sense, but just in virtue of say its inscape or topological mode.

As for 'transcendental', I think its characteristic categorial connotations should be retained.* But I want to insist (1) on the distinction between transcendental arguments and transcendental idealism (and, in parallel, between dialectical arguments and absolute idealism), (2) on an expanded (geo-historicized and/or domain-specific) concept of categories amongst which the commodity, for instance, would be included, and (3) that transcendental arguments are merely types of the retroductive-explanatory argument form familiar in science. Both transcendental and dialectical arguments, as defined in the first paragraph of this section, are, like retroductive-explanatory arguments, when achieved, two-way interlocking arguments, in which the order of epistemic discovery − in the retroductive, conjectural, critical phase of scientific breakthrough to a new level of ontological structure or of totality − is reversed in the order of explanation, matching the ontological order. The explanation is transitive, but it is *of* an intransitive object or domain. It establishes (normally) at best (in an open systemic totality) necessary conditions of being or existence (and hence also conditions of possibility), precisely at the point where referential detachment of the explanans becomes, in the judgement of the relevant scientific community, legitimate and inexorable. The science of the day then moves on to discover the explanans of the explanans. Science never stops still for a moment. It is always on the move. The Baron Münchausen position,

---

* However, it is not clear whether 'category' is supposed to be (a) a necessary condition for being (or, in idealist terms, for our apprehension of being) as such; (b) a necessary condition for some particular (e.g. geo-historically transient or otherwise conditioned) mode of being; (c) just a higher-order condition of a circumstance; or (d) even whether it can be defined other than negatively and/or in terms of the role that 'categorial' errors play in, say, ideology.

of pulling oneself up by one's own boot straps, on which philosophers have spilt so much ink, just never arises. The scientific neophyte is from the beginning confronted with inter-subjectively established facts, which have become referentially detached. Her job is to discover the real reason or truth of these ontic entities, the S_j of S_i. Starting life as a subjective hunch, it may become for her colleagues an empirical certainty. When its reality is established beyond reasonable doubt, science now knows the reason for, or one could say the truth of, S_i — the *alethic* or dialectical reason (dr') of the phenomena it set out to explain. But by now the scientific avant-garde will be searching for the reason of S_j, S_k (which, once known, can be said to be *its* truth).

This scientific process can fairly be called dialectical, if we bear in mind that en route from any level of structure and/or margin of totality to the next, falsification and the elimination, that is to say, absenting, of inadequate theories, corresponding to the nodal dialectical comment (dc'), and retrospective correction of the account of the already established level of structure or realm of totality will occur. It is important to see that there are two distinct moments of criticism. There is the epistemically progressive moment after (1) referential detachment — say at S_i. This is when an absence or anomaly or contradiction generated by, say, a relevant incompleteness (or the tedious homology induced by replication of already well established results), leads to the (2) retroduction of explanatory hypotheses. If (1) is 'D' (description), (2) is 'R' (retroduction). The known fragility of glass is explained by conjectures as to its molecular structure. In general a plurality of hypotheses will be considered (Feyerabend's moment) in a multiplicity of research programmes (Lakotos's moment) until all but one are (3) eliminated (Popper's moment) — 'E'. This is the fallibilist absenting determination within the epistemically progressive movement in the dialectic of science. Now comes the moment of identification 'I' of the new level of structure — S_j — after which time referential detachment at that level will occur and a new round of scientific progress begin. But there is almost always some secondary epistemically regressive work to be done — detailed correction ('C') of the original level. This, like the tedium of initial replication, is part of Kuhnian, normal science; and yields a second moment of falsification in the overall model of theoretical science, which may be dubbed the *DREI(C)* model. The epistemically progressive and regressive moments are depicted in Figure 2.12. After the regressive correction of the facts at S_i we now have the best possible grounds for both asserting the *truth* of those facts and demonstrating their *natural necessity* (via their deducibility

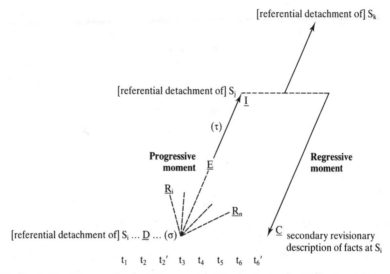

[referential detachment of] S_k

[referential detachment of] S_j

$\underline{I}$

(τ)

**Progressive
moment** $\underline{E}$

**Regressive
moment**

$\underline{R_i}$

$\underline{R_n}$

[referential detachment of] S_i ... $\underline{D}$ ... (σ)

$\underline{C}$ secondary revisionary
description of facts at S_i

t_1 t_2 $t_2{}'$ t_3 t_4 t_5 t_6 $t_6{}'$

Figure 2.12 Progressive and Regressive Moments in the Dialectic of Science

from a description at S_j).* This is what I have called the Lockian
level.[62] After a further elapse of time the firmly established structure
may be held to be definitional of a natural kind and we are now at the
Leibnizian level in the dialectic of science. In this process we have
now considerably refined our rudimentary Hegelian epistemological
dialectic of C1.9.

I have already noted that the epistemological dialectic in science
consists in or progresses largely by a process of immanent critique.
However, it is important to register the vital point that in dialectical
explanatory expositions — which in Hegel must accord with the order
of discovery, but in Marx, as in a scientific textbook, or in the ex post
Lockian or Leibnizian, explanation, need not — as distinct from the
epistemological dialectic, what is false (as well as necessary) is in the
ontological order itself, not (merely) in the epistemological order. This
is a distinction which a Hegelian, whether on a hyper-intuitive,
transformational or descriptive-phenomenological interpretation of
his method, will find it difficult to sustain in virtue of his commitment
to the principle of subject—object identity and the epistemic fallacy it
entails. One final comment on Hegel's dialectical argumentation. I
think in his emphasis on the immanence of critique, particularly in its

---

* This is the analytic moment within the dialectic of dialectical and analytical reason
in science.

Achilles' Heel form, he has brought out the characteristic pattern of disputational argument in science and philosophy, and in addition in civilized culture and conversation generally. But a much more typical dialectic will not be autonomous, smooth, continuous, unilinear and closed, but heteronomous and materially circumscribed, jagged, zigzag and cross-cutting, clumpy (interspersed by sidetracks, non-sequiturs and pauses) and open. This will also tend to be typical of conversation generally.

I now want to consider the effect of the unholy trinity of irrealism: *ontological monovalence, the epistemic fallacy*, both of which derive ultimately from Parmenides (although monovalence was mediated by Plato and Kant and epistemic fallacy by Aristotle, Hume and Hegel), and *the primal squeeze on natural necessity*, established on the Platonic/ Aristotelian fault-line. The effects of monovalence are easy to demonstrate. If thought is included within being, no change is possible; if it is excluded from being, epistemic but not ontic change is possible and so the world must be assumed to be *closed*. If being is now defined in terms of knowledge, as in Aristotelian hylomorphism, Humean empiricism or the Hegelian notion, and it is further assumed that knowledge is *achieved* as, for instance, Aristotle, Hegel and nineteenth- and twentieth-century positivism do, then the absence of the absenting of being established by monovalence entails actualism at the level of general knowledge, itself a presupposition of particular knowledge. As in practice the definition of being in terms of knowledge, viz. the epistemic fallacy, merely masks the dogmatic complacency that *our* knowledge is determined by being, i.e. the ontic fallacy, in the achievement of generalized subject—object identity theory, that is, paradigmatically knowledge as universal and necessarily certain. Whether the objective/ontic moment is dominant, as in hylomorphism, or the subjective/epistemic one (after the Cartesian turn), as in positivism, achieved subject—object identity theory entails the mutual presupposition of epistemic and ontic fallacies. And monovalence merely reinforces the impossibility of epistemic error or ontic change, or of disentangling the two; and hence we have the closed *positivization* of knowledge and being alike. Aristotle's critique of the middle Plato's doctrine of Forms led him directly to the aporiai of substance and essence. Because only accidental features could individuate substances (and the world was by definition closed) thus lacking a concept of the possibility of the achievement of natural necessity — of alethic truth (at the Lockian or Leibnizian levels) in science — which is what in his substantive work he actually did — Aristotle had to fall back on intellectual intuition (nous) as a supplement to induction. The problem of induction was already present on the Platonic/Aristotelian fault-line. Once intellectual intuition was discarded, the only answer was fideism of one kind or another. When rationalist epistemological criteria, following its inwardization and subjectivization by Descartes, eventually became unachievable, empiricist ontology came into its own. Now no concept of ontological stratification, indeed of ontology itself, or natural necessity (ultimately, in Quine, of necessity itself) became tenable. Science became unintelligible while a *triple* but now *aporetic* positivization of knowledge and being occurred. The quest for an unhypothetical starting point had led to a viciously interlocking circle. No absence meant, on the one hand, (a) no alterity, intransitivity or possibility of critique and, on the other, (b) no change. Both consequences of monovalence reinforced achieved subject—object theory and the tacit complicity of epistemic and ontic fallacies (which we have already witnessed at work in Figures 2.8 and 2.10). The primal squeeze between the speculative and positivistic illusions eliminated the middle terms of *scientific theory*, in the transitive, and *natural necessity*, in the intransitive dimensions essential for that knowledge of structure vital for that ontic and epistemic structural change, which the circle disavowed and only the absenting of ontological monovalence can restore. The outcome was that when fundamentalism was finally abandoned in the second half of the twentieth century, acceptance of epistemic relativism led to the intrinsic irrationalisms that dot our philosophical landscape. Most of these are embedded in a new unholy tetrapolity, of empirical realism, epistemological subjectivism and irrationalism, the linguistic fallacy and ontological monovalence. If this book has the effect of absenting the absence of, that is, in vindicating the concepts of, intransitive being (v. the epistemic fallacy, whether in linguistic guise or not), natural necessity (v. the primal squeeze that led to the victory of empiricist ontology) and absence (that is central to dialectic, and especially rational change) itself, then it will have achieved a good part of its aim.

§ 7 Dialectical Motifs: Tina Formations, Mediation, Concrete Universality, etc.

In this section I discuss some characteristic dialectical mechanisms and manoeuvres, tropes and themes, several of which have already been floated. In §§1 and 6 above I mentioned '*heterology*'. This can mean one or more of the following: (1) not true of, or applicable to, itself (in which case its contrary is autology); (2) not the same as itself (where the contrary is homology); and (3) not true for and/or to itself (which is in part the contrary of autonomy, and which I shall sometimes specify as 'alterology'). Its primary sense is (1), which can be exemplified by the fact that the word 'cheese' is not itself a cheese, whereas the word 'word' is a word. In Hegelian dialectic 'A' is necessarily also 'not A', and as such other than itself and generator of a determinate outcome, 'B'. It is by means of heterology in senses (1) and (2) that the forwards or ex ante movement of the dialectic unfolds, with the dialectical comment (dc') in particular explicating what is true of, but not present in, some base concept or form. Only in the self-realization of the absolute idea in absolute spirit do we reach a plane which is not heterological. And in the translucent ex post or retrospective light — the analytic reinstatement in dialectical connection — it casts, each form building up to it can be seen as, after all, *true of, for and to itself*, as such, as contained within and *mediated* by absolute spirit, auto[U]-hetero[D]-auto[R]-logical (in the terms of C1.6). (This is the constellational identity of identity and difference within identity for the sake of identity.)

This brings us naturally to the key dialectical notion of mediation. Hegel might have remarked that all determination is mediation. Indeed Hegelians often use 'to mediate' as synonymous with 'to negate', and 'self-mediation' with 'self-negation'. Only the beginning of a local dialectic is unmediated or immediate. This does not mean that the posited element is arbitrary, because it itself can be seen as mediated by the Hegelian systemic circle. (Wherever we begin, we will achieve the whole, although for presentational and quasi-transcendental reasons, Hegel usually begins with the intuitively simplest element in some regional domain, e.g. Being in the *Logics*.) Although it has philosophical antecedents in the Aristotelian doctrine of the mean, its most usual philosophical employment is to specify an *intermediary* or means of some sort. Thus Marx conceives labour to be the primary mediator between humanity and nature, with various 2nd, 3rd . . . nth order mediations produced on or within (§2 models A and B respectively) the generative separation wrought by capitalism, including private property and the state.[63] Mediation can connote both indirectness and hierarchy. The former is exemplified by the sense of mediation as a medium, and specifically as involving (a) spatio-temporal stretching or distanciation; (b) communicative mediatization (the press, TV, etc.); and (c) postmodernist virtualization or hyperrealization (as readily accommodatable as the figure of inversion within a stratified and non-detotalizing ontology). The latter is more characteristic of Hegel-derivative dialectics, and here the crucial figure is that of the *concrete universal*, which I shall discuss in some detail below. Typically the concrete universal manifests or individualizes itself via one or more particular differentiations in some (what I will call) *concrete singular*. Hegel identifies each of these terms as necessary moments of the notion and each can be seen to mediate the other two. (I give advance notice that I will object to the Hegelian account of the concrete universal, arguing for a conceptualization of it which is both more nuanced and complex.) Indeed, any aspect, (temporalized) moment or (spatialized) determination of a totality may be said to mediate any others and/or the whole. *Process*, as the mode of spatio-temporalizing structure, can be seen as a mediator, e.g. in the social world between structure and agency, or more generally between transfactual efficacy and eventual effect, or within the tensed tri-unity of causality, space and time. *Most generally, if A achieves, secures or eventuates in C (either in whole or in part) via or by means of B, then B may be said to mediate their relation.* It is in this sense that I will argue, for instance, that the past mediates the transition to the future, rhythmics mediate causality, social relations mediate individual agency and philosophy is mediated by the deep analogical grammars of lapsed science and contemporary society.

'*Alienation*', which will also be the subject of detailed scrutiny later, means *being something other than*, (having been) separated, split, torn or estranged from oneself, or *what is essential* and intrinsic *to one's nature* or identity. What is *intrinsic* to oneself need not be internal to, in the sense of physically inside, one — as in the case of a person's kindness or a magnet's field;[64] and what is still essentially one's own at one level (e.g. one's humanity) may be alienated at another (e.g. by being subjugated to gross indignity). To be alienated is to lose part of one's autonomy. Also conceptually tied to 'heterology' is *alterity*. Thus language use, for instance, establishes a relation of sheer other-being, alterity or existential intransitivity, to what it is about. I have argued this cannot be diachronically reduced to an originary (or end) — the dialectical temptation — or synchronically eliminated in the elision of the referent — the converse mistake. Recognition of irreducible alterity, non-identity or difference is essential to any future socialist dialectics which would avoid the sinking back into a simple undifferentiated expressive unity, the most elementary stage of the Schillerian schema, that was part of the fate of the erstwhile 'actually existing socialist states'.

'*Constellationality*' (although also to be found in Adorno) is my term of art. I have referred to both '*constellational identity*', which is essentially a figure of *containment* (in the sense of being a part of), and '*constellational unity*', which is essentially a figure of *connection* (in the sense of being bound together); and I have used it in both materialist non-pejorative and idealist pejorative ways. Thus one can write, within a materialist context, of the constellational identity of being and thought in the sense that thought is both (a) within being, but (b) over-reached by being, as (c) an emergent product of being. And one can write of the constellational unity of dialectical and analytical reason, meaning that they are bound together as essential and interdependent aspects of the transitive dialectical process of science. Hegel's principle of the identity of identity and difference makes it difficult for him to sustain the difference between identity and unity. And the concept is almost always used by him in a teleological context as a figure of closure: principally of (α) the closure of being within his system — hence the non-actual, non-rationalized *demi-actual existent*; or (β) the closure of the future within the present, as described by absolute idealism — hence the *demi-present future*. This is Hegel's great metaphysical ceteris paribus escape or λ clause (as I have called it elsewhere),[65] which is in effect a *weak actualism*[66] and its blockist analogue, weak blockism, of which (α) and (β) are indeed forms, conveniently detotalizing what Hegel cannot 'explain'. Moreover, it is the principle of the constellational identity of opposites, of science within philosophy and of the future within the present, etc., that generates the centrism, triumphalism and endism that I taxed him for in §5 and which directly link to the three members of the unholy trinity, viz. the epistemic fallacy, the primal squeeze and ontological monovalence dissected in §6.

The theme of constellationality is affiliated to, but not the same as that of, *duality*. Duality normally connotes *the combination of existential interdependence* (or, even sometimes at some ontological level and/or from some perspective, identity) and *essential* (and therefore conceptual) *distinction* (including, at the limit, autonomy). It may be exemplified by the duality of absence and presence in spatio-temporal mediation, of theory or practice in absolute reason, or of structure and agency in social practice — where the figure of the *hiatus-in-the-duality* makes possible such important phenomena as dislocation, as well as preventing voluntaristic or reificatory collapse, of the dualities. Closely related to dualities are *perspectival switches*. Such switches may be realistically *grounded*, viz. in terms of some intransitive feature of the object under study, or given a neo-Kantian or Nietzschean interpretation, viz. in terms of the subject's epistemic or evaluative interests or her will-to-power (or caprice). A perspectival switch may be said to be *transcendental*, insofar as a switch constitutes a necessary condition of that from which it is switched, where the latter may be seen to be transcendentally significant in the sense specified in the previous section. Examples are the dyadic tacit/explicit structure of knowledge as analysed by Polanyi[67] or perception as construed by Merleau-Ponty. There are two types of *dialectical* perspectival switches: (a) those which are the results of a relevant valid dialectical argument, as elaborated in §6; and (b) those which may be said to constitute a '*reflection*'. This term can be introduced by noting that in Hegel each phase of the dialectical process can be regarded as a compounded product or boxed focus, consisting in the cumulative results of successive U-D-R sequences. Now Hegel's practice is not in fact conceptually uniformly linear and there is no reason in principle why any term in an organic totality should not be reflected into any other, including compounds of such. In fact, *perspectival fluidity and multi-facetedness* is an essential requirement for any concrete (and, a fortiori, totalizing) inquiry, particularly in the socio-sphere. It should go without saying that Hegelian dialectic purports to be the constellationally completed reflection on reflection.

The consequential heterological outcome of the ex ante or forward movement of some local Hegelian dialectic is, as I have noted, a theory/practice inconsistency. But what happens, more generally, if a transcendental or dialectical necessity, established (let us suppose) by sound argumentation, is contravened? To contravene such a necessity, in some theory or practice, is, insofar as the necessity pertains to the world in which we must act, to contravene an *axiological* (or practical) *necessity* too. I am going to call such necessities, after the watchword for Mrs Thatcher's commitment to an antiquated monetarism (and to remind us of the fallibility of our claims to knowledge of them), a *TINA* ('there is no alternative') *necessity* imposing *TINA* imperatives. Theories and practices which violate such necessities, if they are to survive and be applicable to the world in which we must — in virtue of the axiological imperative — act: (a) require some *defence mechanism*, safety net or security system, which may well, in systematically related ensembles, (b) necessitate supporting or reinforcing *connections*, in the shape of duals, complements and the like elsewhere; and (c) need to assume the cloak of some conjugated *compromise formation* in a world where axiological necessities press about them. Such mechanisms, connections and formations are Tina ones and the whole complex comprises the '*Tina syndrome*'. All transcendental and/or dialectical necessities, insofar as they potentially implicate our speech action, can be seen by a valid perspectival switch as axiological necessities too.

Thus consider subject—object identity theory, whether of a hylomorphic, (Hegelian) phenomenological or phenomenalist kind.

This will appear explicitly anthropo*centric* from a metacritically realist dialectical perspective. Now such a theory, insofar as it is to be applicable to the transcendentally — axiologically — necessary real world of (relatively or absolutely) independently existing and spatio-temporally causally efficacious things, at the very least, will have to covertly graft onto or transmute itself into an anthropo*morphic* correspondence theory, adopting some amalgamation of them or shuttling between the two positions: a typical Tina compromise. However, for general knowledge to be possible (without which particular knowledge is useless), given such an anthropic base, an actualism, postulating the invariant invariance — or constant conjunctivitis — of the subjectively defined particulars, will be required: a typical Tina connection. Moreover, an empirical (or conceptual) realist actualism, to be applicable to the normal normic open-systemic world, where constant conjunctions rarely obtain outside the laboratory and a few other (e.g. astronomically) locally-temporally closed contexts, will need to invoke a ceteris paribus clause inconsistent with itself (for the generalization cannot be both actual and universal) to survive: a typical Tina defence mechanism — or metaphysical λ safety net; but also, of course, a *performative contradiction* — or theory/practice inconsistency. Metacritically, then, the denegation or violation of an axiological necessity must deploy itself as an auto-subversive, radically negating, internally split, axiologically inconsistent Tina compromise formation, necessarily presupposing what it (explicitly or implicitly) denies. In general, then, *Tina formations* are internally contradictory, more or less systemic, efficacious, syntonic (and, as I shall argue, regressive) ensembles, only demonstrable as such, of course, insofar as they have been transcendentally or otherwise refuted, displaying duplicity, equivocation, extreme plasticity and pliability and rational indeterminacy (facilitating their ideological and manipulative use). Moreover, they generate a characteristic range of paradoxes and effects, including the scotomatic ('Stoicism'), schizoid ('Scepticism') and introjective or projective duplicative, replicative or fragmentary forms ('the Unhappy Consciousness'), so well analysed by Hegel in the justly celebrated chapter on 'Self-consciousness' in the *Phenomenology*. We have already observed another instance of a Tina formation in the tacit duplicity of the dialectical antagonists of subjective empiricism and objective idealism in §6. Insofar as Hegel is aware of his tacit reliance on empirical data (that is, insofar as he wants to avoid *reflexive inconsistency*, another name for performative contradiction) this dialectic must take Hegel back in the direction of Kant: to epistemological heteronomy.[68] Conversely Kantian ethical autonomy — the categorical imperative is the prototype of Hegelian autogenetics — is liable to an exactly parallel charge from Hegel.[69]

The invocation of a Tina λ clause can appear as a 2E inconsistency or contradiction, a 3L split or detotalization, but it can also assume the mantle of a straight 4D auto-deconstruction or the 1M non-identity of a theory besides, and requiring something other than, itself. In this respect is it akin to Derridean 'supplementarity', as comprising at once addition and substitution, and to the other members of what Gasché has described as the 'infrastructural chain'.[70] Together these may be regarded as so many metacritical or dialectical comments — a notion I will generalize to that of the *dialectical remark* (drk†) — on the hierarchies of traditional philosophy. But Derrida's models are too closely tied to the practice of hierarchical inversion, chiasmus and erasure. The more general concept of a Tina formation is required for the analysis of the effects of the violation of any axiological necessity, although the way it manifests itself, on any particular occasion, in a multiply determined, contradictory, agentive and internally and externally related world, will be both contingent and variable.

Tina formations are occasionally, although not always, repressed. They thus inevitably raise questions about ideology, power$_2$ formations, hegemony and resistance. A classic instance, admirably analysed by Alasdair MacIntyre on a number of occasions,[71] is that of 'Diderot's Syndrome'. Diderot asked, in *Le Neveu de Rameau*, what happened when an axiological necessity, such as the sexual impulse — or, one might say, the need for food, recognition, de-alienation or autonomy — is denied overt expression. Freud's life work, from his commencement of the (soon to be abandoned) cathartic method,[72] was, of course, a quest for an answer to Diderot's question. Marxists and Nietzscheans ask it too. More to the immediate point, so does Hegel. Indeed to say that some conceptual or social form is at once both false and necessary (which we have seen in §6 is a distinguishing feature of dialectical argument), incoherent yet indispensable, (for Hegel, logically) contradictory but dialectically essential is just to say that it is a Tina compromise formation. Indeed the Hegelian dialectic may be regarded as a progressive compounding of Tina compromise upon Tina compromise, until in the self-realization of the absolute idea and the final overcoming of its self-compromise, in the absolute spirit of absolute idealism we achieve, at once, absolute clarity and absolute compromise. But in the backwards or retrospective reconciliation that this Palladian vantage point affords, negativity is undone, contradiction is cancelled, the implicit explicit, the absent present, plenitudinous positivity restored and actuality rationalized, and we are offered ex post, as the left Hegelians alleged, another sort of compromise: constellationally conciliatory compromise with the prevailing order of things, rationally transfigured under the configuration of the absolute idea.

Notice that both (a) the Tina compromise form, embodying theory/ practice inconsistency,* performative contradiction or reflexive inconsistency, which the dialectical comment registers, and (b) the vicious regress inherent in the self-predicative and self-referential paradoxes and the Fichtean endless task issue in (α) axiological indeterminacy — in Wittgenstein's terms 'we do not know how to go on [and/or, as in (b), when to stop]' — and (β) the lack of progressive (e.g. informational) import, characteristic of degenerating programmes, practices, systems and pathologies generally. And the rational non-valent/Socratic response to both depends upon the explicit recognition and elimination of absences (e.g. of some relevant incompleteness) which Hegel, in his analytic reinstatement in dialectical connection, forecloses. For in closing a potentially, necessarily and actually open totality, and so shutting out the possibility of further essential progress, Hegel performs two self-deconstructive acts. First, he commits himself to that very Fichtean vicious regress which Hegelians know as the 'bad infinite'.[73] What could be more wearisome than merely replicating the status quo (constellationally/essentially or otherwise)? Second, because in overcoming it, he commits himself to the auto-subversion in the injunctive paradox intrinsic to it. We cannot just bring about what already is (although we can attempt to do so) — at the Plateau-nic incessantly revolving turntable that would constitute the constellational closure of geo-history.[74] The transformational character of praxis will ensure that we are always also transforming the structures that we are in the very process of reproducing. In announcing the constellational closure of history, Hegel re-opened the floodgates of tensed geo-historical processes, most notably through the mediation of Marxism. His injunctive paradox is an ethical displacement of the problem of induction, homologous in form with the paradoxes I have already noted (in C1.9). The (1M) resolution of all these turns on the conception of ontological stratification (and alethic truth) and on an open epistemic and practical totality.

If ideology is most generally conceived, as I shall argue in §9 below, as generated and reproduced and/or transformed at the intersection of power, discursive and normative social, material, inter- and intra-subjective relations, then a narrower concept of it, encapsulating the

---

* The split in Hegel between theoretical and practical reason is epitomized by Hegel's *unreciprocated* recognition of Napoleon at Jena.

pejorative connotations of the term, would see the *ideological intersect* of what I have called the 'social cube'[75] as embodying categorial error, of which paradox is just a surface form.[76] The narrower concept may be exemplified by the view of war as a game or women as inferior to men or Marx's justly famous analyses of the value and wage forms.[77] Ideologies, in this narrower sense, necessarily constitute Tina formations and, as such, are liable to explanatory critique (a concept I will resume in C3.7). But insofar as they are causally efficacious, the social relations and interests underpinning them (and thus also the ideologies themselves) will not bend to explanatory critique alone. Rather this will depend on a type of agency to which I have already alluded: *transformed* (autoplastic [cf. 1M non-identity]), *transformative* (alloplastic [cf. 2E negativity]), *totalizing* (all-inclusive and auto-reflexive [cf. 3L]) and *transformist* (oriented to structural change, informed by explanatory critique, concrete utopianism and partici-patory — animating/activating research) praxis (ideally comprising dr_a' in $d\phi$ at 4D). This will involve the intertwining of politics of at least four types: *life* (including e.g. health, career) *politics*, whose subjects are concrete singular agents, and whose ethical counterpart will be a consequentially derived virtue theory; *movement* (e.g. feminist, green) *politics*, motivated by the aspirations of differential collectivities and oriented to the extension of freedoms qua rights; *representative politics*, expressing the needs and interests of different communities but whose bottom line will be the preservation of existing freedoms qua rights; and *participatory-emancipatory politics*, coordinated by a concern with fundamental structural change in a rhythmic to eudaimonia, understood as universal human flourishing. Each itself depends on ergonically efficient ego-emancipatory existential security systems, grounded in relations of fiduciariness, care, solidarity and trust, oriented to reflexively monitored trans-formation, in the context of hermeneutic hegemonic/counter-hegemonic struggles over discursively moralized (ideologically constituted) power$_2$, i.e. generalized master—slave, relations. The eventual dialectic, the grounds and directionality of which I will attempt to vindicate in the next chapter, will depend upon the sequence: ergonic efficiency → empowerment → emancipation → eudaimonia. A eudaimonistic pluriverse would consist in a plurality of processes in which heterology was minimized to a level in which it could be said that each was *true to, of and for themselves and each other and the trans-specific contexts* which they both contain and are contained by. (See Figure 2.13.)

There are two more major concepts to discuss: totality, including concrete universality; and levels. In respect of my section-unifying

self-esteem ↔ mutual esteem → existential security → ergonic efficiency → empowerment →
(universal) emancipation → eudaimonia

↑

transformed transformative [trustworthy] totalizing transformist [transitional] politics/praxis

Figure 2.13   Dialectic of the 7 E's and 6 T's

concept of heterology, they are, in a certain sense, polar opposites for whereas levels make heterology, e.g. in the form of depth, possible, totality seeks to exclude heterology and to embrace all in a unity (albeit of differentiated aspects).

Totality ignites a principal point of difference between transcendental and absolute idealism, which deposits a source of tension within a materialist framework. The Hegelian dialectic is a concrete totality, generated by contradiction, in a process of continual *Aufhebung*, that is, of preservative superstructuration which, when it is achieved, as Hegel claims it is in his system, constellationally closes both being and knowledge, united by the principle of identity, alike. By contrast the Kantian dialectic is a comment (cf. dc') on the limits of finite human intelligence[78] to the effect that it is incapable of *knowing* the infinite totalities of reason, and that the (perhaps eternally challenging) desire to do so plunges it into an intrinsically antinomic mire. This is dialectic as *limit* (dl'). Now suppose Hegel had claimed merely that we know the world and that it is in part contradictory (and perhaps that it must be so, even if only for us to be able to know it). Suppose, moreover, that Kant, for his part, had maintained that we do not know all of the world (or at the very most know that we do so) and that human powers are at least potentially limited. Then their respective positions would have been negotiably compatible, and indeed arguably acceptable. If, further, neither had fallen sway to the conceptual realist aspiration and thought to ground the conditioned in terms of the unconditioned, but they had been content, instead, merely to ground the more in terms of the less conditioned; and at the same time they had rejected an empirical realist account of embodied, finite being (which Hegel, no less than Kant, accepts) — then their positions would have approximated those of critical realism. (It is, as I have already urged, the squeeze on natural necessity, ontological stratification and scientific theory between metaphysics [the sovereign of necessity] and experience [the clerk of contingency] that accounts for the antinomial dialectical duplicity of conceptual and empirical realism.) Let us speculate further that Kant had self-reflexively attempted to situate the critical philosophy in the context of his day (as Hegel did for absolute idealism). Then he could have

contemplated the possibility of dialectical limits of the applicability of
categories in virtue of the relativity of the geo-historical specificity of
the objects to which they applied (as Marx was later to do) *and*
trumped Hegel in virtue of the latter's constellational closure and fear
of an open totality. Kant could have gone on to strengthen his hand
by pointing out that, as inescapably finite, limited, embodied space-
time voyagers, we are necessarily restricted to some local present, to
some or other particular position on our epistemic-ethical-axiological
world-lines, from which, in analogy to a light-cone, some but not
other possibilities are open and some but not other positions visible to
us. Thus transitive relativity — but meta-reflexively situated in the
context of a common cosmos, punctuated by absence and alterity,
from which we clumpily, chaotically and stochastically emerged to
come to know, transcendentally and scientifically, the intransitive
reality of a 'growing-knowers'' philosophically Copernican-
Darwinian world.*

If, to continue the fable, Kant had rejected the second analogy and,
with it, empirical realism tout court, he could then have discarded the
presuppositions of the third antinomy and treated human beings as
causally efficacious agents, with degrees of freedom (as Hegel
correctly appreciated), in a world that is not determined before it is
caused, so that if S_1 causes S_2 at $s-t_i$ and S_2 causes S_3 at $s-t_j$ it does
not follow that S_3 is determined at $s-t_i$. Suppose, moreover, Kant's
attention now swung to the practical sphere. He could have noted
how the greater proportion of *women* (which has to be italicized, given
his misogyny) and men had powers that could be, but were not,
realized and needs similarly unsatisfied, despite the plenitude of
possible resources; and he could have begun to seek the specific
socio-geo-historical causes of this condition (as Marx was to do). Kant
could then have conceived a practical totality, neither as a
transcendent *Jenseits* nor as a Fichtean endless task, but as
unachieved but realizable — in an open world, shaped and
conditioned but dependent ultimately upon rational agency —
informed by the supreme ethical virtue of wisdom — in a dialectic of
truth and freedom that I will articulate in C3. In this way he could
have played a part in forging that chain of identities-in-difference (or,
if you prefer, non-equivalent equivalences) that unite the
marginalized majority, and proleptically, under appropriately
transformed descriptions, the entirety, of the human race. But then,
of course, Kant would have been a dialectical critical realist.

---

* This should not be taken as an endorsement of neo-Darwinist ideology, particularly
in the light of current research.[79]

The drive to totality in science is given by the need to maximize explanatory power. But it is up to science to discover to what extent a subject-matter is internally related and hence in the domain of the 'intra-active'. We can define three basic kinds of intra-action: (1) *existential constitution*, in which event, one element or aspect (moment, determination, relation, etc.), e_2, is essential and intrinsic to (in the sense explained earlier, in which it is not necessarily a physical part of) another, e_1; (2) intra-*permeation*, when e_2 is present within, although not essential to the nature of, e_1, the sense in which e_1 may be said to *contain* e_2; and (3) intra-*connection*, the sense in which one element, e_2, is causally efficacious on an element internally related to it, e_1. This raises a number of issues. It may be questioned whether permeation is really a case of internal relationality if the permeating element is not essential to the permeated one. But an element may be necessary to the existence of another (under the appropriate descriptions) without being essential to its nature. Do the other modes not depend on intra-connection? Sympathetic as I am to the force of this objection, there is no reason why a *possible* connection should not bind elements. (3) is tantamount to dialectical connection and we have already noted that dialectical connections may or may not be dialectically contradictory. More generally, all the basic modes of intra-activity may be reciprocal or non-reciprocal, transfactual or actual, positive or negative, polyadic or dyadic, and agentive or non-agentive. Can a transcendental deduction be given for totality (the key 3L concept) as has been done for real negation or absence (the principal 2E category in C1.3)?

This seems relatively easy for social life. Consider once more our paradigmatic book (with transcendentally necessary spaces, or level-specific voids, in it) in the library, whether it is 'in' (present) or 'out' (absent). There is an obvious sense in which the book, if recently published, existentially presupposes all, or at least many, of the others, and the spatio-temporal traditions which nurtured it (and may indeed be said to have conditioned, permeated or rhythmically generated it). That is to say, it would have been impossible without the others. Or consider the text itself. It is an internally related totality. As are the elements of a language, or the ebb and flow of a conversation, the sequential 'habitus' of a routine, the systemic interdependencies of the global monetary system, a play, a sculpture, or an experimental project oriented to the demediation of nature. Or consider simply a musical tune, melody, beat or rhythm. Or reflect on the semantic structure of a sentence, bound in a complex of paradigmatic and syntagmatic relations (and metaphoric and metonymic presuppositions). Or on its physical structure — for instance, the location of the spaces and punctuation marks within it. Not to treat such entities as totalities is to violate norms of descriptive and hermeneutic adequacy. In particular, insofar as any or more of the above are transcendentally necessary conditions of science, as reflection will easily show that they are, as good a deduction of totality as transcendental realism demands has been found. (Later I shall consider how one might set about a deduction both of science and of transcendental realism without recourse to science.)

So totalities must exist for social life to be possible. But what of nature? First, it might be entered that unless there were internal, and specifically dialectical, contradictions (which presuppose internal relations), there would be no internal (radically negating) tendencies to change either for individual things or for their types (including natural kinds) or, more drastically, for the world as a whole, so that the emergence of, for example, science would have been impossible. If my first argument turns on the transcendental necessity of ontological change, my second turns on that of the transcendental necessity for taxonomy in science. Thus it could be argued that unless some explanatorily significant things had properties which were existentially essential to them, that is, such that they were not just necessarily connected, but internally related, to them, scientific classification, which depends upon the possibility of real (as distinct from merely nominal) definitions, would be impossible. Internal relationality, and so the conceptual possibility of the analytic a posteriori, is bound to the Leibnizian level of the identification of natural kinds, as natural necessity is tied to the demonstration of explanatory adequacy in the dialectic of explanatory and taxonomic knowledge in science. To revert to the model illustrated in Figure 2.12 on p. 110 above, when scientists have gone so far that they can deduce the reason S_j for the phenomena S_i that their concerns are for the reason for that reason — along the epistemological dialectic to S_k — they make it definitional of the structural entities of S_j that they possess the explanatory essential properties that they do.[80] Without them, the activity of classification, in an open-systemic world (in which events are normally 'conjunctures' and things are usually 'compounds' or 'condensates'), would become as arbitrary as that of explanation. For if classification is justified only on the basis of superficial resemblance rather than real identity of structure, then there is no rationale for the stratification of science. This depends upon grasping suitably groomed structurata as tokens of real structures, whose intransitive existence and transfactual efficacy is a condition not only of science, but also of life. Resemblance, like regularity, theory generates insuperable paradoxes, as we shall note in due course. In what follows I will focus, however, on the social realm, where the concept of totality is so patently at home.

To grasp totality is to break with our ordinary notions of identity, causality, space and time, justified by the 'analogical grammar' of the classical mechanistic corpuscularian world view that I have criticized elsewhere.[81] It is to see things *existentially constituted*, and permeated, *by their relations with others*; and to see our ordinary notion of identity as an *abstraction* not only from their existentially constitutive processes of formation (geo-histories), but also from their existentially constitutive inter-activity (internal relatedness). It is to see the causality of a upon b affected by the causality of c upon d. Emergent totalities generate emergent spatio-temporalities. Not only do we get overlapping spatio-temporalities (whether or not, the [non-]entities concerned are of the same or different kinds) but as the intrinsic is not co-extensive with the internal we also have real problems of identity and individuation. When is a thing no longer a thing but something else? When has the nature, and so the explanation for the behaviour, of a (relative) continuant changed? This may be due to either diachronic change (transition points), synchronic boundaries (borders), and/or changing constitutive intra-activity. Aporiai for philosophy, but real problems of individuation, definition, scope and articulation for science. I am going to argue for spatio-temporal, social and moral (real) relationism; in the domain of totality we need to conceptualize *entity relationism*.

How does one research a totality? Starting from any one element, one must in general investigate two margins of inquiry. At the *intensive margin* we will find more and more elements and/or the whole — and in principle their relations — 'reflections' (see p. 116) — contained, condensed, packed into, implicated in and causally efficacious on the initial element, in any number of modes; for instance, either by their presence or by their absence or both. (Thus 'tomato' and 'sandwich' are co-present even when unuttered [and so actually absent], in their paradigmatic and syntagmatic relations, with an utterance of 'cucumber'.) Similarly totalizing at the *extensive margin*, we will discover the initial element reflected, in different ways, into other elements of the totality and/or the whole. And the same applies to the whole itself. A wide variety of constitutive, permeative and causal relations may occur at the intra-active frontier of an aspect or totality. We must continually remember not to confuse the intrinsic and the (material object) internal, that permeation may show that non-corpuscularian fluidity revealed by physical fields and that, in defiance of the Cartesian-Newtonian paradigm of action, intra-active (organic) causality may be effected across a void, i.e.

comprise action at a distance.* Reflections of whatever type (and in particular their nth order relations) may be exteriorized at the extensive margin and the saturated result re-interiorized or vice versa, and so on recursively. Compounding results of successive reflections may comprise totalities of their own. It is important here to discriminate between (α) *totalities simpliciter* (including allegedly 'complete' ones); (β) *sub-totalities*, which possess discontinuities, hiatuses, spaces, binds, barriers, boundaries and blocks between totalities; and (γ) *partial totalities*, which may also contain external, contingent or no connections between the elements of such sub-totalities. In the social world we are almost always concerned with partial totalities. However, once we introduce such 1M−4D motifs as stratification, intra-position, constitutive geo-histories, emergent rhythmics, multiple binds, reflexivity, openness and transformative agency in a materialist framework shot through by all manner, angle, level and kind of determination (on which more in a moment), the theoretical possibilities increase exponentially, approximating a Hegelian 'bad infinite' — a conclusion Hegel was able to avoid only by the arbitrary devices of constellational closure and generally unilinear presentation. That the exponential does not in practice materialize is due to the finite, limited and conditioned character of real partial totalities; and the requirement imposed by science that it is only after an a posteriori subject-specific inquiry that a totality, such as a mode of production, can be described, or the real definition of an object such as a crystal be furnished. However, thinking of totalities as intra-actively changing embedded ensembles, constituted by their geo-histories (and/or their traces) and their contexts, in open potentially disjointed process, subject to multiple perspectival switches, and in structured open systemic flux, enables us to appreciate both the flickering, chameleon-like appearance of social being and the reason why narratives must be continually rewritten and social landscapes remapped.

I now want to develop a concept of holistic causality and illustrate how it might be used in a dialectic of de-alienation. We already know that causality presupposes structural possibility, transfactual efficacy, possessual exercise, the possibility of mediation and the likelihood of multiple determination of results. It may take milder forms than the rather bold 'determination', such as conditioning, limiting, selecting,

---

* This may make it difficult to say whether a potential causal effect should be attributed to locations within the void, or even, given the conceptual connections between identity, causality, space and time, whether it is wholly intelligible to talk of individuating specific locations within it.

shaping, blocking, influencing, etc.; and it may stimulate, release, nurture, enable, sustain, entrain, displace, condense, coalesce, bind, in addition to the poietic 'generate' or 'produce'. But let me subsume this variety under the generic 'determination'. I will then say that *holistic causality* is at work when a *complex 'coheres'* in such a way that:

(α) the totality, i.e. the form or structure of the combination, causally determines the elements; and

(β) the form or structure of the elements causally codetermine each other, and so causally (α') determine or (β') codetermine the whole.

Case (β') applies where the totality is emergent (i.e. has emergent causal powers as a totality) and/or constitutes the ground of the elements. Several caveats must be immediately sounded. Remember we are dealing with partial totalities; so that my concept of holistic causality necessarily cannot be expressive or centred in the way that Hegel's totality is, although it is quite consistent with a gamut of species of domination. Moreover, one particular element within the totality, rather than the totality itself, may constitute the ground of the totality, which will in general be asymmetrically weighted and involve various degrees of attachment and detachment ('relative autonomy') of its elements. Alternatively, the totality may be grounded in a deeper structure (or totality) in which the holistic causality at work in this instance merely mediates the relationship between the super-ground and the elements of the totality. In either event, the totality is itself *structured*, and so may contain or be contained by dialectically contradictory (and more or less antagonistic) or, on the other hand, mutually reinforcing or supporting (e.g. Tina-connective), relationships. The efficacy of the elements and/or the totality may depend upon dual, multiple, joint or contextual action. Super- or intra-structures may be formed on or within in. The totality, at least partially constituted by its geo-historical formation and context, is in open process, intrinsically and extrinsically, so that its form, elements and effects will be continuously *configurationally changing*. These changes or determinations must be understood as transformative negations or absentings, rhythmically exercised, holistically explained and subject to or mediated by intentional causal agency in the social world. So that here we may talk of the constitutional unity and, to neologize developmentally, 'fluidity' of the concept of '[causal] determination' as transfactual efficacy, transformative negation, tensed (spatializing) process, holistic causality and intentional absenting or agency.

A rudimentary dialectic may illustrate some of the relationships at stake. A generative separation, creating an alterity, may entrain an absence, or transformative negation, rhythmically exercised in virtue of the causal powers of the entities involved. Suppose N is an agent alienated from something essential and intrinsic, but now absented from and extrinsic to her. A happy retotalization occurs as a result of her (and let us suppose, collective) embodied intentional causal agency. And we have a dialectic of de-alienation in which N is reunited with a part of herself, now no longer divided and perhaps aware for the first time of the fact of how essential (transfactually real, although not actually experienced) the estranged aspect of the totality of her being was to her identity, and so, by difference, constitutive of her new sense of self-identity.

I now want to turn to the closely connected theme of the *concrete universal*, already mentioned when discussing mediation above. It is not essential to a concrete universal, as I shall develop the concept, that it, or its components, comprise totalities (although it is so for the restricted notion that Hegel deploys). What does it mean to call something 'concrete'? We can get two purchases on this. First, it really makes sense only in contrast to its co-relative — '*abstract*'. Secondly, insofar as it has a positive meaning of its own, its nearest synonym might be 'well-rounded', in the sense of balanced, appropriate and complete for the purposes at hand. Actualities or their descriptions may be concrete (so that the term has a characteristic intransitive/transitive bivalency), as may my experience. *But the concrete ≠ the actual ≠ the empirical.* If *Capital* is regarded as an adequate description of the capitalist mode of production, the intransitive object of its theoretical result may well be said to be *capital in-concretion*,[82] which will be transfactually applicable wherever the concept of capital is, but the results of which will be codetermined (a) by the residue of other economic modes, (b) by intra-structural mechanisms and intransitive objects only specifiable at a level of generality, detail and/or extension with which Marx did not attempt to engage (including much not set out in his famous 'six brochures' and much else not traditionally included in the Marxian superstructure or base, e.g. the reproduction of labour-power, the ecosphere, gender, ethnicity, the unconscious) and (c) by the other moments of the concrete universal I am about to describe — besides the *pan-concrete* totality (of totalities) that was the ultimate intransitive object of Marx's work. Capital-in-concretion is in turn not equivalent to Althusser's 'concrete-in-thought'. Nor is it the same as the 'synthesis of many determinations' to which Marx refers in his Introduction to the *Grundrisse*, which articulates the logic of the (more or less concrete) *conjuncture*. Nor again is it the same as Hegel's famous example of a rose in his *Introductory Lectures* as 'the unity of different determinations' where he describes the multiplicity of aspects of, in my terms, a *concrete singular*.

The main differences between Hegel and dialectical critical realism turn on the (a) *separability*, (b) *multiple determination* and (c) *spatio-temporalization* of the concrete universal. The minimum formula necessary for the concrete universal (CU) is a *multiple quadruplicity*. Thus once the idea of process, conceived as the mode of spatio-temporalizing structural effects, is combined with the Hegelian emphasis on specificity or particularity (which may itself be more or less structurally sedimented and/or spatio-temporally localized), in addition to the moments of universality and singularity, then it is clear that the CU must reveal itself as a *quadruplicity*. Now, leaving aside for the moment the multiplicity of aspects of a totality, in open systems in any particular concrete instance, a multiplicity of mechanisms, specific differentiae, rhythmic processes and episodic events may all be at work as components of the concrete (whatever the focus of one's interest), so that the CU must be conceived at the very least as a *multiplicity of quadruplicities* or multiple quadruplicity.

For Hegel the concrete universal was constituted typically by a universal, a specific or particular and an individual or singular element; and these elements were inseparable, i.e. could not exist without each other. We can, of course, immediately ask Hegel (and even more pertinently, the British Hegelians) whether the CU is supposed to refer to something real or merely, in neo-Kantian fashion, imaginary; and, if the former, whether the universal is ultimately logico-divine (and therefore possessually space-time transcendent) or material (and so in space-time). Hegel's answer would be to reject the question. For him the real is ideal and the infinite is embodied. And his project is to establish this. So let us not pursue this point; but take up more concrete (less abstract) points of difference with Hegel. First, *separability*. In an experiment, otherwise efficacious determinants on causal outcomes are isolated out or otherwise controlled. This is *demediation*: the instantiation of a universal law in a singular, although of course normally replicable, instance or sequence. Second, let us take the missing term in Hegel. We have seen that once the Plateau-nic end is achieved, because everything is always stable, everything is always changing. The constellational closure of space-time is accompanied by the elimination of (post-Hegelian) structural change and thus of the concepts of periodicity and locality, as indispensable to socio-geo-historicity, where differential rhythmics or processes have to be related in an explanatory hierarchy of structural levels or modes articulated around transitions at the explanatorily most basic (or otherwise interesting) level or its rhythmic (and in relation to which other changes can be ordinated). A similar argument — from deep structural change — furnishes a minimal defence of some synchronic/ diachronic distinction as necessary for explanatory social science. Third, Hegel's irrealism does not allow him the possibility of what I have called 'referential detachment', i.e. the ontological dislocation of referent from the act of reference, which in turn cannot be, in virtue of his commitment to the categorially duplicitous principle of subject—object (transitive—intransitive) identity, clearly differentiated from sense. Hence the genuine indexicality of sense of a word like 'I' becomes the impossibility of referential indexicality (and thence token-reflexivity) of a concrete singular, without which tensing, dating and locating (and hence any science, or even discourse, let alone geo-history) would become impossible. Finally, structures, including unknown ones, constituting sheer unactualized possibilities (which may embrace the dispositional identities of physical fields or agentive selves) or their transfactual efficacy in open systems manifest universalities without singularities — a situation which Hegel's actualism cannot permit.

But at this juncture we come head on to the multiple quadruplicity of the/a/some CU. In general in open systems we will be dealing with a constellation of mechanisms, mediations or differentiae and components of a conjuncture. Open systems characteristically make determination not only non-linear but also non-radical. The mediations may be mechanisms themselves or more or less idiographic contexts, episodes or objects (e.g. uniquely laminated structurata). Thus process was described earlier as the mode of spatio-temporalizing structure. However, there may be a number of such modes or rhythmics for any such structure; and in principle the same applies to the levels of specific mediation and concrete singularity. (Events or social singulars such as persons may have more than one rhythmic.) This gives us four modes of illicit abstraction, viz. destratification, deprocessualization, demediation and desingularization. But even this is too simple, taking into account 2E−4D desiderata. Elements at any one of the four levels of the CU may be totally or partially bound into totalities, and there may be internal relations between the levels. Next 2E. Elements, whether internally related or not, may be efficacious as either absent or present, and if internally related, they may be dialectically contradictory or not, but this does not add a further difficulty of principle. Finally 4D. Human agency implicates a network of social relations, inter-personal action, intra- or interactions, material transactions with nature and inter-subjectivity that not only further complicates the CU but also requires investigative techniques sui generis as well as displaying an emancipatory conatus of its own, as I aim to show. Corresponding to 1M – 4D requirements we have *another* set of four modes of illicit abstraction: destratification (again), denegativization, detotalization and de-agentification. Figure 2.14 illustrates multiple determination in the case of events. Figure 2.15 shows a case of the binding of structures in a totality codetermining a similarly based conjunctural context. Figure 2.16 depicts the basic concept of a CU as a multiple quadruplicity. But increasingly throughout this book I will be thematizing *concrete singularity* as the key to the realm of freedom, including the abolition of human heterology. As for the problems of individuation and articulation which I have left open, there is no resolution for them other than to allow this to be determined in the specific case by the theory or set of theories which maximizes explanatory power. Of course this will depend in part on one's explanatory objectives. This does not, however, subjectivize explanation. For there are clear principles of depth (stratification) and completeness (totality) which allow us to decide whether one theoretical, and, a fortiori, applied, explanation is better than another.

This allows me to move on to the final theme of this section — that of *levels*. If totality permits 'within-ness', levels allow 'about-ness'. We have already witnessed it in the guise of ontological stratification providing both (α) the key to the 1M resolution of a whole class of philosophical problems of which the Platonic self-predicative ('Third Man') paradox and the problem of induction are the best known, and (β) the basic principle of theoretical explanation in science around which the *DREI(C)* model revolves. (α) resolves the problems of what I shall call, borrowing a term from Peter Manicas,[83] 'the transdictive complex', where transdiction for me connotes both the vertical or structural depth and horizontal or transfactually efficacious aspects of

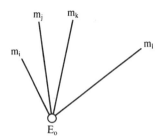

Figure 2.14 Multiple Determination in Open Systems

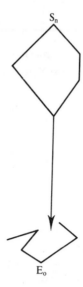

Figure 2.15 Totality of Structures Co-influencing a
Bound Conjuncture of Events

1M transcendental realism. The basic principle behind the resolution
of this problem-field turns around the concepts of ontological
stratification and, as we shall see in C3, alethic truth, and the
corresponding avoidance of vicious regress or cumulative homology,

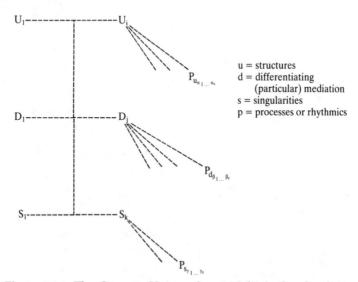

u = structures
d = differentiating
     (particular) mediation
s = singularities
p = processes or rhythmics

Figure 2.16 The Concrete Universal as a Multiple Quadruplicity

i.e. explaining something in terms of itself, rather than a new level of structure (or degree of completion or totality).

Is there a basic schema of *applied* scientific explanation? There is; and it is applicable in the fields of theoretical and practical reasoning alike. Like the theoretical model it has its primary progressive and secondary regressive moments. The first step in the explanation of some concrete phenomenon, say a conjunctural episode, composed, in the fashion of partial totalities, of both external and internally related elements, will be to resolve it into its components. The next step will be to redescribe these components in theoretically significant terms, so that the transfactually efficacious principles of theoretical science can be brought to bear on them. Then, employing those principles, taking into account the particular mediations and the operative geo-historical processes in the case at hand, to retrodict back to possible antecedent causes. Next, comes the elimination of what will always constitute a plurality of possible causes in open systems, until one has identified a full enough set (which may comprise a totality) of causes for a concrete applied explanation to have been said to have been provided, given one's explanatory objectives. There will almost always then follow a regressive movement in which the initial phenomenon is redescribed in the light of its causes. Hence we have the *RRREI(C)* model of applied scientific explanation, with the 'C' standing for correction. However, unlike theoretical explanation in at least many of the natural sciences, viz. from explanatory significant structures to their higher-order structural explanation, applied explanations of concrete singulars, like changes in a particular structuratum, are a much messier affair. In a dialectical pluriverse an event e at a level L is as likely to be (multiply) explained by elements at the same and lower-order levels in addition to higher-order (deeper) ones, and/or even laterally, diagonally, tangentially by elements not locatable in the categorial or generic order at all. Failure to distinguish theoretical and applied explanations, and to discriminate levels of abstraction, as well as topic, scope and perspective, have bedevilled disputes within Marxology in particular. In the first place we have here an intransitive object which is changing so that geo-historically specific theories, e.g. for contemporary 'consumer capitalism', are necessary. Second, one has to consider seriously whether a theory explicating the social presuppositions of capitalism and, allegedly, not just the contradictions and crises tendencies that flow from its deep structure but also its fundamental processual dynamic, should even attempt to explain relative prices (so that the 'transformation problem' may embody something akin to a fundamental category mistake). There is more than a hint of actualism here.

Alongside the 'pure' models of theoretical and applied scientific explanation, one can differentiate *intermediate, regional, local-period-ized* and *idiographic* studies exemplified by work on ecology, party politics, Fordism and biography respectively. Ontological exten-sionalism would disconnect and decompartmentalize phenomena. Despite my warnings about actualism and my stress on the complexity and differentiation of our world, dialectics will always strive to cut across disciplinary boundaries, as phenomena in a mish-mash world do, and to *totalize*, to draw together the intrinsically connected into an internally concrete (= well-rounded) whole.

Level-specific concepts, such as stratification, emergence, em-bedding, recursion, reflexivity, the dialectical comment (dc'), dialectical reason (dr'), are essential to the dialectics we have been investigating hitherto. It is therefore especially important to see that the concrete universal, and totality generally, do not negate, but depend upon them — just as the reverse is true. It is incompleteness (insufficient totality) in the shape of absence that must drive our dialectic on to consider non- and extra-Hegelian dialectics in the next section, before in §9 we turn to transformative agency itself as our paradigm.

§ 8 On the Generalized Theory of the Dialectical Remark, the Failure of Detachment and the Presence of the Past

Since §3 we have been witnessing a materialist dialectician on the scene, namely Marx, in counterposition to Hegel. In the present section I will be introducing motifs from other personnel, most notably Aristotle. Aristotelian dialectics, particularly in the notion of dialectical distinction (dd'), Kantian dialectics, most notably as dialectical limit (dl'), Derridean deconstruction, the Habermasian dialectical counterfactual ideal speech situation (and more generally his more recent theory of communicative action) and Engels, who I am summoning up here principally as the formulator of his so-called 'dialectical' laws, all share this feature in common with Marx's critique of and dialectical comment (dc') on political economy and capitalist society: namely that they must be understood as meta-level comments, and at least implicitly metacritical *remarks*, on some prior or pre-existing assertion, assumption or state of affairs (which need not be discursive). I am going to call such generalized comments, to discriminate them from Hegel's particular and limited dialectics (while possessing some connection with it), *dialectical remarks*. Such dialectical remarkers or their remarks typically find it difficult to *detach* themselves from the situation upon which they would remark. This may be regarded as typical of relational dialectics (and I will be viewing it in this light anon) but here I am more concerned to link it up to the theme of the all-pervasive *presence of the past*, to which it in a way testifies. My chief objective here is to press for a much more adequate and *complex ontology* than the one with which we have been hitherto provided. En route I hope to resolve the antinomy between deconstruction and speech action theory, showing it to be at once a case of the *interdependence of the mediate and immediate* and of the *tacit complicity of dialectical antagonists*. I will be developing the concept of a *meta-reflexively totalizing situation* to three main ends: (a) to show why we need not engage in the practice of Nietzschean forgetting (the truth of the talk about truth), Heideggerian erasure or Derridean play; (b) to redeem my earlier promise to show why, despite being ineluctably linguistified beings, we need not (epistemo-)logicize (or linguistify) being; and (c) to show how, despite its all-pervasiveness, we can escape the fate of being prisoners of the past. To illustrate this last point immediately here, the past brings possibilities and openings for the future and the best 'ecstasis' or orientation to it is one of *creative transformative* use of these.

The dialectical remark is characteristically contextualized, dependent upon the past and inexorably invoked and implicated in the hermeneutic and other struggles around ideologically discursively moralized power$_2$ relations (into which Foucauldian 'knowledge/ power' can be inscribed, as will become clear in the next section). I shall start by focusing on 'the philosopher'. But I am going to trifurcate Aristotle into Aristotle$_1$, the actual historical philosopher to whom I referred in C1.6 and §5 in connection with 'Aristotelian propaedeutics'; Aristotle$_2$, a very broad-minded lover of wisdom who not only tolerates the dialectical suspension but also appreciates the dialectical over-reaching of analytical reason; and Aristotle$_3$, a narrower (but by no means shallow) contemporary codifier of non-deductive procedures of inquiry.

I have already remarked on Aristotle's practice of dialectic as that of working through received opinions and aporiai until some sort of consensus was achieved as to a starting point for more rigorous — analytical — reasoning. Such an *archē* can be conceived as a dialectical comment or remark on the existing state of the subject. Now this procedure embodied two great insights. The first is that *probative-introduction* moves, such as that made possible by the decisive testing of genuine existential questions (which I am arguing the ontologically monovalent tradition cannot sustain), are just as important as — if not more so than — probative-derivation moves in science (and elsewhere). The second is that, *provided that one remains tied to a particular level of ontological stratification*, that is to say, that one cannot get a purchase on greater ontological *depth* (or, by 3L extension, totality), which I shall associated in C3 with a new *alethic* concept of truth, such dialectical non-deductive reasoning is the only way of augmenting the probative power — *probative-augmentation* — of a theory, position or proposition. Broad Aristotle$_2$ sees the crossing in and out of the sphere of formal reasoning, in a dialectic of fact and meaning, as endemic to the hermeneutics of social life,[84] understood as endlessly propaedeutic; even more to the point he sees it as essential to the creative and accomplished σ and τ transformations vital to the C1.9 epistemological dialectic in science which I have described in detail in earlier studies. Nietzsche would not have exaggerated if he had said that (a) meaning *is* and (b) truth *depends upon* a mobile army of metaphors — at least in science, as where in reading a contemporary research report in micro-physics one will find all manner of secondary and tertiary qualities, such as strangeness and colour, attributed to charges and particles (metaphors too). In this zoo the reader will find the bricolage of the past and outside ruthlessly and relentlessly exploited (what Bachelard politely referred to as 'scientific loans'). Here day is night and the exploitation of exterior cognitive, linguistic and material resources — of dead labour — whether affected by some lateral or polysemic condensation of the imagination, in a dream or over a cup of tea, (α) depends upon the bracketing of errors applicable only to signs fixed in meaning and assigned a uniform value (the 'suspension') and (β) presupposes a transformative practice and social-relational network, mediated by inter-subjective dia-logical inconsistencies, for the consensual understanding necessary for the intelligibility of the formal derivation of the consequences of the conceptual mutation (the 'over-reaching'). Suspension, over-reaching and formal derivation are often co-occurrent facts of science. But both locally and globally the sciences are periodizable too. (Names: Copernicus, Galileo, Dalton, Darwin, Marx, Einstein, Aristotle [the formal logician and biologist].)

Aristotle$_3$ codifies a non-deductive logic, in which (contra Aristotle$_2$) meanings now remain stable, at any level of discourse (so, for example, there can be a discourse about meanings) but truth-values do not. This is essentially disputational in form. It proceeds by the assertion and contra-diction (denial), whether categorical, cautious or provisoed; qualification, distinction, limitation (the move I have already connected with Kant as, metacritically, in effect, a dialectial comment on pre-critical metaphysics) and refinement of theses. This kind of dialectic — as ordered and disputational controversy between antagonists, typically a proponent and opponent of some thesis — has pre-Socratic origins, corresponds to the Roman and medieval tourneys or jousts or combat, to put it in Habermasian language, by the force of the better argument, and has been in contemporary times itself admirably mooted by Nicholas Rescher.[85]

Aristotelian$_3$ dialectics has a number of interesting features. First, although two (or more) parties are in an obvious sense in contra-diction, which is indeed, as in Hegel, the mechanism of the dialectic, the principle of non-contradiction is not broached, as in Marx, in the sense that the same person cannot both assert and deny the same proposition p at the same (space-)time in the same respect (including from the same perspective) in the same context (e.g. moot), definitionally at the same level of discourse. Second, as in intuitionism and constructivism, the law of excluded middle fails. Neither p nor −p may be the case for all the evidence to hand; that is, we may have to attribute a third epistemic truth-value — undecidability.[86] Third, negation does not annul; instead, it typically takes the form of refinement (e.g. by a suitable qualification). And double negation does not reinstate the original thesis, but takes the form of its *progressive refinement*; so that the dialectic is cumulative and increasingly mediated. Fourth, it is inexorably (geo-)historical. Each utterance can be understood only in the context of what has gone before. Each such remark may be regarded as a dialectical comment on the one preceding it. As such, in an Aristotelian$_3$, as in Hegelian, dialectic a position never sheds its probative origins, and any distinction between context of discovery and justification falls down. Next, let us consider what Rescher has dubbed 'the most characteristic and *creative* of dialectical moves':[87] distinction (dd'). A disputant may be prepared to accept that P supports Q but contend that the operative situation is not P itself, but say P and R − P qualified by the presence of R — and that this motivates against rather than for Q — in effect a dialectical comment on it. In quasi-Hegelian terms a new mediation or determination has been added to the developing argumentative structure, which becomes progressively richer, in a not dissimilar way to that in which the category 'being' cumulatively unfolds to appear as the absolute idea in the *Logics*, and eventually absolute spirit in the *System*.

Finally, let us turn to what is perhaps the most interesting feature of the species of dialectic: *the failure of detachment*. In deductive logic one can argue from 'if P then Q' and 'P' to 'Q'. But in Aristotelian$_3$

dialectics one can at best argue from, say, P on the condition R to Q normally, generally, usually or ceteris paribus, or as a rule obtains, that is to say, writing Q/P, and dropping the condition R for expository convenience, one cannot detach Q from Q/P. Now looked at from a single-tiered (e.g. empirical realist) standpoint this is indeed the case in open systems. But this is so with all laws in such systems, which must be interpreted 'normally'.[88] But if we break free of the grip of actualism, and no longer see laws as empirical regularities, accept the ontological stratification posited by critical realism, then laws can be conceived as transfactually (universally) efficacious, even if their consequences are, as they normally are, outside the laboratory, unactualized. Detachment now *does occur*. Q is a real agency in the conjuncture, but it is now no longer interpreted actualistically (or empirically). This remains ontologically true of laws, whether or not we have epistemic grounds for asserting a particular law. Rescher's actualism and failure to differentiate ontological from epistemological considerations (the hallmark of the epistemic fallacy) leads him to confuse the ontological status of law-like generalizations with our (geo-)historical evidence for asserting them. In his actualism he mirrors the real Aristotle (and Hegel).

The reason why detachment fails in Aristotelian₃ dialectics is twofold. The first is the 'vertical' actualism that would deny any ontological stratification. Now Aristotle did indeed seek (and sometimes find) good scientific explanations, but he failed to theorize ontological structure and he plugged the gap between induction and the deducibility (of a tendency), achievable at the Lockian or Leibnizian moment in science, with nous or, to anachronistically apply a Feuerbachian line of criticism, his own not inconsiderable intellectual intuition, as already noted in C1.6. But even if Aristotle had successfully accomplished the vertical leap to ontological stratification, his 'horizontal' actualism, of which the symptoms are his aporiai of matter, and accident,[89] that is, his absence of the concept of transfactually efficacious tendencies (in any of the senses I distinguished earlier) in a differentiated, as well as structured, and open, world, would have let him down and made detachment impossible. If Aristotle's scientific analytics depends upon his dialectics, no Aristotelian science could ever get off the ground. Mutatis mutandis, the same considerations tell against Kant's and Hegel's actualism too. The absence of a concept of a transfactually efficacious natural necessity means that without their (so I shall show) illicit resort to the synthetic a priori and *Geist*, detachment should have failed them too. It is Hegel's merit, by seeing the dialectical process as always dependent upon a cumulative memory store (or 'negative referral'), to have realized this. But I shall argue that, on any plausible epistemological interpretation, Hegel makes science impossible.

Before going on to explain legitimate senses in which, in virtue of the presence of the past or outside, detachment may be said to fail, it is worth adding a word or two on dialectic as argument. This leads back to the etymologically primordial sense of dialectic as the art of dialogue or conversation. And post-Schleiermachian hermeneutics may be regarded as a form of dialectic, with the four characteristic hermeneutical circles, each involving a fusion of horizons (in the Gadamerian image) or meaning-frames — of inquiry, communication, inquiry-into-communication and inquiry-into-text or text-analogue[90] — be they real or groundedly imputed — seen as dialogical or dialectical ones. This gives us an important range of connotations of the term of dialectic to which I shall return.

I now want to pass from the logical (or more properly ontological) failure of detachment, rooted in actualism, to the real material spatio-temporal failure of detachment. Specifically I will be thematizing *the presence of the past*, and analogously of the intrinsic outside, in four basic modes — breaking from the (α) ego-present-anthro-centric, (β) punctualist and (γ) blockist conceptions of space-time characteristic of the irrealist tradition. One way (corresponding to one mode) is to think of existentially constitutive geo-historical process as the 2E counterpart to the existentially constitutive intra-active (internal) relationality at 3L discussed in the previous section. I will be motivating the presence of the past (and outside) in a much stronger sense than as a 'negative presence' in the moving finger of punctual time in a cumulative memory store such as in Hegelian dialectic, although I would not underplay the role of memory and one of my main modes will involve what I will call 'strong negative presence'. My argument will also turn on stronger considerations than the partiality of all transformations, important again though this is, especially for the critique of voluntarism. This motif, considered as signifying the absence of the past (one of the four contraries of the presence of the past), has recently been much fussed over by Žižek under the rubric of 'vanishing mediators'.[91] But vanishing, or absenting, is integral to any non-preservative transformative negation, or transformative practice; and it is the fate of everything finite to perish, and thus truistic to say that all, not just some (as Žižek seems to suppose), mediators must vanish.

My four primary modes can be distinguished as:

(α) *existential constitution;*

(β) *co-presence;*
(γ) *lagged or delayed efficacy;*
(δ) *agentive perspectivality.*

(α) This first mode includes mere containment, mentioned in §2. The sense in which the geo-history of a thing is constitutive of its nature or identity is different from the sense in which a thing would not be what it is but for its process of spatio-temporal formation. The former — process-embodied-in-product — from an essential disposition to a merest trace (such as that of a pox-marked face), represents a clear sense of failure of material detachment (as distinct from the latter — a mere product of a process). It may sometimes be difficult to decide between the two in geo-historiography. Was the countryside constitutive of the mid-eighteenth-century town? (α) may be manifest collectively as ritual, habitus, tradition; individually as routine. But it may be petrified, congealed, inert. As we are in the realm of the fourfold polysemy of real negation discussed in §6, let us consider the other senses. First the past may be present as product. For instance, a statue as dead labour, literally past commodified time. Or as sediment, residue, deposit. Think of a disused coal site. Or of soot or dust. Or, and here we intersect with (β), think of the paradigm of the presence of the past as a rock containing layers of many ages, a compound or condensate or different epochs. Or, if it be said that this is merely a case of overlapping durations,* think of a tree trunk as cohering as a whole. Secondly, the past may be present as product-in-(actual or potential)process — in any form from the possibility of cognitive exploitation (of the kind that Darwin used in constructing his theory) to the onset of a neurosis, the origins of which lie in early childhood (cf. paradigm γ).

(β) We have already examined the dialectics of the co-presence of the past in the present (in §3 above). This depends on differentially distanciated space-times, established by disjoint, and possibly contradictory, rhythmics. This paradigm includes the 'intersecting' combination of rhythmically differentially sedimented structures on a single episode, such as that illustrated in §2 by the Queen's opening of Parliament; or by the launch of a ship; or a visit to a 'theme park' (but here the rhythmics, although intransitive, are 'virtual', so that the phrase 'virtual reality' is not a misnomer). Again the past may be

---

* Even this, constituting a case of (β), instances the presence of the past. To get an empirical purchase on overlapping spatio-temporalities we must choose a zero- or base-level space-time. In explanatory contexts the choice should be made in terms of the most explanatory significant rhythmic; for merely nominal purposes convention or consensus will suffice.

encrusted, embedded in a landscape, say, or as an active part of the present. This is perhaps the point to state that in the case of all the modes I am discussing the past may be present as transfactual or actual, latent or manifest, agentive (and, if so, as living or dead) or not; it may have been continuously or discontinuously present; it may be internally related to other elements of the past and/or present and/or to processes oriented to and/or in anticipation of the future, and it may be present in a positive or negative mode. To illustrate this last prima facie paradoxical form, consider the presence of the absence (in the simple sense established in §1) of men of fighting age in Budapest after the uprising of 1956, which may be causally efficacious even now in 1993. It is worth stressing the role that explanatorily grounded localization/periodization plays within an internally tensed distanciated space-time in the dialectics of co-inclusion. Although the loco-periodization is a transitive act, the locations and periods are real, grounded in the real differentiations and changes in underlying (explanatorily significant) structures. There may be any number of important processes within a location/period and hence any number of potentially different tenses, coordinated by the most explanatory significant or just a conventional base or zero-level space-time.

(γ) This takes me to my third paradigm of lagged, delayed potential or realized efficacy carried across a (spatio-)temporal level-specific void. This, which has an obvious paradigm in psychoanalytic explanation, is the temporal analogue of action at a distance. We can see it literally as such, when with powerful telescopes the past in some distant region of space is perceptually present to us now. (γ) depends upon explicit recognition of causality as not only a perfectly proper criterion for ascribing reality, but also that upon which the empiricist 'esse est percipi' ultimately depends. No one should underestimate the causal grip that the past exercises on any present, however inert it may appear to be. Think of a volcano. I referred earlier to Hegelian 'negative presence'. One could develop a concept of 'strong negative presence' in the case of causally efficacious memory, but as the remembered is always liable to play a causal role and we are no longer dealing with purely Hegelian dialectic I would prefer not to embark on that road.

(δ) Perspective is ineliminable in dialectic. In §9 I shall discuss the duality of social structure and human agency as transcendentally necessary conditions for each other. So it might be thought that they are on a par. But from the agent's point of view they are not. She is always treading on pre-trodden ground. Wherever she goes 'metaphorically' there has always been someone else before. She is

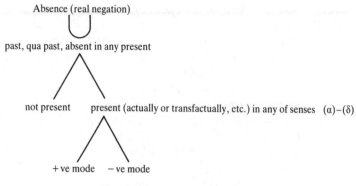

(in the simple sense, exemplified by the absence of men
in Budapest in late 1956, established in §1, i.e. as de-onts)

Figure 2.17 Recursive Embedding of Absences

always — from birth to death — living in a pre-constituted world. She
is always living in the past.

This discussion is connected to absence in the tree diagram (Figure
2.17) illustrating, inter alia, the recursive embeddedness required for
the more complex ontology I am seeking to develop.

I mentioned earlier that the presence of the past has (at least) four
contraries. The two most obvious ones are (a) the absence of the past,
which needs no further discussion once non-preservative
determinate negation (including 'vanishing mediators') is situated,
and (b) the presence of the future. Now I have already argued in §4
above against the possibility of backwards causation, i.e. an effect
preceding its cause. So the sense(s) in which the future is present has
to be different from the sense in which the past is present, viz. as
(potentially determining) *determined*. But I am going to argue in C3.6
for the reality of both time and tensing, the irreducibility of tense and
the reality of the future. So it would seem prima facie paradoxical if I
was to be committed to the reality of the future but not its presence.
In fact I am going to argue that, if the future is paradigmatically
shaped possibility of becoming (a possibility which may be closer or
more distant from us, more or less about, and more or less likely to be
actualized), the presence of the future is a perfectly kosher locution,
but that it is always mediated by the presence of the past (up to the
limit of the indefinite present). Thus we have to think the concept of
the presence of the future as the presence-of-the-future-in-the-past-
in-the-present. There are parallels or analogues of all at $(\alpha)-(\delta)$.

(α') Pregnancy is constitutive geo-historical process of coming-to-
be. Or consider the anthropic and/or causal closing of possibilities as

an impeding event comes upon us. Or the pre-programming of a genetic code. Or a time bomb. Or salivation, exacerbated by routine (the presence of the past). As structured, entities such as people and institutions contain various possibilities (powers, liabilities and tendencies of the type discussed in §4, including recursively the power to acquire powers) some of which are more likely to materialize than others. (This is why the future must be seen as *increasingly shaped possibility*.) And so there is a sense in which we, and entities generally, may be said to contain possible futures within us, and these may be vital to our being. But there is also a sense in which these possible futures are so qua product-in-process, that is, as possibilities existentially constituted by their geo-histories; and therefore a sense in which the most interesting case of the present as a future is mediated by or even *dependent* upon the presence of the past.

(β') By symmetry of argument it could be said that the dialectics of co-inclusion must allow for the presence of the future. If x, a tensed past, is co-included within y, then y must be a tensed future co-included within x. But there is a trap here. The dialectics of co-inclusion is made possibly by the necessary but indefinite temporal stretching of an episode, event, or period. It lies either in the past or in the present. And in the latter case it defines a boundary state between what is determined and determinate and what is, even if it is practically inevitable, not yet. Suppose we are in an episode which is ongoing, tense is defined by the moment of becoming in the episode we are in. If we are living in or constituted by a multiplicity of differential rhythmic processes then we may indeed have to talk about the simultaneity of non-simultaneous becomings. There are two considerations here. Suppose we are in a episode which is ongoing, tense is defined by the moment of becoming in that particular episode. And in the case of differential rhythmics, if coordination is by reference to a future, the grounds for its *expected* causal efficacy must lie in the past and its not having become remains unaffected. Secondly, some socio-geo-historical processes representing world-lines which are future in respect of some other notional or possible world-lines are always *past*, in the sense of existentially intransitive and determined, in respect of any observer's/classifier's/explainer's world-line, and so can only be *known as past*, and so as mediated by the past, relationally. We will never come across a future which is either determinate or completely closed.

(γ') The correlate of lagged efficacy is the role that anticipation, planning and projects play in action. The future is prevalent in the geo-historically mediated social present, from 'futures markets' and discount rates in the economy to trust in railway timetables or a

parent's return. But we need not look so far away for the analogue of
the presence of the past here. For the very paradigm of intentional
agency is defined by its orientation to the future: rational agency is
well grounded and executed intentional bringing about of a state of
affairs that of necessity lies in the future and (unless it is
overdetermined) would not have otherwise occurred, even if this
event is only a redescription of the past. The future is the intentional
object of every act. But it is always in a present and mediated by some
past.

(δ') Does the transcendental perspectival switch have an analogue?
Yes. For agents can, while deposited in the past, *prefigure* in their
transformative praxis the future. A minimal condition for this would
be that it be insofar as possible consistent with the intentional object
of the praxis (ends/means consistency). But prefigurative politics
should in some sense embody as a promissory note the vision of the
future society it aims to bring about.

The two other contraries of the presence of the past worth
mentioning are (c) the absence of the present and (d) the presence of
the present. (c) has two paradigms. The first is provided by the
observation of a distant present, which I will discuss in C3.6. The
second is yielded by the phenomena of lapsed time, most obviously
when asleep, but also in the case where a phenomenon is described
as 'late' or, to take the opposite case, when the contemporary is
described as 'post'. This depends upon some present context being
loco-periodized in a putatively explanatory or, perhaps, tendentially
predictive theory. Once more the intelligibility of this locution
depends upon the mediation of the presence of the past in senses
(α)–(δ) above. The final contrary, (d) — the presence of the present,
the obverse of (c), paradigmatic simultaneity — only has a
philosophically or sociologically interesting meaning when it is once
again taken as mediated by the presence of the past. In short, the past
is all pervasive.

In the sequel to this book, *Dialectical Social Theory*, I will set about
developing the complex ontology that is required for a dialectical
social theory fully adequate to the dialectical pluriverse in which we
must act, and which in the next section I am going to begin to explore.
Here I have time for only a few general pointers. First we should note
the significance of the possibilities of recursive embedding, systematic
intermingling and multiple mediation of concepts and their referents.
Thus we have noted how the transfactual efficacy of a tendency,
processually exercised through a rhythmic, may be multiply mediated
by specific differentiate before contributing to the multiple
determination, via the intentional causality of agency of a mixed

(naturally circumscribed, socially-materially conditioned, contextually positioned) conjuncturally bound result. But the rhythmic may itself be transfactual, and the mediation processually spatio-temporalized, and the structured system which exercises its causal powers may, like any part of the 'causal chain', systematically cohere in a nexus or totality, which contains, as the ground of or as grounded in, dialectically contradictory radically negating tendencies. A stratified schema is represented in Figure 2.18. Take an even simpler case. In Figure 2.19 we have iconic representations of natural or social absences and hidden depths.

In §4 I distinguished different concepts of causal powers and tendencies. But one might well ask why cannot causal powers not just be processually exercised, but there be powers to process (consider 'maturing', 'growing', 'developing')? And, of course, one must think of the power (or liability) to acquire powers or needs; give full weight to the implicit, the latent; the delayed and distant; allow relations to be as real as their relata; break down, as the concept of the fourfold polysemy of real negation discussed in §6 does, the distinction between process and product, that is, see the synchronic/diachronic distinction, although realistically justifiable, as not categorially constitutive, any more than the distinction between the large and the

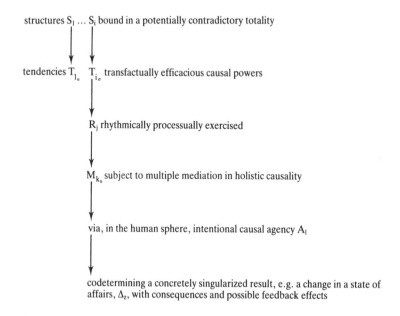

structures S_1 ... S_i bound in a potentially contradictory totality

tendencies T_{1_a} T_{i_σ} transfactually efficacious causal powers

R_j rhythmically processually exercised

M_{k_n} subject to multiple mediation in holistic causality

via, in the human sphere, intentional causal agency A_l

codetermining a concretely singularized result, e.g. a change in a state of affairs, Δ_z, with consequences and possible feedback effects

Figure 2.18 The Complexity of Causality

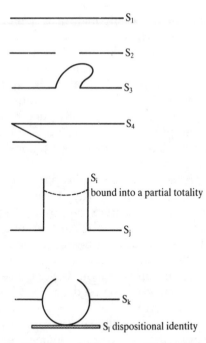

Figure 2.19   Natural Absences, Hidden Depths

small is. Considerations of this sort indicate that the geo-historicization of social theory is long overdue and that concepts like centre and periphery, with the periphery representing a marginalized (de-totalized) more or less essential split-off, may be as useful as (or more so than) the macro/micro contrast. Pursuing my catalogue, we must allow for a disjunctive plurality in addition to a conjunctive multiplicity of causes in open systems, and when one thinks causality, think in terms of categories of negation and their derivatives (such as contradiction); conceptualize intra- as well as inter-activity, -dependence and -connection; investigate both margins of inquiry in totalities, etc. Formalization can play a role here too — thus modal, relevance and tense logics have illuminated structure, differentiation and change respectively.

I now want to take the antinomy between Habermas (and more generally speech action theorists such as Searle) and Derrida (and deconstructionists generally) as illustrating the tacit complicity of dialectical antagonists to which I referred to §§4 and 6. I may here perhaps be guilty of anachronism in interpreting Derrida as a transcendental philosopher and dialectical commentator, as the disseminating remarker between 1967 and 1974 (i.e. up to *Glas*). His main dialectical comment has been on the traditional hierarchies of philosophy, from speech/writing on, which he typically juxtaposes, then inverts and subjects his inversion to erasure. It is less contentious to see Habermas as a transcendental philosopher and dialectical commentator from *Knowledge and Human Interests* (also 1967) on. Thus in his development of the concept of an ideal speech situation in the seventies, he metacritically claims to show how what is everywhere presupposed by communicative interaction is counterfactual, i.e. seldom if ever (and then only partially) realized. In a sense the communicants are guilty of performative contradiction, and form a normative Tina formative compromise. He then goes on to develop his counterfactual commentary in *The Theory of Communicative Action* into a systematic metacritique of the colonization of 'life world' by 'system' under the auspices of the steering media of money and power.[92] Habermasians and speech action theorists can point out that Derrida is no Cratylus: he obviously intends to be read, and so communicate, which presupposes a necessary minimum quotient of logocentricity, and is thereby guilty of self-referential paradox. Deconstructionists, on the other hand, can respond by pointing out how the critiques of action theorists rely upon all kinds of unreflected metaphors and tropes, the genealogy and sense of which they do not even begin to thematize, invoking the non-self-present, tacit, past, absent, networks of networks, and more generally the tacit presuppositions of infrastructural spacing, iterability and so on, in practice self-deconstructing themselves. Thus we have a stalemate in which both sides accuse the other of self-referential paradox.

I will concentrate on the tradition which begins with Nietzschean negligence, traverses Heideggerian b̶e̶i̶n̶g̶ and can only end in writing itself *out* by erasure. But it is not my intention here to take sides. *Properly conceived* the programmes of deconstructive semiotics and reconstructive hermeneutics are not only consistent but interdependent, betokening the interdependence of the mediate and the immediate,* the duality of structure and agency, characterized by

---

* I shall want to insist on this point. Axiologically, and from the standpoint of practice (and hermeneutics), no action or understanding or communication would be possible — without interminable regress — unless some actions,[93] including perceptions, were just done and sentences simply understood, not by virtue of other actions or sentences. Conversely, ontologically, and from the standpoint of theoretical reason (and semiotics), arguably any action, including our discourse, would be impossible except on the basis of an indefinitely extended geo-historical formation of the conditions that make basis actions and understandings possible.

non-arbitrary dialectical interconnection. What they share in common is an irrealist, unstratified, actualist, and arguably a punctualist and/ or blockist and/or closed ontology — and in particular an insufficiently stratified and distanciated concept of the self and space-time.

The paradigm of the tradition of writing *sous rature* — under erasure — is that of the Nietzschean theses of the necessity and impossibility of knowledge, requiring an active forgetting of the illusory character of truth. *But what is necessary is not what is untenable.* It is not science, experience, signification, etc. which are untenable but metaphysical conceptions of them, on which the Nietzschean tradition imposes a quite appropriate dialectical comment. What it replaces them with are concepts like the trace structure of the sign, metaphoricity, etc. which are indeed conditions of the *possibility* of science and the like.* But it holds these equally to be conditions of their *impossibility* in that they cannot be lived by the *agents* concerned. And this depends upon unreflected and transcendentally refuted concepts of agency, experience, space-time, generally upon an unacceptable ontology. Let us take a temporarily stretched and spatially spread practice like a research project. Consider an agent N's participation in, say, an experimental programme. Amidst a multiplicity of practices and spatio-temporal paths she engages in a distanciated and self-reflexively monitoring participation in a particular aspect of it. Suppose she has to test, as a member of the research team, a particle's spin. She is focusing on untying a knot in a cord. She is competently doing so. She is aware of the role of her task in the context of the overall programme and in the context of the hierarchy and plurality of projects with their own rhythmics in her life. She could recall last night's TV, she is aware that she has an unconscious, that the sign has a trace structure, of the metaphoricity of language use, the very language she is using now, that she is subject, in a multiplicity of dimensions, to the inertial drag of the past and its delayed causal efficacy. She knows that she will die as so much cosmic dust at the same time as she is untying the knot and attending to the matter at hand; just as she knows about, and perhaps is skilfully employing, the metaphoricity of language while chatting to a colleague about last night's TV. She knows all this in a *meta-reflexively totalizing* (reflection on her praxis and) *situation of her life*. She is a

---

* A more nuanced judgement of these Derridean concepts would have to note his elision of the referent from the semiotic triangle which I will develop in C3.2, the exaggerated character of Derridean claims and his relative silence on material infrastructures.

stratified agent engaged in transformative practice, including inter-subjective communication, immediately understood because mediately contextualized in an extended (non-punctualist) and open (non-blockist) stretch of time, who, *in virtue of a being a stratified self*, no more has to forget her Nietzsche in untying a knot than lose her capacity to speak French in saying 'yes please'. This is illustrated in Figure 2.20, which will be amplified further anon. If one wanted to ask in what did such an agent's subjectivity or self consist, one could reply only that it consisted in her dispositional identity with her (changing) causal powers. To be is to be able to come to do.

The same concept of a meta-reflexively totalizing situation allows the agent to understand both that her engagement with reality is inexorably linguistic and that reality must be referentially detached from her language use in a recognition of alterity or existential intransitivity that is a transcendental presupposition of the satisfaction of our most bodily urges. Her baby must 'intuit' the reality principle, perhaps first disclosed by the absence of her breast, just as she must understand the complicated experimental project in which she is at work. This can be put another way. At the level of ontogeny, language is being-expressive. But at the level of ontology,

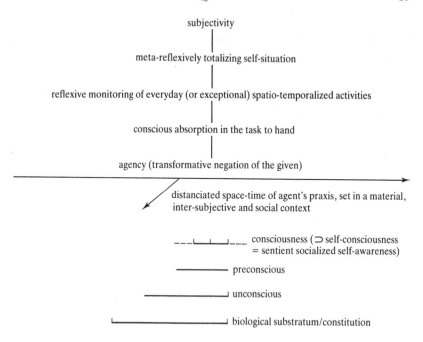

Figure 2.20 A Stratified Model of the Self

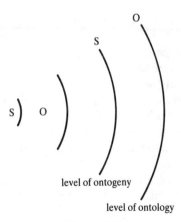

Figure 2.21

once we metacritically detach ourselves from the premisses of our transcendental arguement, we can come to see that a world without humanity is a condition of the possibility of everything we call 'human', that the epistemic – ontic, expressive – referential duality of function of language which occurs within language is ontologically within an overarching objectivity. Only this standpoint allows us to ask the existential question that the tradition of monovalence forecloses; can we as a species survive and flourish? In C4 I will show the metacritical effects of not asking this question, which presupposes the possibility, for most of actualized space-time, of being without *Dasein* or human being. Figure 2.21 attempts to depict this situation. In C3 I will show how a genuinely ontological, rather than merely ontic, concept of truth is possible (and used).

It is also the concept of a meta-reflexively totalizing situation that allows us to appreciate how we can have a future despite the saturation of social (and to an extent natural) life with the past. We make use of some part or aspect of it against other parts to transform the transformative situation in which we must act or die. We change the mediations which project us into the future, and in so doing we claim it as our own.

Engels is the first of a line of dialectical commentators on both the Marx–Hegel relationship and the scientificity of Marx's metacritique of political economy. I promised to say something about Engels's dialectical laws. These, he argued in his *Dialectics of Nature*, can be 'reduced in the main to three' — viz. (1) the transformation of quantity into quality and vice versa; (2) the interpenetration of opposites; and (3) the negation of the negation. There are ambiguities in Engels's various discussions. It is unclear whether the laws are supposed to be more or less a priori truths or super-empirical generalizations; and whether they are indispensable for scientific practice or merely convenient expository devices. Besides the notorious arbitrariness of Engels's examples, the relevance of *his* dialectics for Marxism, conceived as a nascent social science, may be questioned, especially as Engels is opposed to any reductive materialism. While the evidence strongly indicates that Marx agreed with the general thrust of Engels's intervention, his own analysis of capitalism neither presupposed nor entailed any dialectics of nature. At the same time his critique of a priorism, mentioned in §5, implies the a posteriori and subject-specific character of claims about the existence of dialectical or other types of processes in reality. The relations between the Marxian, Engelsian and Hegelian positions can be represented as in Figure 2.22.

Engels's first law specifies *dialectical thresholds*, and might be exemplified by the phenomena of emergence, and levels generally. Its ancestry clearly lies in Hegel's nodal line of measure relations. Despite Engels's examples, transcendental arguments are constructable to the effect that in an originating, developing, non-reductionist totality at least the transformation of some quantitative into qualitative differences must be true, although, of course, as such it licenses no particular empirical claim. In any event Mao was wrong to reduce it to a special case of a second law which, after Stalin had abolished the third law, increasingly discharged the burden of the Marxian dialectic. A cynic might take the second law's popularity as referring to the 'interpenetration' between the USSR and the West. The term 'opposite' is notoriously vague, while 'interpenetration' suggests 3L dialectical connection without any necessary contradiction (which was perhaps why Stalin continued to approve of it). Insofar as it is supposed to stand for the unity, qua interdependency (which may take the form merely of existential dependency or internal relationality; or of tacit complicity; or of conflict, e.g. around a structure of domination), of dialectical

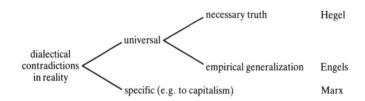

Figure 2.22

antagonists, it may be highly contingent, localized and variable. But it is clearly meant to designate such phenomena as the internal relationality of proletarians and capitalists in capitalist society — which is not saying very much, especially if the tacit implication is that the abolition of the wage contract will result in the toppling of the potential transfinity of relations of subjugation (power$_2$ relations). It is the third law which has the clearest meaning. In fact, in its Hegelian and Stalinist forms, it stands for the cancellation of contradiction. But in its Marxian and dialectical critical realist forms it indicates *the geo-historical transformation of geo-historical products*. As such it is a genuine dialectical comment on Hegelian preservative dialectical sublation. Moreover, insofar as it designates the *absenting of absence*, it correctly specifies what I am arguing dialectic is. *Hegel lost not absence — of this he is full — but the concept of absence.* In virtue of this absenting, plenitude, repletion, saturation (and the restoration of monovalence — positivity) were, it was hoped, secured. In it this 'third law' mediated by the tri-unity of (empirically grounded) causality, transformative praxis and (irreducibly specific and spatializing) tense that is crucial to any dialectic of human emancipation.

I have treated Aristotle, Kant, Hegel, Marx, Engels, Habermas and Derrida as dialectical commentators and introduced the concept of a meta-reflexively totalizing reflection and situation. It might be asked what is the dialectical status of *this* book. This is not the place for reflexivity, which I will attempt in due course. But in the meantime it can be thought of as a dialectical comment on dialectic. Moreover, it stakes a further claim: namely to achieve the dialectically rational resolution of the contradictions and lacunae it identifies in hitherto dialectics, namely in dialectical critical realism. It is a metacritical comment at the τ transformation of C1.9, where I sketched a Hegelian (epistemological) dialectic — the basic form of which Marx rightly claimed Hegel glimpsed only to envelop (and transfigure) in mysticism. Whether it has succeeded in this is only for the reader to judge at the end of the book.

§ 9 Dialectical Critical Naturalism

In this section I want to explain what critical realism has done; why, unwittingly, it is a perfect vehicle for, or at least an exemplar of, social dialectics; and why, despite this, it must be itself dialecticized, and further generalized and substantialized. In prefigurative application of this I shall show both how the mechanism at the core of critical naturalism, the transformational model of social activity (henceforth TMSA), is a model of transformative praxis, *absenting* the given (and typically *driven* by and *against* absence) — that is, a model of *transformative negation*, now understood as incorporating the essential insights of §7 and §8, viz. the intra-active relational and geo-historical processual constitution of social products (people, institutions, etc.); and how the two-way interlocking pair of transcendental arguments necessitating a conceptualization of the duality (with the vital hiatus) of structure and agency establish, on the one hand, (α) in the argument from agency to structure, the possibility of a *dislocated dialectics of structure and agency*, and, on the other, (β) in the argument from structure to agency, through the theorem of the necessary embodiment of intentional causality, the inexorable spatio-temporality of social life, and a fortiori its processual (and contingently globalizing) character. (α) connects to the refrain of the presence of the past, (β) to that of emergent and differential rhythmics. Significantly (α) portends the *negative* (and other) *generalizations of the TMSA*, which, in my initial formulations of it, still bore the imprint of ontological monovalence.

Four dialectically interdependent planes constitute social life, which together I will refer to as four-planar social being, or sometimes human nature. These four planes are (a) of *material transactions with nature*; (b) of *inter-personal intra- or inter-action*; (c) of *social relations*; and (d) of *intra-subjectivity*. Important discriminations must be made at each level, thus at (c) we can differentiate *power* (including hegemonic/counter-hegemonic), *discursive* and *normative* relations (to which there correspond at [b] power, communicative and moral relations). And within the power sub-dimension of what I have characterized as the 'social cube', which I will briefly summarize below, it is essential both to distinguish between *power$_1$*, as the transformative capacity intrinsic to the concept of agency as such, and *power$_2$*, as the (possessed, exercised, mobilized, manifest, covert, indirect, mediated or their contraries; globally, nationally, regionally, sectorally, locally; economic, political, military, symbolic, etc.; more or less ideologically legitimated or discursively moralized, more or less resisted or opposed, more or less successfully, etc.*) transfactually efficacious capacity to get one's way against either (i) the overt wishes and/or (ii) the real interests of others (grounded in their concrete singularities); and to thematize the plurality, which approximates to a *potential transfinity* of power$_2$ or *generalized*

---

* Needless to say all these, and other differentiations which could be added, transmute power from Steven Lukes's '3-dimensional' to a poly-dimensional concept.

master—slave-type relationships from class and gender to age and ethnicity.

The use of the notion of generalized master—slave relations is deliberate. For in the first place, one can map certain general attitudes, from the sections immediately following Hegel's master—slave dialectic, which are conventionally associated with geo-historical periods, on to contemporary orientations to relations of domination, exploitation, subjugation and control. Thus to *stoicism,* corresponds *indifference,* and to *scepticism* the *denial* (or rather denegation — rejection in theory, acceptance in practice) of those relations. And one can align the *unhappy consciousness* (with which the chapter ends) to two phases, namely (i) the *introjective internalization* of the master's viewpoint or aspirations or ideology and/or (ii) the *projective duplication* of what the slave, lacking the imaginary world of religion (Kantian 'rational faith'), finds in fantasy, film or soap in a surrogate compensatory existence.* In the second place, use of the master—slave trope enables us to pinpoint a characteristic feature of the capitalist mode of production: *the exploitative relation intrinsic to the wage-labour/capital contract is hidden at the level of inter-personal transactions* by fetishism and the causally efficacious category mistakes upon which it depends. This is one reason why any emancipatory axiology under capitalism requires the methodological resources of a *depth-explanatory critical social science* of the kind critical realism aspires to provide.**

As critical naturalism is relatively well known, and since I have elaborated it in detail elsewhere,[95] I will restrict myself to a statement of its most distinctive features. It attempts to overcome three dichotomies: (a) in opposition to the voluntaristic tendencies of the Weberian and the reificatory ones of the Durkheimian traditions alike, it articulates a conception, the TMSA, upon which social structure is a necessary condition for, and medium of, intentional agency, which is in turn a necessary condition for the reproduction or transformation of social forms; (b) against both individualist and collectivist conceptions of social science it argues (i) that all social life

---

* In Hegel scepticism is the archetypal figure for theory—practice inconsistency, as the unhappy consciousness is for split. At the same time the stoic may be regarded as the paradigmatic detotalizer.

** As Anthony Giddens's model of structuration is similar to the TMSA it might be worth noting that (1) a tendential voluntarism prevents Giddens from undertaking the negative generalization that dislocates structure from agency (a position championed from such different positions on the sociological compass as adopted by Margaret Archer and Ernesto Laclau alike) and (2), as Alex Callinicos has correctly pointed out, he fails to differentiate power as analytic to action (power$_1$) from power expressed in relations of, albeit reversible, domination (power$_2$).[94]

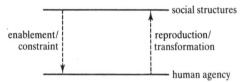

Figure 2.23 The Transformational Model of Social Activity

is embedded in a network (say a partial totality in the sense of §7) of *social relations*, and, more contentiously, (ii) that social relations constitute the paradigmatic subject-matter of social science and (iii) that social identities are constituted relationally, viz. in virtue of the changing/differentiating system of differences and/or changes; and (c) in contrast to positivistic hyper-naturalism and hermeneutical anti-naturalism, it claims to give an account — critical naturalism — of how the social sciences can be sciences in *the same sense* as the experimental sciences of nature, but *in ways which* are as different from the latter as they are *specific* to the nature of societies. Transformationalism. Relationism. Critical naturalism.

(a) is argued by showing, on the one hand, that intentional causality would be impossible without material causes which pre-existed it; and, on the other, that social material causes exist only in virtue of the embodied intentional agency which reproduces and/or transforms them. Thus we have the connected themes of (α) the *duality of structure and agency* — with the hiatus preventing a reductionist collapse in either direction; and (β) the *duality of mediation and transformation* — with the hiatus enabling non-substantial process and disembedding mechanisms. At the heart of this conception is the idea of *praxis* comprising the *transformative negation*, or change, *of the given*. Think of sewing, cooking a meal, or making conversation. *Doing is making. Homo faber.* At the same time this transformative activity reproduces and/or more or less transforms, for the most part unwittingly, its conditions of possibility, including, most notably, what, when fleshed out, appear as social structures and their generative mechanisms (e.g. ways of cooking, making micro-chips or production generally), the agent herself and, generally, what was given, the *donné*, and which has now been reproduced or transformed (e.g. by consumption, dissipation or less drastic changes). Figure 2.23 illustrates the basic model. The relationship between the social structure which constrains or enables the human agency which reproduces or transforms it can be regarded as mediated by *process*, the way in which structural powers are exercised and their causal effects materialize. This is the general form of the spatio-temporality of social life. Figure 2.24 situates the TMSA as a species of transformative negation. The TTTTφ (to which I have already alluded) stands for the transformed (autoplastic), transformative (alloplastic), totalizing, transformist (oriented to deep structure global and dialectically universal change) praxis which may come to reverse a simple dialectic such as

absence → alterity → detotalization (alienating split-off or marginalization) → impotent self.

It should be noted that unintended consequences and unacknowledged conditions at the level of social structure and unconscious motives and tacit skills at the level of human agency immediately afford social science a cognitively enhancing and putatively emancipatory role. I will return to the negativization of the TMSA made necessary by the critique of monovalence when the other basic features of critical naturalism have been demonstrated.

(b), at least (b) (i), is readily understood. Try the mental experiment of subtracting from society for a moment the human agency required for it to be an ongoing affair. What we are left with are *dual points of articulation* (and process) of structure and agency, which are the differentiated and changing *positioned-practices* human agents occupied, engaged, reproduced or transformed, defining the system of social relations in which human praxis is embedded.

(c) is also relatively easily established, on the premiss that the tensed intentional causal agency upon which the TMSA depends entails that the social field is open. But one can quite easily establish this empirically. There are no explanatory significant empirical regularities yielded by social science, so the social domain is de facto open. To establish the limits on naturalism let us take, say, inorganic chemistry as a comparative backdrop (although in principle a variety of sciences should be considered[96]). The activity-dependence of social structures entails its auto-poietic character, viz. that it is itself a social

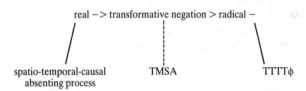

Figure 2.24 The TMSA as Transformative Negation

product, that is to say, that in our substantive motivated productions, we not only produce, but we also reproduce or transform the very conditions of our production. The same premiss, of intentional embodied human agency, grounds both the conceptuality and the geo-historicity of social structures. (In both cases the relation is one of dependence not identity.) Thus we can situate the *auto-poietic, conceptualized and geo-historically dependent* character of social structures alongside their *social relation dependence* as four ontological limits on naturalism.

Epistemologically, the openness of social existence implies the necessary transfactuality of its subject-matter (if it is to be the object of science) and the impossibility of crucial experiments, its conceptuality establishes the necessity for a hermeneutic moment in inquiry, and its geo-historicity the transient character of social structures. This sets the basis for *dialectical explanation*, including concepts of contradiction, crisis and struggle and at least potentially *dialectical arguments*. The co-incidence of the causal efficacy of ideas and their material conditioning will lend to any social dialectic a crucial *relational* (subject – object, agentive – structural, epistemic – ontic) aspect. Finally the condition that, as conceptualized, social forms are quasi-propositional (or even propositional, as in the case of the mediation by ideas of deep structures), and, in addition, normally quasi-propositionally justified or legitimated under some or other description,* renders them liable to one or both of two modes of *critique*.

First, social forms are subject to immanent critique, in terms of their theory/practice inconsistency. I have already remarked on the role that this plays in the context of hermeneutic hegemonic/counter-hegemonic struggles over discursively moralized $power_2$ relations. Second, they are liable to critique, and especially to metacritique, as false — and in particular as at once necessary and false (or at least limited) — hence, as explained in §6, rendering them vulnerable to *dialectical argument*. (Such forms will typically necessitate Tina compromise and supplementarity, stoic compartmentalization [detotalization] and metaphysical λ's. They will be coupled in illicit exchange and tacit complicity, showing the duplicity and equivocation characteristic of the unhappy consciousness. Moreover, as axiologically, viciously and regressively indeterminate, they will display great $power_2$ manipulability and ideological plasticity.) The

---

* In C3.2 I shall show how this requirement is intrinsic to the judgement form as such and also in turn flows from the sole premiss, activity-dependence, that we are employing to deduce the character of any conceivable social science.

ensuing model of *social science as explanatory critique*, which will be
substantially developed in C3.7, can then be generalized to take in the
non-satisfaction of other human interests besides truth and
consistency (although some such interests, for example education,
are straightforwardly necessary for them), for instance help, shelter
or equity. Critical naturalism thus establishes a series of *ontological*,
epistemological, *relational* and *critical* differentiations for the social
sciences from a natural science like inorganic chemistry. There will be
important differences within the various social sciences, of course.
But the retroductive explanatory (DREI(C)) and retrodictive
explanatory (RRREI(C)) models of theoretical or 'pure' and applied
sciences developed in §§6 and 7 will be applicable to the social
domain, including the possibilities that the explanatory moment in
the transitive process of science will be dialectical in content and/or
form.

So far I have presented the TMSA in a positive light. But there is its
negative generalization to consider. For a structure may survive in
one or more of the following modes:

(i) *without* any human agency, and even (i') despite any human
agency;

(ii) in virtue of our (conscious or unconscious) attentive or
inattentive (ii') *inaction*;

(iii) in virtue of our *compliance* or our passive or tacit acquiescence
(or, in virtue of our neutrality or 'neustic' indecision); and/or

(iv) in virtue of the *indirectness* of the human agency which
reproduces it.

(iv) is the least contentious. A power$_2$ structure may be maintained
via various institutional, ideological and personal intermediaries,
mechanisms, delegacies and functionaries, or in virtue of its
systematic interconnections in a totality. But this is quite consistent
with the TMSA, which in no way requires understanding the range of
unintended consequences of our actions (or not). Similar considerations apply to (iii). (ii) simpliciter may be said to involve
forbearance, or leaving alone. But 'letting be' is, or may be, an act
consciously performed. And this would be the essence of my
rejoinder to Ted Benton's 'ecological critique', in which he proposes
models of 'eco-regulation' and 'primary appropriation' as correctives
to Marx's Promethean materialism and my TMSA.[97] In the same way
the 'feminist critique' which proposes a heuristic in which concepts
such as 'care' and 'nurturing', convincingly formulated by Kate
Soper, among others, in a number of places,[98] take the place of male-

oriented 'working-class work' is a valuable corrective, not least inasmuch as it focuses attention on the reproduction of labour-power. Also worth bearing in mind are the phenomena of, on the one hand, unemployment without leisure, and, on the other, dissipative collapse of either structure or agency. Other models, such as those based on a military paradigm, are much more readily locatable within the mainstream of the Hegelian (cf. the continuing reprise of the life-and-death struggle up to and including the non-sublation of war in absolute spirit) and Marxian traditions.

The negative generalization proper takes the form of (i) and (ii'). It recalls Adorno's famous adage that not just theory, but the absence of theory, becomes a material force 'when it seizes the masses'. Two facts are of paramount importance to register. First, that inaction (whether held accountable or not) is as axiologically irreducible as non-being is ontologically. We cannot do everything at once or be aware of all the consequences of any one of our actions. What is open to us is to become aware of roundabout connections (cf. [iv] and the putative 'holistic' critique of the TMSA) and screened deep structures (cf. [ii] and the potential 'transformist' critique), and where the structures and connections are oppressive and congealing engage in the totalizing depth praxis necessary to negate them. But this leads into my second point. Given the presence of the past and the exterior and the depthless atomization characteristic of bourgeois individualism, but accentuated by certain features of late- or postmodernist society,[99] by the merest transcendental perspectival switch, structure is always going to seem dislocated from, and pre-existent to, agency. We are faced starkly with the predicament posed by (i'). Only the mobilization of the totality of the globally oppressed by power$_2$ relations can transform, rather than transfigure, this state of affairs.

Can the negative generalization be itself negatively generalized? Certainly there is no reason why the structures, mechanisms or forms in question should be positive. Negative existence is not the same as non-substantial process. Pierre's absence does not entail action at a distance. And, even if it did, both may be allowed in dialectical critical naturalism. Not *all* the components of the social cube may be negative if society is to be an ongoing affair, so that we may talk, if one likes, in terms of 'inaction in virtue of our agency'. However, here again, employing a spatio-temporal perspectival switch on the negative generalization, we can sustain the thesis of the activity-dependence of social structures on the condition that they are seen as dependent upon the activity of the *dead*: of past as distinct from present praxis, labour or care. That is, as long as we conceive the TMSA as intrinsically tensed, geo-historicized, rhythmicized. But though,

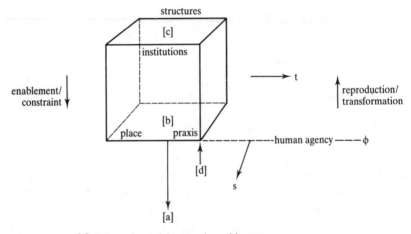

[a] = plane of material transactions with nature
[b] = plane of inter-/intra-subjective [personal] relations
[c] = plane of social relations
[d] = plane of subjectivity of the agent

Figure 2.25 Four-Planar Social Being Encompassing the 'Social Cube'

rejecting monovalence, there is, as we shall see in C3.5, a sense in which the positive and negative, paradigmatically, may be considered to mutually presuppose each other, both conceptually and causally, all the *decisive* moments in social life are *negative*.

I now want to further generalize, dialecticize and substantialize the TMSA. Figure 2.25 represents four-planar social being, encompassing the 'social cube', in terms of which we must understand social life. It has not been possible in this figure to represent the depth of the stratification of the personality, which we shall investigate anon. The separation of space from time in the figure is artificial and we should think instead in terms of a multiplicity of (potentially disjoint) rhythmics, conceived as tensed socio-spatializing process. The social cube should be thought of as a cubic flow, differentiated into analytically discrete moments, as I have detailed elsewhere,[100] as rhythmically processual and phasic to the core. This is a feature which, as Margaret Archer has convincingly demonstrated,[101] distinguishes it from structuration, or more generally any 'central conflation', theory. Moreover, the elements of each plane ought to be conceived as subject to multiple and conflicting determinations and mediations and as displaying to a greater or lesser extent (more or less contradictory) intra-relationality and totality; more generally, as embodying all the moments of the concrete universal. As should be clear from my earlier discussion, the power$_2$, discursive/ communicative and normative/moral sub-dimensions of the social cube at planes C and B can be thought as ones whose point of intersection is ideology as exemplified in Figure 2.26. All power$_2$ relations are power$_1$ relations but the converse is not the case. Correspondingly, turning back to Figure 2.24 above, we must differentiate that constraint$_2$ which is the effect of power$_2$ relations and that constraint$_1$ which is not. Constraints$_1$ may be socially caused, and, as such, the object of rational transformative praxis, but some such contraints (such as those imposed by the laws of nature, and the material, ecological, [spatio-]temporal, ecological, entropic, and axiological asymmetries to which social life is subject) must be taken as unsurpassable. Power$_1$ relations are manifest on plane A, but power$_2$ relations, though they may be mediated by material transactions with nature, are limited to planes C, B and D (the last two of which are directly connected by the homonymy implicit in 'intra-subjectivity'). As already mentioned, power$_2$ relations may not be recognized; or they may be recognized on one plane but not another. Social or inter-subjective power must be distinguished from material power. This is not quite the same as Giddens's influential distinction between (power over) authoritative and (power over) allocative resources. For the former refers, inter alia, to ideologically legitimated power and the latter — economic power — depends upon social power$_2$ relations.

The plurality of modes of power$_2$ relations has already been aired. But discursive and normative relations can also be seen as or as dependent upon types of power$_2$ relations. Moreover, when institutionalized and globalized, political power may take the form of 'The New World Order', economic power assumes the shape of the rapidly shifting structure of the global capitalist economy, moral-normative power is displaced by the sanctions of inter-national, intra-

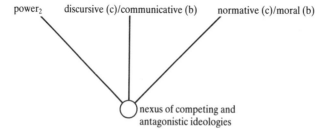

Figure 2.26 Ideology as an Intersect of Three Sub-dimensions
of the Social Cube

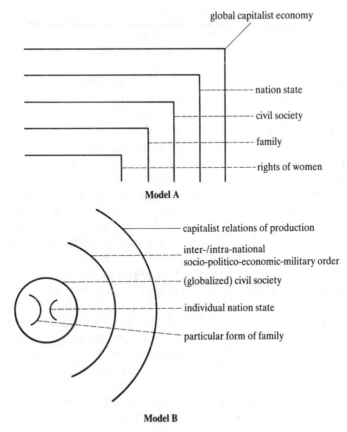

global capitalist economy

------- nation state

---- civil society

---- family

----rights of women

Model A

------- capitalist relations of production

inter-/intra-national
socio-politico-economic-military order

--- (globalized) civil society

--- individual nation state

--- particular form of family

Model B

Figure 2.27

national or ethnic violence and discursive power is displayed by a
homogenized ideological mediatization of 'the news' in a cultural
matrix dominated by the co-existence of Disneyfication/
McDonaldization, poverty and waste. Any attempt to put further
institutional flesh on a model of this type depends on some
hierarchization and this in turn is at least in part a function of which
of the two models of superstructure outlined in §2 we deploy. Thus in
model A in Figure 2.27 the global capitalist economy sets the
boundary conditions on the nation state which sets the boundary
conditions on civil society which sets the boundary conditions on the
family which sets the boundary conditions on the rights of women. In
model B capitalist relations of production constitute the conditions of
possibility of the inter-/intra-national socio-politico-economic-military
order which constitutes the conditions of possibility of civil society,

state and family alike. These are merely exemplifying schematisms. What is vital to stress is that power$_2$ relations are, when recognized, potentially or actually sites of *struggle* which may be of hermeneutic or more 'material' kinds, hegemonizing or detotalizing, readily reversible or not.

If a particular social cube is dialectically contradictory it may induce crisis tendencies which are (a) systemic and/or (b) structural and/or (c) implicate power$_2$ relations and/or (d) effect legitimizing and/or (e) motivating ideologies. Unfortunately we must think 'crisis' with the negative generalization of the TMSA in mind — the possibility of inaction within zero-level agency. Crises may mark nodal points or episodes[102] and/or stimulate or release transformative mechanisms and agencies. The social cube can be used to cast light on the Hegelian 'speculative proposition' and vice versa. The speculative proposition designates a subject (in this case, society) which is not fixed, but is in a process of formation (reproduction, transformation or dissipation), which can only be caught in a network of relations (or as Hegel would have it, predicates), i.e. as a concrete totality; which succeeds, insofar as it does, by bringing out the condition of possibility (dr') of the totality, sublating it via totalizing depth practice (TTTTϕ). The social cube can also be used to criticize one-sided social epistemologies — such as a non-critical hermeneutics at B (or discourse theory at C). Thus, focusing on the face of communicative interactions from situations of co-presence to telephone calls takes in only one mode of social and inter-personal subjectivity (reducing the former to the latter), ignores such modalities as force, and such phenomena as power$_2$, and ignores the plane of material transactions with nature or socialized material objects characteristic of work, the depth stratification of the personalities of the communicators (and the sense in which their speaking and writing expresses other aspects of their personality), the meshwork of institutions in which their exchange takes place and the social relations which are a condition of its possibility, and the criss-crossing of their communication by a differential array of causal space-time paths and rhythmics. Let us consider some of the rhythmics in which an agent may engage:

1. the narrative of her life, her biography;
2. the lagged causal efficacy of her unconscious, her unwritten biography;
3. her life cycle as an organism (a human being) and specifically as a woman;
4. the flow of her daily praxis (engaged in a variety of social practices with rhythmics of their own) as tracked by her space-

time routes through the cities, dwellings, worksites, landscapes
in which she lives;

6. the *longue durée* of differentially sedimented structural
   institutions and the social relations upon which they depend;
7. the development of specifically civilized geo-history in the
   context of human geo-history, inserted in the rhythmics of
   species, genera and kinds, located in a geo-physical
   development of a solar system, embedded in the entropy of an
   expanding universe.

At this point I want to switch perspectives (which is ineliminable in
dialectic) from structure to agency. Figure 2.28 illustrates schematic-
ally the stratification of action, the existential intransitivity of
intentionality and the distinction between real reasons for action
(which may be more or less unconscious, and to a greater or lesser
extent ideologically formed) and mere ex post or pre-rehearsed
rationalizations. Actions are accountable, even if they are routinized
or habitual, and even if their reason lies in custom or convention. It is
real reasons for action which comprise the existential agent's
intentional causality, and without this concept structure would float
free, in a noumenal or virtual cloud, of agency. It is embodied
intentionality which earths social life. Figure 2.29 is a more
complicated model of the components, or, if you like, the springs of
action. *It is informed* (or misinformed) *desire*, propelled by absence,
that powers transformative praxis or negation (and the *durée* of
agency in Figure 2.25).

Properly conceived, action should be understood as a cognitive-
affective-conative-expressive-performative vector, with a form, content, mood, style and efficacy of its own. A few brief comments on
the model. Amour de soi is the basis of altruism, while amour propre
is intrinsically egoistic. I believe that curiosity is a basic urge or
instinct, essential to the learning process, in which the dialectic of
desire becomes the dialectic of freedom. I have included as an
example of mood an optative moment, incorporating that neo-
Blochian hope which fuels that *concrete utopianism* that plays a crucial
role in emancipatory axiology. I have also situated 'motivation' and
'drive', which encompasses an agonistic aspect and may be taken as
one indication of the agent's sense of ease and confidence generally.
Of course, there will be internal relations between the components or
bases of action. Undergirding them all is a more or less ego-syntonic
or ego-emancipatory existential security system, initially formed in
the processes of primary polyadization in early childhood and

ultimately nurtured and sustained by relations of fiduciariness, care, solidarity and trust. All the components of action constitute causal powers (or liabilities) of the agent, but I have differentiated powers (competences and facilities qua access to resources), in the sense of transformative capacity, from the rest.

Figure 2.30 is an elaboration on Figure 2.20. On this model *the self is nothing other than the dispositional identity of the subject with her changing causal powers*. The agent is consciously absorbed in a practice. This constitutes her praxis, i.e. her causal agency. But an agent may engage in a number of social practices on a particular day (child-minding, cooking a meal, driving a car, designing a book jacket, making small talk with Jemma, participating in a rally, etc.), so social practices cannot be identified with human praxes. Nor can the latter, as the flow of intentional agency, be identified either with specific actions (such as making a cup of coffee) or with the acts performed in

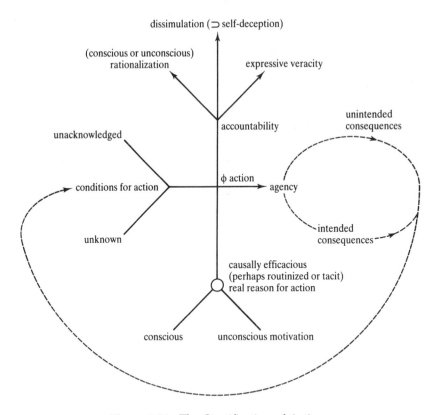

Figure 2.28 The Stratification of Action

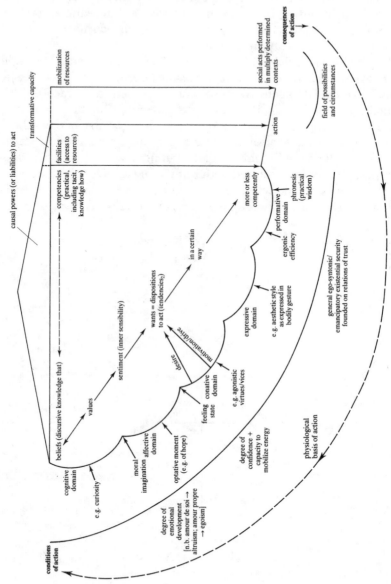

Figure 2.29 The Components of Action

or by the actions in which her intentional agency is the transformative force. Figure 2.30 does not identify the multiplicity of rhythmics involved, nor does it bring out the degree of centrification, fragmentation or alienation of the subject, or the fact that the double stratification of mind — of beliefs constituting a psyche and of projects articulating a life — have both conscious and unconscious aspects. Finally none of the models do justice to the open systemic, multiply and conflictually determined nature of the aspects at play in our internal pluriverses.

At this point I want to revert to the topic of ideology, and in particular ideology in the narrow sense as embodying categorial error. The archetypal figure of alienation for Hegel is the *'beautiful soul'*, the pure agent who will not reconcile herself to the norms of, and so is

Figure 2.30 The Stratification of Agency: A Moment in a Person's Life

alienated from, her community. She is split off from just one of the four dimensions of the social cube. In contrast the prototypical Marxian *generative separation*, which articulates the conditions of possibility of capitalist society, produces a split both in all four dimensions or planes and in the agent's labour or activity itself — a fivefold alienation. The immediate producers, in being alienated from their labour, are cut off from (a) the means and materials of their production, (b) each other, (c) the nexus of social relations and ultimately (d) themselves. Let me approach the topic of categorial error by considering two of its basic forms — illicit categorial (a) *fusion* (e.g. of the transitive and the intransitive dimensions in subject—object identity theory) or (b) *fission* (e.g. the detotalization of being involved in an actualist account of laws). (These examples should show that these category mistakes are by no means opposed, rather they tacitly complement one another.) Now one example of illicit fusion is (a') the *exchange of non-equivalents* pivotal to the wage-labour/capital contract, made possible by the commodification of labour-power and the fetishism in which capitalist relations of production are enveloped. And from this — or rather the theory in which it is embedded — Marx hopes to demonstrate the dialectical *necessity and falsity* of the 'wage form'; and, more generally, as conceptualized, the mode of production which is defined by it. A social example of illicit fission is the (b') *non-parity of equivalents* involved in paying female or immigrant workers less than native male workers for the same work. From considerations such as this I would like to derive an argument for a basic or *core equity* in C3. Now one of the chief ideological configurations at work in contemporary society is the cloaking, or, more generally, (a") representation of sectional interests as universal ones. This is characteristic of free market ideologies. Less noticed is its inverse, (b") the *representation of universal interests as sectional*. An example may be the British miners' strike of 1984—85. Of course there are other prevalent ideological mechanisms, including the naturalization, and thence eternalization, of the status quo (cf. §5); the screening of contradiction and conflict; organicism (natural law theory), social conventionalism, e.g. social contract theory, voluntarism (e.g. decisionism), etc. etc.

We have already seen that despite the particular value of immanent critique in hermeneutic struggles in discursively moralized power$_2$ relations any social (and so conceptualized) system violating an axiological necessity will induce a range of responses from Tina compromise formations through theory/practice inconsistencies to pathologies of action entraining crisis tendencies and the like. Two questions immediately arise:

1. By what mechanism are the oppressed in power$_2$ relations to achieve their emancipation?
2. In accordance with what standards of consistency and universalizability are they to reason?

1. It is *informed* desire that drives praxis on. Desiring agents have an interest in removing the constraints (including constraints$_2$) on their freedom to satisfy their desires, more generally wants. Knowledge is intrinsic to power. (And focusing on the model in Figure 2.29 would show curiosity as intrinsic to the desire for knowledge.) Power, and so knowledge, is essential to the satisfaction of desire. Definitionally, then, there is a conatus to deconstraint or freedom, in a depth dialectic I will articulate in C3, and to the knowledge of the power$_2$ relations constraining the satisfaction of wanted need. *Absence* will impose the *geo-historical directionality* that will usher in a truly humane human global society, mediated (or so I shall argue) by explanatory critical and emancipatory axiological social science.[103]

2. It could be said that to show an inconsistency or other weakness in an opposition's position does not oblige one to advance a position of one's own, especially if one is not in a situation to do anything about it.* Moreover, it could be argued that one need only put forward criteria of consistency and universalizability if one does not accept the dialectical critique of analytical reason, to which I turn in the next section. Further, it could be said that, following the line of the materialist diffraction, there is no reason why a *single* criterion or formula applicable to every situation should be forthcoming, and that the whole point of dialectical practice is that it requires the meta-ethical virtue of *phronesis*, demanding skilful application case by case. Moreover, it could be argued that judgements are per se patronizing and diminishing of the autonomy of the agents to whom they are addressed — that the most one can do is to assert a hypothetical second-person with a possible assertoric imperative embedded within it, along the lines of 'if I were you and wanted shelter (which you do) then do x'. Every expressively veracious fiduciary remark would then have to take into account the concrete singularity of the agent to which it is addressed. It could additionally be claimed that perspectival relativity and pluralism are intrinsic to dialectic for which some kind of algorithm is being demanded. The value of these

---

* Thus there is a difference between being inconsistent and not being consistent in the sense of not being willing to formulate or act on a policy in terms of which one's consistency could be judged — akin to the difference between being immoral and being amoral.

responses, individually and collectively, should not be under-rated. However, it seems unlikely, in the context of counter-hegemonic struggle, that any objective such as emancipation from the constraints$_2$ imposed by, say, the capitalist mode of production could be achieved without (α) a sketch of the principles and mechanisms under which agents would flourish without it, or (β), more generally, a plausible strategy for advance in such a direction. The question is what is T/P consistency (which implies universalizability), *unless* there are specific grounds for withholding it?

It should be said that the provisional formula that I offered in §1 for T/P consistency in a praxis in a dialectical process, viz. as transfactual, processual, concrete, agent-specific and transformative, not only needs full elaboration, which I shall supply in C3, but also remains a purely formal criterion with a content that has yet to be explicated. However, it is not an objection to a criterion that it is formal, if it can inform a substantive one, as the Lockian/Leibnizian moment of science is able to do. At this point one needs to distinguish between (a) dialectical universalizability, which is both a test for consistency and a criterion for truth, (b) the T/P consistency, which refers to the praxis that the logic of dialectical universalizability may inform, and (c) the developmental consistency or coherence that designates the process in which the praxis is embedded. The point about developmental, directional or dialectical consistency is that no general formula for it can be given. It is necessarily intrinsic to the process concerned. Science seeks to resolve analytical inconsistencies but their very resolution depends upon the suspension of the axiom of (analytical) consistency; and an open totality will always convey the possibility of such inconsistencies. Think of it like this: at the end of the day, the cherry must blossom. (Once this book is finished, it must hang together.) But the cherry will perish. (Other books will be written.) This is existential contradiction expressed in the form of the finitude of any concrete singular. To be developmentally consistent is to know when to be inconsistent, when to grow, when to mature, when to apply a dialectical comment on dialectical comments, when to stop and when to wait until the agents concerned have made up their own minds into what their freedom consists. Dialectical processual consistency recognizes the authenticity of every concretely singular agent's own narrative or story no less then than the rights of her being.

In turning to the praxis embodied in the process one must make the obvious point that only detailed skilled judgement will do. But can one say anything in general about the criteria for the praxis and the theories that ground it? The praxis will obviously be processual, it should conform to all the moments of the concrete universal (thus the universality should be transfactual), and be grounded in theories which are themselves transfactual, concrete, agent-specific and transformative, i.e. oriented to change in the desired direction. Transfactuality does not restrict, but generally enlarges, the scope (and hence universalizability) of a judgement insofar as it includes the vast majority of open systemic instances in addition to closed systemic ones. Similarly a core human equality based on our shared species-being concretized as equity will vastly extend the scope of the criterion of consistency (and a fortiori universalizability). The requirement that the grounding be agent-specific or actionable might be thought to be covered by the criterion of concrete singularity. But it is worth stressing in its own right. For it not only guards against (non-concrete) utopianism, but also avoids the fallacy that ought implies can. The Kantian doctrine produces a double split: first, between the phenomenal and the noumenal; and then between the world within which we must act (though perhaps can choose mysteriously before life) and a second world or after-life in which happiness is in accord with virtue. Moreover, the criterion of agent-specificity stresses the *self-emancipating character* of the praxis that it is designed to inform. Can one say anything about the objectives to which the praxis in the dialectical process is oriented? In C3 I will show how the absence explicit in desire and judgement form alike presuppose a eudaimonistic society founded on universal human autonomy. Its logic will be totalizing and oriented to the real needs and interests of the *concrete singularity* of each individual as a condition for the free flourishing of all. The key value of such a society will be freedom, conceived as self-determination and as necessarily oriented to the abolition of constraints, such as structural power$_2$ relations and gross inequities, which impede it; a massive extension of rights (which are freedoms), universally recognized, and as much participation-in-democracy (self-government) as is consistent with time, place and nature — in particular, as is consistent with the massive redistribution of resources required for an asymptotic approach to global equity, the needs of future generations, other species and the environment generally. It might be thought that the particularities of the mediations at work in the orientation to concrete singularity will lessen the scope of any (positive or negative) evaluative judgement. To the considerations already advanced in relation to transfactuality, shared species-being (equity) and actionability, we can add two further points. The first is that the specific mediations must be both relevant and significant. The second is that we have to take account of the enormous non-parity of equivalents (cf. [b'] above), inequities

	U	P	S
Politics	Emancipatory/ Transformist	Representative/ Syndicalist	Life
Ethics	Explicitly Universalistic	Particularist	Emotivist/Personalist
Contemporary Site	Multi-national Corporation (Global Commodification)	Political Parties (Complex and and Disjoint Development)	Patriarchal Family and/or Career (Manipulation/ Fortuna/'Fate')
Political Theory	Liberal Universalism (e.g. Rawls)	Pluralistic Communitarianism (e.g. Walzer)	Voluntaristic Pragmatism (e.g. Rorty)

Figure 2.31

generally and the lack of reciprocity involved in existing power$_2$ relations in contemporary global society.

Earlier I differentiated emancipatory/transformist, representative/ syndicalist, movement and life politics. If we conceive movement politics as part of emancipatory politics, then we can align the kind of politics under the traditional UPS schema of the triadic concrete universal as illustrated in Figure 2.31. Another perspective can be got by reinvoking the social cube, but introducing a mediating plane between social relations and personal inter-/intra-actions. Representative politics can then be aligned to the plane of social mediations, life politics affixed to the domain of intra- and inter-subjectivity, and emancipatory-transformist politics to the domain of social relations.

Let me sum up by asking in what sense dialectical critical naturalism is so. It is *naturalist* in the threefold sense (1) that it entails an emergent powers materialism, in which society is materialized ultimately in virtue of embodied intentional causal agency reacting back on the kinds of materials out of which it was formed; (2) that, subject to the qualifications noted earlier, it legitimates the possibility of an explanatory social science; and (3) that it licenses us to pass from purely factual to evaluative conclusions.* It is *critical* (1) insofar as it

---

* For instance, if one can show that a belief is false, ceteris paribus, then any action informed by it will be wrong. More importantly, if one can show *why* it is false, say in virtue of some power$_2$ relation, then one can pass, ceteris paribus, to a negative evaluation on that power$_2$ relation and to a positive evaluation on action rationally directed at overthrowing it.

is established by transcendental argument, (2) inasmuch as the explanatory social science it situates is (contingently) critical and (3) the model of explanatory critique can be generalized to constraints on the satisfaction of needs other than truth as a general agentifying axiology, as I will show in C3. It is *dialectical* (1) insofar as it situates the possibility of dialectical explanations of the origins, structures (where dialectical argument itself may play a pivotal role), transformative tendencies, struggles and crises in principle at all four planes of the social cube; (2) insofar as it non-monovalently situates the dislocation of structure from agency, concretizes the social totality, allows for contradictory and generally disjoint processes, while grounding its ontology in transformative praxis; (3) insofar as transformative praxis, paradigmatically absenting the given, is sparked by absence in the shape of desire, to absent the constraints on desire, and in a dialectic of truth mediated by wisdom (to be developed in C3) to absent the $power_2$ relations which $constrain_2$ the realization of the wellbeing and potentialities of each and every concrete singular individual agent.

§ 10 Towards a Real Definition of Dialectic

Insofar as, for better or worse, discussion of dialectic has been dominated (since his time) by Hegel, in the first two chapters of this book we have been working our way, mainly through the explicitly immanent and contrastive critiques of Hegelian dialectic, towards a real definition, as distinct from the purely nominal one issued in C1.2, designed to capture the essence of the concept.* This was already prefigured in the first section of this chapter as the *absenting of absence*, and in the human realm as the specifically causally efficacious *agentive*, as distinct from dummy (proxy, surrogate or epiphenomenal), *absenting of absence*, a concept that Hegel cannot sustain. The positive identification and elimination of absence, entailing the critique of ontological monovalence, yields the barest sketch of a definition of dialectic. In this section and the chapters to come, some flesh will be put on the skeleton. But two caveats must be straightaway sounded. We have seen in §6 that the multiple diffraction of the concept enabled by Marx's critique of Hegel's philosophy of identity permits a plurality of dialectical configurations,

---

* On real definition as a crucial scientific procedure, see RTS2, C3.

topologies, perspectives and inscapes, which it would idle to suggest could be captured by a single formula. In particular I noted the possibility of a very wide sense of 'dialectic' as indicating merely any sort of relationship between differential elements, which can obviously be put through a variety of hoops. Connectedly, although through its 1M−4D relations, dialectical critical realism attempts to explicate the essence of the concept, it has no wish to be proprietorial about (to invoke scholastic idiom) its *proprium*, let alone legislate its accident. This is perhaps the place to mention that dialectic is the *process* or set of processes, or more generally phenomena, (in the intransitive dimension) which critical realist, like Hegelian, dialectic sets out to *describe* (in the transitive dimension) and dialectically and reflexively connect in the philosophical *system* or meshwork of dialectical critical realism. This is perhaps also the place to make two other points. First, that critical realism will be extending its realism, in dialectical critical realism, to cover an aspect of the concept of truth (which I will call alethic realism), morality and spatio-temporality. These extensions cannot be fully explicated until C3.2, 3.6 and 3.7 respectively. But it is worth remarking that, in particular as applied to the social world (in, for example, the case of morality), they open up the possibility of *constitutive falsity, constitutive morality* and *constitutive perspectivality* to set alongside that *constitutive geo-historical processuality* and *intra-relationality* already explored. By *alethic realism* I mean to connote the reason for or *truth of things* as distinct from propositions (in the intransitive dimension). Moral realism specifies a first-person action-guiding *relation* to, in the social world, typically a set of relations which includes, but is not reducible to, *actually existing moralities* which may be described, redescribed, critically explained (in *descriptive, redescriptive* and *explanatory critical morality*), accepted or changed (reproduced or transformed). What is most distinctive about the spatio-temporal realism I will be advancing is its insistence on the *reality* of *tense* (as spatializing process) and becoming (in the intransitive and transitive dimensions alike). Second, the reader should be forewarned that dialectic achieves its full purchase only in relation to its analytic antipode which, although treated here, can be fully developed only when our journey has been completed. There is dislocation as well as interdependence in the duality of theory and critique.

In articulating dialectic as absenting absence, and socio-substantively as the conatus for freedom (and, further, universal human flourishing in the context of other species and nature generally), I am going to employ three complementary approaches:

1. a retroductive-explanatory derivation of the concept from its genealogy;
2. a metacritical exposition of the concept within dialectical critical realism, in its 'positive', 'negative (critical)' and systemic extensions, prefiguring the fuller elaboration in C3;
3. a critique, traditional ('transcendent'), immanent and proto-explanatory (metacritical$_2$), of analytics, or more generally the analytic problematic.

I will then reprise the central themes of this chapter in the context of the argument of the book as a whole.

1. The affinities between Aristotelian dialectical distinction (dd'), Kantian dialectical limits (dl') and Hegelian dialectical comment (dc') as species of dialectical remark (drk†), on the one hand; and, on the other, the connections between the generalized dialectical remark and civilized conversation oriented to trust-worthy or fiduciary communications are apparent. But in the relatively unknown Ionian tradition, which I differentiated from the Eleatic mainstream in C1.6, dialectic connoted contradiction, conflict and change. From communication as opposed (sic) to conflict, the practice of argumentative moot, never far removed from rhetoric, embodied conflicts *in* communication, as a putative alternative or complement to force, in a sense of dialectic *as* argument — a sense which could be naturally evoked as late as John Stuart Mill, despite his anti-Hegelianism. It is this sense that I have conceptualized around the idea of hermeneutic struggles. Dialectic understood as essentially involving contradiction, and as a dynamo of conceptual and social change, was heavily reinforced by Hegel and Marx (and the Marxist tradition) and a century dominated by class conflict, war and increasing global *intra-dependencies*, (partial) colonial and female emancipation and argument about rights. These may be seen as occurring in the context of what I have characterized as generalized or master–slave-type power$_2$ relations of exploitation, domination, subjugation, oppression, repression and control, whether maintained directly or indirectly, by force, ideological legitimation and/or surveillance. So we have here dialectic as the 'logic of change', but also from Hegel as immanent critique and dependent upon the detection of theory/practice inconsistencies (and conveying a consequent lack of universalizability). Hence too the motif of the unity of theory and practice in absolute reason. But change involves transformative negation; and hence absenting, most notably of constraints on desires, wants, needs and interests. Foremost among such constraints will be those flowing

from power$_2$ relations.* Thus the definition of dialectic as absenting absence; and, since all ills can be seen as absences and absences as constraints, as absenting constraints. Furthermore, since all lack of freedoms can be seen as constraints (and vice versa), the definition of dialectic as *absenting absentive agency*, or as the axiology of freedom. The directionality imposed on the education of desire by the reality principle, i.e. alethic truth, mediated in practice by the meta-ethical virtue of wisdom, will lead, so I shall shortly argue, not to an end state, but to an objective process of universal human self-realization, eudaimonia or flourishing(-in-nature). Reverting to dialectic as dialogical argument, presupposing (in a potentially recursive meta-hermeneutic) the fusion of meaning-frames, whether it takes the form of ideology-critique or not, it is easy to see that this too depends upon that positive identification and removal of mistakes, definitionally absences, whether they take the form of and/or are based on inconsistencies, incompletenesses or irrelevances. And this too is part of the process of liberation. A real definition of dialectic as the absenting of absence and, socio-substantively, as the process of the development of freedom suggests itself inexorably. Figure 2.32 illustrates this.

Two final remarks here on the definition of dialectic as absenting absences. First, this definition can be recursively applied to incorporate the absenting of constraints on absenting constraints, or the absenting of absences (such as constraints$_2$) on absenting absences (or more generally ills). Second, in praxis what is absented is absence itself (be it subjective, inter-/intra-subjective, social or natural [material]). Insofar as thought is involved it may be mediated by the absenting of mistakes, and insofar as the absenting is not immediate it may involve the abolition of constraints, i.e. the augmentation of freedom. Absenting is the causally efficacious *transformative* negation or spatio-temporally distanciated (or rhythmically processual) or (more or less) holistically totalizing intentional change. From this standpoint, analytics expresses the ontology of stasis; and, inasmuch as a praxis is mediated by constraints$_2$ justified or dependent upon it, an implicit ideology of *repression*, grounded, I shall argue, in the logic of reification, fetishism and commodification, ultimately as homogenized time. Analytics assume, then, the shape of an *unself-*

---

* I shall label socially derived constraints as '*constraints$_2$*'; but although all power$_2$ relations constrain$_2$ '*subjects$_2$*' (the constrained/oppressed in relations of domination), some constraints$_2$ are not the result of power$_2$ relations or power$_2$ relations alone. Consider, for example, the profligate use of resources in a society free of power$_2$. Of course, not all constraints are social constraints, just as (at least arguably) not all subjects are oppressed. Hence the need for the subscripts.

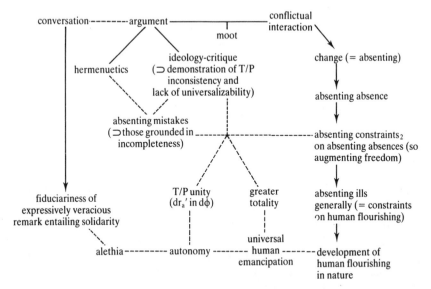

Figure 2.32 A Genealogy of Dialectic

conscious ideology of the normalization of past changes and freedoms, and the denegation of present and future ones.

2. I have been arguing that *absenting constraints on absenting absences* is the *alethia of dialectic.* I now want to develop this perspective from a position intrinsic to dialectical critical realism. Every expressively veracious judgement, whether in the fields of theoretical or practical reason, has to be *universalizable* in three different ways, in accordance with the different aspects or components it has:

(α) (assertorically) *imperatival-fiduciary;*
(β) *descriptive;*
(γ) *evidential.**

(α) The judgement has to be (a) *trustworthy* and (b) *universalizable* (i) in the minimal sense that if in exactly the same circumstances the addressor would not follow his own advice, he would be guilty of theory/practice inconsistency, subject to a dc' and heterology, and (ii)

---

* In C3.2 I shall treat expressive veracity as a component of the judgement form. Here for ease of exposition I take it as a presupposition.

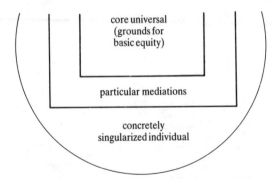

Figure 2.33   The Concrete Singularity of the Human Agent

more strongly, in that it has to be oriented to the concrete singularity of the addressee (this is why, to use Kantian terms, the imperative has to be assertoric rather than a hypothetical or categorical one) and universalizable to any other concrete singular so situated.

(β) The judgement has to be (a) *descriptively accurate* and (b) *universalizable* in the sense that in exactly the same circumstances the situation would repeat itself, as the regulative presupposition of science of sufficient reason (for changes and differences, and, by perspectival switch, for identities and stabilities), or what I have elsewhere called 'ubiquity determinism',[104] demands.

(γ) The judgement has to be (a) *grounded*, for which there are several degrees of strength, the strongest one of which is alethic, which implies that it is (b) *universalizable* in the sense that in exactly the same circumstances the explanation or reason or the truth for the descriptive adequacy of the judgement, or rather what it describes, would be the same, expressing the totalizing depth stratification of being that the principle of sufficient reason itself presupposes.

These three aspects can be loosely associated with three aspects of the concrete universal — (α) with singularity, (β) with particular differentiae or mediations and (γ) with universality as such; and (α) is clearly correlated with the plane of inter-/intra-personal subjectivity in the social cube. More interesting, perhaps, is to picture both the expressively veracious addressor and the person or agency to whom his remark is made as comprised of a core universal humanity, particular mediations and rhythmics and a concrete singularity or duality of his own, that is, as a concrete universal = singular himself, as depicted in Figure 2.33. Communitarians should not get unduly worried here. Universalizability functions as both a test for consistency/sincerity and a criterion for truth. The mediations involved in the case of both addressor and addressee will give the communitarians most of what they want. (Personalism, the characteristic moral ideology for slaves$_2$, invariably abstracts an ideal-typical individual from an a-socio-geo-historical situation.)

In C3.7 I will show how both ethical naturalism and moral realism are justified. Here, although I have elaborated the former on several occasions,[105] this must be taken — as a promissory note — on trust. There are two complementary arguments one could use here. First, if the addressee is constrained in the satisfaction of her wanted needs, the addressor in his fiduciary judgement implies both his solidarity with her and his commitment to the content of the explanatory critical theory of her situation, including the alethia of her concrete singularity, involving, inter alia, a theory of human nature-(needs and interests)-in-society-in-nature. As any social ill can be seen as a constraint on freedom, this entails that any expressively veracious moral utterance implies a commitment to universal human emancipation and a society in which the concrete singularity of each and all is realized. This gives us so far only a commitment to an end-state process. Both imply a commitment to the *totalizing depth praxis* and the research inquiry necessary to inform it, including practical help in the subject$_2$-addressee's self-emancipation from her current situation. All of which requires balanced *phronesis*. The second approach is to ask is there ultimately any state of affairs which is sincerely universalizable other than a society in which, to use Marx's words, 'the free development of each is a condition of the free development of all', that is, which is grounded in the concrete singularity of each and every one (and the former as a condition for the latter), based on the core human equality derived from our shared species-being (cf. Figure 2.33 above), and oriented to the processes of human flourishing in the context of concern for future generations, other species and nature generally. This does not depend upon any Rawlsian 'veil of ignorance' or Habermasian 'ideal speech situation': it is a simple transfactual, concrete and singularized criterion of moral truth: dr$_p$'.

Finessing the first line, the general schema we have is furnished by

axiological commitment in expressively veracious moral judgement → fiduciariness → solidarity → totalizing depth praxis (including inquiry) → content given by explanatory critical theory → emancipatory axiology (= TTTTϕ).

We get a *transition from form to content* in at least three ways: (i) in the reciprocity-universalizability of the content of the initial judgement which, important though it may be from the point of view of immanent critique, may be put down as relatively trivial; (ii) to the action entailed by the formal requirements of solidarity and the totalizing depth praxis (including inquiry); and (iii) to the end-state process. Now by the merest transcendental perspectival switch — viz. from practical to theoretical reason — *any* expressively veracious assertoric utterance at all (and even by a further switch any intentional act) can be seen to imply a commitment to the project of universal human emancipation, involving the abolition of the *totality of master–slave relations*.

The desire to overcome constraints (including especially constraints$_2$) on the satisfaction of desires, wants (causally efficacious beliefs) and needs (what is necessary to an agent's survival and flourishing) implies a conatus or tendency$_2$ to knowledge of all four planes of the social tetrapolity at the hub of which I placed the social cube. And this, mediated by the political skills and practical wisdom shown in collective totalizing agency, will take humanity to the eudaimonistic life for all. In C3 I shall sketch some of the directional ends implied by the *dialectic from absence to freedom*. For instance, the maximum feasible participatory democracy, understood as self-determination, autonomy or self-government, or at least the maximum feasible participation-in-democracy, consistent with self-defined efficiency, size and other relevant considerations. Suffice it to say for the meantime that we shall go from *primal scream to universal human flourishing*.

I now want to resume a theme developed in §9 on p. 168 above. There we drew connections between

(α) illicit fusion and (α') the exchange of non-equivalents and (α'') the representation of sectional interest as universal; and
(β) illicit fission and (β') non-parity of equivalents and (β'') the representation of universal interest as sectional.

Dialectic depends upon the art of thinking the *coincidence of distinctions and connections*. Fusion involves the absence of a *distinction*, such as the transitive dimension/intransitive dimension one implicit in the epistemic fallacy, and necessitates internal complicity or counterparts. Fission involves the absence of a *connection* such as is involved in actualism between laws in open and closed systems (or detotalization generally). Fission characteristically requires *external* complicity or counterparts. Fusion commits an error; fission omits the truth. The former is characteristically driven by monism or other reductionisms, the latter always results in detotalization (hence

dualism or pluralism at best, eclecticism and fragmentation at worst
— e.g. in moral non-realism, of values from being). Now I have two
interests here: to show how this couplet can be put to critical (1)
politico-ethical (2) systematic-diagnostic use. (β') licenses an
argument, with the support of the principle of sufficient reason and
bearing Figure 2.33 in mind, in favour of *equity*, a core basic human
equality in resources and opportunities subject to the constraints of
any further over-riding principles of justice and in the context of a
balanced human life. This immediately, ceteris paribus, entails an
argument for the abolition of power$_2$ differentials, at least of the
present gross kind.[106] This immediately augments our argument for
freedom and shows the sense in which freedom and equality,
particularly when intertwined with solidarity, are not necessarily at
loggerheads as they are stereotypically portrayed.

Second, I show in Figure 2.34 how the initial illicit fusion of the
epistemic fallacy at work in empiricism and rationalism coheres with
the fissions caused by ontological monovalence and the primal
squeeze at the Platonic/Aristotelian fault-line — 'the unholy trinity' of
§6 above — to produce the dominant — and analytic — irrealist
problematic within a potentially infinite array. At the level of
particular knowledge the fusion at work in subject—object identity
theory produces an anthropo-ego-present-centric atomism and
punctualism of an empiricist kind and is subject to aporiai of
solipsism. These manifest themselves, as the effects of an illicit
fusion, in internal duplicity and equivocation (do or do not either or
both facts and things exist independently of us?), and hence illicit
fission and theory/practice inconsistency, susceptibility to dc', etc. At
the level of general knowledge, the criterion historically laid down by
rationalist epistemology's detotalization of the negative (change, etc.)
assumes the form of an anthropomorphic or divinized (and hence, by
Feuerbachian critique, anyway anthropomorphic) actualist blockist
regularity determinism. The effects of the generalized fusion
(subject—object identity theory) again manifest themselves in a
splitting. As the fusion has excluded the non-actual real, a split occurs
between weak actualism, which would save the empirical at the
expense of regularity (science at the cost of philosophy), and strong
actualism, which would have things the other way round.[107] Once
more we have theory/practice inconsistency, the formation of Tina
compromises, etc. More covertly, we have the illicit fission
engendered on the fault-line (really an effect of the fusion involved in
generalized subject—object identity theory), producing the aporiai of
fideism. For, in lacking a conception of natural necessity, induction
requires an external counterpart — in intellectual intuition, religious

faith, social convention, etc. The result is the overt conceptual split of the unhappy consciousness between enlightenment (of an empiricist and de-ontologized kind) and faith of one sort or another. Why did empiricism win? Bourgeois individualism, Newtonian science and the post-Hegelian kenosis of reason.

The core idea that I have been concerned to develop up to now is that any ill can be seen as a constraint and any constraint as the absence of a freedom. This does not entail, as we shall see, that there are not degrees and modalities of freedom. A person may possess a capacity to live well and not be disposed to exercise it. What I want to do now is look at some of the conceptual labyrinths that can be developed from the key notion, structuring dialectic, of absence itself. Hitherto we have been primarily occupied with dialectic as that species of real negation which turns on change, but dialectic is not only about change or even negation. It is concerned with presence,

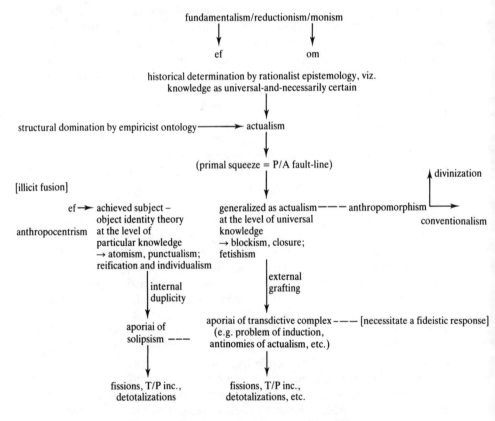

Figure 2.34 Categorical Error and Its Effects

and the co-presence of the absent and the present (with constitutive sedimentation, dislocation and lag — in the senses of both decay and delay) and of the absent-in-the-present and vice versa (cf. §§2 and 8), and with alterity, sheer difference (cf. §6) and much else besides. In §1 I stressed the mutual irreducibility of difference and change. The unifying concept of absence can designate synchronic difference, 1M non-identity, mediated by distance in space as easily as diachronic change over time. But these differentiations can be established by an argument from 1M stratification or emergence, from 2E spatio-temporal divergence as readily as contradiction, which, if only in the guise of constraint by at least one other, perhaps intrinsic, element, must be seen as essential for change, from 3L reflexivity or totality, or simply from 4D agency (e.g. in an objectified act). Only if token monism were true would difference and change not occur. Such monism would rule out qualitative differentiation and change, stratification and emergence and thence agency and discourse alike. Hence our world must be synchronically pluralistic for any extension. Despite their irreducibility, there are close conceptual connections between difference and change. Thus any sound argument from absence qua non-identity will establish the case for absenting qua change, and vice versa. They presuppose each other but are not equivalent. They exemplify in fact dialectical connection. Subject—object identity theories make both impossible. Corresponding to the errors of fixism and fluxism are those of monism and destratification (which would undermine underlying identity-in-difference or unity-in-diversity). Moreover, consider the paradigm occurrence of the 2E problem of induction, when a thing remains the same but acts in accordance with changing (e.g. waning) causal powers. One response is to apply contrary, a third or no predicates to the thing in question. In thinking the *constellational unity of identity* (qua continuity of spatio-temporal personality) and *change*, as I have argued we must do in conceptualizing the self as the dispositional identity of the embodied agent and her changing causal powers, but applying a perspectival switch here, we can also see it is as a case when we want to say that a thing both is and is not itself. Here we have the *constellational unity of identity* (qua sameness of subject) and *difference*, as I would press we must think the widespread phenomena of constitutive intra-relationality. (When a person loses a loved one, do they remain the same?) At the nodal moment of transition and in the case of intra-constitution the constellational unities encompass *identities* — of identity and change and identity and difference: blows at the heart of analytic reason where, in Bishop Butler's famous pronouncement, 'everything is what it is and not another thing'.

Absence, either qua gulf or qua split, is essential to metacritique and, when it takes the form of immanent critique, the absence, when pressed, displays itself as theory/practice inconsistency, together with the Tina connections and compromises the latter entrains. But absence also implies detotalization or split-off, characteristically resulting in de-agentification, fragmentation, impotent indifference (cf. stoicism), self-deceiving denial (cf. scepticism) or the introjection or projection of power$_2$ relations (cf. the unhappy consciousness) and/or a variety of other forms. Absence is the blind spot of the tradition which unifies not only 2E but also 1M−4D relations. The unification of 2E around the notice of absence is represented in Figure 2.35, one transcategorical unification achieved by the same notion in Figure 2.36, while one sequencing of categorical relationships within dialectical critical realism is represented in Figure 2.37. These are designed to show that although absence may be the missing metacategory par excellence, what we are dealing with in dialectical critical realism is a *systematic intermingling* of categories, concepts, critiques and figures rather than a unilinear procession, although I will consider in C3.11 whether there is one particular way in which dialectical critical realism can be said to be most adequately dialectically presented.*

It is difficult to say whether it is ontological monovalence, through the absence of the concept of absence and armed with a de facto generalized concept of reference, or the epistemic fallacy, mediated by subject−object identity theory and generalized as actualism and licensing duplicitous equilibrating exchanges, which, reinforced by the ontological destratification (primal squeeze) it implies, is the prime mover in the positivization, reification and eternalization of current knowledge and more generally the status quo — for they function to the same effect, buttressing each other — typically in an ensemble characterized by ontological extensionalism, ontological de-agentification, a-spatio-temporalization, detotalization and fetishism, together with the theory/practice inconsistencies, Tina compromise formations, complementarities and metaphysical λ clauses they necessitate. However, it is important to see that, despite my talk of the 'unholy trinity', there are really only two category mistakes involved. The epistemic fallacy leads to ontological actualism which

---

* T. Smith's otherwise persuasive *The Logic of Marx's Capital*, New York 1991, is flawed by (a) over-emphasis on the presentational and epistemological aspects of Marx's dialectic to the neglect of the ontological, explanatory, critical and relational dialectics essential to it, and (b) an acceptance of the Platonic analysis of change in terms of difference — dialectic is reduced to the triad of unity, difference and unity-in-difference iteratively re-applied to a pre-appropriated subject-matter.

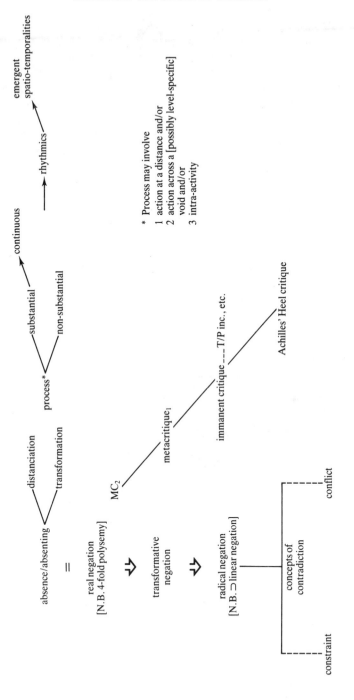

Figure 2.35 Unification of 2E Categories around the Notion of Absence

generates primal squeeze; and ontological monovalence results in the
elimination of absence and error, producing a purely positive account
of knowledge and being alike. Moreover, it should be stressed, in
respect of Figure 2.34, that the aporiai of solipsism, no less than those
of the transdictive complex, necessitate a fideistic response.
Historically the epistemic fallacy has generated the problem of the
one and the many, while the doctrine of ontological monovalence has
generated the other great problem of philosophy, the problem of the
one and the/its other (negation, opposite, etc.). We shall see in C4
that the aporiai of subject—object identity theory, whether in its
particular (atomistic) or generalized (actualistic) form, inevitably
generate a new transcendent — God or the social structure being the
most typically invoked. That is to say, that identity theory inevitably
generates a dualism (or pluralism) incompatible with itself.

If we focus on the human world, where the openness of the
dialectic will be especially clear, a contradiction, or an ensemble
(perhaps in disjoined and antagonistic articulation), may stimulate or
release either (α) a good or positive dialectic leading to a greater

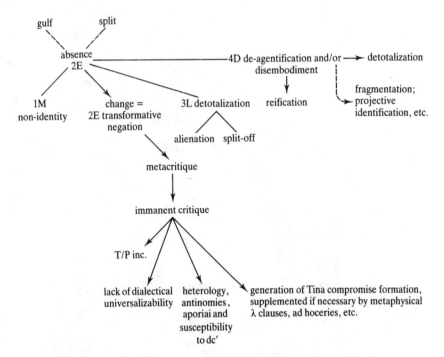

Figure 2.36 One Transcategorical Unification Achieved by the
Notion of Absence

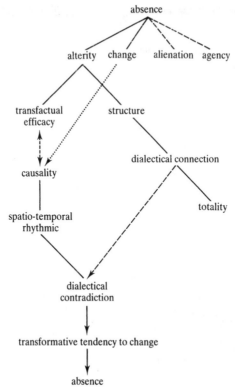

Figure 2.37 One Sequencing of Categorial Relationships within DCR

totality incorporating that totalizing depth inquiry informing the transformed transformative totalizing transformist practice (encompassing a synthetic unity of life, movement, representative and emancipatory politics) oriented to universal human emancipation or (β) a bad or negative dialectic generating alienation, fragmentation and sectional-sectarian splits inducing disempowerment and de-agentification, sustaining or reinforcing, in a context of encrusted social stratification, the multiplicity of master−slave or $power_2$ relations and the network of ideologies of subjugation and legitimation, underpinned by the real alienation or generative separation or fission of the immediate producers from their labour and the four planes encompassing the social cube of §9 (that is to say, from nature and material objects, each other, the nexus of social relations and ultimately themselves). An example of a good dialectic of the former kind (cf. also Figure 2.1 in §1) is represented in Figure 2.38.

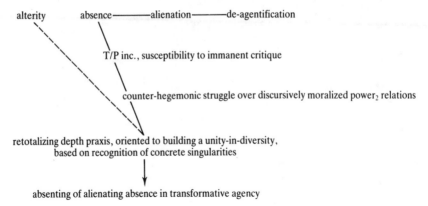

Figure 2.38

3. I now turn to a brief resumé of the traditional critique of analytical reason and a fuller account of the immanent and proto-explanatory critiques I am developing. The essence of the traditional critique is that the principles of identity and non-contradiction (falsely) *abstract* from categories such as process, interconnection, context, ground, totality — *organic* categories vital to the understanding of social life. I am not without sympathy for such critiques. But they are non-immanent and I am going to be tough on them. I will take as a good example of such a critique that offered by Allen Wood in his book *Karl Marx*,[108] who argues that dialecticians hold these principles to be either trivial (and so obvious), or, if given an interesting interpretation in the context of an organic world view, false. First, as in most of such critiques, it is very difficult to find *precise* statements of the principles. Wood writes 'the logical principle of identity says only that we cannot speak truly if we deny that a given thing is the same thing as itself, or affirm that it is the same thing as something which is wholly diverse from it' (p. 203). But what exactly does 'wholly diverse' mean? Why not just a little bit diverse? And what if it is not quite the same as it was, or as another of its kind? What are the criteria of identity for the identity of a thing? Obviously these are context-dependent. In science millions of different hydrogen atoms are the same — that is, possess the same electronic structure (share the same real essence). In the same way, why cannot a given thing *also* be the same as something else — for example, if it is existentially intra-constitutive of it. We have already seen the necessity to think the *co-incidence* of identity and difference and identity and change. As stated, the principle seems wholly false,

ruling out stratification, change, internal relationality, etc., not to mention more recondite phenomena such as the presence of the past which I have been at pains to defend. An entity can be identified with an indiscernible one, viz. if it belongs to the same *kind*; or, if we try to make Leibniz's principle truistic by introducing spatio-temporal location, different entities may occupy the same space-time slice if they belong to different *categories*. When I die am I the same as my corpse? Wood's principle would make agency impossible. Similar objections apply to Wood's principle of (non-)contradiction which 'says only that if we affirm a given predicate of a given subject, we cannot speak truly if we also deny that same predicate of that same subject at one and the same time and in one and the same respect' (ibid.) — except that this time it is formulated more exactly, apart from leaving out subject/agent, context, perspective (just think of the different space-times implied by the theory of relativity — and from a cosmic point of view, Xegel [of §4] is right, every moment is transitional, a frontier), level, category, etc. Taken literally it prohibits non-valent responses, nodal or intersecting points, problematic axiological choice situations, which we have explored earlier at length. More seriously it offends against science, which depends upon the σ and τ transforms for the normal science—revolutionary science (dc')—post-revolutionary science (dr') dialectic at work in the DREI(C) logic of scientific discovery. Indeed, strictly speaking, no science (certainly neither Newtonian science nor contemporary physics) has ever completely conformed to it. 'Respect' seems to denote 'property', 'class' or perhaps 'aspect'. If so I can certainly affirm a given predicate transfactually and deny it actually, just as depending on the stretch of the pertinent time I can include both positive contraries and negative sub-contraries (see §3).

Second, I reject Wood's hermeneutics. The main objection, when the principles are cashed out ontologically, is supposed to be that they abstract from an organic unity. But this is consistent with a closed world view, a constellationally closed totality that Hegel, but not Marx, possesses. The world is in open process. Trivial though this is, being is becoming (or, at least, being able to become). Third, I dispute Wood's exegesis of Hegel. For, on my interpretation, he entirely accepts the analytical critique of dialectical reason. His novelty is that he uses it as the motor of his dialectic, which proceeds from the identification of an inconsistency, or more usually an incompleteness, at the nodal moment in the U-D-R schema, to its repair in speculative reason. Fourth, I suspect that Wood is tacitly (epistemo-)logicizing reality, a view about which I have already complained enough, though I will shortly display its mechanisms and effects. And with that I switch over to the more satisfying mode of immanent critique.

If a simple epigram could sum up what is essential to thinking dialectically it would be that it is the art of thinking the coincidence of distinctions and connections. Its essence is fluidity structured around the hard core of the concept of absence and the 1M−4D relations it implicates. It is the case that identity presupposes non-identity, and non-contradiction incompleteness and change. Thus identity is always an abstraction from a process or set of processes of formation; and re-identification of a token not only depends upon differentiation from others of the token's type, but also turns on the possibility of a situation in which the individual is constituted by something other than itself and/or becoming something other than it was (the co-incidence of identity and difference and identity and change, respectively). Any piece of deductive reason presupposes the establishment of a common context of utterance. And its existence presupposes the possibility of its re-establishment. We are immediately involved in a meta-hermeneutics dependent upon transformative praxis or absenting agency, and a meta-semiology implicating the changing intra-relationality of a nexus of signs. Thus we arrive at the fount of the dialectical critique of analytical reasoning — the conceptuality or meaning-dependence in the acceptance of semantic identity to the effect that the graphemes or phonemes involved are instances of the same, tokens of a type. From the most elementary to the most recondite, analytic reasoning is entirely *dialectically dependent* upon the processes of transformative negation necessary to ascertain, in an open-ended hermeneutic, 'what x means' or when two instances of A are to count as the same. Such hermeneutics is a constant, like the speed of light, or the 'universal whore', necessary for any inter-subjective exchange, communication, measure or intelligibility and presupposing our 'vehicular' thrownness — thrown into a pre-existing ongoing network of social and material and semantic relations affecting four-planar social being. To make this point seem as important as it is, remember that when the analytic hour arrives or the Lockian bell strikes in the transitive process of science in the *dialectic of dialectical and analytical reasoning* — in which it was Hegel's great insight to see embedded a dialectic of incompleteness and inconsistency — this is only in virtue of the occurrence of another cycle of transformative negation dependent upon conceptual-epistemic distanciation, involving the absenting and cumulative presenting of novel epistemics, entraining a trace structure of their own, metaphors, only intelligible (at least at first) to some, designating a deeper or fuller intransitive ontic field or domain.

What the analytical critique of dialectical reason does is to *detotalize* from all these learning, non-identity and anomalous processes upon which it itself depends. In the course of this, analytical reason is not just suspended (as in Aristotelian propaedeutics), or bracketed (which is what Hegel actually does) or 'transcended' (which is what he claims to do), but, rather, dialectically *over-reached* and contained as a *precious* gem, vital for grounding truth claims and attributions of natural necessity and deducing consequences for experimental tests.

Properly conceived, *logic is* only, but *is* a vital *moment in the process of thought*. But I will finish with a final re-emphasis on the *fertility* of contradictions, and the partiality of any gnoseology that leaves them out. And here I take my leave from this aspect of the immanent critique of analytical reason.

There are characteristically different complementary 1M–4D critiques of deductivism. If at 1M this turns on the normal multiple determination of the results of a tendency's exercise, at 3L it hinges on the mediation of the exercise of the tendency (as in Marx's strictures against Ricardo's violent abstractions), while at 2E it depends on the rhythmic processuality (including geo-historical specificity and its normic directionality) of the tendency and at 4D upon the conceptually dependent transformative negation which is praxis. Of course when it is legitimate, deducibility depends upon the transitive epistemological dialectic in science.

We began to scratch the surface of the analytic problematic in (2) when discussing the effects of the categorial errors depicted in Figure 2.34. I want to focus on the categorial error which is crucial to the analytical problematic, viz. (a) the irrealist *epistemologization of being*, implicit in subject–object identity theory, generalized as actualism and undergirded by the epistemic fallacy. This goes together with (b) the ontological contra-position (or transposition) of the logical principles of identity and non-contradiction. This is the *logicization* of being. There then follows the *ontification of knowledge*, overseen by the ontic fallacy (the dual of the epistemic fallacy, together effecting subject–object equivalence), characteristically producing what, following Adorno, I will call (c) identity-thinking. This ensemble (see Figure 2.39) has presuppositions, corollaries and efects, including Tina connections and compromises and consequences. Let us examine the fine structure of the identity-thinking that the analytic problematic encourages. This can be classified into (i) token–token identity, presupposing the constancy of particulars; (ii) token–type identity, presupposing the particular examples or tokens instantiate one and only one universal or generalization, that is, closed systems and the fetishism of empirical regularities (or constant conjunctions of

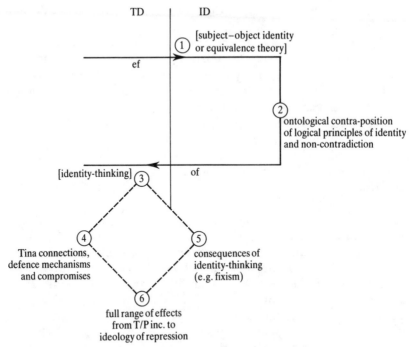

Figure 2.39 The Analytic Problematic

events) that the latter entails; and (iii) type—type identity, presupposing the universal or generalization is unchanging. Ontologically (i) entails fixism and (ii) and (iii) actualism, blockism and fetishism; epistemologically, (i) presupposes fixed subjects (in contrast to the developmental subject negation which is the heart of the 'speculative proposition' in social science) correctly identified, and therefore rigidly, and thus arbitrarily, defined, (ii) subsumable under known generalizations, (iii) the terms of which are rigidly defined and which are reified and eternalized, resulting in the elision of the possibility of error or accommodating change in empirical regularities or former incompleteness, eventuating in epistemological stasis and complacency to correspond to the ontological stasis already achieved. The net upshot of my argument could be summed up by saying that *the very concept of analytical reason embodies mystification and confusion.*

Ontologically actualism, presupposing fixism, entails blockism and fetishism. Whether it is atomistic-punctualist (allegedly Heraclitian, certainly Humean), monist (Parmenidean), eidetic (Platonic), kinetic-(quasi-)eidetic (Aristotelian) or expressivist-kinetic-eidetic (Hegelian), conceptual realist (Leibznizian) or empirical realist (Kantian), it tendentially leads to fundamentalism and reductionism (whether empiricist, rationalist or transcendental [or dialectical] idealist) in epistemology. And it strongly encourages, for reasons I shall go into, ontological extensionalism (whether nominalist or Platonist), atomism and punctualism at the level of particulars, coupled with the positivist illusion in metaphysics (the illusion that there is no illusion), together with de-agentified (reductionist or dualist) agency rather than intentional embodied agency and (tacitly descriptivist) personalism/ emotivism in ethics. Its fundamental tents could be written as:

[I] empiricist ontology ↔ individualist sociology.

But the irrealist tradition is compatible with the speculative illusion in metaphysics, a conceptual realist and holistic ontology, and intentionalist logic and a collectivist sociology; as in

[II] rationalist ontology ↔ collectivist sociology.

Of course, much finer discriminations are possible. Hegel's hyperintuition, on Marx's critique of it (we have yet to declare final judgement on it), functions as a smokescreen for an empiricist epistemology, so we could write it as:

[III] conceptual realist gloss on empiricist ontology ↔ individualist civil society glossed by concretely universal state.

Erstwhile actually existing socialism was characterized by a rationalist metaphysics, a command economy, a collectivist party state, a simple undifferentiated organic expressive unity underpinning a non-hegemonic ideology which eventually no one believed in:

[IV] rationalist metaphysics + command economy + collectivist party state + expressivist ideology.

To revert to simple formulae, as against [I] and [II], dialectical critical realism could be represented by:

[V] dialectical transcendental realist ontology ↔ dialectical critical naturalist relational sociology.

If we return to Figure 2.34 we can see the anthropocentric (characteristically empiricist) left-hand side as subjective and typically involving the positivistic illusion. Rationalism, classically the victim of the speculative illusion, historically defined the criterion to which empiricism must conform and so fixes *actualism* and *monovalence* as the ultimately determinant moments in irrealist problematics. This gives us subjective and particular ontological and epistemological atomism, spatio-temporal punctualism, logical extensionalism, sociological individualism (its underlying model of man [sic] will become increasingly important as my argument unfolds), corpuscularianism and action by contact. It presupposes the reification of facts and the reduction of theory (a consequence of the positivistic illusion). Objectively, on the right-hand side of the figure, we have anthropomorphism, in its dominant empiricist form, epistemological and ontological actualism yielding nomothetic determinism, and the fetishism of constant conjunctions and spatio-temporal blockism. The aporiai of solipsism stem from the absence of a concept of *primary polyadization*, while those of the transdictive complex (such as the problem of induction) derive from the absence of ontological stratification (cf. 'primal squeeze') and alethic truth. Both, as already remarked, can be overcome only by sociological or religious (Descartes and Kant) fideism. In its recessive rationalist forms, whether of dialectical or non-dialectical kinds, we have the possibilities of logical intensionalism and ontological organicism (of a processual or non-processual kind). Typically rationalists, hypostatizing ideas and tendentially eliminating a posteriori controls on theory, have faced the aporiai of matter and of contingency, which can be resolved only by a detotalizing split of reality such as in Hegel's actualism and closure manifest in the concepts of the demi-actual and the future (i.e. the demi-present) in Hegel's constellational closure with both the demi-actual and the future explicitly consigned to empiricism.

I have argued against analytics that only intensional semantics can sustain logical extensionalism. It could be further mentioned that bourgeois individualist civil society needs the fallback of an authoritarian state with a high degree of superveillance to sustain the power$_2$ relations intrinsic to it. If my argument is correct we have here a case of neither simple internal duplicity nor external complementarity, but of the interdependence of dialectical antagonists. I should like to pursue the theme of philosophy, or rather irrealism, as intrinsically aporetic-antinomial, in which its tensions are constitutive of it, but this must await a future occasion. Within this matrix I have been describing, dialectic has always been subordinate to analytics. It is not difficult to see why. For its leading modern exponent, Hegel, lends his whole effort to the transfiguration of an actuality that has already been defined in bourgeois individualist, that is to say, analytical and empirical realist terms (as Kant correctly divined). Thus it is not only that Hegel accepts the analytical critique of dialectical reason, but in his negation of negation, i.e. his speculatively rational transfigurative result, he is guilty precisely of the reinstatement of analytics (cf. §3) as the 'hard-core' of his redescription, undoing his own philosophical innovations.

Now the ensemble, in any one combination of its declensions, produces all manner of splits, false abstractions, detotalizations, inconsistencies, paradoxes, duplicities, equivocations, Tina compromises, and hence grafting, supplementarity, metaphysical λ clauses, etc. One attempt at a dialectical critical representation of the irrealist tradition, which I will discuss in greater historical detail and broader structural depth in C4, is depicted in Figure 2.40 below.

If most dialectics hitherto have been irrealist, how can dialectical critical realism accept a dialectical pedigree? It can do so via the heritage of the left Hegelians, and Marx and the research programme he inaugurated. It is true that the left Hegelians, in trying to extract method from system, misunderstood the point and presuppositions of Hegel's method, but they did try to sustain the key notions of negativity, an open totality and transformative praxis. A reflexive, microcosmic situation is shown in Figure 2.41 and more macroscopically in Figure 2.42. It is worth noting that the notion of deep structure itself gets off the ground only if one possesses the concept not only of absence from consciousness, but also of absence from actuality.

Note that the essence of my critique of the irrealist tradition is that it is constituted by voids — and the chief and unifying void is the category of absence itself. If we add to this a characteristically lagged dependence on the past and the outside, we can see why I tentatively defined philosophy in §1 as the unconscious and aporetic normalization of past changes (and freedoms) and denegation of *present* and future ones. This gives philosophy a potentially bipolar character. But if we add to that the causal efficacy of both itself and its ideological effects we can see how, particularly at certain geo-historical *turning points*, philosophy can come to play a potentially repressive — or emancipatory — role. The other side of its Janus-faced character will be explored anon. It is worth re-emphasizing that if the prototype for irrealism is the Hegelian figure of Stoicism itself, that of the theory–practice inconsistency which we have seen to be at the heart of the immanent metacritique is that thematized in the immediately following section of the *Phenomenology* on Scepticism, and the form of introjected or projected ideational alienation is that

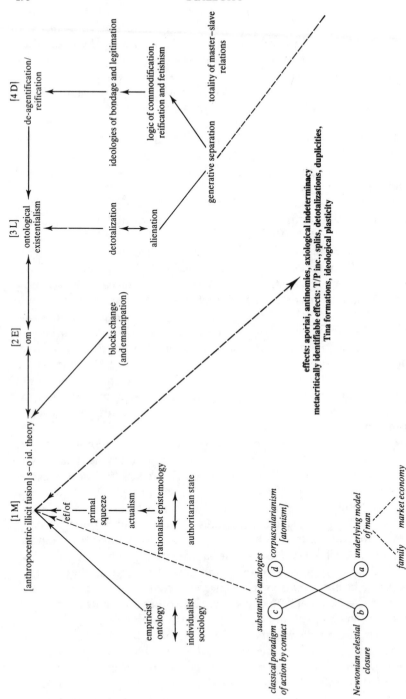

Figure 2.40 The Logic of Irrealism

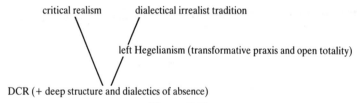

Figure 2.41

discussed in the next and final section on the Unhappy Consciousness. At the same time the stereotype for alienation, including real (not just ideational) absenting generative separation, is the Hegelian figure of the Beautiful Soul, but these function as more general social ideologies too, as forms of legitimation of master—slave relations. There are, of course, much more specific ideologies, some of which will be considered in C4, such as that of personalism as a characteristic moral ideology for slaves and emotivism as a characteristic moral ideology of masters.

I will now conclude this chapter with a brief survey, followed by an indication of the multiplicity of dialectics of different types the

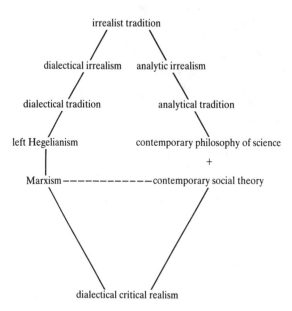

Figure 2.42

diffraction allows, and a thematic reprise of some of the new ideas and perspectives I have been floating. In §1 I critiqued ontological monovalence, asserted that it makes sense to say that non-beings exist and even argued that the negative has an ontological priority over the positive. I took care to distinguish and connect the notions of transfactuality and negativity, and differentiation and change. If there was a single pivotal manoeuvre it was to bring the concept of change under that of absence, seeing that changes are absentings; and so unifying the concepts of space, time and causality, under the sign of the fourfold polysemy of absence (process, product, process-in-product, product-in-process), in the idea of tensed rhythmic process as spatio-temporalizing causal efficacy. Human agency must be understood as embodied intentional causal absenting, as I stressed in §2, where I also discussed the topics of emergence and multiple control, arguing for an emergent powers materialism — itself a figure of constellational identity — that bypasses physicalistic reductionism and spiritualistic (or other) dualisms alike. I introduced two concepts of superstructure (one more properly called intrastructure) and two types of emergent spatio-temporality. Existentially constitutive geo-history and the theme of the presence of the past and outside were broached here, to be developed in the course of the chapter.

In §3 I mapped a variety of dialectical relations from constraint to overt struggle. The character of the Marxian dialectic was seen to be quite different from that of the Hegelian one. Marx does not breach the norm of non-contradiction (though Marxism must, if it is to make any progress as a science). Hegel, on the other hand, can only really sustain dialectical connection as distinct from contradiction (which may be reasonably argued to be essential for change). He annuls negativity, cancels contradiction and resorts to constellational closure and surds such as the demi-actual (irrational existents) in his quest to reconcile himself (and his readers) to the actually existing order of things. On my exegesis, he accepts the analytical critique of dialectical reason and achieves in the end merely an analytic reinstatement (albeit in dialectical connection). In §3 we started to consider a great variety of other dialectics which I shall come on to in a moment, beside Hegel's epistemological one. In §4 criteria for distinguishing good and bad dialectics were advanced and the problem of the Janus-faced character of axiological indeterminacy and the possibility of a non-valent reponse to a wide class of problematic choice situations as a prelude to problematizing the problem itself were considered. The concepts of the constellational, dispositional and rhythmic identity of a thing with (the exercise or not of) their possibly changing causal powers was entered. In dialectic to be is to be able to become.

In §5 the possibilities opened up by the multiple materialist diffraction of Hegelian dialectic were explored. This is perhaps the point to re-emphasize that dialectic is, or can be, a very broad concept (which, in this book, I am *essentially* retotalizing through the 1M−4D network of dialectical critical realism); and that dialectics and formal logic are not *necessarily* at loggerheads, despite my strictures on the pretensions of the latter. Just as logical and dialectical contradictions can intersect, viz. when they are grounded in a common mistake, many types of dialectic involve no breach with analytics. Throughout I have been arguing for a dialectic of dialectic and analytical reason, with analytical reason representing an invaluable moment in the process of scientific thought. In §6 I argued that dialectical arguments are a species of the genus of transcendental arguments of the kind of retroductive-explanatory arguments familiar to science, distinguished by the fact that they establish *false necessities** as ontological conclusions. I defended ontological arguments and up to now have developed two basic models of scientific explanation: the theoretical DREI(C) and the applied RRREI(C). The fact that dialectical arguments vindicate ontological results flies in the face of the epistemic fallacy, which together with the doctrine of (voidless) ontological monovalence and the primal squeeze on natural necessity I identified as the terrible trinity — of Parmenidean-Platonic and Platonic-Aristotelian provenance — structuring western philosophy up to its contemporary analytical (neo-Humean or neo-Kantian) and postmodernist (post-Nietzschean) forms.

In §7 I developed a variety of dialectical motifs from heterology to totality, the most important of which were totality itself and the concrete universal = concrete singular, which I argued had to be understood in principle as a multiple quadruplicity. In thematizing totality, intra-relationality of three kinds were considered: intra-constitution (the existental constitution of one element by another), intra-permeation (containment) and intra-connection (causation). By now we had some prima facie bizarre figures — alongside the dialectics of transition (node, frontier and threshold), dialectics of co-presence (co-inclusion of absence and presence in a potentially much greater matrix of possibilities) within distanciated space-time, shortly to be joined by dialectics of dislocation of structure and agency, as in the §9 negative generalization of the transformational model of social activity, and dialectics of the co-incidence of identity and change and of identity and difference; constitution by the past, outside, another

---

* This is an idea as shocking to the pretensions of analytical reason as that of the false analytic a posteriori when a real definition is corrected.

entity, and even morality, perspective and truth (or falsity); Tina compromises, connections and defence mechanisms; internal, external and intra-complicity; the dialectics of fusion and fission; and of the Achilles' Heel critique (such as I have attempted of Hegel). In §8 I introduced the generalized notion of a dialectical remark, which shows both the limitations and the affinities of the Hegelian dialectical comment with Aristotelian dialectical distinction, Kantian dialectical limit and Derridean deconstruction. In resolving the antinomy between hermeneutics and semiology, I showed how it was a failure of ontological stratification (and distanciated time) which necessitated Nietzschean forgetting, just as it led to Aristotelian non-detachment.

By §9, developing critical naturalism, a variety of substantive social concepts had been introduced: the concept of hermeneutic (alongside other) hegemonic/counter-hegemonic struggles over generalized master—slave-type $power_2$ relations (of exploitation, domination, oppression, repression, etc.), where $power_2$ was differentiated from $power_1$ or power simpliciter, i.e. the transformative capacity intrinsic to action; concepts of life, movement, representative and emancipatory politics; of that transformed transformative trans-formist depth practice under conditions of global intradependence necessary to totalize the human race; ideologies of legitimation and bondage; the figures of generative separation and the unhappy consciousness, in the context of developing commodification, reification and fetishism. A four-planar social topology was sketched in which ideology was located at the point at which discursive, power and normative sub-dimensions of the social cube intersected. Although the transformational model of social activity perfectly represents the geo-historical transformation of geo-historical products (the genuine negation of the negation), I noted why and how critical naturalism had to be dialecticized. In the present section I identified the void at the heart of philosophy as the notion of absence. If there is a second great discovery I would like to claim to have made in this book it is that of a genuinely ontological notion of truth: alethia — the truth of things, as distinct from propositions — to be fully justified in C3.2. *The alethia of dialectic is the absenting of constraints$_2$ on the absenting of absences.* I argued that this can be fully achieved only in a society in which the free flourishing of each concrete singular individual is a condition for the free flourishing of all. So the alethia of dialectic is also universal human emancipation, which I argued, following on analysis of the universalizability of the components of the judgement form, and an ethical dialectic from form to content, is implicit in every expressively veracious assertoric sentence. The simple existential alethia of absence is finitude (transitoriness) and the alethia of the absence of the concepts of absence (non-dialecticity) and alethia (irrealism) is not least that it sequesters ideologically unwelcome existential questions from what Habermas calls the 'public sphere'.

The diffraction makes possible the distinction of epistemological, ontological, relational, ethical and other dialectics. It is a fault of Bertell Ollmann's otherwise convergent book *Dialectical Investigations* that he reduces dialectic to 'a way of thinking', albeit one 'that brings into focus the full range of changes and interactions that occur in the world'.[109] Epistemological dialectics (of various genres) there certainly are. There is the epistemological dialectic that depends upon conceptual distanciation and transformation, 'our vehicular thrownness' and the trace structure not just of the signifier but also of human subjectivity in the dialectic of dialectical and analytical reasoning. But there are also ontological dialectics of super-stratification and emergence in our entropically expanding universe, in which there occurs a metacritically Copernican-Darwinian moment of self-consciousness (i.e. sentient socialized self-awareness) in a geo-historical-social dialectic that may be nearly over or may only just have begun. There are ontological dialectics of intersecting, overlapping, disjoined and condensing differential emergent spatio-temporalities, of contradictory rhythmics, of alienated split-offs, of partial totalities, of mediatization and hyperreality. There are relational dialectics dependent on the causal efficacy and material conditioning of ideas. There are metacritical dialectics in which ideologies are subject to immanent and explanatory critiques on grounds of their theory/practice inconsistency, lack of universaliz-ability, heterology or just their plain oppressive role in countering human needs and interests such as, but not only, that of truth. There are ethical dialectics like the dialectic which will take us in the next chapter all the way from the womb to universal human emancipation or that describe the dialectic of agents, acts and outcomes that settles the dispute between the advocates of virtue theory, deontology and consequentialism. There are practical dialectics of numerous types.

There are different modalities of dialectics. There are dialectics of figure and ground that can be used as referential perspectival switches or, like the dialectic of centre and periphery that I discussed in C1.4, that can be used to highlight the plight of the marginalized majority. There are dialectics of generative separation, whose fivefold character I have described, resulting in alienation, split, and split-off, which may then be ideologically eternalized or compartmentalized, resulting in the fragmentation, decentrification or ideological saturation of disempowered agents. But alongside dialectics of repression, or compromise formation, there are dialectics of reagentification and resistance. There are elongated dialectics and dialectics of balance, but also of the evanescent trace or the shooting star. There are dialectics of participatory, representative and delegatory democracy. There are dialectics of position and manoeuvre, process and result (including process-in-result-in-process), empowerment and constraint, condensation and displacement, metaphor and metonymy. There are dialectical reversals of structural, strategic, tactical and conjunctural kinds (and in dialectical critical realism we shall see more than a few of the first). There are dialectics of contra-position and paradox (the surface form of categorial error). There are dialectics of truth, desire, freedom, equity; of expressive veracity, fiduciariness, self and solidarity, concrete utopianism and participatory-activating research. There are dialectics as struggle, as hope, as hermeneutics, as polite conversation. There are dialectics as argument, intra-action, change. But above all there is the dialectic of freedom, and the absenting of ills, which may be looked upon, for they function, as constraints.

At 1M the essence of dialectic is the provision of a non-arbitrary principle of stratification, and emergence which together with the figure of the hiatus in the duality is enough to resolve most of the textbook problems of philosophy, as we shall see in C4.2. At 2E, the hub of dialectics, there are modalities of negation and critique, of tensed process and emergent or divergent spatio-temporalities. At 3L, there are dialectics of totality and the detotalizing absence (which plays a part in most dialectics), reflexivity and concrete singularity. At 4D there are dialectics of transformative practice, which is causally efficacious absenting agency, for instance, in remedying remediable ills. In the next chapter in the systematic exposition of dialectical critical realism I will elaborate, on the basis of a combination of ethical naturalism and moral realism, the dialectic of freedom.

Moving from dialectical explanation to explanatory critique to dialectic as the axiology of freedom, I proceed from desire generated by absence, through the reality principle, in its 1M−4D moments, and mediated by the dialectic of truth to the directionality imposed on our wants (rationally assessable dispositions to act) by the reality principle and the logic of dialectical universalizability, to a society which is a rhythmic process, not an end-state, in which concrete singularity is the relational condition of concrete universality (which should be compatible to liberals, as well as to socialists, feminists, greens, etc.). Such a society — in which the free flourishing of each is the condition for the free flourishing of all — is not post-ed, but an immanent and tendential possibility. It is necessitated by structural conditions held in check by global discursively moralized $power_2$

relations and frustrated by the failure of its intrinsic enabling conditions. Socialism, if that is what we should call such a society, is, like Ethelred, unready. Only absolute reason in the form of the unity of explanatory critical social theory and emancipatory axiology can put this right. This is the ultimate absence this book aims to repair.

Dialectical Critical Realism and the Dialectic of Freedom

§ 1 Ontology

In C2.6 I differentiated two senses of 'ontology': the sense in which everything is within being and the sense in which we might want to demarcate specifically ontological as opposed to, for instance, epistemological, relational or ethical dialectics. I defended ontological arguments and contended that it was inconceivable that the term 'ontology' not refer. I constrasted three compatible uses to which the concept might be put: (1) to distinguish *philosophical* from *scientific ontologies* (the latter consisting in the specific ontics of determinate transitive epistemic inquiries); or as a unified concept either (2) picking out different orders of abstraction, levels of inquiry, domains of extension, perspectival angles, etc. or (3) designating some characteristically dialectical mechanism or manoeuvre, such as contradiction or emergence, master—slave relations or constellationality, and applying it across disciplinary boundaries. I have also argued in previous publications that philosophical ontology in sense (1) need not be dogmatic and transcendent, but may be immanent and conditional, taking as its subject-matter just that world investigated by science (presupposed or acted on by other social practices) yet from the standpoint of what can be established about it by transcendental argument. This counters the traditional Humean-Kantian objection to ontology, but leaves the necessity of the conclusions contingent upon the acceptability of the premises. Hegel claims to get round this in an immanent self-entailing/validating phenomenological circle. In this chapter I shall explore how one can establish transcendental arguments both (a) for, as distinct from, science and (b) for transcendental realism (or, more generally, for dialectical critical realism) without recourse to science, so tying the metacritical knot without Hegelian metaphysical rope.

I have also argued that any theory of knowledge presupposes an ontology in the sense of an account of what the world must be like, for knowledge, under the descriptions given it by the theory, to be possible. Thus Hume, Kant, Mill, Nietzsche and Rorty all presuppose an empirical realist theory of causal laws, on which empirical regularities are at least necessary, if not sufficient, for them. For example, it is Rorty's failure to thematize ontology — epigrammatized by his inane remark that he wishes Heidegger had never used the word 'being'[1] — that is responsible for the antinomies of agency, which duplicate those of Kant, that spoil his work.[2] Failure to be explicit in one's ontology merely results in the passive secretion of an *implicit* one. From the critical realist perspective, the *epistemic fallacy*, enshrined in the dogma that statements about being can and will always be analysed as or explicated in terms of statements about our knowledge of being, is a multi-consequential disaster. In the first place, as just indicated, it merely masks the generation of an implicit ontology — in the dominant modern form, a Humean one of atomistic events and closed systems; and a fortiori of an implicit realism (here, empirical realism); and, insofar as critical realism (which not only problematizes ontology but also gives it a radically different content) isolates axiological/transcendental/dialectical necessities, in a triple series of *Tina compromises*. Ontology — and realism — are *inexorable*. The crucial questions in philosophy are *not whether, but which*. Second, it conceals a deep-seated anthropocentric/anthropomorphic bias in irrealist philosophies and western thought generally — the *anthropic fallacy* — the exegesis of being in terms of human being. Thus, being is explicated, in both the conceptual realism of rationalism and the empirical realism of empiricism, in terms of an attribute of *human* being. Even Heidegger does not escape the charge of anthropism. For in *Being and Time* being is always mediated by *Dasein* or human being; and, in his later works, he rethematizes ontology in terms of its human traces from the pre-Socratics to the contemporary age of nihilism and technology. In other words, Heidegger does not so much redefine or overcome as evade 'the scandal of philosophy'.* Third, it co-exists symbiotically with an esoteric naturalization of knowledge — e.g., in the Humean case, with the reification of facts and fetishism of their conjunctions; that is to say, with the compulsive determination of knowledge of being by

---

* This is, 'not that their proof has yet to be accepted, but that such proofs are expected and attempted again and again'.[3] Compare Bertrand Russell at about the same time: 'if you are willing to believe that nothing exists except what you directly experience, no other person can prove you wrong, and probably no valid arguments against your view exist.'[4] I shall shortly give such a proof.

being. This is the reciprocal, equilibrating *ontic fallacy*. Fourth, transposed to the social domain and set in a hermeneutic, semiotic or otherwise linguistified key, the collapse of the intransitive dimension or the denegation of ontology takes the form of the analysis of being as our discourse about being — the *linguistic fallacy*. Indeed this, or some displacement of it, is the guise which the epistemic fallacy now customarily wears in each of (a) ordinary language, linguistic — or just plain analytic — philosophy, (b) Marxist philosophy and (c) post-structuralist and, more expansively, postmodernist thought. In this chapter I am going to (α) longitudinally, theoretically deepen and (β) laterally, topically enrich the ontology of critical realism which I am dialecticizing. At (α), already committed to a stratified, differentiated and changing world (in contrast to the flat, uniform depthlessness of empirical realism), critical realism is developed to encompass the categories of negativity and totality. As this chapter proceeds we shall move through the four moments or levels of dialectical critical realism outlined in C1.4, displaying the concepts, implications, resolutions, critiques, explanations and dialectics most characteristic of each level in turn. The dialectical critical realist dialectic is a four-term one in contrast to Hegel's three-term dialectic, but the structures of the two terms nominally shared with Hegel are very different. At *1M* (prime moment) the categories are of *non-identity* (in opposition to Hegelian identity). At *2E* (second edge) they are those of *negativity*; at *3L* (third level) *totality*; and at *4D* (fourth dimension) *transformative agency*. The critiques here take the forms at 1M of ontological actualism, at 2E of ontological monovalence, at 3L of ontological extensionalism and at 4D of ontological de-agentification. Laterally, at (β), already committed to an entity (perceptual), causal (explanatory) and predicative (taxonomic) realism, dialectical critical realism is broadened to embrace a spatio-temporal, moral and alethic (truth) realism. The effect of not making these extensions would be to *detotalize* being. Thus moral irrealism literally *devalues* social life.

Hitherto the most significant theses of critical realism, if we leave aside its extension onto the social terrain, have turned on relations of non-identity. Thus both (a) the distinction between the *intransitive and transitive dimensions*, which makes ontology possible and necessary again, and (b) the distinction between the domains of *the real and the actual*, which situates ontological stratification and transfactuality (and the corresponding analysis of laws as the tendencies of deep structures) posit distinctions or *non-identities within a constellational identity*. The motif of non-identity connects to a familiar post-structuralist refrain, and encompasses (c) the *critique of centrism*. The chief centrism which 1M dialectical critical realism identifies is that at work in the anthropic fallacy. This is the common unifying bias in (a) and (b), viz. the tying of being and knowledge alike to the realms of subjectivity and actuality (nowhere more transparent than in Hegel's doctrine of Essence, the supposedly most realist book of the *Logics*), and which has as its prima facie paradoxical condition and result the 4D de-agentifying reification of facts and their conjunctions. From (a) flow the issues we have just rehearsed of the quadruple ineluctability of ontology, realism, critical realism and dialectical critical realism; and of the duplicities and equivocations, pliabilities and compromise formations, manifest as absences, splits, reifications, theory/practice inconsistencies and susceptibility to dialectical comment and explanatory metacritique$_2$ implicit in subject−object identity theory and its necessary duals. The concept that blocks subject−object identity is *alterity*, particularly in the form of referential detachment; the concept that it masks is *absence*. (b), like (a), is susceptible to immanent critique, transcendental refutation, metacritical diagnostic and proto-explanatory analysis. The overall critique at 1M turns on the non-identities at stake in the relationships described by $d_r > d_a > d_e$ (which links [a], [b] and [c]) where d_r includes the causal (transfactual) as well as the existential (structural) aspects of depth realism. The arch criminal here is anthropic actualism or generalized subject−object identity theory. All this will be systematically articulated in §4 after discussion of its emergence and derivability in §3 and the dialectic of scientific discovery and truth it entails in §2. In this block the outstanding questions of (i) dialectical or developmental consistency and the nature of (dialectical critical realist) (ii) theory/ practice consistency and (iii) universalizability are clarified — the last two of which link directly to the concepts of the dialectical comment and heteronomy, dialectical reason and autonomy (a practico-theoretical bridge concept) and the unity or coherence of theory and practice in practice (dr_a' in $d\phi$).

2E is the abode of absence — and, most generally, negativity, the dialectical category par excellence. Indeed it can be viewed as implicated in all the other moments, categories and dialectics and 'a simple dialectical presentation' would proceed from it as we shall see in §11, rather than the more topical route followed in the bulk of this chapter. Many of the principal issues have already been mooted in the preceding chapters. The cardinal points turn on appreciating that absence exists, causes effect absentings (changes — that is to say, changes *are* absentings), ills can always be seen as absences, which act as constraints, and that (empowered) praxis can always be seen as potentially absenting (causally efficacious) agency, which can remove remediable ills. In the course of this chapter these aphoristic mottos

are presented in a dialectic of negativity, which terminates in a state
of the good (emancipated, eudaimonistic/free flourishing) society.
Some brief points, resuming earlier themes. (a) *The critique of
ontological monovalence* and the related assertion of the reality (in
nature as well as society) of non-existents, inefficacies, omissions,
voids, etc.; the relatively humdrum formula of 'non-being (or
inaction) within zero-level being (or agency)' (which in the social
world dislocates structure from agency) to the more daring arguments
for the ontological priority of the negative; the progressively more
exclusive concepts of real, transformative, radical and linear negation
with multiple process/product, real/actual, ontological/epistemo-
logical ambiguities; the essentiality of contradiction — from external
constraints to overt (for example, hermeneutic hegemonic/counter-
hegemonic) struggles over power$_2$ or master–slave-type relations —
for change; the mutual implication of causal determination and
transformative negation, and the minimal definition of dialectic as
absenting absence. (b) *The reassertion of the geo-historicity of being*, of
tense and place as irreducible and spatio-temporality as real, of the
tri-unity of space, time and causality in tensed spatializing process, of
emergent, divergent, possibly convergent, causally efficacious spatio-
temporalities and rhythmics, of the constitutive presence of the past
and outside. (c) *The unity of the 'two' senses of negativity*, the
intertwining of the notions of absences and ills, which will transport
us from the notion of social science as explanatory critique through
emancipatory axiology to the radical implications of the dialectic of
freedom to be sketched in §10 — understood as absenting constraints
(especially constraints$_2$) on absenting absences or more generally
remediable ills (which act as constraints). At this point we are able to
substantiate our maximal definition of dialectic as the progressive,
though contingent and non-linear, development of freedom; and the
transitions from form to content, centre to periphery and figure to
ground become explicit.

3L is the home of totality. The chief sin here is *ontological
extensionalism*. This functions to *disconnect*, as monovalence operates
to *deny change in, being*, and anthropo-actualism *necessity* in it
(squashing structure and eliding difference). Ontological extensionalism is manifest in, for example, the hypostatization of thought, but
most generally in and as *alienation*, detotalization, disintegration,
repression and split-off. The materialist prototype of alienation stems
from the generative separation which is the condition of possibility of
a *fivefold* alienation of the immediate producer/reproducer/
transformer from (a) their product and (b) the four planes of social life
— in virtue of their alienation from their labour. These four planes are

of course (i) material transactions with nature (and material objects generally), (ii) intra-/inter-personal relations, (iii) the network of social relations in which the former are embedded, involving power, discursive and normative dimensions and their ideological intersect, and (iv) the domain of an agent's own subjectivity. Totality depends upon internal relationality, and to the extent that a subject-matter shows it, we have to think it under the aspects of *intra-activity*, including *existential constitution* of an element by another, permeation (or containment) and connectedness (or causality). The topics of mediation, margins of inquiry, perspective and concretion — both qua *concrete universality* ↔ *concrete singularity*, conceived as multiple quadruplicity, and qua the constitutive role of creative fantasy in the *concrete utopianism* that yields at once hope and possibility to the totalizing depth praxis — have already been broached. At 3L we have dialectics of unity and diversity, of intrinsic and extrinsic, of part and whole, of centrification and peripheralization, within *partial totalities* in complex and dislocated open process, substantively under the configuration of global commodification. The internal aspect of totality is *reflexivity*, a world geo-historical phenomenon, which we have seen deployed in the concept of a meta-reflexively totalizing situation in the context of a stratified distanciated self, defined ultimately by the dispositional identity of a person with their changing causal powers. Ethical dialectics fall under totality and dialectical critical realism's dialectic of desire to freedom, in which the totalizing logic of dialectical universalizability plays a crucial role, is mediated not only by the reality principle (which we can now call alethia) but also by the virtue of practical wisdom or *phronesis*.

4D is the zone of transformative agency. This may be omitted *three* times in a philosophy. First, in the lack of a concept of *embodied intentional causal agency*. This may take the form either of a physicalistic reductionism or a spiritualistic dualism — the former entailing de-agentification, the latter disembodiment — or *both*. Second, in the *reification* of facts, where 'reification' means the attribution of a purely thing-like characteristic to human beings, their products and/or relations, and in the *fetishism* of conjunctions, where 'fetishism' means the attribution of animistic (ultimately, anthropomorphic) magical powers to things, attendant upon empirical realism. Third, in the logic of *commodification*, which makes in reality the 1M category mistake of reducing powers to their exercise, reifying labour-power and fetishizing its product. (In this way a scientific worker may come to be doubly alienated — from her product in reality, and from the thought that it is her product.) Crucial here to the avoidance of the first error is an *emergent powers materialism*, in which reasons are, and good reasons may be, causes. 4D is the site of dialectics of *reversal*. And in a dialectic of consciousness and self-consciousness in reason in §7, or that of material interest which will take the agent via instrumental reason from critical to depth totalizing explanatory critical rationality in §10, I make out a case for imparting a certain, if highly contingent, *directionality* to geo-history, presaging a society in which the free flourishing of each is the condition of the free flourishing of all. In any event here the critiques of cognitive and political triumphalism, finalism and endism, i.e. of the constellational closure of the future, are resumed and it is shown how these and the injunctive paradox intrinsic to right-wing Hegelianism and indeed arguably conservatism generally, viz. to reproduce the status quo, are auto-subversive. Agency, whether in the shape of mowing a lawn or in what I shall call the transformed transformative *trustworthy* totalizing transformist *transitional* praxis which would unite the interests of the human race-in-nature, is a species-specific ineliminable *fact*. It is worth bearing in mind, in the context of the world historical problem of agency for the radical libertarian left, that even inaction makes a difference.

Let me turn now, rather more briefly, to the lateral extensions to the ontology of critical realism. There is nothing at all anthropocentric about the reality of space, time, tense and process. I defend the irreducibility of MacTaggart's A series (past, present, future) to his B series (earlier than, simultaneous with, later than), that is, to be more specific, the *reality of tense* and the *irreducibility of space-time* on any world-line both for the transitive observer and for the intransitively observed. In C2 I stressed the tri-unity of space, time and causality in tensed (spatializing) process, understood as the mode of becoming of effects. But what exactly is the reality of the tenses? *The reality of the past* is that of the *existentially intransitively caused and determinate* (where caused means produced, determined and it is the case that a thing can be determinate even if not determinable); that of the *present*, of the (indefinitely extendable), indeterminate *moment of becoming*; and that of the *future*, that of the more or less *shaped* (conditioned, circumscribed, grounded) *mode of possibility of becoming* (under some set of descriptions) and hence becoming in due course existentially intransitively determined and determinate. My immediate antagonists here comprise an uneasy alliance of ego-present centrism or indexicalism (on which only the present exists), blockism (on which all times co-exist), punctualism and closure.

A transitive-relational/intransitive distinction plays a key role in morality too. Morality specifies an action-guiding relationship to the systems of intra- and inter-subjective, social and social—natural relations. But, though in this respect it is analogous to tense, it *is* (α) anthropic or social-relation dependent and (β) lies on the transitive-relational side of the divide. Because of (β) we must distinguish (a) *descriptive, redescriptive* and *explanatory critical morality* (in the transitive-relational dimension) from (b) the *actually existing,* constitutive or participants' *morality* or moralities (in the intransitive dimension), which sustains the *irreducibility of 'ought' to 'is'*, i.e. the possibility of criticism and a fortiori critique. As a moral realist I hold that there is an objective morality. But how can it be known? This is where ethical naturalism comes in. It lies in the *transition from fact to value* (and theory to practice). So there is an ethical alethia, ultimately grounded in conceptions of human nature, in the context of developing four-planar social being, with the moral consciousness of the species in principle *open*. Just because we can get, through explanatory critique, from fact to value, the first-person activating character of moral judgements poses no problem for dialectical critical realism's moral realism. Secondly, the anti-naturalistic fallacy often functions merely to screen the generation of an implicit emotivist or descriptivist morality reflecting the status quo ante of actually existing morality — it de-moralizes (in the transitive dimension) by reflecting the morality of an actually existing already moralized world (in the intransitive dimension). Here we have dialectics of practical problem-resolution, consciousness-change and emancipation. *Universalizability* serves as both (1) a test of consistency and (2) a criterion of truth. But the so-called 'communitarians' are right to insist on the epistemic *relativity* of moral judgements (in the transitive dimension) and the *diversity* of actually existing moralities (in the intransitive dimension). Dialectical critical realism holds, however, that epistemic relativity is quite consistent with judgemental rationality, here, in the practico-ethical realm, as in the realm of the descriptive-explanatory work of science (including the description and explanation of actually existing moralities).

My alethic realism consists in the *truth of things* not propositions, and is satisfied just as that moment when *referential detachment* of an explanans in an explanatory process becomes legitimate and necessary in the dialectic of science. Briefly, an adequate analysis of truth will show it to comprise a *tetrapolity*, involving four components or moments: (α) *normative-fiduciary*, in the communicative sub-dimension of the social cube, (β) *adequating*, in the transitive dimension, (γ) *expressive-referential*, in an ontic-epistemic duality, and finally (δ) *alethic*, in the intransitive dimension. Recognition of the alethic moment — truth as dr' or dg' — in a genuinely ontological employment, resolves, as we shall see briefly in §4 and more fully in C4.2, a host of philosophical problems — in fact, almost all those standard aporiai which depend on homology or vicious regress. *In the moral realm, alethic truth, the good, is freedom*, depending on the absenting of constraints on absenting ills.

I have talked about two kinds of ontological extensions in the ontology of dialectical critical realism, (α) longitudinal and (β) lateral. But there is a need for a third kind — (γ) scalar. Most (implicit) ontologies are *simplistic*. Hegel might just as well have defined dialectic as seeing the *complex* in the simple, as seeing the positive in the negative. Indeed this is part of the meaning of 'concretion'. We have seen in C2 the prominence that dialectical critical realism gives to notions such as recursion, embedding, intermingling, the hiatus, constellationality, perspective (and perspectival switches), reflections (in the sense of C2.7) both within and between different categories and categorial groups and/or levels. Thus we have to think of social beings as constituted by the presence of others and of their formation; and of at least four distinct types of tendency; of phenomena such as natural absences, empty selves, hidden depths (cf. C2.8), of the penetration of philosophy by science and society, of the presence within the absence of the future, of the whole in the heap, the void at the heart of being.

But it might be objected at this point, what exactly is the argument for ontology, not in the philosophy of science (which may indeed meet the criteria dialectical critical realism describes) but in general? The argument for *ontology* is just the argument for *existential intransitivity*, which is just the argument for *referential detachment*. Realism in the sense that involves existential intransitivity is a presupposition of *discourse* which must be *about* something other than itself, of *praxis* which must be *with* something other than itself* or of *desire* which must be *for* something alterior to itself. To someone who doubts whether referential detachment exists just ask them to repeat and/or clarify what they have said, and then ask them what it is that they have repeated or clarified. It must be a referentially detached (social) entity. Any creature capable of differentiation must be capable of referential detachment. This does not immediately establish the case for alethic truth. For that we must have a creature capable of dividing the world into essential and non-essential attributes, and of appreciating that the former do not always manifest themselves in

---

* Cf. the critique of foundationalism I have elaborated elsewhere.[5]

actuality. With the *first referential detachment* of structure and the transfactual efficacy it affords, we get the first taste of *alethic truth*, the dialectical reason or ground for things. And now we are doing science, from a position in which the primordial activities of referential detachment and the necessity for ontology may be readily forgotten. But also, insofar as differentiation is itself a causal act and causation is absenting, we are on the terrain of dialectic, upon which 1M non-identity and transfactuality can thus retrospectively be seen to depend.

It will be recalled from the *Phenomenology of Mind* that the Stoic (be s/he Aurelius or Epictetus) is indifferent to reality, the Sceptic denies its existence in theory but affirms it in practice (and so is guilty of theory/practice inconsistency), while the Unhappy Consciousness makes it explicit in the introjection or projective postulation of another world. After the demise of positivism in the wake of the double blow of relativity theory and quantum mechanics, philosophy found itself in a double bind. In failing to thematize (or at least reproblematize) ontology and so to articulate a new one — which could accommodate transitive and intransitive change and stratification alike — it tended to transmute along the transitive dimension into a variety of forms, which I will treat in logical, not necessarily chronological, order. First came a sociological conventionalism, exemplified by writers such as Bachelard and Kuhn, like Stoicism indifferent to reality yet at the same time aware of the context of master−slave or oppressive power$_2$ relations at work. Thus the scientific neophyte was pictured as accepting on purely 'positive' grounds (in the early Hegelian usage, that is to say, acceptance on the basis of authority) the craft of her trade. Meanwhile there would be sporadic outbursts of internecine warfare as new ways of thinking and probing things were vaunted, which resembles nothing so much as the section of the *Phenomenology* entitled 'the spiritual kingdom of the beasts, or the affair itself'. This stoic indifference to reality gave rise to a post-structuralist collapse to scepticism, in which Derrida can write 'there is nothing outside the text'[6] and probably neither mean, definitely not believe and certainly not act on it, entailing palpable theory/practice inconsistency. The duplicity implicit in post-structuralism then became explicit in the unhappy consciousness of a pragmatist like Rorty, who considers that there is a reality (even if only in the guise of incoming causal impacts) but forbids us to talk about it. This convoluted introjection gives way to the explicit Dadaist contradiction of Feyerabend who sees no reason for imposing any constraints on the 'doubles' of the real world we can make. But on close inspection all these beautiful souls of 1967 turn out to be still at work in the struggle for symbolic capital, money and power.* The history of post-positivist philosophy thus mimics certain famous dialectical topographies.

The self-referential paradoxes and theory/practice inconsistencies attendant upon the denial of referential attachment = existential transitivity = ontology are so patent that it might seem that the difficult task is not to give a transformed transformative response to the Heideggerian 'scandal of philosophy', but how to begin to explain irrealism. For that is the *real* scandal of philosophy. I postpone attempting to unravel it until C4.

§ 2 The Dialectic of Truth

'Truth' seems at once (a) the simplest and (b) the most difficult of concepts. (a) Saying 'true' to a proposition is to give one's assent to it — this is its primary function, whereby redundancy and performative theories derive their plausibility. But one is thereby committed to a claim *about* the world, roughly to the effect that that is how things are, from which correspondence theories since the time of Aristotle have drawn their currency. This claim carries the normative force 'trust me — act on it', whence pragmatic theories gain their footing. At the same time this claim, if challenged, needs to be *grounded*, a requirement that seems to point in the direction of coherence theories. So a truth judgement will typically carry or imply a fourfold dimensionality, possessing (i) *expressively veracious*, (ii) *descriptive*, (iii) *evidential* and (iv) *imperatival-fiduciary* aspects. This four-dimensionality is intrinsic to the judgement form as such, and is not limited to truth judgements. Each aspect is universalizable, albeit in different ways, and aspects may be loosely attached to the concrete universal and the social cube (as mentioned in C2.10). To these matters I will return. For the moment it is sufficient to appreciate that it is in virtue of its basic *world-reporting* meaning (its descriptive 'this is how things are in the world' component) that truth-talk satisfies a *transcendental-axiological need*, acting as a steering mechanism for language-users to find their way about the world.

(b) But 'truth' is at the same time the most difficult of concepts in

---

* The life-and-death struggle is a continuing theme of Hegel and cannot be reduced to the chapter on 'Self-consciousness'. It is explicit in the dialectics of nobility, wealth and war. In the same way the struggle for recognition to which the life-and-death struggle is indissolubly linked is a continuing refrain in Hegel. Moreover, I think the metaphor can be taken quasi-literally in referring to scientific and philosophical social systems, in addition to politics and life generally.

which, as I will briefly indicate, there is hardly an extant theory without some flaw but in which it is equally hard not to recognize some truth or power. Moreover, it has ramifications for theories of meaning and reference (which I will address), perception, causality, agency, experiment, communication (and thus also philosophical sociology and ontology generally, which will also be pursued in the course of this chapter). In respect of the familiar distinction between meaning and criteria of truth, although the latter must be (α) universalizable in *form*, (β) their *contents* may well be as *variable* as the contexts in which truth claims are made. Thus in particle physics repeatable registration of tracks on a monitor brings out both these aspects.

After a short comment on some of the aporiai of recent truth theories — and a slightly more detailed look at the concept in the Marxian canon — I proceed to give my own stratified theory of the meaning of truth and then show it at work in the dialectic of scientific discovery. I then pass on to the implications of what I have already in §1 prefiguratively nominated the 'truth tetrapolity' before an excursus into questions of dialectical, T/P consistency and universalizability returns me to issues of meaning, reference and criteriology in the sciences.

The most important historical theories of truth this century, outside the Marxist camp, have been the correspondence, coherence, pragmatic, redundancy, performative, consensus and Hegelian theories of truth. Correspondence theories had their heyday during the mid-century supremacy of logical positivism, although they were also supported by some critics, such as Austin, of the latter. The basic objection to the most influential correspondence theories — the early Wittgenstein's picture theory, Tarski's semantic theory and Popper's theory of increasing verisimilitude or truth-likeness in the development of science — applies to all alike: there seems no 'Archimedean' standpoint from which a comparison of the competing items can be made. Together with a rejection of immediate knowledge, and of the reification of facts (the realization that facts are established results, made, not apprehended[7]), the recognition that matching is a metaphor (that a transitive theory is not *like* what it is about) and that semantic theories are homologous (say the same thing — albeit at different levels), it seems correspondence theories must be abandoned, especially when they act as the non-compacted component of subject – object identity = duplicity theories. That said, it has to be recognized that there is an inherent TD/ID bipolarity or ambivalence in concepts like 'facts' and 'truth', which cannot be completely gainsaid in an adequate truth theory.

Coherence theories seem most plausible as an account of the criteriology rather than meaning of truth. Hegelian theories may be regarded as a special case of them in which it is the conformity of an object to its notion (ultimately the whole, closed totality), rather than vice versa, that defines truth. But, whether in Hegelian dialectical or more analytical declensions, coherence theories seem to presuppose something like a correspondence-theoretic account of 'correctness'. However, if the world were regarded as a text it could be argued that there could be no better account of correspondence than coherence.

The two main influential species of pragmatism derive ultimately from (1) Peirce, James and Dewey and (2) Nietzschean perspectivism. (1), which has been recently popularized by Rorty and seems currently to be accepted by Putnam and possibly Davidson, maintains that the only workable concept of truth is warranted assertability (and dovetails neatly with constructivist and intuitionist theories of mathematics). It is vulnerable to the objection that a proposition may be warrantedly assertable but false. (2) For the Nietzschean tradition which informs post-structuralism, truth is 'a mobile army of metaphors', ultimately an expression of the will-to-power, which must be thought, as both necessary and impossible, 'under erasure' (cf. C2.8). It is hard to see this position, whether in its Derridean or Foucauldian guises, as anything other than palimpsesting itself out of existence, self-erasing.

The other theories must be handled even more briefly. The redundancy theory, initially formulated by Ramsey, seems either to smuggle in truth by the back door or to deny the axiological necessity of the truth predicate. Performative theories of the kind advocated by Strawson, Hare and Searle seem more satisfactory in this respect, but they in turn underplay the extent to which the use of the truth predicate needs to be grounded, a requirement stressed by Kripke. Consensus theories are subject to the dilemma that if given a strict interpretation, twenty million Frenchmen can be wrong; or, if given an ideal-typical formulation, that they do not explicate our existing concept of truth.

Slightly longer on the Marxian tradition. In the writings of its founders (a) 'truth' normally *means* 'correspondence with reality', usually interpreted under the metaphor of reflection or some kindred notion, while (b) the *criterion* for evaluating truth claims normally is, or depends upon, human practice. 'Reflection' enters Marxist epistemology at two levels. Marx talks of both (1) the immediate form and (2) the inner or underlying essence of objects being '*reflected*'. But while what is involved at (1) is an explanatory postulate or methodological starting point, at (2) it is a norm of descriptive or scientific adequacy. Thus whereas at (1) Marx criticizes vulgar economy for merely reflecting 'the direct form of manifestation of essential relations',[8] his concern at (2) is precisely with the production of an adequate representation or 'reflection' — a *task* which involves theoretical work and conceptual transformation, not a single passive reproduction of reality. Note that a 'reflection', as normally understood, is both (α) *of* something which exists independently of it (in the ID) and (β) *produced* in accordance with certain principles of projection or representative convention (in the TD). However, if (α) is not to become epistemically otiose (as, for example, in Althusser) there must be some *constraints* on the representative process generated by the real object itself (in the way in which an experimental outcome depends upon the structure under investigation).

Marx and Engels talk of 'images' and 'copies', and Lenin of 'photographs', as well as reflections. These metaphors readily encouraged collapse of case (2) to case (1), of the cognitive to the causal functions of the metaphor, of Marx's deep correspondence theory to the simple reflection theory of dialectical materialism. In reaction to the latter, western Marxism typically comprehended truth as the practical expression of a subject rather than a theoretically adequate representation of an object, whether in coherentist (as Lukács), pragmatist (as in Korsch) or consensualist (as in Gramsci) form. If the generic weakness of 'reflectionist' (objective empiricist) Marxist theories of truth is neglect of the socially produced and geo-historic structure of truth judgements, that of epistemically idealist western Marxist theories is neglect of the independent existence and transfactual efficacy of the objects of such judgements. What is needed clearly is a theory which neither elides the referent nor neglects the socially produced character of judgements about it.[9] It is to the development of such a theory that I turn now.

An adequate theory of truth must take account of the fact that there are four basic concepts of it, or components in its analysis:

(α) truth as *normative-fiduciary*, truth in the 'trust me — act on it' sense, in the communicative sub-dimension of the social cube;

(β) truth as *adequating*, as 'warrantedly assertable', as epistemological, as relative in the transitive dimension;

(γ) truth as *referential-expressive*, as a bipolar ontic-epistemic dual, and in this sense as absolute; and

(δ) truth as *alethic*, as the truth of or reason for *things* and phenomena, *not propositions*, as genuinely ontological, and in this sense as objective in the intransitive dimension.

I have already labelled these moments as the 'truth tetrapolity'.

Some comments on the tetrapolity. It is best illustrated by being situated in the context of a rudimentary dialectic of truth, which can then be filled out. A group of scientists are (a) subjectively empirically certain about the reason S_j for some well-attested phenomena, S_i. They succeed in convincing their colleagues about the (b) inter-subjective facthood of S_j, so that it becomes referentially detached at t_2 as (c) the reason for S_i or the objective truth of S_i, while the new wave of scientists is at the same time heading the search for the reason S_k for S_j in the next round of scientific discovery (which will produce the alethia of S_j). So we go from *subjective certainty* → *inter-subjective facthood* → *alethic truth*. The key moment occurs at $(\gamma)-(\delta)$ in the dialectic of S_i → S_j → S_k, when scientists are no longer concerned with verifying statements about S_j, accept its bipolar facthood and regard themselves in the DREI(C) moment of the logic of scientific discovery as having identified the reason(s) for S_j, referentially detached them and moved onwards in the direction of S_k. Typically at this moment the scientists will have the best possible (Lockian/ Leibnizian grounds) for the attribution of natural necessity to, and the truth of the propositions designating, the phenomena of S_i. $(\alpha)-(\delta)$ may also be regarded as expressing degrees of groundedness. Thus the axiological imperative in social life means that we may sometimes have to act on propositions that are not even warrantedly assertable (β). Note that on (γ) truth is still ontogenetic, tied to language use; but at (δ) we are concerned with the truth, ground, reason or purpose of things, not propositions. Of course, such alethic truths must still be expressed in language and are subject to correction in the regressive moments of the dialectic of scientific discovery. But this does not alter the fact that it is a fundamentally different, though dialectically interconnected, concept at stake. Epistemological relativism at (β) (in the TD) is, of course, consistent with judgemental rationalism (in the IA) and ontological realism (in the ID), but the concept of the transitive dimension should be metacritically extended to incorporate the whole material and cultural infra-/intra-/superstructure of society. It is the being-expressive bipolar concept at (γ) which accounts for philosophical intuitions about the difference between 'truth' and 'warranted assertability', but the point of (judgement of) correct identification and referential detachment is marked primarily by the change in the direction of scientific inquiry rather than perceptual and/or causal revelation of the truths of S_j, which are (alethically) of S_i. Notice that truth at (δ) is praxis-dependent (2E), totalizing (3L), in the sense that it is oriented to maximizing explanatory power, and

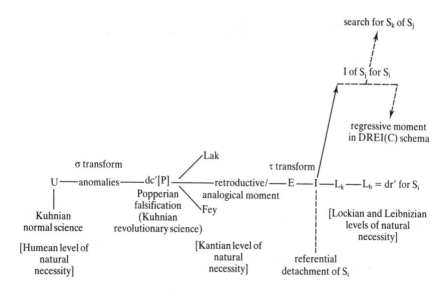

P, Lak and Fey stand for the Popperian, Lakatosian and Feyerabendian moments in science
L_k and L_b refer to Lockian and Leibnizian levels of natural necessity respectively
cf. also Figure 2.12 at p.110

Figure 3.1 The Epistemological Dialectic of Science

contextualized (4D) by the dialectic of the science concerned, as well as, of course, expressing ontological stratification (1M).

The dialectic of truth can be articulated in two obvious ways:

1. by being situated in the context of gradations of natural necessity — with 'D' describing the Humean, 'R' the Kantian, 'I' first Lockian (synthetic a posteriori) and then Leibnizian (analytic a posteriori) moments of knowledge of natural necessity in the dialectic of explanatory and taxonomic knowledge I have already rehearsed (DREI(C));
2. by superimposing this dialectical transcendental realist model on the Hegelian epistemological dialectic first elaborated in C1.9, as illustrated in Figure 3.1 above.

Alethia, as we shall see, is the resolution of the standard textbook 1M problems of philosophy. It is dialectical reason and ground in theory and the absence of heterology; it is true to, for, in and of itself. It furnishes the non-arbitrary principle of ontological stratification that powers the dialectic of scientific discovery. Transposed to the ethical domain, the true = the moral good = freedom, in the sense of universal human emancipation, as will be shown in §§7–11. For the moment we have to return to more quotidian matters.

We are concerned with three distinct phenomena:

(α) *dialectical*, or, as I have sometimes called it, *developmental consistency* in a process;
(β) *theory/practice consistency* in a praxis in some process;
(γ) *dialectical universalizability*.

(α) may be social, as in the case of a progressive research programme (where one's criterion may be, for instance, optimization of the rate of scientific advance measured on some scale), or natural, as in the case of the maturation of a caterpillar into a butterfly or an acorn into an oak (where, if one wants to impose a criterion, it may be beauty, or normalicity of development or whatever). The point about consistency here is that no general formula for it can be given: criteria are necessarily *intrinsic* to the process concerned. There may be a Lockian Hour in science (and perhaps philosophy) but then there may not be, as is readily verifiable from reading a range of novels of different genres. Normally one would be talking here, as in the case of the more tractable (α) and (β), about a *process-in-product-in-process*.

Two metatheorems may be immediately stated:

I. Universalizability is both (a) a test for consistency and (b) a criterion for truth in the fields of theoretical and practical reason alike.

II. End-states, which should be universalizable, are not always realizable by agents (e.g. one can't get from x to everywhere and one can't go to y from just anywhere). However, in general it is plausible to suppose that one can progress towards them, or mitigate regress away from them. [P]

(β) T/P consistency on the part of an agent N should

1. be practical,
2. satisfy P (and, if possible, prefigure the end-state or at least be as far as possible consistent with it),
3. be grounded in an explanatory theory or set of theories of

    (a) the current situation,
    (b) the desired end-state and
    (c) the transition from (a) to (b).

(γ) Both an agent's praxis and its groundings (3) should be universalizable in the senses that they be

1. transfactual,
2. concrete — satisfying all the moments of the concrete universal (including, of course, concrete singularity),
3. actionable, in the sense of agent-specific, and
4. transformative, in the sense that it is oriented to change (in the direction of the postulated end-state [P]).

(δ) All the aspects of the judgement form — in theoretical and practical reasoning alike — are universalizable — although in different ways:

(a) expressive veracity: 'if I had to act in these circumstances, this is what I would act on';
(b) fiduciariness: 'in exactly your circumstances, this is the best thing to do';
(c) descriptive: 'in exactly the same circumstances, the same result would ensue';
(d) evidential: 'in exactly the same circumstances, the reasons would be the same'.

(c) and (d) are merely implications of the principle of sufficient reason (which I have elsewhere called ubiquity determinism). We need not quarrel with this, save to note that if a normic (transfactual) and concrete interpretion is not given of the 'same circumstances' they fail. Fiduciariness carries with it the 'conversationally candid' implication of expressive veracity, so (b) might be said to imply (a), as (d) might be said to imply (c). Note that the four moments of the judgement form are internally related. And that in the ethical sphere, taking into account the concrete singularity of the particular agent entails that the imperatival aspect be only, in Kantian terms, 'assertoric' (i.e. in accordance with the agent's wants, in a potential dialectic of wants, needs and interests) rather than (personalistically) categorical or (technologistically) hypothetical. This is also pre-supposed by the criterion of actionability. It is worth mentioning too that the judgement form through its fiduciary-imperatival and descriptive-plus-evidential aspects has a *theoretico-practical duality* built into it. Theoretical reason, which merely says the world is so-and-so, still implies a commitment to act on it. And so by a perspectival switch it informs practice. This is important because the expressively veracious aspect stipulates, and through its implication of fiduciariness presupposes, not only (1) that if the agent addressor A was placed in a situation of the agent addressee this is how she would act, but also (2) that she shows *solidarity* with B in degrees running from minimal advice as in (1) through forms of moral and material assistance (including speech and writing, of course) to (3) empowerment and (4) engaging in a totalizing depth praxis designed to bring about the desired state of affairs — that is, either, in the case of practical reason, in accordance with some grounded end-state or -process; or, in the case of theoretical reason, in accordance with the descriptive implications of saying how the world is so. So every speech act must be regarded as making an *axiological commitment*. Moreover, given that to say how the world is is implicitly to advise agents to act on that basis, not to assist or empower them when it is in one's capacity to do so is to be guilty of T/P inconsistency ceteris paribus. That is, in the context of a balanced life, bearing in mind that amour de soi is the basis of altruism (only the empowered can empower) and that A's object is not to substitute her action for that of B but rather to solidarize with it.

(ε) Less importantly, the descriptive component and the expressively veracious and fiduciary components of the judgement form can be loosely associated with the levels of particular mediations and concrete singularity in the concrete universal; and the expressively veracious and fiduciary moments as representing respectively the plane of the stratification of the personality and the plane of interpersonal transactions in our four-planar theory of social being.

The significance of these results will become clear in the dialectic of freedom. But for the moment it is sufficient to note the alignment of dialectical reason, alethia, T/P consistency, dialectical universalizability, non-heterology in an expanded sense of being true to, for and of oneself and each other and autonomy; and that of susceptibility to dialectical comment, T/P inconsistency, immanent critique, Tina formation, heterology and non-autonomy, absence, detotalization and split.

It is incumbent upon me to say something about the concepts of meaning and reference, traditionally associated with that of truth. The centrepiece of any adequate theory of meaning must be the semiotic triangle (see Figure 3.2). If the traditional nominalist error has been to elide the signified, the customary post-modernist stance has been to elide the referent. If it is the signifier that transmits the locutionary force in the communicative sub-dimension of the social cube, and the detachable referent which enables us to talk *about* something (including what we are currently saying), it is the role of the signified, that may be bound in layers of differentially sedimented semantic stratification, which enables the conceptual distanciation, exploiting perhaps the slightest of analogies, metaphors and metonymies, which plays such a creative role in the paramorphic model-building essential to science. Each of signifier, in the communicative sub-dimension, signified, in the transitive dimension generally, and referent, in the intransitive dimension, may (a) be caught up in eddies of their own and (b) have attached to them, e.g. through paradigmatic and syntagmatic, structured and differentiated relations, multiple other semiotic triangles enfolding on the element which must be thought under the aspects of (c) geo-historical process-in-product(-in-process) and (d) intra-activity. Together (c) and (d) explain the acuity of the notion of the trace structure of the signifier. Each may, moreover, act as a proxy for, or simply as, an other, and they are typically internally related which explains the poverty of a purely extensionalist analysis of language use. Identity here is constituted through difference and change.

The most important ingredients in an adequate dialectical critical realist account of reference are already caught in Figure 3.2, viz. (i) the notion of referential detachment and (ii) the generalized concept of the referent with which I am working. Once one breaks from atomistic-punctualist-monovalent-extensionalist justificationalism one can treat of *any* significant chunk of reality (irrespective of whether this makes it easy to handle logically); and to treat of it non-anthropically one must be capable of non-anthropically detaching the referent from the human act which picks it out, which is also to detach oneself from the referent. Problems about the status of the referent — is it real or imaginary, transfactual or actual, positive or

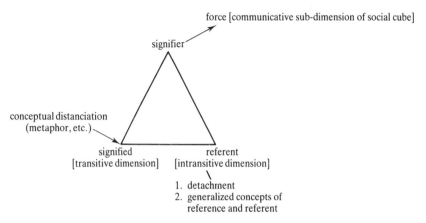

Figure 3.2 The Semiotic Triangle

negative, in relation or a self-subsistent entity, an aspect or a totality, social-relation-dependent or not? — then become much more tractable.

Finally a word on the criteriology of the sciences. Practical reason is, or depends upon, an applied science. But both the natural and social sciences may be pure or applied; so there is no unique way to carve up the sciences. All we can say is that in the ethical realm we will typically be dealing with a complex of applied social sciences in which the third 'R' — signifying 'retrodiction' — depends upon the multiple application of law-like tendency statements with prior DREI(C) retroductive-analogical theoretical credentials.

§ 3 On the Emergence and Derivability of Dialecticized Transcendental Realism

Critical realism arose as transcendental realism from the crisis and demise of positivism in the philosophy of science. The philosophy of science itself emerged as a discipline distinct from epistemology (the general theory of knowledge) in the mid-nineteenth century — at about the time that separate sciences bearing names such as 'physics', 'chemistry' and 'biology' were becoming 'professionalized'. The leading figures of its first generation were Comte, the inventor of the signifier 'positivism' (in addition to 'sociology'), the ultra-empiricist J.S. Mill, who thought that even mathematical propositions were empirical — a confusion of theories of explanation (in the EA) and justification (in the IA) — and the Kantian historian of science Whewell. Much of the subsequent trajectory of the philosophy of science can be presented as a continuation of the controversy between Mill and Comte, on the one hand, and Whewell, on the other, with the former hegemonic until circa 1970. The dominant view of science has been squarely based on Humean empiricism, epitomized in Mach's claim that natural laws were nothing but 'the mimetic reproduction of facts in thought, the object of which is to replace and save the trouble of new experience'.[10] Thus the late nineteenth century witnessed such spectacular triumphs for the empiricist camp as Benjamin Brodie's construction of a chemistry without atoms, which were widely held to be, in Alexander Bain's words, 'representative fictions'.

The positivist vision of science turns on a *deductivist* theory of scientific structure and a *monistic* theory of scientific development, in the other of which each can be embedded. Modern scientific realism takes off from criticism of the logical positivism of the Vienna Circle of the twenties and thirties, which forged Machian epistemology and

Fregean logic to form the received conception of science until the late sixties. One of the first decisive attacks on this was mounted by Quine, who urged, as early as 1953, against the canonical analytical/ empirical and theory/fact distinctions for a *holistic* view of knowledge as in effect 'a field of force whose boundary conditions are experience'. Drawing upon this, Mary Hesse, amongst others, claimed that scientific language should be seen as a dynamic system continuously growing by the metaphoric or metonymic extension of natural language. Observational predicates were not isomorphs of a physical, sensual or instrumental kind, but 'knots' attaching the semantic network to the object-world in a theory-dependent and mutable way. This was powerfully reinforced by a growing awareness, induced by the work of Popper, Kuhn, Lakatos, Feyerabend and, in France, Bachelard and Koyré, of the reality of scientific change. Theories were social constructions, offering competing descriptions and explanations of a theory-independent world. Wittgensteinians, such as Scriven, Hanson, Toulmin and Sellars, latched onto and developed this line of attack, making explicit the *sociality* of what critical realism has come to call the *transitive* (epistemological and social) side or dimension of science. And monism was on the way out.

Meanwhile Rom Harré, like Hesse and Scriven, indebted to the tradition of Whewell and his early twentieth-century successor Campbell, drew attention to the role of (especially paramorphic) models in raising *existential* questions — in the *intransitive* (or ontological) dimension of the transitive process of theory growth. Theoretical entities and processes, initially imaginatively posited as plausible explanations of observed phenomena, could come to be established as *real*. This could be done either through the construction of sense-extending equipment, in which case the criterion for describing reality was perceptual, or through the design of instruments predicting the detection of the effects of theoretically posited mechanisms, in which case the criterion was causal. These different influences all converged slowly to suggest a *structural*, theoretical, vertical or *existential* realism. This was further supported by the linguistic arguments of Kripke and Putnam that the use of natural kind terms, such as 'gold' and 'water', presupposed that the substances had real essences, although not necessarily known to us.

At this time I was systematizing and generalizing the results of what was being hailed as an (in effect anti-Kantian, but *Copernican*) 'Copernican revolution' in the philosophy of science in my system of transcendental realism. But I argued that the anti-deductivist moment had to be completed by the development of a 'horizontal' *causal*, *transfactual* or depth dynamic nomic realism, alongside the structural or entity realism already established. These were related as follows: generative mechanisms were the causal powers of structurally efficacious things. Empirical regularities or constant conjunctions of events were no more a necessary than a sufficient condition for the attribution of natural necessities (of natural kinds), which had therefore to be analysed as tendencies. And I produced transcendental arguments which showed that it was a presupposition, or condition of possibility, of experimental and applied scientific activity that the intransitive objects of scientific work both existed and acted *transfactually* (or to use words other critical realists have employed), transsituationally or transphenomenally, irrespective of the closure or otherwise of the system in which they occurred. This is an argument against actualism and for the categorial distinctiveness of the domains of the real, the actual and the empirical.

Arguments for scientific realism *within* the philosophy of science may be divided into the following:

1. *Transcendental arguments* of the type I used, which, insofar as they are (like mine) immanently critical are ipso facto transcendental refutations of irrealist (roughly non-realist) positions in a metacritical circle. A full metacritical$_2$ explanation of the transcendentally refuted position would yield its explanatory critical dialectical necessity or the alethic truth of the falsity of the theory critiqued. Here dialecticized philosophy joins hands with the sociology of science, at least in the form of the Edinburgh School, as represented by Barry Barnes and David Bloor, which is both materialist and realist in orientation in contrast to, for example, the Paris School of Latour or the work of Knorr-Cetina. It is also of some significance to note that the attack against deductivism was initiated, complemented and carried through by critical realists such as Russell Keat, Ted Benton, William Outhwaite, Andrew Collier, Peter Manicas and Andrew Sayer or erstwhile critical realists such as Rom Harré with a deep interest in the human sciences where what one commentator has called the 'law-explanation orthodoxy'[11] was never really plausible.[12] One final word on social objects. Although the processes of knowledge and their objects are causally interdependent, the latter must still be regarded as existentially intransitive,[13] so that realism is an a priori condition of any investigation, irrespective of domain. Thus it applies even to Cartesian doubt.[14] Two consequences: social dialectics are relational dialectics; and the transitive dimension of even natural science includes the whole matrix and four-planar, including technological, character of society in principle.

2. *Inductive arguments* from the directionality, history or success of

science. Thus Putnam and Boyd argued that the cumulative character of scientific development strongly indicates that theories are (fallible) attempts to describe real states and structures as they succeed one another in providing more complete accounts of a theory-independent reality. However, Putnam now rejects this on the grounds of a 'disastrous meta-induction' from the failure of reference in some actual cases. From a transcendental realist meta-perspective this is a double mistake: (a) one cannot argue from an isolated counter-incidence to an emergent principle of structure of totality (cf. the critique of actualism — deductivism); (b) in any event, Putnam should have welcomed both the instance and his meta-induction as evidencing the fallibility of all claims to knowledge (cf. the critique of monism — inductivism). Hesse also criticized the Putnam—Boyd argument on the grounds that the history of science reveals no such convergence. If she means that the latest descriptions in the transitive dimension are constantly changing then she is certainly correct. But if she means that the directionality of science shows no cumulation in the knowledge of existents and their causal powers then she is either joking or misunderstanding what in §2 I dubbed the dialectic of truth, that is to say, the essential dynamic of science (which constellationally incorporates redescription of past results). Harré and Aronson have produced a similar inductive argument from the determinate outcome of searches for hypothesized beings, staking the ground for what they call a pragmatic policy realism.[15]

3. *Reductiones ad absurdum*, of irrealist positions. Examples of this are, of course, the paradoxes, antinomies and aporiai with which irrealist philosophies abound (such as the problem of induction), which will be touched on as we move through the 1M−4D vertical column of this chapter and systematically diagnosed and explained in C4. But one kind of problem may be specifically mentioned. If realism is transcendentally/axiologically necessary, then irrealist philosophies must presuppose in practice some ontology, exposing the epistemic fallacy as a sham, and thence some or other realism (e.g. an empirical, conceptual or intuitional realism). And if a particular form of realism, such as a dialecticized transcendental realism, is necessary, this implies that geo-historically grounded and efficacious philosophies will always take the form, as we should by now expect, of multiply internally inconsistent Tina compromise formations.

If dialecticized transcendental realism is the sublation of positivism two questions inevitably arise. First, can one give transcendental arguments for science? Second, what are the current alternatives and does one need further argument against them? To take this second question first. We have already observed in §1 the transition route from positivism via conventionalism, pragmatism, constructivism to superidealism that inevitably flows from a continuing commitment to the epistemic fallacy, involving the denegation of ontology or the failure to rethematize being outside an empirical realist framework. (One should mention here a neo-positivist backlash in the form of the work of van Fraassen and Cartwright.) The answer to the second part of the second question is: yes. Positions on the transmutation route are attractive; and one must expose the dilemmas and antinomies, the splits and detotalizations which they entrain, as well as their underlying categorial error. Take Rorty's pragmatism. For all his other influences, his paradigm is Kuhn's *The Structure of Scientific Revolutions*. The essence of this book is the possible (and actualized) incompatibility, even incommensurability, of conceptual schemes. This is Rorty's argument for metaphor, creativity, the new. And yet the arch-concept, on which his rhetoric swings, that of different conceptual schemes, is one which, following Donald Davidson, he explicitly disavows. The *new anthropism is the same*, as we always knew, with its continuing commitment to empirical realism, it would be *bound* to be. Then there are the possibilities of all sorts of half-way houses and the necessity for transition paths. Charles Taylor is a brilliantly innovative philosopher who explicitly identifies as a realist, the logic of which dialectical critical realism attempts to articulate. Consider his concluding article in an important collection of essays, *After Philosophy*.[16] Taylor identifies three main failings in what is essentially the Cartesian-Lockian representationalist view of knowledge: (1) the disengagement of the subject from practice, (2) a punctualist view of a (generally disembodied) self and (3) an individualist-atomist conception of society. And he locates correctives in Heidegger (to whom I will shortly come), Merleau-Ponty and Hegel and in a conception of transcendental argumentation close to mine. And yet he can say that we cannot draw 'a neat line . . . between my dealing with an object, such as a football . . . and that object', i.e. the football itself.[17] But, without scouting the difference between the *Geisteswissenschaften* and the *Naturwissenschaften*, upon which I as much as he wants to insist, this is precisely what we *must* do. In order to *pass* a football we have to *practically referentially detach it*; and in order to understand our passing of it we have to believe that it is not only referentially detachable, i.e. *existentially intransitive*, but subject to *transfactually efficacious* laws of nature. Dialectical critical realism is implicit in every practical deed.

If dialecticized transcendental realism is transcendentally necessary for the intelligibility of science, can we produce (a) transcendental arguments for science or (b) transcendental or other valid arguments for dialectical critical realism without immediate recourse to science? (a) The transcendental argument for science turns on its *causal efficacy*, which can be *rationally assessed*; and may — indeed does — vary from science to science (western medicine, as Feyerabend has justifiable cause to complain, has a very poor record in many fields; econometrics, as Tony Lawson has amply demonstrated from a critical realist standpoint, barely deserves the name of 'science') and from research programme to research programme, as we all know from the work of Lakatos and Laudan. More interesting are arguments of type (b). First there is an Heideggerian-type argument from the *pathology of everyday life*. N is driving a car as *das Zuhande*, the ready to hand, concernfully engaged in being-in-the-world-with-others, mindful of the *ecstases* of her assignment. N is in the realm of the Heideggarian ontological, as distinct from the ontic realm of science. The car breaks down. N fiddles around unsuccessfully and finally calls the emergency rescue service. They arrive and are similarly concernfully oriented to their task. No luck. N's car is driven away to the garage, thence transferred to a depot. A mechanic finally isolates a design fault in the vehicle and this is relayed back to the design unit of the manufacturing firm. To all intents and purposes we are now in the Heideggerian ontic realm. Existential intransitivity, referential detachment (and with it the critique of the epistemic fallacy), structure, difference and transfactual efficacy are all being presupposed. Suppose the design fault raises issues of substantial scientific concern. Let us treat science itself as an *existential*, employing *categories*. Experiments are carefully designed and undertaken. They presuppose the transfactual efficacy and, unless special conditions are stipulated, the non-anthropocentricity, of the structures, mechanisms and laws which they enable us to identify. That is to say, they presuppose an ontology which would apply without the mediation of human being (i.e. *Dasein*), i.e. a non-Heideggerian ontology, although, of course, we can *know* this, tautologically but inevitably, only as human beings. To put this another way, they presuppose a counterfactual. But if one is a sceptic about counterfactuals, one cannot take a walk in the Black Forest, or hammer a nail in the door. (The agent must know that if she hammers too hard the door might — and, at a certain limit, will — break.) Heideggerian ontology, taken seriously, yields its own immanent critique. We can study science as everyday life, in the laboratory or in the classroom. And when we do, we find that it presupposes a transfactually efficacious and at least non-anthropic world of both enduring and transient things, punctuated by absence and powered by contradiction (in the broad sense of C2.10), bound into partial totalities (in the sense of C2.7) and dependent in epistemic actuality upon the agentive agency of human beings. Such agency presupposes a world, which has occurred and will come again to pass, without them.

But reflection upon the conditions of intelligibility of the most quotidian activity, like making a pot of coffee, presupposes the whole ontology of dialectical critical realism. We presuppose referential detachment of the pot and the coffee, that the nature of water, coffee, pots and cups will not change, that if a cup breaks there is a reason for or alethic truth of it. The exercise is one of real determinate transformative negation, absenting the absence of coffee. The causality of the animated discussion that ensues is holistic and dependent upon the efficacy of reasons as causes in the praxis of materially embodied human agency.

To drive the point home let us return to the argument at the end of §1. The first intuitive acts of referential detachment occur with the experience (later recognition) of desire, lack or absence and the connection of these absences to that of another, the continuing presence which constitutes the condition as one of *primary dyadization* or *polyadization*. (The necessity for this is the reductio ad absurdum of monism and solipsism alike. Whoever autogeneticized themselves?) After referential detachment of material objects and in the context of individuation within the primary polyad comes the recognition that the referent has causal powers of its own. At this point there occurs the first acknowledgement of axiological necessity and what I have been calling, in a deliberate echo of Freud, the 'reality principle'. As knowledge of the reality principle deepens, we will find our way, as this chapter will show, on to a *dialectic* which is equally of *desire* (from desire to the desire for freedom) and of *freedom* (from desire to freedom).

Discourse, it is important to stress, must be *about* something other than itself or else it cannot talk about itself at all. For this presupposes an act of referential detachment. The same applies to thought, be it Cartesian doubt or Hegelian *Denken* (conceptual thought). In the context of the stratified conception of the self and the distanciated conception of space-time for which I have already argued (in C2), this is quite consistent with *reflexivity* (a 3L category I will discuss in §9). It is also crucial to appreciate that the category around which the dialectic revolves, absence, is already implicit in the possibility of referential detachment. For this presupposes the possibility of absenting oneself or one's discursive act or one's pre-linguistic intuitive acts from what they are about. 2E negativity is therefore already implicit in 1M non-identity qua existential intransitivity. Conceptually close to referential detachment is recognition of the contingency of being of both referrer (and life, and human being generally) and referent, and with it critique of ego-present-centricity and anthropism.

Desire, we said, must be *for* something other than itself or else it cannot be satisfied. (On our conception of self and space-time this is quite consistent with narcissism.) Similarly praxis must be *with* something other than itself, otherwise it cannot do or make anything. This is the basis of the argument for the TMSA. But it is equally a critique of every foundationalism (from the Cartesian cogito to the conventionalist cogitamus); scepticism (modern Cratylans who are sceptical about whether it makes sense to talk about a real world of causally efficacious interacting and impinging things at once refute and detotalize themselves); absolutism (which abruptly and arbitrarily halts an ongoing process); and irrationalism (which swings on the illicit fusion of levels in not seeing the possibility of the constellational identity of the possibility of judgemental rationality [in the IA] within the actuality of epistemic relativity [in the TD] within the necessity for ontological realism [in the ID]). It is now time to systematize the landscape of 1M non-identity.

§ 4 1M Realism: Non-Identity

The dominant thematics of 1M realism is non-identity most unequivocally expressed as *alterity*, sheer other-being, whether of determinate or indeterminate types and whether knowable, known or not. The three principal motifs of 1M have already been sounded in §1: (α) the critique of anthropism, incorporating the epistemic fallacy; (β) the transitive/intransitive distinction which the critique of the epistemic fallacy situates; and (γ) the differentiation between the domains of the real, the actual and the empirical, which the systematic argument for ontology in science and our everyday existence entails. But 1M is the traditional stamping ground of epistemology and before the dialectical critical realist's explanation of it can begin we must disconstruct the unitary and undifferentiated concept of 'knowledge' which which received philosophy until circa mid twentieth century operated. Thus the philosophy of science was for the most part treated as a substitution instance of a chronically underdifferentiated theory of knowledge, with the philosophy of social science tacked on as in turn nothing more than an illustration of the general philosophy of (natural) science. Textbooks would treat of cracked radiators with an occasional footnote about the *Azande*. These elisions must be dismissed out of hand. Thus discriminations must be made between (a) ordinary and scientific knowledge, with the latter requiring an arduous socialization process of its own; (b) the social and the natural sciences, with the former (i) subject to a whole series of ontological, epistemological, relational and critical differentiations, (ii) characterized by the dislocated dialectics of structure and agency, and (iii) conceived as describing a (synchronically) emergent power of matter, ultimately embodied in the intentional causality of agents; (c) practical knowledge how, propositional knowledge that (Ryle) and the more generic knowledge of; (d) tacit and explicit knowledge (Polanyi); (e) following Wittgenstein's separation of form of life from theory, practical and discursive knowledge; and finally (f), after Chomsky, competence and performance.

Positivism is the achieved subject—object identity knowledge theory against which contemporary philosophy reacts. Critical realism is a fallibly and dynamically critical non-identity theory. Following a phenomenological method, it starts from actually generated kinds of knowledge and asks what the conditions of their possibility are. Theorems of non-identity turning on conceptions of intransitivity, transfactuality and so on quickly follow from this, but let us stay with identity theory for the moment. As realized, it was epistemologically reductionist, logically extensionalist and ontologically atomist with respect to particular, and actualist with respect to general, knowledge. It was, as achieved identity theory, anthropic. The Humean theory of causal laws on which it was based implied philosophies of space and time — atomism entailed punctualism and actualism blockism; and, qua anthropic, ego-present-centric punctualism (which it became the fashion to dub 'indexicalist') and God's-eye view or Laplacean blockism respectively. *Subject—object identity theory failed* ultimately because, at the level of *particular* knowledge, it could not solve the problems of solipsism — of how the one (subjective instance) could sustain any other; and because, at the level of *general* knowledge, it could not solve the problem of what I am going to call the *transdictive* complex. Transdiction denotes inference from the observed to the unobserved. Most obviously it includes the problem of induction — inference from past to future, which I generalized to the problem of *transduction* — inference from closed to open systems.[18] But it also includes retroduction, or the alleged fallacy of the affirmation of the consequent — which disappears when we reach the level of alethic truth, and retrodiction, that is to say, of inference to structural and antecedent causes respectively.[19] The problem of induction is an instance of one of the root problems of philosophy to be investigated in C4, the problem of the one and the many. Historically, both solipsistic and transdictive problems were accorded *fideistic* resolutions and philosophy was set on the transmutation path through irrationalism to superidealism *or* critical realism. Both internally antinomic problem-fields, constituted by duplicitous anthroporealist exchanges, most notably of thought and things, necessitated the generation of a new transcendent, traditionally God, now social convention or some other surrogate for the missing term of 'ontological stratification' (the effect of 'primal squeeze' of the unholy trinity of C2.6) and the resultant incapacity to generate a concept of *alethic truth*. Together the *anthroporealism* (i.e. anthropocentrism and anthropomorphism) and the *new transcendent* constitute an *irrealist ensemble* and ineluctably require in practice a *Tina compromise form*. The whole problem-field was sustained in the discipline of philosophy by an *unserious scepticism*. It has now paved the way for an *irrealist irrationalism*, or a neo-positivist backlash. These are the contestants in contemporary science-oriented philosophy.

What is its pathology? An irrealist denial of the independent existence and transfactual efficacy of things coincides in equivocal plasticity with the reification of facts and their conjunctions. There is another missing term here: the absence of transitive science as *labour* or work which, in the context of the TMSA, could have made it clear why science must be understood as a process of *transformative negation*. This merely masked the tacit sociological individualism, in profound resonance with the ontological atomism of what we can designate as a *theory problem-field solution set*. But the primary absence *necessary* for that exercise was the absence of the concept of absence, and a fortiori of ontological causality generally as absenting change. Instead the uniform, flat, undifferentiated implicit ontology intoned more (and more) of the same, i.e. under some set of descriptions. Once again we find negativity implicit in 1M ontology — here in two respects: qua 'simple' causality, as absenting change and, qua transfactuality, as possibly absent from actuality. So, although the d_r/d_a and $d_{positive}/d_{negative}$ distinctions are not, as I made clear in C2.1, the same, a grasp of absence, negativity and hence dialectic is conceptually necessary for the understanding of causality. What is the historical source of ontological monovalence? It lies in a triple transposition of Plato's:

1. the analysis of statements about non-being into false statements,
2. the analysis of change in terms of difference, and
3. the presupposition of the satisfaction of reference.

In (1) we already see the effects of the epistemic fallacy, traceable, so I have argued, to Eleatic monism. But in (3) as well we observe the sequestration of *existential* questions which is the primary effect of monovalence, as the primary effect of actualist destratification (of the possible and the necessary alike) is the sequestration of *essential* ones. So the generative matrix of subject—object identity theory and its irrationalist sequel is the absence of concepts of work, ontology, structure and absence.

For 1M realism the world is characterized by intransitivity, stratification, transfactuality, multi-tiered depth, emergence (a condition of possibility of agency), multiple control and change. It thus presupposes transformative negation, contradiction, at least partially connected nexuses or fields and reflexively monitoring socialized agents with the causal power to intervene in nature if they wish to do so. The domains of the real, the actual and the empirical are characterized by a fourfold distinction:

(α) they are categorially distinct and ontologically irreducible;

(β) they are normally disjoint or out of phase with one another;

(γ) the activity necessary to align them for epistemic purposes normally involves practical and conceptual distanciation, typically dependent on the past and the exterior; and

(δ) they may possess radically different properties (e.g. in fetishism, mediatization or virtualization they may invert, or otherwise occlude, the properties they purport to describe).

Can we be a little more precise about the chief villain, actualism, and its deductivist and determinist accompaniments? We must first distinguish actualism from the actual. The following senses of actualism can be distinguished:

1. generalized identity theory;
2. the specific Humean theory of causal laws, closely associated with Laplacean or regularity determinism and the linchpin of deductivism as a philosophy of science;
3. reduction of the real, necessary and possible to the domain of the manifest, evident or apparent, the most obvious sense in Hegel;
4. reduction of structures and generative mechanisms to events or states of affairs, of change to difference, and difference to generality;
5. the eternal, qua universal-and-necessarily-certain, the sense most evident in Aristotle;

6. strictly a blockist corollary of actualism, the absence of an open future.

The concept of the actual as an instance of the necessary, possible or universal, divorced from actualism, is unobjectionable.

Now in a world of open systems, actualism in any of senses (1)–(6) must split and detotalize itself. For consider (2), the actual cannot be both universal and empirical: universality can be retained but then empirical regularity must go, or empirical regularity can be accepted but then universality is lost. *The actual is necessarily divided against itself.* The world cannot be both law-governed or necessary *and* actual. Similarly in open systems, actualist philosophy can be saved but only at the expense of science; or science can be retained but only if actualist philosophy is jettisoned. There are similar dilemmas in the cases of determinism and blockism and the concept of the actual as an instance of the possible.

Let us pursue the track. Deductivism is unobjectionable if it specifies the deducibility of a transfactually efficacious tendency, but it is false and pernicious if applied actualistically outside a few experimentally or locally (e.g. astronomically) spatio-temporally closed contexts. Again determinism is unobjectionable if it implies only that there must be reasons for changes and differences (ubiquity determinism), but it is totally unacceptable if it is taken, as it normally is, in an actualist sense, to imply that because an event happened (or, including blockism, will happen) it was bound, in the sense of predetermined, to happen before it was (or will be) caused to happen by the particular matrix or conjuncture of mechanisms, agencies and circumstances which caused it. This is to conflate epistemological predeterminism and ontological determination. The case against determinism, as conventionally understood, can be backed up by two other considerations. Relations of natural generation are not, as a general rule, logically transitive. Thus it is not the case that because S_1 produced S_2 and S_2 produced S_3 that S_1 produced S_3 — if, for example, S_2 possessed emergent powers (see C2.2) or the system in which S_3 is formed is open or if some of the processes at work are stochastic. The development of catastrophe and chaos theory has dealt another blow to regularity determinism, illustrating that non-linear dynamic systems can yield highly irregular (chaotic and unpredictable) results. Closely associated with this ensemble of theories is reductionism. Two instances may be taken. In physics it is not the case that we must stop the in principle indefinite regress of strata at the point where our technological equipment, or *Umwelt*, is affected by the unknown substrate: that is to say, there is no need for a positivistic interpretation of contemporary physics. Even if we never succeed in penetrating the barrier imposed by the complex of the latest scientific technology and nature, that there is an ontological cause for an epistemically repeatable result is a presupposition of science and a realist exegesis of the more fundamental than actualized particles or fields is satisfied, even if it consists only in the constellational, dispositional or rhythmic identity of a thing with its possibly changing, possibly exercising, causal powers and tendencies. Reductionism has plagued the human sciences but so long as absentive agency exists it will not replace the question of what is to be done. For this is a *decision* which has to be taken in the intentional intrinsic stream of social life, which can never be replaced, although it may be informed, by our knowledge of substantial extrinsic constraints. Even the deduction of the intrinsic from the extrinsic would be an intentional task that could not be substituted.

1M problems of philosophy typically turn on the destratification of knowledge. The archetypal problem for explanatory knowledge is, of course, the problem of induction, only a special case of the much wider transdictive complex, as the archetypal problem of taxonomic knowledge is the problem of universals, which can be subjected to a similar generalization. But we must include within this group the twentieth-century self-referential and the Platonic self-predicative paradoxes, the set-theoretic paradoxes and the paradoxes of material implication. These will be systematically investigated in C4.2. In all these cases the solution is provided by an alethic concept of truth. It provides a reason distinct from, but explanatory of, the fact that all metals conduct electricity (namely in virtue of their possession of a free electron), that Socrates is a mortal, that water tends to boil at 100 degrees centrigrade, that the pen with which I am writing is blue (it reflects light of the wavelength of 4400Å), that if I took a walk now I would get wet. In all these cases what is required is not deductive generalization (alone), but the introduction of a new explanatory concept and principle, reflecting a new and deeper level of reality, typically driven by the ongoing dialectic of science from manifest appearance at a base level to essential (and/or totalizing) structure *at the level which explains it*. Almost all the conventional problems of philosophy can be attributed to the lack of the concept of alethic truth and the social dynamics which enables us to discover it, as I will show in *Plato Etcetera*. The result of the failure to sustain ontological stratification is vulnerability to immanent critique, T/P inconsistency, dc', and, as I shall show, dr', detotalization, split, Tina compromise formation, repression (Diderot's Syndrome), grafting, the invocation of metaphysical λ clauses, etc.

Dialectics of 1M are typically dialectics of superstructuration, stratification and emergence. Specific examples are the dialectics of mechanisms and events and structure and agency which play so large a part in real geo-history. Then there is the dialectic of the real and the actual which occurs in emergence; or of wants and needs which occurs in subjective learning processes and will play a role in the dialectic of freedom; of figure and ground which occurs in perception, reference and perspectival switches (which can also be used to highlight the plight of a marginalized minority — or majority); and of form to content, of which we have already had a foretaste in §2 and will be fully developed in §10; of identity-in-difference and of radical alterity; the dialectic of depth-stratification; of juxtaposition and chiasmus, or the dialectic of simple and complex. Then there is the epistemological dialectic in science itself and with it a dialectic of explanatory and taxonomic knowledge, of natural necessity and natural kinds; of dialectical reason (dr') and dialectical ground (dg'); of truth; of abstract and concrete (or concretion); of incompleteness and inconsistency, of metaphor and metonymy, of displacement and condensation; of signifier and trace. Metacritically we have dialectics of stasis, glaceation; of homology, vicious circle and endless regress; of reification, fetishism and hypostatization, reflecting or doubling the *dynamic* of commodification. Here we also have ideologies of de-agentification, of the impotent and the empty, of radically decentred and fragmented selves. This is in fact the net effect of anthropism: de-agentification. A dialectic of liberation would essentially depend on a dialectic of recentrification and re-empowerment; a dialectic from anthropocentricity to humanism, involving all the moments of dialectical critical realism from 1M to 4D. This is not the last paradoxical *reversal* that we will find in the dialectics of critical realism. But the theoretical key metacritical dialectic here must be the dialectic of illicit fusion, cloaked by the epistemic fallacy, spawning subject–object identity theory and its generalized form, actualism. This involves the illicit equilibrating exchange of non-equivalents, thoughts and things, including the reciprocal ontic fallacy, some of the effects of which I traced in C2.10 and more of which will be investigated in C4. This, generating duals, complements and inverses, necessitates consideration of the ways of dealing with the splits, which we have seen, as in the case of actualism, inevitably arise. Repression can result either in symptom-formation, or in the generation of a Tina compromise (the most system-syntonic response) or in an alienating, detotalizing split-off, as for instance in the compartmentalizing devices of relevance theorists or, to take a diametrically different case, the delusions of the unhappy consciousness. Close to this are the dialectics of supplementarity and grafting, virtualization and hyperreality. But on this tendentially postmodernist note we must take our leave of the 1M realm of non-identity and repair to the heartland of dialectic itself: the sphere of 2E — negativity.

§ 5 2E Realism: Negativity

Negativity is the motive of all dialectics, including Hegel's analytic reinstatement in dialectical connection and that of critical realism's dialectic of desire to freedom. It is the single most important category, more general than negation because it spans charge or force, the consciousness which isolates a positive lack, the absent without a present or positive; it connotes more directly the negating process whereas negation suggests merely the outcome or result. Negativity embraces the *dual* senses of the (evaluatively neutral) *absence* and the (pejorative) *ill*, united in dialectical critical realist explanatory critique, the aim of which is precisely to *absent ills*, underlying which is the metatheorem that *ills*, which can always be seen as *absences*,* are *constraints*, and that *to change is to cause is to absent* (that is, that changes are absentings), and which forms the backbone of the C2.10 real definition of dialectic as absenting constraints on absenting ills (or absences) — or, in effect, *the axiology of freedom*. But in dealing with negativity we are also taking on board figures like the hiatus, the margin, the void, the hidden, the empty, the anterior, the exterior, the excluded, the omitted, the forgotten and the feared. Some senses of to negate were mentioned in C1.3. Here we can list, with specifically philosophical implications in mind: to absent, to constrain, to condemn, to injure, to refine, to qualify (cf. Aristotle), to limit (cf. Kant), to cancel, to suspend, to undo, to erase, (notoriously) to nihilate, to annihilate; and more technically to mediate, transform, contradict, marginalize, sunder and void.

Systematically I have argued that real > transformative > radical > linear negation, concepts which all possess (a) an epistemological/ ontological, (b) a transfactual/actual and (c) a determinate/ indeterminate ambiguity; and that the concept of real negation has a fourfold polysemy with its social paradigm comprised by geo-historical-processes-in-product-in-processes, revealing not just their

---

* Thus illness can be conceived as the absence of health (e.g. on a notional or actual graduated scale) — and, linking with the 3L realm of totality, health can be explicated in terms of the concept of a functioning whole, so that a disease, or even an un-ease, is a detotalization. In the same way poverty can be understood as consisting in or entailing an absolutely or relatively inadequate standard of living.

causal formation by, but the constitutive dependencies of entities and relations on, their past and their outside. But one can add further organizing mediations (such as the fourfold polysemy of radical negation recursively embedded within the fourfold polysemy of real negation [cf. C2.6]). Both of these stem from the bipolarity of negation as absence and absenting. Thus negativity is systematically connected with *space-time*, and negation with geo-history — a connection to be explored in the next section. So transformative negation can be endogenously or exogenously generated, transfactually efficacious, rhythmically exercised, holistically mediated, stretched out and/or split off, agent-dependent or not. Negativity is also systematically connected in its pejorative sense with critique and criticism, as I shall briefly indicate below and more fully elaborate in §7.

Let us begin with some of the things we have established so far. A transcendental deduction of real negation was issued in C1.3. It was established in C2.1 that real non-being exists (so that we have ontology > ontics > de-onts); and that absence refers. At this point I want to re-emphasize, contra Sartre, that the category of negation is no more animistic or anthropic than the physical concept of force. Whether a being is absent in some context-level-specific region of space-time is irrespective of its humanity. I argued for the ontological priority of non-being over being on a number of grounds including, inter alia, that in a totally compacted space, i.e. a space without spaces, material objects such as corpuscles could not move, so that the Cartesian-Newtonian paradigm of action is fatally flawed. Voids are necessary for motion, and motion necessary for causality and hence change over time (transformation) but motion or substance is not conceptually necessary for voids, although it is, of course, necessary for their human identification.* Contrary to almost all philosophers, although the Heideggerian question has a certain piquancy for me, in that I argue negative without positive being is possible but the contrary is not the case, I am not primarily concerned with nothing or nothingness, but with *real determinate non-being*, the concept of which Hegel, Heidegger and even Sartre fail to develop. And my base concept of non-being is absence, *the simplest and most elemental concept of all*. It is easy enough to see that any world containing change must contain absence. And not to conceive agency as absenting is to reify the agent and detotalize her from the system in which she acts. Moreover, insofar as all transcendental arguments turn on agency (including Kant's original one, once one rejects an

---

* This argument applies only to material objects. Fields, potentials and forces may be continuous but classical concepts of density and compactness do not apply to them.

impossible empiricist account of experience), all transcendental argument must be seen to presuppose the category of absence. Even more simply, a sentence without absences, pauses or spaces, would be unintelligible. Thus absence is a condition of any intelligibility at all.

The slogan which has dominated nineteenth- and twentieth-century discussion of the concept of negation is Hegel's famous inversion of Spinoza to produce the formula 'all negation is determination'. But this is simply not true. There are three main objections to it. In the first instance we have to distinguish logical from (real) natural (including dialectical) negation and connectedly (a) epistemological from ontological determination and (b) definition from determination proper (all of which Hegel elides). Second, we need to appreciate the simple facts that (i) some negation, like that at work in unresolved contradictions (an uninstantiated concept for Hegel in his endist [Mark II] incarnation), is *indeterminate* in outcome and that (ii) even those which are in process of resolution (e.g. at the moment between the σ and τ transforms in the Hegelian epistemological dialectic) possess a time of indeterminacy. Third, contrary to linear Hegelian autogenetics, most results are *multiply* (whether radically or not) determined including codetermination by a host of contingencies, whose constellational necessity for Hegel does not transcend their causal impact. It is in fact far more interesting to take the Spinozan equation. Thus, *definitionally*, we can say that things are defined by what they exclude (this is not quite true, as intra-activity attests) or, better, by their differences, or, even better, by their position within the system of changing differentiations and differentiating changes. And, taking *determination* proper, all determination is negation can be understood as asserting the *negativity of causality*. *To cause is to change is to absent is to transform and so redetermine.* Causation is absenting. And we can develop a 1M−4D *causal chain*. The dynamization, which is also the spatialization, of causality begins with the concept of the transfactual efficacy of the generative mechanism or the causal powers of a structure (1M). It is continued in the notion of the rhythmic exercise of that tendency in some more or less determinate and more or less mediated field (2E). The processualized and mediated tendency may now be bound into an intra-active totality at work in holistic causality, multiply reflected and interiorized and exteriorized at both margins of inquiry (3L). The, or an, eventual result of the initial structural efficacy may be dependent, in the human sphere, upon the conceptualized absenting agency or praxis of embodied persons in the four-planar (cf. C2.9) context of social life (4D). So we have the result that *negativity* is the *hub* not only of existence but also of *causality*. Quite simply, to cause is to absent.

It is sometimes said, e.g. by Istvan Mészáros, that there is a mutual dependency of the positive and the negative.[20] In a continuing, e.g. social, process this is true in that determinate transformative negation depends upon positive (social and natural) material resources and structures and issues in a more or less determinate outcome. But once more the *priority* of the negative over the positive asserts itself: (a) when we situate this process as a *process*, it then appears as the negation of the negation, i.e. the geo-historical transformation of geo-historical products, and (b) when we remember that the positive is radically *constituted* by the negative qua formative process and the presence of the absent in the guise of the past and outside, this apparent duality is dependent upon a negatively charged asymmetry, in which, especially if we employ a distanciated concept of spatio-temporality (so as to incorporate the dialectics of co-inclusion), so that there remains in the negative in the positive in addition a further negative residue or trace structure, an absent in a present, never co-identical with itself. Hegel was fond of saying that the essence of dialectic was seeing the positive in the negative, and in his dialectic of reconciliation this is indeed so.* For us, it is more correct to say that it is to see *the negative in the positive*, the absent in the present, the ground in the figure, the periphery in the centre, the content obscured by the form, the living masked by the dead. The same writer's other point about the dependency of the logical primitives of saying 'yes' and saying 'no' (neustic ticks and crosses) upon material processes of formation is more solidly grounded.

In this book I have been systematically exploring a variety of concepts and connections unified around the notion of absence. We have considered subject and developmental negation, the tri-unity of space, time and causality, rhythmic process, the critique of both fixism and fluxism and the situation of the metacritical limits within which we must act. We have noted the very different concepts of contradiction employed by Hegel and Marx, and traced the interrelation between the concepts of connection, constraint, struggle, critique, T/P inconsistency, detotalization (alienation and split) and transformative praxis. We have considered problematic axiological choice situations, the pervasive mediation of the future and present by the past and outside, the co-incidence of identity and change and of identity and difference, polar oppositions such as those

---

* Brecht caught the flavour of this well: 'The best school for the dialectic is emigration. The keenest dialecticians are refugees. They are refugees because of changes and they study nothing other than changes . . . . If their enemies triumph, they calculate how much the victory has cost, and they have a sharp eye for the contradictions. The dialectic, may it always flourish.'[21]

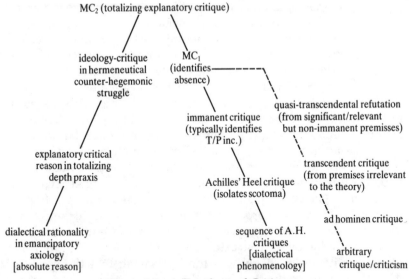

MC₂ (totalizing explanatory critique)

ideology-critique
in hermeneutical
counter-hegemonic
struggle

MC₁
(identifies ──── ─── ─── ───┐
absence)
          quasi-transcendental refutation
          (from significant/relevant
          but non-immanent premisses)

immanent critique
(typically identifies
T/P inc.)

transcendent critique
(from premises irrelevant
to the theory)

explanatory critical
reason in totalizing
depth praxis

Achilles' Heel critique
(isolates scotoma)

ad hominen critique

dialectical rationality
in emancipatory
axiology
[absolute reason]

sequence of A.H.
critiques
[dialectical
phenomenology]

arbitrary
critique/criticism

Figure 3.3   A Topology of Critiques

involved in discursively moralized power₂ relations, and in C2.10 I showed the unification of 2E categories around real negation and of dialectic around 2E. All of this could be summed up by saying that in dialectical critical realism *the negative constellationally over-reaches the positive*. In this chapter we are going to examine dialectics of desire, critique and freedom. In the dialectic of freedom *explanatory critique* plays a crucial role. In Figure 3.3 I sketch a topology of critiques. All the critiques depicted result, if successful, in showing T/P inconsistencies, splits and detotalizations, but it is clear some are more powerful and significant in their upshot than others. In the social world praxis is typically dependent upon wants, which are rationally assessable, causally efficacious beliefs, dependent upon a conative component which is most radically captured by the concept of *desire*. Although desire is not necessary for absence, absence is paradigmatically a condition for desire.

In this chapter I have already noted the connection between desire and referential detachment and so existential intransitivity and, by a more circuitous route, transfactual efficacy. In any event, desire presupposes an absence, viz. of the intentional object, in Brentano's sense, of the desired. Ceteris paribus, this presupposes a meta-desire to remove any constraints (including those constraints₂ which derive from oppressive power₂ relations) on its satisfaction. And thence we derive a series of meta-meta desires, only two of which I will mention here. (1) To absent constraints on the satisfaction of the desire and thus, mutatis mutandis, the power$_2$ relations from which any such constraints might flow; and thus, by the logic of dialectical universalizability, as I will show in §7 below, the totality of power$_2$ (master−slave-type) relations. (2) To acquire the practical knowledge how to absent the sequence of constraints. And this generates a conatus to knowledge, or the mediation of wants by the reality principle, cognitized as alethic truth, which paves the way for the dialectic of freedom, to be articulated in §10, which radically extends, generalizes and deepens the dialectics of mutual forgiveness in Hegel (which includes forgiveness about the persistence of master−slave relations) and that of de-alienation in Marx respectively (cf. C4.5). But desire includes the famous desire to be desired which the Hegel of 1806, but not of 1796, glossed as a desire for recognition. The younger Hegel had been explicit that *desire*, in love, includes *the desire to be desired*, and loved, and that this drive incorporates the desire to be united with the loved one — a paramorph for the desire for *de-alienation*, that is, for the restoration, perhaps in a much more complex and differentiated totality, of the unity between the agent and everything essential to her nature (i.e. from the standpoint of totality, a part of herself). What is not usually taken into account is that the Hegelian life-and-death struggle is between two of the *same kind*, i.e. under the same description (not, say, between man and beast), and this is already susceptible to a dialectical critical deepening, even in its own terms. For to say of two strugglers that, prior to the outcome of their struggle, they are of the same kind is, ab initio, to grant them the same rights, equities and freedoms.

Negativity, and 2E generally, is involved in all dialectics, not only those specific to critical realism. Thus alongside dialectics of critique, we have the absenting of errors involved in dialectics conceived as argument. As transformative praxis consists in transformative negation the dialectics of 2E can subsume and unify the dialectics of 4D. Thus we have here the dialectics of interchange and reversal, of hegemonic/counter-hegemonic struggle, of position and manoeuvre, of structural and conjunctural inversion presaging the abolition or restoration of power$_2$ relations, of all the modalities of ideological conflict. 2E has a particular connection with the dialectics of node, frontier, transition and change, of process and spatio-temporal rhythmic, the dialectics of spatio-temporality generally, and those of development and directionality; of subjectivity and sociality, self and solidarity and, as we have just seen, of desire, critique and freedom; in short, with everything encompassing our transformative negation including praxis, from the dialectics of problematic axiological choice situations to the dialectics of the excluded and the marginalized, of power$_2$ relations generally, of their reversal and abolition, and of emancipation. Within the field of 2E lie dialectics of dislocation and distanciation, decay, delay and lag, disjuncture and constitutive geo-history, differential rhythmics and deposited residues. Foremost among 2E dialectics must be the dialectics of generative separation producing the fivefold alienation of the immediate producer from her product and the four planes constituting social life, the splits, detotalizations and fragmentations that result, hopefully to be transcended in a recentrification of the marginalized majority and the TTTT agency, informed by a totalizing depth praxis, resulting in a dialectical unity-in-diversity. Metacritically, the omissive critique, and thus the very concept of metacritique itself, turns on the identification and elimination of relevant and significant absences, which must be extended to incorporate the kind of 'shortfall' identifiable in Hegel's own dialectic of freedom. But 2E plays a role in *all* dialectics, from the simple dialectic of

absence → alterity → detotalization → de-agentification
or disembodiment

to those of the most complex partial totalities that is the stuff of real geo-history.

What problems of philosophy are associated with 2E? Those that stem from the positivization, which includes the uniformalization and lack of positionality, of being, i.e. ontological monovalence. These include those paradoxes (such as those involved in problematic axiological choice situations) that arise when the deeply unserious scepticism of the academy gives way to the so-called 'real' problems of philosophy. When, for example, we have to stand Tyndall's famous criterion on its head and ask whether we can continue to accept our imagination. Indeed, a crisis point in philosophy could be defined as one in which scepticism became real. Thus at the point of change in an ultimata or some emergent entity we have real occurrences of the problem of induction. Such crisis points can vary from the state of affairs in late scholasticism when everything possessed its own quiddity (and reality was overdifferentiated) to the situation just described when induction breaks down, when the course of nature (on the epistemic fallacy, easily identified with intellectual conformity) changes, i.e. when one and the same entity manifests changing causal powers, when we have to talk about the co-incidence of identity and change, or at its spatial analogue, the boundary, the co-incidence of identity and difference (just as the principle of individuation breaks down, in the field of 3L, when two or more entities of the same kind occupy the same region of space and time, in contexts of intra-activity). The absence of an intransitive dimension makes it impossible to rationally think intellectual change, and this is what happened when the implications of relativity theory and quantum mechanics seeped through into philosophy. The TD/ID distinction depends upon absence qua sheer alterity (as totality depends upon the absence of omissions and agency upon the absence of disempowered negating agency, i.e. de-agentification); and incorporation of epistemic relativity depends upon the notions of transformative negation and absenting process. At the ontic level, the collapse of absolutist concepts of space and time and the concomitant notion of radically divergent world-lines and of the assumption of the independence of position and momentum in what is in effect contextual intra-action are readily accommodatable within a dialectical critical realist framework, whether they should prove to be scientifically tenable in the long run or not.

However, if there is a problem that dominates 2E it is the problem of opposites. In the dirempt world of early modernity and the sundered intellectual climate deriving from Kant's multiple dichotomies, Hegel was obsessed by this problem. Indeed, philosophically his main motive was to close the Kantian subject—object gap (cf. *The Phenomenology of Spirit*) and to generate content from form alone (cf. *The Science of Logic*) as Kant had tried to do in ethics (in the categorical imperative). Under the spell of the principle of the identity of exclusive opposites, it seemed to him that one could only go from A to something other than A* in a purely ex ante autogenetics of form from content if one asserted −A, thus its opposite (contrary), so generating a (logical) contradiction, which could then be resolved (in a process which involved the transmutation of the positive contraries into negative sub-contraries, whence they were to be retained as negative presences in a cumulative memory store), in an imaginary or real sublation of speculative reason. From Hegel's analysis there has arisen the superstition that contradiction depends upon the generation of a multiplicity out of an original unity,[23] but, as I have tried to show in C2.3, the reverse is more the case in at least genuine dialectical contradictions. These depend upon dialectical connections i.e. inseparable but distinct (and therefore multiple) elements. Once more monism rears its head.

---

* Incidentally Hegel accepted the Platonic analysis of change in terms of difference, as does Smith in an otherwise excellent exegesis of Marx's presentational dialectics.[22]

But is there a genuine problem of opposites? Richard Norman has argued, in a variety of publications,[24] that there is and it turns around the historical confrontation between reductionism and dualism. In some cases, such as the society−nature,[25] reason−cause and mind−body problems, there is a clear dialectical critical realist mechanism which resolves it turning on an emergent powers materialism, which is a figure of (materialist) constellational identity (e.g. society is contained within but over-reached by nature from which it is emergent and onto which it reacts[26]). And I think this links up with a double polemic that Marx and Engels waged: on the one hand, against dualistic idealism, and on the other, against contemplative (in Marx) or vulgar (in Engels) reductionist materialism (e.g. of theory to experience or society to nature).* Now in some cases a mediating position seems, if one can put it this way, immediately correct. But in what sense is human agency contained within social structure or vice versa? This is a case of a hiatus in a duality. But there is no reason not to combine this figure with that of constellationality, as in the duality of practical and theoretical reason within the constellational coherence of theory and practice within practice. Or in the case of social structure and human agency, to consider the hiatus as necessitating the constellational *dislocated* duality of social structure and human agency (within the overall concepts of four-planar social being). Does the stratification of the world tell against this form of resolution? The world is multiply stratified and its strata are real. Desks aren't particles. But they are contained *within* the level of particles, and the figure of constellational identity, and in a changing world of dispositional and rhythmic identities too. If there is a real problem of opposites it is surely a function of discursively moralized power$_2$ relations of oppression, exploitation, domination and control (reflecting the Hegelian oppositional or coupled logic of essence), no less apparent today than in the self-divided world at the dawn of modernity which were expressed in Kantian dichotomies and which Hegel tried to overcome transfiguratively.

I have argued against Hegel's conflation of logical and natural necessity and negation. But it might be claimed that my own thesis of the quasi-propositionality (belief-expressive) character of acts threatens to do the same thing, and in particular undermine my distinction between logical and dialectical contradiction. The answer to this is fourfold:

---

* This cannot be too closely linked to the dispute between subjectivism and objectivism as collective voluntarism or objective empiricism, for example, are possible and not infrequent.

1. The quasi-propositionality may allow us to identify, in the context of a dialectical contradiction, a T/P inconsistency, but this is still not the same (necessarily) as a logical contradiction unless the dialectical contradiction was an epistemological one or otherwise immediately involved in theory/theory contradiction.

2. The distinction between theoretical and practical reason, and theory and practice, is not abolished by their duality. There is still a difference between changing our beliefs about the world and changing the world.

3. Even if axiological underdermination flows from T/P inconsistency this does not mean either (a) that there are no rational criteria for action or (b) that in a world without T/P inconsistency axiology will be determined, as distinct from autonomous. T/P consistency leaves options open. A world without T/P inconsistency would not be, as the Stoic-Spinozan-Hegelian tradition has thought, a (rationally) determined one. It would be *open* and up to the agents to do what they wanted within their causal powers.

4. By the same token, where there is either logical or T/P contradiction and axiological underdetermination results, this does not leave us bereft of criteria. Consider an epistemological dialectic. We may have good reasons for knowing whether the non-actualization of an instance under apparently closed conditions gives genuine grounds for non-falsification of a hypothesis or not. Or we may come to a favourable decision on a research programme in which its cognitive capacities and the possibilities were already well proved, e.g. by legitimating the deduction of a more significant set of tendencies or results (i.e. attaining their alethic truth) than that of competing programmes.

Is there a dialectically compelling order of presenting the main theses of 2E? One could go about it in a different way from the one in which I have presented it, or the sequential ordering I posited in C2.10. Thus one could start by criticizing the Platonic analysis of change in terms of difference. Then one could show, with an intransitive realm already established, that the presupposition of change is real negation, easily exemplified by non-existential proofs in science. This introduces the theme of process (to which I come in the next section) and also takes us on to look at the illicit fusion which generates the esoteric anthroporealist exchanges of the irrealist ensemble and the Tina compromise form that results. This would lead us, on the one hand, to the metacritical voids that saturate irrealism and, on the other, to the subjective deduction of the underlying model of man (sic) in a totalizing metacritique of the logic of commodification, grounded in generative separation, and the totality of power$_2$ relations with which it is conjuncturally or epochally intertwined.

All the categories of 2E can, however, be derived from absence. It might, however, be doubted whether this is in fact the case. For have I not argued that dialectical contradictions presuppose dialectical connections? But this is to take dialectic very undialectically. For I have argued that one can get from absence to structures, and thence it is an easy step to derive dialectical connection and thus contradiction too.* Moreover, the basic categories of 1M−4D can also be all derived from absence. To illustrate the latter: 1M can be derived from absence in the form of desire (referential detachment) or distance (alterity), or, if some licence is allowed, from the absence of actualism. 3L can be derived from the absence of absence, with detotalization the result of the presence of an absence, or the absence of a presence (including a causal connection). 4D can be derived from the absenting of absence which is agency.

Constellationality, which resolves the problem of opposition, is a 3L figure of totality. One can show how these 'problems', such as that of subject and object, which are resolved in the domain of totality, arise from identity theory. More generally we can follow up the argument of C2.10 by tracing the implications of the congealing solidification of the analytic problematic flowing from subject−object identity theory (see p. 192, Figure 2.39). Let us see how identity theories spawn each other as a prelude to a possible integration of the valid insights of non-identity theories under the umbrella of dialectical critical realist 1M non-identity. It will be remembered that subject−object identity theory (1), covered by the epistemic fallacy, generates the epistemo-onto-logicization of being (2), against which I railed in C2 enough. This immediately generates the reciprocating 'ontic fallacy', and what I called, following Adorno, identity-thinking, generating Butler's principle of self-identity (4) which in its wake gives rise to various Tina compromise formations (5), connections and defence mechanisms, together with aporiai, antinomies, T/P inconsistency, detotalizations and splits, as depicted in Figure 3.4. The possibilities of (a) token−token, (b) token−type and (c) type−type identity can be considered in this context. Ontologically, if there is a single token, we get a monism (6), if a plurality of tokens then a monodology (6'); at (b) a reductionism (7) which normally, and tendentially$_b$ necessarily, takes the form of an atomism (7'); and at (c) an actualism, or generalized subject−object identity theory (8),

---

* Of course lots of other routes are possible. For instance, absenting separateness totalizes.

so that actualism > reductionism > monism. Epistemologically, (a) implies (9) the presupposition of fixed subjects, in opposition to our category of subject developmental negation and Fischer's contradictio in subjecto. Historically this ultimately derives from the Platonic analysis of predication, and it entails (9′) fixism. (b) in turn implies that the fixed subjects are known, i.e. subsumable under generalizations, entailing cognitive triumphalism (10). At (c) these

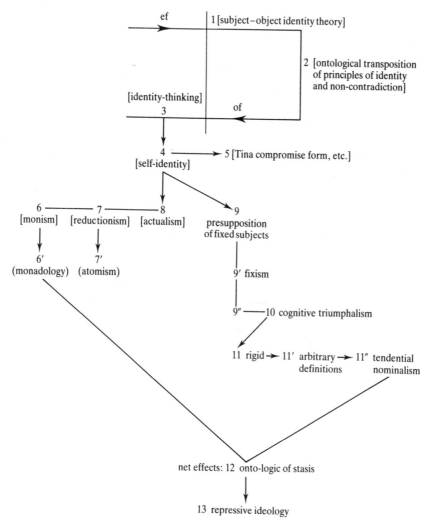

Figure 3.4 Consequences and Mechanisms of Identity Theory

fixed subjects are known in terms of rigidly, and hence arbitrarily, defined terms (11). This, of course, renders conceptual, and the accommodation of ontic, change impossible, in what is in effect the return of the Eleatic one, reflecting the illicit but primal con-fusion of (2). It is obvious that the effect of the (1)−(11) (theory problem-field) solution set is *stasis* (12), which, in the context of existing power$_2$ relations, identifies it as a *repressive ideology* (13). The presupposition of fixed subjects has been the subject of independent critiques by Hegel, Adorno and Derrida. Hegel objects to it on the grounds of the principle of the identity and difference in identity in his spiritual constellational monism. But we have seen that the result of his unprincipled use of this principle results in a form of stasis as congealing as that of the analytic problematic. Adorno warns, by contrast, that the whole project of reducing subject to object or vice versa is fundamentally mistaken. But it seems intuitively, scientifically and philosophically unsatisfying and indeed refutable not to see subjectivity as grounded in *some sense*, or over-reached, by objectivity, if only in a meta-reflexive totalizing sitution of the couple. Derrida argues for the inversion, where there is a priority of object to subject (or, in principle, vice versa), chiasmus and erasure of the pair. But apart from his welcome disrespect for tradition, there is, as I have already argued, nothing to be said for erasure as a solution to philosophical problems. After displaying the spatio-temporality and explanatory critical aspects of 2E, we can then take a retrospective glance at 1M non-identity in the context of totality to see if, in §8, we can do any better than Hegel, Adorno or Derrida.

2E not only unifies but itself satisfies all the moments of dialectical critical realism. It is stratified in a hierarchy of concepts, grounded in absence. It is dynamic in its essence (real negation is absenting process). It is totalizing in that it coheres the system as a whole. And it is transformative, in that it includes transformative praxis understood as absenting absentive agency, oriented to change. It is the dialectical moment par excellence.

§ 6 Space, Time and Tense

A full treatment of the subject-matter of this section would require a book of its own. Instead of that let me begin it by listing some of the topics either already, or about to be, broached in this book, bearing in mind that dialectical critical realism extends realism about existence and causality to spatio-temporality, and specifically to realism about tensed spatializing process:

1. (A) the reality and (B) the non-anthropocentricity of space, time and tense and process.
2. The transcendental deduction of tense, and process.
3. The nature of past, present and future.
4. (a) The necessity for MacTaggart's 'A series', in which events, etc. are related as past, present and future (cf. 2) and;
   (b) its irreducibility to MacTaggart's 'B series', in which events are compared as earlier than, simultaneous with or later than.
5. The irreversibility of time, and its connection with associated asymmetries, and the phenomena of directionality.
6. The connection between causality and process, the character of rhythmics and the tri-unity of space, time and causality.
7. The fivefold character of space-time.
8. The two types of emergent spatio-temporalities and the phenomena they make possible, including the four modes of the presence of the past and the presence of the future as mediated by the past and the outside; and the problems they raise, e.g. of loco-periodization.
9. The dialectical character of time and of space.
10. The implications of the bipolarity of absence (as process and product) and of its fourfold polysemy.
11. The phenomena of historicity (and geographicity) and the futuricity of praxis.
12. The (a) disembedding and (b) emergence of space from time and vice versa, thematized in particular respect to conditions of late/post-modernity.
13. The critique of irrealism about space, time, tense and process and its connections with irrealism about causality, and even existence.

Space-time has a fivefold character: (a) as a referential grid; (b) as a measure; (c) as a set of (initially) mutual exclusion relations (initially) abstracted from the changes and differences in the network of material things; (d) as a property with causal powers sui generis, which may be transfactual or actual, positive or negative, bound into a totality or not, agentive or not, so that neither space nor time is causally inert (just think of the considerations that go into the location of an engineering plant or the timing of an investment decision); and (e) as a (macroscopically currently entropic) process. The irreversibility of time is established by the impossibility of backwards causation. Antecedence is essential to causality as becoming and is implicit in all transitive action verbs.[27] Moreover, for a power to be exercised it must first be possessed, just as for its exercise to be mediated and/or manifested these must be subsequent, even if only notionally, to its rhythmic exercise, which can be identified with its world-line. The assumption of backwards causation is in fact plausible only on the deprocessualization of causality, in which case the order of a pair or more of events is indifferent to the attribution of causality. The irreversibility of time is profoundly connected with other asymmetries, including the axiological asymmetry, the divergence of world-lines, entropy, the ecological asymmetry, the relational asymmetry, directionality as such and the (constellational) embedding of psychic within social within physical within cosmic space and time. I have argued for the tri-unity of space, time and causality (and will argue for the tri-unity of geography, history and social theory) especially in the notion of the irreversibility of tensed spatializing process, as absenting or negating transformation (or merely distanciation [without change other than in spatio-temporal position]), the efficacy of which I have called its rhythmic. But a rhythmic is not just a mediation which may be mediated, viz. by the other members of the causal chain, which may be aligned to the other moments of both dialectical critical realism and the concrete universal. Aside from actually or potentially possessing causal powers, it may eventuate from the generation, stimulation or release of what I characterized in C2.8 as powers to process (maturate, develop).

Let us get to the heart of the matter: the reality of tense. Now I have argued against indexicalism (ego-present-centrism) and punctualism for non-anthropocentric and distanciated concepts of space-time and against blockism and closure for an unactualized and open future. But in what sense are past, present and future real? The or a or some past is real as existentially intransitively determined and determinate (or fixed in its indeterminacy), whether it is knowable or not. The/a/some present (which is an indefinitely extendable boundary state*) is real as the moment (or, within the moment, the node) of happening. The/a/some future is real as (generally, increasingly) shaped possibility of happening (and of coming to be determined). These are implicit in the descriptions under which we must act as embodied beings, even if it is only to effect or record a measure, and therefore presuppose a change in the system of material things upon which we must act — for to act is to bring about a state of affairs which (unless it were overdetermined) would not otherwise have occurred. Process is inexorable, directional change, which cannot be extruded from the

---

* The exact extension depends on the character of the causal process under way. Is it a shower, a lunch, a cricket match or a revolution?

material world if we are either (α) to sustain the conditions of the intelligibility of our embodied agency (and hence of science, or emergence, or cosmic development) or (β) to avoid the dualistic disembodiment or the de-agentifying reification of our agency, and hence split us from the matter on which we must act. (β) entails the detotalization of the cosmos, unless we are prepared to invoke a miraculous Leibnizian harmony of monads. To put this another way and more generally: if agency *or* absenting *or* transformative change is real, then (a) actualism must be false and (b) process, becoming and tense must be real.

Before — for this is very short — I develop this line of argument let me make it plain that in the transcendental deduction of the A series I am not denying that facts in the A series can be, once known (and hence determined), reported in the B series, suitably mediated if necessary. But to say that an event e_o has happened doesn't *mean* the same as to say that it is earlier than some other event, which is quite consistent with its not having (yet) occurred; unless, that is to say, we are tacitly and ego-present-centrically identifying the second event with our own now. But our now is *not* the only moment of becoming. That way lies indexicalism, and ultimately a solipsistic punctualism, in which we cannot even speak of our past (which, to re-emphasize, is not the only past), causality or ultimately, via the argument for referential detachment, about anything at all. Nor does there lie any joy in a blockist response, for again this elides the distinction between what has yet and has not yet happened, as all events simultaneously co-exist. Neither indexicalists nor blockists can sustain a genuine concept of causality as directional absenting or change. For this we need the concept of tensed spatializing process or rhythmic.

But this takes me directly to the non-anthropocentricity of space, time, tense and process and the causal irrealism involved in any position that denies the irreducibility of the A series to the B series or the reality of tense or process. Ego-present-anthro-centrist (indexicalist) punctualism cannot even sustain the idea of a past on our world-line: the *causes* of the effects we experience are irreal. Blockist closure, on the other hand, holds that the future already exists, having been predetermined (e.g. by the hand of God or in accordance with the empirical regularities of a Humean-Laplacean determinism and actualism). Hence it cannot sustain the idea of a directional *change*, e.g. as the effect of human agency. For indexicalism no time is possible but the present; for blockism there is a conjunctive simultaneity of all times, i.e. there is neither past nor future. In other words neither can sustain a genuine concept of causality. Neither position is compatible with either embodied agency or cosmological theory, which posits a rapidly expanding divergent and, therefore, as yet unmade universe increasingly unknowable for any given state of technology, in which causes bring about qualitative and quantitative changes, that is to say (to be laborious about it), events do not happen before they are caused to occur. Irrealism about tense and process inevitably entails irrealism about causality. But, it might be interspersed here, I have not considered a 'God's-eye' blockist closure of a future which already exists, even though it is in practice and perhaps in principle unknowable to us. For instance, we can certainly in principle and in practice observe other pasts at our present. Hence how do we know that other futures are in principle not observable at our present? Now even if, per impossible (because of the finite speed of light), we could see now at time t_1 on our own world-line, E_w, an event that has not yet occurred on another world-line, Z_w (i.e. that lay in the future for its inhabiting space-time travellers), that does not mean either (a) that the event on Z_w happened (existed) before it occurred, as the blockists postulate, or that it was pre-ordained to take place before it was caused, as the Laplacean determinist would have it; or (b) that time (and with it becoming, process, tense and rhythmics) is not irreducibly real. The confusion comes from illicitly transposing our, viz. E_w's, present onto Z_w, producing paradox, namely that the event is both present with respect to E_w and future with respect to Z_w. The fundamental mistake is to think that my present is the only present, which includes most blockists as well as indexicalists, except that the more sophisticated blockist anthropormorphically transposes his or her own present onto the present of an omniscient being usually called 'God', eternal and outside time. What underlies this failure to come to terms with the implications of relativity theory? It is nothing but ontological monovalence. The past and the future are both *negative*, but in different causal directionalities — one is gone (spatially behind us), the other is ahead (not yet). Moreover, there is nothing ontogenetic about the A series, which would again tie time, causality and existence to my/our/God's existence. The A series and tense are non-anthropically real. Both irrealist positions effect a T/P inconsistency, split or detotalization as a result of the disembodiment or de-agentification of the agent who must act. Blockism presupposes a Laplacean determinism, without the categories of emergence, finitude, novelty, contingency and accident, open systems and negativity in the form of the past and the outside. Moreover, it implies that all events can be uniquely ordered in the A series and it makes the completely unwarranted assumption that space-time is continuous, unique and fixed in spite of the implications of relativity theory. It is not worth commenting further on the solipsistic consequences of indexicalism.

A distinction may be made between reflexive and unreflexive truths. In C2.4 I argued that we were situated within metacritical limits — in a world between the absence and ubiquity of change. This means we have the possibility of a dialectic of reflexive and unreflexive truths. (It does not follow from the fact that a truth is unchanging that it cannot be included in a dialectically [temporally transformative; spatially alteriorizing or distanciating] absenting process, nor need it apply everywhere — its conditions of applicability may be absented.) I argued in C2 that some of the ultimata in our pluriverse must consist in their rhythmic identities with the exercise of their causal powers, and that at nodal points of transition we may have to think the co-incidence of identity and change and/or identity and difference. If geo-history in 'hot' societies has become reflexivey self-monitoring, so that we can talk of the phenomena of historicity (and, indeed, increasingly geographicity), action, as such, is always *futurized* (and localized). The characteristic structure of intentional action can therefore be given by the following formula:

present absence → orientation to future → grounding in the presence of the past → praxis.

Thus to be committed to the existence of space (first implied by the reality of difference) and time (initially entailed by the reality of change) and hence causality* is to be committed to the *reality of process* which may be substantial or non-substantial, i.e. rhythmically traverse level-specific voids or constitute action, including intra-action, at a distance. This last point establishes the difference between geo-history, which must be substantial, and space-time, which need not be. Process is directional absenting, and, in the human world, I have argued that we must think in terms of concepts such as developmental or dialectical *consistency* (cf. §2), referring to the manner in which a result is arrived at (cf. prefiguration in politics) or, at the limit, just the achieved result (e.g. alethic truth in science) — or by analogy with the way in which a caterpillar matures into a butterfly, or an acorn into an oak.

---

* The reader should be reminded here that (1) most causality has both spatial and temporal components, and (2) spatio-temporality has emergent sui generis causal properties, whose spatial and temporal aspects may be independent of, discordant with, and emergent from, each other.

Since all agency is A-serial and a fortiori token-reflexive, something more should be said about the character of the present. The present is the moment of becoming on an agent's world-line, which was becoming when it is in fact in the past, and will be becoming, when it is in the future. The nature of time consciousness implies that the present cannot be punctual, so for the coherence of the event which is perceived it must always be distanciated and open-ended. Just how *much* is a contextual affair, dependent on the nature of the episode concerned (e.g. is it a coffee break, a friendship, a life, or a geographical epoch?). This means that the present is always liable to contain (several) pasts in the manner of the dialectics of co-inclusion. The B series is not token-reflexive. One may want to highlight the changing attribution of the value of the predicate 'true' and, in particular, the intransitivity of tense, by countenancing a (spatio-) temporally indefinite C series, e.g. 'p' was true between $T_i \ldots T_j$ and false between $T_j \ldots T_k$. ('It is raining' was true yesterday but false today.) The famous dispute between Quine and Prior turned precisely on whether one can analyse substantial change in terms of formal difference. It is clear that Prior was right: one cannot. But by the same token one cannot construe substantial difference (alterity) in terms of tensed change. The celebrated Aristotelian aporia of so-called 'future contingents' could have been avoided by recourse to an open-ended C series. We can simply say that even if it is logically necessary that a sea fight either will or will not occur tomorrow (a position against which I have already militated), we do not know which is true (in part because it has not been fully determined).* But Aristotle's blockism led him to the conclusion that, even if it was contingent (a position difficult to reconcile with Aristotle's actualism), its truth must, in some sense, be already fixed, that is to say, blockistically actualized. In which case it could not really be *either* future *or* contingent.

Closely connected with the causal irreducibility and directional asymmetry of space-time are axiological, relational, social and psychological asymmetries, and embedded with the entropy of cosmological time, which is quite consistent with emergent local negentropy, is the ecological asymmetry, the shaping of a part by the whole. Both space and time are many-layered concepts which can be used formally, as Lefebvre does, to define different modalities of space (physical, social, psychological) or employed metaphorically to model epistemic relativity in space-time on physical relativity. In such

---

* This opens up the fascinating vista of a dialectic between reflexive and non-reflexive truths which I cannot go into here.

a case the irreversible character of causal process could provide an analogue of ontological realism, which is in part a homeomorph, considering that causality (or the absence of it) is the most general criterion for ascribing reality to beings. Questions of loco-periodization must be resolved by reference (a) to the purposes of the inquiry, allowing again for perspectival fluidity and variability, and, (b) given these, by the differential explanatory and taxonomic powers of the emergent spatio-temporalized structures, rhythmics or totalities involved.

Space and time may be used not only to designate the difference between distanciation or difference (alterity) and transformation or change, but also to highlight two modes of absence, implicit in, for example, alienation or T/P inconsistency, the mode of *gulf* (in space) and the mode of *split* (in time). Both are clearly prominent features of the contemporary world. I have been deliberately avoiding siding in the battle between those who hold that we are in the epoch of post-modernity and those who hold we are not. It is often said that post-modernity is characterized by the re-emergence of space from its Marxian or Heideggerian eclipse by time for the pre-postmodern period. Certainly the importance of the globalization of commodity production and the spatiality of the city and the spatialization of culture, together with the re-emergence of the thematic of the end of history, cannot be gainsaid any more than the disembedding of space from place. But the flip side of this is the implicit (indexicalist) privileging of the present, and its ideological effect is, as always, the naturalization of a (McDonaldized) status quo, the normalization of the recent past and local customs in the context of increasingly homogenized and commodified 'values' before it can be reflected upon, and the repression of the possibility of future change and absent freedoms. The intersect which is ideology will always try to play off, in a duplicitous complicity of dialectical counterparts, blockist time against indexicalized tense and the politics of space against those of place according to its advantage. But we must resist these inducements. Sociology, geography and history must match the equipoise of causally efficacious rhythmics.

One last word on emergent spatio-temporalities. I have argued for them as either new relata of an existing system of things or else relata of a new system of things; and for overlapping, intersecting, disjoint spatio-temporalities, and thence for the fourfold presence, as distinct from mere dependency, of the past and the outside, viz. as constitutive process, as co-inclusive, as lagged, delayed efficacy and as perspectivally pre-existent structure; and I have argued for the way in which the presence of the future is characteristically embedded in the presence of the past. But one must not forget that in conceptualization time is emergent from space (although concepts, of course, have a physical basis); just as in the most characteristic form of disembedding, mass mediatization, space is effectively emergent from time (although, of course, it depends upon, like everything else, a process).

§ 7 Social Science, Explanatory Critique, Emancipatory Axiology

In C2.9 I argued for a position in the philosophy of the social sciences that I characterize as 'dialectical critical naturalism'. Dialectical critical naturalism posits a series of ontological, epistemological, relational and critical differences between the social sciences and the experimental sciences of nature which mediate and transcend the dichotomy between hypernaturalistic positivism and dualist or syncretic hermeneutics which has split the social sciences since the hermeneutics of Schleiermacher was taken up by Dilthey.[28] In particular it argues (i) that the necessary conceptuality of the subject-matter of social science does not exhaust, and may indeed mask or distort, it in a manner which a critical social science can expose; and (ii) that the existence of unacknowledged conditions, unconscious motivation, tacit skills and unintended consequences afford to the social sciences a putative enlightening role for lay actors. Its transformational model of social activity avoids the twin errors of reification and voluntarism in a dislocated duality of structure and agency, while the relational conception of social life evades the pitfalls of individualism and collectivism alike. A four-planar conception of developing human nature in society, embedded in non-human but partially socialized nature, is composed of the stratification of the personality, material transactions with the physical world, inter-/intra-personal relations and social relations sui generis defining the position-practice system in virtue of which more or less structurally sedimented institutions are causally efficacious (ultimately via past or present human agency which is intentional under some description). The 'social cube' has power, normative and discursive sub-dimensions, which intersect in ideology. Ideology in a strong sense embodies categorial error, but is, at any rate in its broad sense, the site of hermeneutical alongside other struggles over power$_2$ relations of exploitation, domination and control. These relations are in principle subject to tactical or strategic reversal and may be the object of conjunctural suspension or structural abolition.

In §1 I briefly described the way in which dialectical critical realism (which comprises naturalism as a special theory of the social sciences) is committed to a combination of (α) *moral realism* and (β) *ethical naturalism*, which I shall now detail. Its moral realism contends that morality is an objective real property, but the first present (and universalizable) action-guiding character of moral claims and judgements entails that a distinction has to be made between (a) the real transitive-relational moral property, which connotes a position on a set of intra-subjective, inter-subjective, social and social — natural relations; and (b) the intransitive morality of an always already moralized (or a-moralized) world. The distinction between (a) and (b) allows my moral realism to be critical and to sustain the irreducibility of ethics to descriptive sociology. In particular it would be useful to differentiate *descriptive, redescriptive* and *explanatory critical morality* in the transitive (more properly relational, because morality is practical, designating an *action-guiding* relation on or to something) and *actually existing morality* or moralities in the intransitive dimension, and, inter alia, to characterize, taken in combination with (β) my ethical naturalism, the *constitutive morality* of a society as *false* and to demonstrate it, in the manner of an explanatory critical dialectical argument, as a *false* (or limited) *necessity* (cf. C2.6). For my ethical naturalism implies that moral propositions can be *known*; and, in particular, social-scientifically vindicated; so that, contrary to Moore's supposed naturalistic fallacy, there is no unbridgeable gulf between fact and value, or theory and practice. I am going to argue against the conventionally accepted base assumption of [1] the evaluative *neutrality* of social science, not only through the easy demonstration of the evaluative character of its discourse but also through the prima facie more difficult demonstration of the scientific legitimation of values, for [2] the conception of social science as *explanatory critique* and thence to [3] the idea of social science as *emancipatory axiology* and ultimately [4] to a notion of it as *dialectic*. The naturalistic transformation from 'is' to 'ought' — which is not only compatible with, but also *grounds*, the moral realist *irreducibility* of 'ought' to 'is' — that is to say, the transition from *fact to value*, presages the transitions between and dialectics of *theory and practice, form and content, centre to periphery, figure to ground, desire to freedom*, and to the sensitized solidarity of the totalizing depth praxis and the dialectics of de-alienation and emancipation.

Conceptually, the most important thing to appreciate at the outset is that any ill (and indeed, ceteris paribus, any object of practical reasoning) can be looked upon, or dialectically transposed, as an absence, and any absence can be viewed as a constraint. Such constraints include constraints$_2$ and inequities. Such ills may be seen as moral untruths. Thus we have the metatheorem: *ills → absences → constraints* (including *inequities*) → (moral) *falsehoods* → (and, if categorially absurd, I shall write them as 'ideologically†' so). From the standpoint of practical reason inasmuch as they are (i) *unwanted*, (ii) *unnecessary* and (iii) *remediable* or removable, they should be transformatively negated, i.e. *absented*. I shall negatively generalize the concept of constraint, so that there is an *equivocity* of *freedom from* and *freedom to* (and Isaiah Berlin's celebrated distinction appears as two poles of ultimately the one concept). The root conception of freedom with which I shall be working is that of autonomy in the sense of self-determination. Rational autonomy will then incorporate cognitive, empowered and dispositional or motivational aspects. Reason as such may constellationally embrace the disposition to reason, but if the reason concerned is cognitive, then empirically they are distinct items. Conversely human beings may indeed desire to be free, as such and in general, but lack the concrete power and/or knowledge to achieve particular freedoms, say the right to suffrage, literacy or health care. Thus as criteria for rational agency one must

- (α) possess the knowledge to act on one's own real interests (the cognitive requirement);
- (β) be able to access the skill, resources and opportunities to do so (the empowered component); and
- (γ) be disposed to so act (the dispositional or motivational condition).

Of course the 'knowledge' referred to in (α) may be tacit competence, knowledge how rather than propositional knowledge that, practical not discursive.

There are some other matters to clear up before I commence my deduction of [1]−[4]. Moral reasoning is a species of practical reasoning, characterized, inter alia, by the fact that it is (non-uniquely) dialectically, and so specifically transfactually, concretely and actionably, 'binding' and universalizable in form, and that its ultimate object is flourishing human beings-in-nature. Practical reasoning may arise from a failure to satisfy some desire, want or interest. It logically presupposes both a *negative* (proto-)*critique* and a *positive* (proto-)*theory* of how to remedy the situation — an aspect of the duality of theory and critique. To be slightly pedantic for a moment, what is required is clearly to *d*iagnose the problem, *e*xplain it and then take appropriate *a*ction to absent it. This is the *DEA model* of *practical* problem-resolution or *reasoning*. It is important to note that when applied in the sphere of moral reason this has to satisfy a *prefigurative condition* or moment, which stipulates (1) that the action concerned, and the process more generally, do not undermine the end or objective and be as far as possible consistent with it and (2) that, insofar as it is possible, it in some way expresses or embodies the principles or values of the end-state or -process. The DEA model may depend on the exploitation of the RRREI(C) model of applied social scientific explanation, which itself depends on the iterated applications of the DREI(C) model of pure scientific explanation. All this will involve the meta-ethical virtue of *phronesis* or practical wisdom, a virtue that the good applied scientist typically has. Suppose one's objective in a DEA context is normative change, then a simplified praxis would turn on the *d*escription *e*xplanation and *t*ransformation of actually existing morality (the *DET model* of *normative change*), as part of a *totalizing depth praxis* incorporating, inter alia, a posteriori participatory research inquiry (including a detailed and specific analysis, for the conjunctural situation will in general be novel and unique), explanatory critique and concrete utopianism (I will sometimes refer to the conjunct just as the explanatory critical theory†) leading into a theory and practice of transition, including the sensitized solidarity to which I have already referred. There is one final preliminary. I want to differentiate (1) instrumental (including technical), (2) critical, (3) explanatory critical, (4) depth explanatory critical, (5) totalizing depth explanatory critical and (6) dialectical rationality, appended by (7) geo-historical directionality.

It is pretty obvious that social scientific discourse is in fact evaluative, as is the principal reason for it, the value-saturated character of what social scientific discourse is about, so I will not discuss this side of the equation any further here.[29] The value-implicational, rather than the value-impregnated, character of social science is much more interesting. Charles Taylor, John Searle, A.N. Prior, Philippa Foot, Elizabeth Anscombe and many others have all tried to refute 'Hume's law' stipulating 'no ought from an is'. Valuable though their attempts have been, which I have discussed elsewhere,[30] a morally irrevocable refutation of Hume's law has to be from processes that are constitutive of purely factual discourse. Now the subject-matter of social science is composed not just by social objects but by beliefs about social objects, and if such beliefs are false (a judgement which is within the remit of social science), and one can *explain* the *falsity*, then, subject to a ceteris paribus clause, in virtue of

the openness of the social world and the multiplicity of determinations therein, one can move without further ado to a negative
evaluation of the explanans and a positive evaluation of any action
rationally designed to absent it. This is the heart of the missing
transcendental deduction of facts from values. It turns on discovering
the *alethic truth of falsity*, and thus, as should not surprise us, on both
1M ontological stratification and 2E ontological bi-/poly-valency.
Actually there are even simpler transitions, which I shall go into
shortly, but they do not possess comparable diagnostic value and the
immanent critical force of the argument form just advanced. Thus, at
level 2 of critical rationality, to criticize a belief is implicitly to criticize
any action based on or informed by it. But in this case the dialectical
ground (dg') for the criticism and the dialectical reason (dr') for its
falsity is not brought out. Similar considerations apply at the level of
purely technical reason. Notice that even at the level of instrumental
rationality in the context of power$_2$ relations social science — at least
at the degree of alethic truth — is not neutral in its implications for the
oppressor and the oppressed. The oppressed have a direct material
interest in knowledge of these relations that the oppressors do not. Is
this why there is a constant tendency for those in power in times of
(or in revenge for) crisis to repeat the sin against Socrates and
education generally? The real importance of the explanatory critical
derivation of values from facts and practices from theories[31] is that it
can be *generalized* to cover the failure to satisfy other axiological needs,
necessities and interests besides truths, including those which are
necessary conditions for truth, such as basic health, education and
ergonic efficiency.

But an even simpler argument is to hand. For a nominally
descriptive statement has, in virtue of the fourfold character of the
judgement form discussed in §2, the assertorically sensitized
normative fiduciary implication 'act on the basis of it'. It will be
remembered that the four internally related components of the
judgement form are comprised by (a) expressively veracious, (b)
descriptive, (c) evidential and (d) normative-fiduciary aspects.
However, the argument I employed in §2 for assertorically
imperatival sensitized solidarity applies with equal force here. This
immediately takes us into a conception of social science as not only
non-neutral (against [1]) and as implying explanatory critique [2], but
as *emancipatory axiology* [3]. This is through what I will denominate as
the *'ethical tetrapolity'*, which may be expressed as follows:

[axiological commitment implicit in the expressively veracious
moral judgement] → (1) fiduciariness → (2) content of the

explanatory critical theory† complex ↔ (3) totalizing depth praxis of emancipatory axiology → (4) freedom qua universal human emancipation.

The transition from form to content is a logical extension of the transition from fact to value. It may be regarded as spelling out the substance that the fiduciary remark implies, prefiguring a society based on a normative order of trust, just as the totalizing logic of the depth praxis follows from the dialectical universalizability of the (especially the imperatival and evidential) components of the judgement form.

What is the content at (2) which *trust* presupposes? It is the positive *naturalistically* grounded four-planar theory of the desired end-state or -process which encompasses (as the positive to the negative moment) the explanatory critique in the strict sense, which itself must be ultimately naturalistically grounded in a four-planar theory of changing and changeable human nature-in-nature. This latter may be suggested as an exercise in concrete utopianism, postulating an *alternative* to the actually existing state of affairs, incorporating unacknowledged and even hitherto unimagined possibilities for the satisfaction of wanted needs and wanted possibilities for development, grounded in sustainably potentially disposable resources in the context of a different social order. There is no gulf, but a two-way flow, between (2) and (3), which will incorporate a theory and practice of *transition* to a proximate or ultimate objective. As each moment of the judgement form is universalizable in the ways made explicit in §2, i.e. is transfactual, concrete (qua quadruple so as to include rhythmics, mediations and singularities), actionable and transformative, the logic of the ethical tetrapolity will be inexorably totalizing, finding identity through difference and unity in diversity. This is the moment of the dialectic of mutual recognition of, and action in accordance with, shared *contra-central* interests in the fragmented *periphery*, the dialectical perspectival switch from the systemically mediatized (even virtualized) reality of the *figure* to its unseen but dialectical *grounds* (e.g. from capital to the generative separation that sustains it).

So far I have not shown how the ethical tetrapolity encompasses step (4), the goal of universal human emancipation. This I will now rectify. We have the theorem of the dialectical equivalence, or at least transmutability, of ills, absences, constraints, inequities and falsities. Insofar as an ill is unwanted, unneeded and remedial, the spatio-temporal-causal-absenting or real transformative negation of the ill presupposes universalizability to absenting agency in all dialectically similar circumstances. This presupposes in turn the absenting of all similar constraints. And by the inexorable logic of dialectical universalizability, insofar as all constraints are similar *in virtue of their being constraints*, i.e. qua constraints, this presupposes the absenting of all constraints as such, including constraints$_2$ (i.e. the abolition of all master−slave-type relations) and other inequities. And this presupposes in its wake a society oriented to the free development and flourishing of each and all, and of each as a condition for all, that is to say, universal human autonomy as flourishing, the dr_p', the free = the good = the moral alethic society. So the goal of universal human autonomy is implicit in every moral judgement. But, as by a valid transcendental perspective switch, theoretical can be seen under the aspect of practical reason (cf. C2.3), the objective of the eudaimonistic society is contained in every expressively veracious assertoric utterance. Furthermore, in virtue of the quasi-propositional character of every act, it is arguably implicit in every intentional deed. But as the logic is totalizing, and every absence can be seen as a constraint, this goal of universal human autonomy can be regarded as implicit in an infant's primal scream. This argument, however, supplies us with only the *formal* criterion of freedom qua universal human flourishing. The *substantive* criteria have once more to be fleshed out by a *naturalistically grounded* four-planar theory of the possibilities of social being in nature in the direction indicated by the formal criteria. That is to say, by a concretely utopian exercise in social science conceived now as absenting constraints on absenting absences or ills (cf. C2.10); that is, as *dialectic* or the *axiology of freedom* [4]. The formal desiderata are characterized by an orientation to the criterion of *concrete singularity* — truly the key to the realm of freedom — of each and all, and of each as a condition of all, by absolute reason, autonomy and the absence of heterology, that is, each agent is true of, to, in and for herself and every other. As I stressed in C2.10, it requires no Rawlsian veil of ignorance or Habermasian ideal speech situation to justify it. As a check on the validity of the formal criteria one can ask are there any others, which are not contained or sublated by it, which are sincerely universally universalizable? Its converse is marked by susceptibility to immanent critique, dc', T/P inconsistency, heterology, alienation, inequity and oppressive power$_2$ relations. Alethically it would be a normative Tina compromise form. This indeed is our existential now.

Now for some comments on the substance of the ethical tetrapolity. First on steps (2) ↔ (3). This raises, predictably enough, a number of problems. How are the subjects, whom I will call 'subjects$_2$', who are committed to actually existing morality while occupying subaltern poles of discursively moralized power$_2$ relations, to be brought into this dialectic, which I have hitherto described essentially as one of social science? We may sketch a typical *dialectic of morality* thus:

> descriptive morality → immanent critique (T/P inconsistency, dc')
> → redescriptive morality → hermeneutic and material counter-hegemonic struggle → metacritique (MC$_1$) → explanatory critical morality (dg', dr', MC$_2$) → totalizing depth praxis (incorporating a self-reflexive monitoring process and the prefigurative and thus means/ends consistency condition) → emancipatory axiology.

Personalism, perhaps the dominant moral ideology for subjects$_2$, is characterized by the attribution of responsibility to the isolated individual in an abstract, desocialized, deprocessualized, unmediated way, with blame, reinforced by punishment (rather than the failure to satisfy needs), as the sanction for default. But emotivism, decisionism, prescriptivism, descriptivism, sociological reductionism, nihilism, all — like personalism — trade on the assumption that values cannot be naturalistically grounded, based on the assumption that no transition from fact to value (and a fortiori from form to content) is possible. But through the theoretico-practical duality of the judgement form, it is the easiest thing in the world to pass from fact to value, and as *rational causal/absenting agents* we do it all the time. However, any such dialectic of morality as I have described will presuppose both a subjective dialectic of desire → wants → interests → emancipatorily oriented purposes; and an objective dialectic in which the constraints upon action are perceived as dependent on the reality of social, including screened power$_2$, relations and hence their transformative negation as dependent upon collective and ultimately totalizing agency. Totalizing praxis requires a vast stretching of the *moral imagination*. In considering this it should be borne in mind that only the empowered individual can assist or effectively solidarize with the powerless, so that amour de soi, rather than amour propre, is the true fount of all 'altruism', and that it is enlightening not egoistic for the individual to acknowledge her real self-interests. Here one might envisage the following dialectic (of 7 E's):

> self-*e*steem ↔ mutual *e*steem (where the intra-dependence of action itself reflects both the fiduciary nature of the social bond and the reality of oppressive social relations) ↔ *e*xistential security ↔ *e*rgonic efficiency ↔ (individual → collective → totalizing) *e*mpowerment ↔ universal *e*mancipation ↔ *e*udaimonia.

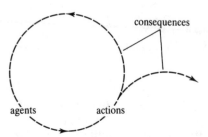

Figure 3.5 The Ethical Circle

The success of the immediate goals of the totalizing depth praxis will depend to a large extent on whether the emancipatory agents are capable of latching on to immanent emergent or partially manifest tendential processes (including cultural ones) and stretch them in the desired direction. Insofar as fiduciariness or trustworthiness both underpins esteem in the dialectic of the '7 E's' and is both an initiating moment in and an essential condition for the success of the totalizing depth praxis, we must add a fifth 'T' to our formula of the TTTTϕ of C2. But this is the politics of *transition* and so we can add a sixth alliterative 'T' to characterize the politics of the totalizing depth praxis as:

> *t*ransformed *t*ransformative (marking the coincidence of autoplastic and alloplastic change, subjective needs and objective possibilities) *t*rustworthy *t*otalizing *t*ransformist (committed to deep structural change) *t*ransitional praxis.

Any dialectic of liberation from ills (qua absence) is committed to the possibility of changing four-planar human nature, so that we must regard the *moral evolution of the species as open.* A beneficent objective dialectic, relating the strengths of virtue theory, deontology and consequentialism, which may be called the 'ethical circle', and which should be understood as inserted in the context of the transformational model of social activity advanced in C2.9, is depicted in Figure 3.5; and a related topology of the four kinds of politics I discussed in C2 is illustrated in Figure 3.6 in the figure of the concrete universal, with the rhythmic component of the quadruplicity represented by movement politics. Finally the *practical* character of the knowledge required should be re-emphasized.

The orientation of the free society to concrete singularity is represented in Figure 3.7. Is it possible to second-guess the substantive criteria? Clearly it is posited on a massive change in four-

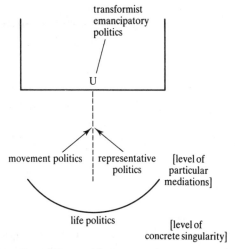

Figure 3.6 Four Types of Politics and the Concrete Universal

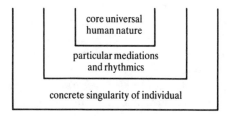

Figure 3.7 The Concrete Singularity of the Human Agent

planar human nature. The totality of master–slave-type relations would be done away with, including the end of the generative separation of the immediate producer and the fivefold alienations which result from it. For to be alienated is to be separated from oneself or something essential to one's nature or being. One can envisage a vast extension of (reciprocally, thence universally, recognized) rights, which are precisely freedoms; and a greatly extended constitutional democracy, including as much local autonomy and participatory democracy (precisely collective self-government) as would be consistent with the rational regulation of the massive redistribution, transformation and limitation of resource use dictated by considerations of equity and ecology alike.

Considerations of size are pertinent here. For participatory democracy, or just participation-in-democracy, suggests decentralization and local autonomy, while global constraints and inequities point to circuitous decision-making routes. At the global level one might consider a Council of the Peoples and a Council of the States or Regions. The normative order would be based on trust, solidarity and care, if not indeed love. If so, economic arrangements might be structured around a minimal viable standard of living in exchange for caring duties without the compulsion to work, in the sense of selling one's labour-power. But the dispositional or motivational aspects of free rational autonomy, including its agonistic and expressive ingredients,* would be given free rein in a socialized market[32] with a bias to empowering the tacit knowledge of the immediate producers and collective enterprises organized on a cooperative basis. As transitional slogans one might venture 'from each in accordance with their wants, abilities and needs' (since people may possess different needs to work) and 'to each according to their essential needs and innovative enterprise'. Global, regional and local informed democracy (which may well incorporate a syndicalist component as representative of particular mediating and/or disadvantaged groups) would ensure the rights of future (and differential) generations and other species were taken into account and decide upon such issues as the rate of depletion of scarce resources and feasible population growth. Education in a creative flourishing of the arts and sciences would be at a premium in such a society. Indeed this would in essence consist in a continually *reflexive learning process*, appropriate to a transitional dialectical rhythmic to a goal which, as in a Fichtean (but not endless) progress, may only ever be asymptotically approached.

Even with this reservation, one has to step back a little. What about phenomena like 'moral distance' despite global intradependence, the presence of the past, the inequities induced by the failure of expectations, the genuine psychopath, the virtualization of actuality, totally contradictory conceptions of efficiency grounded in different objective functions? One has to ask whether there is not any constraint on the lack of constraints or limit to the principle of dialectical universalizability? First a principle of *balance* (cf. Aristotle)

---

* It is neglect of this component of singular freedom, together with a planning apparatus expressing productive relations only consistent with an economically basic level of technology, inscribed sociologically within an undifferentiated expressive unity, which, in the context of global intradependence, especially in the form of the constitutive intrinsic outside, and the presence of the past, especially in the form of constitutive geo-historical process, accounts for the economic and civil kenosis of the erstwhile actually existing socialist states.

would place a limit (cf. Kant) on an emergent (cf. Marx) totality (cf. Hegel) that does not apply, or applies only in special cases, to the constituents of a totality in the way in which I will elaborate further in §§8–10 and C4.2. Second, it should be remembered that I am to an extent second-guessing what naturalistic substantive social science might discover about the unrealized possibilities of four-planar social being. (Even so, whatever this comes up with, progress in the direction of the formal criterion will be in general possible, even if it consists in halting [further] regression away from it.) Third, four-planar social being is always everywhere changing, and changeable. Process in open totalities entails that all politics are transitional, and that all causally efficacious transformative praxis is continually negating the status quo.

In §10, after further exploring the realms of totality and agency, I will return to the dialectic of desire, mediated by the axiological necessities I initially called the reality principle but which we can now know as alethically attainable truth and practical wisdom, to freedom, in the sense of universal human autonomy as flourishing. But it is worth making three concluding points here. First, one needs only a _conatus_ to knowledge to get the dialectic of freedom going. Agent N desires x but is constrained. Ceteris paribus, N wishes to remove the constraint on x and hence to know how to absent the absence of x. That is to say, the intrinsic releasing conditions for knowledge of the generative mechanism which will overcome the constraint on x are satisfied and then, by the logic of dialectic universalizability, to all similar constraints, and thence to all constraints qua constraints, corresponding, in Hegel's phrase, to the knowledge that man, as such, is free. Second, to the extent that the constraints on knowledge, or more generally on any other of the aspects of rational autonomy, are social, as they necessarily are in the case of constraints$_2$ on subjects$_2$, then only knowledge about constantly developing four-planar human nature, including, of course, social relations and hence the social sciences in sensitized solidarity with the tacit know-how of the subjects$_2$, can rationally inform emancipatory praxis. It is material interest in the form of the reality principle that will drive the dialectic of freedom on. Third, if a case can be made out for saying that natural science and technology can satisfy material desires in the epoch of consumer capitalism, it can equally be argued that looking at the contemporary phase from the standpoint of the forces of production, three phenomena stand out:

(a) a drastic reduction in necessary labour time;
(b) new, information-based ('post-Fordist') technologies requiring

a socially aware workforce with implications for knowledge about the character of the relations of production, i.e. for social science;

(c) the developing globalization of commodity production, which increasingly makes transformative tendencies radically negational (auto-subversive) in character.

This suggests the possibility of a dialectic of globalizing self-consciousness which may presage movement in the direction of a totalizing depth praxis partially offsetting the dialectical lag of transformative agency behind social structures, with endemic crisis tendencies, so that the extrinsic enabling conditions for change are satisfied too. If this were so, the unity of theory and practice would be satisfied in practice and geo-historical directionality (level 7 on p. 261 above) would catch up with dialectical rationality (dr_a' in $d\phi$). And we would be on the way to universal human autonomy.

§ 8 3L Realism: Totality

The inherent impulse of totality is to connect, so it is as well to register at the outset of our investigation of the realm of 3L realism that there are times when it is essential to disconnect, separate, distinguish and divide, that differentiation is a necessary condition of totality and diversity of unity. All good dialecticians have understood this. It is no accident that it is in the domain of totality, in the spheres of the notion and the philosophy of spirit, that Hegel is most impressive; and I have in fact argued that Hegel does sustain a genuine concept of dialectical connection — though only literally at a (temporal) stretch one of dialectical contradiction. But his transfigurative analytic reinstatement in dialectical connection, underpinned by his philosophy of identity, affects even the coherence of his totality — partly because his totality is (constellationally) closed and partly because his unprincipled use of the postulate of the identity of identity and difference undermines the possibility of a sufficiently strong concept of alterity necessary for true totality. The result is a polymorphous expressivism — in effect a huge illicit fusion or mélange of fusions centred on the realized absolute idea. In fact, ultimately, to sustain any of the four moments — 1M non-identity, 2E negativity, 3L totality, 4D transformative agency — of the critical realist dialectic you have to do justice to them all. I have already partially prefigured this discussion in C2.7 by arguing that the only plausible concept of a totality is that of a *partial totality*, rife with external as well as internal, and (not the same thing) accidental as well as necessary connections, replete with gaps, discontinuities, voids as well as pockets of thoroughgoing (sub-)totality. And that the most appropriate concept of causality for 3L, *holistic causality*, is that of a structured, asymmetrically weighted, differentially charged nexus. Moreover, contrary to Hegel, that the concrete universal is a *multiple quadruplicity* (in which rhythmic processes play an integral part alongside specific mediations), whose moments are in principle separable.

I have already hinted in §5 that it is totality — the realm of emergence, mediation, the *intra-active* (constitutively, permeatively, causally), the concrete (including concrete utopianism), the perspectival switch (with its necessary flexibility, fluidity and variability), the compounded reflection, the balanced whole — which will resolve the traditional problem of opposites. Where this problem is indeed genuine, it does this mainly through the key figure of *constellationality*. Let us take the problem of the relationships between subjectivity and objectivity, epistemology and ontology, language and the world, the intrinsic and the extrinsic, or its close correlate, reasons and causes. At the level of adequation, and even more so of expressive–referential duality, in the dialectic of truth I outlined in §2, we can make use of metaphors like matching or expressing to capture the relationship between subject and object, and this relation is clearly within subjectivity, not, as naïve realists think, within objectivity — just as we can articulate the relationship between language and the world only in language. The picture is rather as Figure 3.8 illustrates. But then, by a strategy of dialectical argument, we come to a position of *transcendental detachment*. We see that it is a condition of the possibility of our premises — the unity of world and language linguistically articulated — that being is quite independent of our articulation, knowledge of this accord, and even of our existence. We can argue this philosophically starting from the re-identifiability of every speech act, going through to playschool

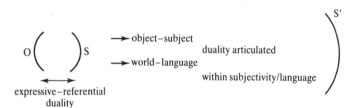

Figure 3.8

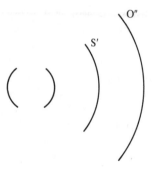

But in a meta-reflexively totalizing situation (cf C2.8) this articulation is situated,
in transcendental detachment, within an over-reaching objectivity

Figure 3.9   (cf. Figure 2.21 on p. 150)

scientificity from the pre-existence of dinosaurs, to cosmological speculations on the origins of our universe. So we must redraw Figure 3.8 as in Figure 3.9 where the outer hemisphere represents an over-reaching (and open) objectivity. And the figure that results is that of the constellational unity of the unity of subject and object (or being and language) within subjectivity (language) within objectivity (being). We do not need erasure, or the formula the condition of the possibility of x = the condition of the impossibility of x, to cope with what in another publication I have called the neo-Kantian predicament. Figure 3.9 depicts the case, does it not? Moreover, this objectivity is knowable, both philosophically and scientifically, at the alethic level of truth. It is in a similar way that we can think the distinction between transitive and intransitive dimensions, or between epistemological and ontological/ontic dialectics within an over-reaching being from which, of course, knowledge is geo-historically emergent. Again reasons can be constellationally contained, as a vitally important sub-set, within the larger category of causes, at least when they are acted upon, i.e. are efficacious. There are constellational identities, unities and other modes, and in any particular case it is essential to get the exact relation right. Thus the dialectic of dialectical and analytical reasoning, and, within it, the dialectic of incompleteness and inconsistency, exemplify unities, not identities. So does the history of irrealism, or at least arguably so. (I say arguably because if we accept the youthful Marx's critique of Hegel [see C2.6] he was actually a closet positivist — for whom the term 'logical positivist' would seem particularly apt.)

It will be remembered that we gave transcendental deductions of totality in C2.7. I am not going to repeat them here. Reflexivity is the inwardized form of totality. Both are global as well as distinctively philosophical phenomena. Indeed it is the urge of totality to break down the philosophy/science divide, as that between science and everyday life. We have witnessed it at work in the concept of a meta-reflexively totalizing situation — another dialectical perspectival switch in the key of constellationality. Particularly significant here was the concept of the dispositional identity of a person with her changing causal powers in the context of a stratified conception of the self, four-planar social being and distanciated emergent spatio-temporalities, incorporating a notional moment of the co-incidence of identity and change. Totality is the mainspring too in the logic of dialectical universalizability that we have already seen at work and to which we will return in §10. It is the fount of the totalizing depth praxis in the axiology of freedom, a praxis which just expresses the *reality* of social relations and global intradependence. It is totality that inspires hope, but it is equally behind the superveillance techniques that Foucault has described. It is the drive for totality that begins discursive argumentation, inspires participatory democracy, the Habermasian 'public sphere', but it is also at the root of colonialism, neo-colonialism, capitalist accumulation and empire-building generally. There is a methodological lesson here: dialectical arguments and figures are neither good nor bad in themselves — they are necessary or possible, and, when the latter, they leave the field of phenomena underdetermined. That is to say, our totality, unlike Hegel's, is open both synchronically (systemically) and diachronically (to the tensed spatializing causal processes of the future). Moreover, our totality ethically prioritizes the individual — the concrete singularity of each is the *condition* for the concrete singularity of all — while recognizing the determining role played by material circumstances (including, of course, ideas), particularly in the form of structurally sedimented institutions interlocked with discursively moralized oppressive power$_2$ relations. It is totality too that closes the hermeneutical and epistemological circles and explains why texts or reality respectively, insofar as they appear as such, are always bound to appear at least potentially intelligible to us.

It is worth dwelling a moment on reflexivity. In its most basic form it specifies the capacity of an agent or an institution to monitor and account for its activity. It is thus intimately connected to the phenomena of the historicity of social spatialized processual change and the futuricity of praxis discussed in §5: to the growth of superveillance techniques and mass (and increasingly globally homogenized) mediatization as much as to the possibility of a meta-reflexive situation. It is also systematically connected, in virtue of the intradependence of social being, to the phenomenon of *trust*. We can differentiate at least four (as should not surprise the observant) kinds of trust/mistrust:

(a) *Abstract* trust in expert systems of which the trustor has no knowledge and which is accepted purely on the basis of instrumental reason either out of necessity (there are no other feasible options to flying across the Atlantic) or as a result of perceived efficacy in the past (i.e. inductively).

(b) *Mediated* trust in domains, such as the realms of economics and politics, where the trustor is an active participant, knows something about the mechanisms at work and has good grounds for scepticism about their fiduciariness or reliability and that of those in power.

(c) *Concrete* trust, ideally singularized, such as is shown in the solidarity entailed by the expressively veracious judgement or in the totalizing depth praxis its grounds imply.

(d) *Personalized* trust, such as is expressed in relations of intimacy, demonstrated in phenomena such as personal loyalty, in friendships and acts of nurture and care in primary polyadization.

Irrealist philosophy almost inevitably detotalizes being. 1M identity theory necessitates a dual, producing a split and/or T/P inconsistency between the portion of reality it seems able to accommodate and the portion that it cannot. This detotalization results in repression, Tina compromise and/or split-off. This entrains in turn in the resultant detotalized system either de-agentifying reification or a human–nature dichotomous dualism (e.g. of two-world [Kantian] or a two-language [linguistified neo-Kantian] kind). Thus Hegel's actualism, for example, gives rise to the intransigent class of demi-actual and demi-present surds, irrational existents such as Krug's pen or eventuates in a constellationally closed future. But it is manifest more globally in Hegel's philosophy, in the fissure between Hegel Mark I and Mark II and the split between theory and practice which runs through Hegelian dialectics. Kant's own detotalizations are as numerous as, and explained by, his dichotomies — contradictions are denied reality, the 'I think' is hypostatized, the third antinomy necessitates the projective duplication of the phenomenal realm within which we must act into the noumenal realm, where the origin of agency lies. Ontological extensionalism (externalism or separatism) is manifest too in the Humean doctrine and post-Weberian orthodoxy, that there can be no transition from an is to an ought — i.e. values are detotalized. Self-referential paradox, reflexive inconsistency, performative contradiction, have their roots in a real problem: *alienation*. With Marx's analysis in mind, we could say that it is the generative separation at 2E that is the source of the illicit fusion and exchange of non-equivalents implicit in the wage-labour/capital contract which induces alienation at 3L and reification, fetishism and mystification at 4D. More generally we could delineate the following sequence for irrealist ideologies:

1M identity theory → 2E split → 3L detotalization → 4D disembodiment of de-agentification (or both).

The philosophical problems that arise at 3L stem from detotalization, directly induced by an absence (just as detotalization stands at 3L to T/P inconsistency at 2E as a principle of critique) — even if it is only the absence of a distinction or a connection. Thus totalities are emergent entities with sui generis causal powers. As such they are endowed with *emergent principles of structure* (the absent distinction) and cannot, as in the paradox of the preface or the set-theoretical paradoxes, be reduced to an aggregate of their components. I can assert that I will die without knowing how or when, just as in the same way an author can be sure that her work contains errors without being able to specify exactly what or where they are. In this case error is constellationally enclosed within an ignorance that is justified by epistemic relativity or the author's rhythmic positionality on her epistemic world-line.

The dialectics of 3L include the dialectics of totalization, detotalization and retotalization, centre and periphery, inner and outer, part and whole, inclusion and exclusion, fission and fusion, equivalence and equilibration, explosion and implosion, globalization and localization; of recursive embedding, systematic inter-/intra-mingling, of the compounding and condensation of reflections (in the sense of C2.7), of transcendental and dialectical perspectival switches. Substantively, they revolve around the figure of unity-in-diversity and include the dialectics of democratic decision-making. Ideologically, they include the dialectics of the illicit presentation of sectional as universal or universal as sectional interest, the screening of contradiction and conflict, the rhetoric of organicism and collectivism. Metacritically, 3L encompasses the dialectics of alienation and de-alienation and of all the modes of detotalization from repression to compartmentalization or externalizing exclusion. As totalizing, however, they subsume the dialectics of stratification, contradiction and change, and of desire to freedom at 1M, 2E and 4D. This does not mean that totality has the last word in dialectical critical realism. In an open future that must go to the transformative negation of the contemporaneously existing order of things by that transformative praxis which is agency.

§ 9 4D Realism: Agency

My discussion of 4D realism should be understood as presupposing the dialecticized critical natauralism of C2.9 — in particular:

1. the negative and other (feminist, ecological, holistic, transformist) generalizations of the transformational model of social agency, to produce a dislocated dialectics of structure and agency and a conception of what I have been calling four-planar social being encompassing the social cube depicted in Figure 2.26;
2. the stratified conception of the self illustrated in Figure 2.31 and the stratification of action, as presented in Figure 2.29; and
3. the model of the components or springs of action represented in Figure 2.30.

Taken together, my argument in C2 suggested that persons are best conceived as intra-active processes-in-laminated products[see C2.2]-in-pre-existing/ongoing processes. Now in considering the stratification of the agentive self it is important to bear in mind the 'internal' dialectical pluriverses (complete with internal and internalized master – slave-type relations) with multiply determined components, streams, arrays and aspects of consciousness, self and agency, in potential or actual discordance, or contradiction, disjoint or coupled rhythmics and bound into sub- and partial totalities. This radical decentring, emphasized in late/postmodernity, by no means prevents the possession of well-grounded and causally efficacious reasons, ordinated in a hierarchy of projects,[33] but it certainly makes clearly focused self-conscious agency, particularly on a collective scale, more difficult. We start immediately with real problems — of vacuous, disempowered, emasculated selves, which are psycho-somatic-social mixes, and the world historical problem of agency. This last must be situated in the context of the growth of new technologies, the differential spatialization of production locales and markets in the crisis-prone and internally antagonistic global capitalist economy; and in the context of growing inequities and a periphery subject$_2$ to a plurality of oppressive power$_2$ relations each ready to play the others off, in a society exceeding sustainable ecological limits, containing pockets of intra-ethnic violence, saturated with mass mediatization and informed with fundamentalist and/or irrationalist ideologies.

At a philosophical level this is reflected in a profound *dualism* between embodiment and agency such that inevitably irrealist philosophies are unable to sustain a concept of *intentional embodied causally efficacious agency*, that is, of bodily agentive (transformatively negating) agency, absenting absences, informed necessarily with real, and potentially with good, reasons for action. Instead of the constellationality of reasons within causes and of the emergent powers traditionally associated with mind within a partially socialized nature in an unsocialized cosmos we have detotalization and dualistic split or reification. Irrealism is unable to think the concept of intentional causality. 4D subsumes both metacritical and ethical dialectics. The former will be considered in detail in the next chapter. At the ethical level, in contrast to the combination of moral realism and ethical naturalism I have been motivating, we are faced with a combination of *emotivist* moral ideologies for masters and abstract universalist *personalist* moral ideologies for slaves and religious or ethnic *fundamentalist* ethics, accepted on a purely positive basis, i.e. on authority alone. In this situation there is a crisis for de-ontology over competing and antagonistic rights, for virtue theory over which dispositions are to be acquired in routinized practices and for consequentialism over its incapacity to sustain an equitable humanism, grounded in a conception of our core common humanity.

The figure of constellationality which I have already invoked needs to be complemented by that of the hiatus in the duality in the case of the theory/practice, society/individual or structure/agency relations. One should take the latter as constellationally dislocated unities not identities. On the other hand, it is equally enlightening to switch perspectives and see the over-reached term of the constellationalities as involving a tensed hiatus or quantum leap from the term from which it is conceptually or naturally emergent. But then in the case of some dialectics it makes little sense to accord a priority. Thus it is true that moral realism is grounded in naturalistic ethics, but it is moral realism which also by imperiously demanding grounding necessitates the transition from form to content. The single most important conceptual move that dialectical critical realism can make here is to accompany the negative generalization of 'constrain', so that to constrain an ill is to disempower, contradict, overthrow or otherwise constrain a constraint, with a *positive generalization of the concept of freedom*, so that this includes not only rights, democracies and equities (including the absenting of constraints$_2$) but also needs and possibilities or potentialities for development. To amplify this slightly, if we take the goal of freedom to be human autonomy then what is to be liberated is the concrete *self* so that a genuine self-determination is obtained. That is to say, our object is self-emancipation. There is no reason why states of affairs such as health (3L qua wholeness, totality or balance), de-alienation, education, access to information, etc. should not be seen as rights and so as freedoms. Second, we have seen that differentiation is a condition of totality and diversity of unity. This has two implications: on the one hand, the universal recognition and realization of such rights, and generically of freedoms; on the other, the requirements of maximum individual, local, cooperative, associationalist, autonomy and pluralism consistent with the first desideratum — which must be extended to include the rights of other generations and species — and the rational resolution, at the level of scale, of the matter at hand. Thus ecological policy would have to be decided at a global level, and be designed conceptually, to liberate concretely singularized individuals from the constraints of, for example, pollution.

The intentionality of praxis is shown in the capacity to transform the world in a way which, unless (as in a firing squad) it was freakishly overdetermined, would not otherwise have occurred. This is the starting point of all the major transcendental arguments that critical realism has employed, without Kant's objectivist, absolutist, idealist, dualist and irrealist commitments. It is also the starting point of most of the dialectical arguments I have employed in the present work, including the dialectic that will take us from desire to freedom in §10. The problems of philosophy that arise at 4D all stem from *de-agentification* via disembodiment or disintentionality — hence my stress on embodied *agentive* agency. The dialectics characteristic of 4D are those of human praxis, encompassing most of the others we have discussed and many more for which we have had no time. Thus harking back to the sense of dialectic as argument or conversation we have dialectics of hermeneutical struggle. There must be immediate knowledge for any hermeneutic context to arise (so I argued in C2.8). But corresponding to the four forms of hermeneutics — of inquiry, of communication, of communicative inquiry and of textual inquiry — that I have elsewhere differentiated,[34] there are four distinct modes which hermeneutic struggles may assume. Thus just think of the consequences of struggles over the interpretation of religious tenets, even if these have been in part rationalizations — at the level of accountability in personal, and ideology in social, stratification — of deeper causes. As problems of philosophy, hermeneutic circles give rise to Meno's paradox,* the paradox of originality — what is truly novel cannot be immediately understood — and display isomorphs in the post festum paradox and the predicament of the Beautiful Soul. In the context of the dialectic of centre and periphery we have dialectics of the recognition of identities-in-difference, posited on differences-in-identity, of selves-in-solidarity forging a unity-in-diversity that will defragment the marginalized majority of the human race. Thus it is in the ethical domain that 4D is perhaps most at home and the question that dominates it, following an immanent critique of the status quo, is not whether, but *how*, to negate the given.** For agency will always negate the given, even if, pace Hegel, the negation does indeed perpetuate existing structures.

§ 10 The Dialectic of Desire to Freedom

The dialectic of desire to freedom is at once a dialectic of desire and a dialectic of freedom. In this section I will be resuming some earlier themes, especially those elaborated in §§2 and 7, tracing several dialectical pathways to the eudaimonistic society and exploring some of the implications of my argument. I should make it explicit at the outset that here I am, in a sense, engaging in an exercise of metacritical (metatheoretical) concrete utopianism; that this is not a historicist enterprise of anticipating the trajectory of a future which has yet to be caused, but rather depends in part upon us; instead I am attempting to articulate the tendential$_b$ (see C2.4) *rational directionality of geo-history.* Our 'vehicular thrownness' establishes the explanatory primacy (in the EA) of the political over the ethical, while the extended argument of this chapter from absence to referential detachment to the logic of scientific discovery and alethic truth, entailing, when consistently pursued, the conception of social science as emancipatory axiology, suggests the normative primacy (in the IA) of the ethical over the political. (This is the constellational unity [and fluidity] of the ethical and [into] the political within the political.) My project is normative. I shall be making much use of the logic of dialectical universalizability. But, because we are in transitional

* 'A man cannot inquire either about that which he knows, or about that which he does not know; for assuming he knows he has no need to inquire; nor can he inquire about that which he does not know, for he does not know about that which he has to inquire.'[35]
** Moreover, the best therapy for the narcissistic fragmented self of late/postmodernity[36] is the dialectics of alloplasticity and autoplasticity in the transformed transformative agency of the totalizing depth praxis.

rhythmics or processes, this logic must be embedded within a developmental *dialectic of the logic and practice of dialectical universalizability* incorporating *a dialectic of dialectical universalizability and immanent critique.* Because we are inhabitants of a dialectical pluriverse, characterized by complex, plural, contradictory, differentiated, disjoint but also coalescing and condensing development and antagonistic struggles over discursively moralized power$_2$ relations, subject to regression, entropy and roll-back, we cannot expect the *dialectic of real geo-historical processes,* from which the logic of totality, i.e. of dialectical universalizability, starts and to which it always returns, to be anything but a messy affair. This logic is a spatio-temporally, multiply and unevenly distanciated developmental process, in which so long as dialectical universalizability is not seen as a *transfactual, processually oriented, concretized, transformatively directional norm, subject to the constraint of actionability* in a world in which agents act on their perceived interests (including their perceptions of the interests of others), it is often going to seem to be falsified. But norms, although they can be broached and discarded, cannot be falsified by the irrationality of actual geo-history. They can be falsified, but only by the provision of a better, nobler, norm more fitting to the needs and propensities of developing four-planar socialized humanity. Pluralism, diversity, is intrinsic to the logic of totality, but as we are dealing with a dialectic encompassing immanent critique in counter-hegemonic struggle, inconsistency too must be conceded a value in its own right. It is a dialectic, not an analytic, of dialectical universalizability that I am about.

I will be arguing that just as the concept of *constraint* must be *negatively generalized* to include unwanted and unnecessary, and so remediable, ills qua absences and hence that to constrain such a constraint is to liberate, the concept of *freedom* must be *positively generalized* (and substantialized) so as to encompass not just such obvious items as rights, equities and (participation-in-)democracies, but needs and possibilities, such as possibilities for self-development and self-realization. In the dialectic of dialectical universalizability and immanent critique, the former may be related to the positive, the latter to the negative generalization. My orientation here is, as always, to concrete singularity and the goal of a society in which the free flourishing of each concretely singular agent is a condition of the free flourishing of all.

I start with some metatheorems, say something about the pivotal concept of autonomy, before delineating various conceptions of freedom and rehearsing the character of the judgement form, T/P consistency and dialectical universalizability. We know (1) that a reason can be a cause, and to cause is to negate is to absent (transfactually, rhythmically, potentially holistically and possibly intentionally); (2) that ills which are unnecessary and unwanted (conditions that I will take as presupposed for expository convenience) can be considered as absences, and so constraints, but also as falsehoods to concretely singularized human nature; (3) that dialectic is, in the human world, most basically, the absenting of constraints (including the constraints$_2$ on subjects$_2$ which derive from exploitative or oppressive power$_2$ relations, and the inequities that flow from them); and (4) that by a negative transcendental perspectival switch, to constrain is to contradict is to absent; and finally (5) that the moral truth or alethia, the good, is dialectically universal freedom.

The most basic meaning of autonomy is self-determination. 'Complete autonomy' would imply the absence not of causes, but of prior or external ones (e.g. subjugation). Of course, the world in which we act is always going to be constrained by (a) natural laws and ecological limits, (b) the nature of globalized and temporally distanciated four-planar social being, (c) one's values, projects and rationality in attempting to accomplish them, including, for instance, the balance of the four types of politics in one's life. Autonomy presupposes freedom of choice (and hence a degree of axiological underdetermination).* But freedom of choice does not imply the absence of grounds for choice (as in complete axiological indeterminacy). And, in one sense of 'free', one will be free just to the extent that one possesses the power, knowledge and disposition to act in one's real interests, e.g. wanted needs, or development or flourishing, including one's wants *for* others. However, this is perhaps better looked at as a *criterion for rational agency* (a departure from my earlier usage). And one can then say if one uses one's *autonomy* both *rationally* and *wisely* (i.e. in accordance with the virtue of phronesis, including its connection with the criteria of mean, balance, totality, health and wholeness) then one will be able to, or tend to be able to, realize one's ideas in practice. Hence the connection between autonomy, functioning as a theoretico-practical dual concept potentially linking truth to freedom, and the unity — or, better, coherence — of theory and practice in practice, i.e. absolute reason. The concept can be extended or its presuppositions explicated, in many directions. Thus nothing which was reified, i.e.

---

* It was a disastrous mistake of Hegel's to identify freedom and necessity — the sign of his actualism and acceptance of authority, i.e. of his 'positivity', and his equation of freedom with fate.

like labour-power treated as a commodity, could be said to be truly autonomous. Self-determination is normally a necessary condition for self-realization, and if one's self includes one's potentialities, then one can reasonably be said to be alienated from them. And only a self which, in solidarity, has emancipated itself can be said to have become self-determining, i.e. autonomous. This is at once a prefigurative ('presence of the future') condition on emancipation and a process-in-product ('presence of the past') condition for autonomy. It is the same requirement that makes the imperatival aspect of the judgement form, in Kant's terms, an assertorically imperatival one. This presupposes that the addressee of the judgement wants advice and discussion and the same applies at the level of more material forms of solidarity. This is also an implication of both the concrete singularity and the actionability or agent-specificity implicit in dialectical universalizability.

Now to the even broader concept of freedom. At its root level, to be free is to be without, i.e. to have no/absent, constraints in some respect, and liberation is the absenting of the respects (concrete constraints). To be free *from* constraints on x is to be free to *do* x. Hence the equivocity of Berlin's alleged contrast. But we can distinguish various degrees of freedom, which may be fruitfully compared with the various levels of rationality I set out in §7:

1. (a) agentive freedom, viz. the capacity to do otherwise which is analytic to the concept of action;
   (b) formal legal freedom, which neither implies nor is implied by (1a);
2. (a) negative freedom from, which, I have just argued, is tantamount to
   (b) positive freedom to (a disempowerment, for instance, can be seen as a constraint).
3. Emancipation from specific constraints, where emancipation is defined as the transformation from unwanted, unneeded and oppressive to wanted, needed and liberating (including em-powering) states of affairs, especially structures. Clearly this can be universal, collective or individual. By this point one will have become interested in criteria for rational agency and be susceptible to the logic of dialectical universalizability.

At what point in the ethical tetrapolity does the logic of dialectical universalizability bite? At the transition between the ground of the fiduciary remark and the remoralization of the world that is the object of the explanatory critical theory which both informs and is informed by the totalizing depth praxis I discussed in §7. Thus take the simple judgement 'smoking harms health': we can postulate the transition → the harming of health as such is wrong → absence of health is an ill → ills such as that, which function as a constraint on life, are wrong → all such constraints should be absented → all constraints, as such, should be absented. What makes a dialectic of such (dialectical) universalizability necessary? My ethical naturalism implies that an epistemological dialectic will be necessary for the transition to the realm of freedom, which paradigmatically violates norms of purely analytical consistency. In addition T/P inconsistency is characteristic of all formative/learning/maturation/developmental processes. Note that the fact that my moral realism, in the context of developing four-planar social being (or, as I shall sometimes say, 'human nature'*), makes substantive moral truth changing counts for, not against it; and provides another point of linkage with the 'communitarians'.

Let us, after this necessary digression, resume the progression of degrees of freedom. We now have the concept of

3'. universal human emancipation from (unnecessary) constraints as such.

The next level of freedom is

4.   autonomy, in the sense of self-determination discussed above; and corresponding to it,
4'. rational autonomy; and
4". universal human autonomy.

This must be conceptualized as in nature and, as such, subject to the rights of other species and over time, so that it extends to the rights of future generations. At this point the positive generalization or stretching of the concept of freedom mentioned earlier becomes possible. First to *needs*, whether absolute, in the sense of necessary for survival, or relative, in the sense of necessary in the context of geo-historically grounded possibilities. Thus freedom as:

5.   wellbeing, with the emphasis on the absence of ills and the satisfaction of needs; and corresponding to it,
5'. universal wellbeing.

The next extension is to see the realization of concretely singularized *possibilities for development* (including the potential for possibilities of

---

* The first locution is better, because if an independent meaning can be put on human nature then it may function as a norm against which, for example, social institutions can be judged.

development), in the context of developing, and by a further level shift, the possibilities of further developing, four-planar social being as *rights*, and a fortiori as *grounded freedoms*, subject only to the requirement of totality, that it is consistent with the universally reciprocated recognition of such rights, i.e. that it does not transgress the concretely singularized grounded freedoms of others. We thus have freedom as

6.   flourishing, with the emphasis on the presence of goods (benefits) and the realization of possibilities, which entails
7.   universal human flourishing, or the eudaimonistic society.

By now, of course, de-alienation and the totality of structurally sedimented master−slave relations will have long been abolished and, in the context of the open moral evolution of humanity, the erstwhile power$_2$-holders and oppressors will see their interests under transformed descriptions. My task now is to show how this most (ontologically) negative philosophy can generate the most (ethically) positive results.

The simplest way of introducing the logic of consistency and universalizability is to register that you cannot say 'you ought to ϕ' and not ϕ in materially the same circumstances without committing a practical or performative contradiction, i.e. being guilty of T/P inconsistency. It is this simple principle, taken to the limit, that binds the trustworthiness of any sincere statement to T/P consistency, dialectical universalizability, dialectical reason, autology, autonomy and universal human autonomy; and, conversely, the lack of dialectical universalizability to T/P inconsistency, performative contradiction, reflexive inconsistency, susceptibility to dc', heterology, heteronomy and Tina compromise. More fully, now, we know from the treatment of §2 that universalizability is both a test for consistency and a criterion of truth (an acceptable experimental result must be repeatable in principle); that T/P consistency is a matter of *praxis* (in a *process*), which should be *practical, progressive* (in the sense specified in p. 220) and *theoretically grounded*; and that both praxis and grounding should be universalizable in the sense that they be *transfactual, concrete, actionable* (agent-specific: ought presupposes, not implies, can) and *transformative*, i.e. oriented to the objective(s) of the praxis, which, in the field of practical reasoning, will be ultimately grounded in a theory of four-planar human nature. At this juncture two objections may be mooted. Will not the particularities of each concrete situation be so great and specific as to render nugatory the criterion of universalizability? No — for the onus is on the backslider to show that mediations and singularities of a situation are both (a) *relevant* to and (b) *significant* for the matter at issue. It is no objection to the payment of taxes to cite the fact that one is red-headed — *unless* such persons are systematically discriminated against on such grounds. How do I know a priori that the *substantive* naturalistic criteria will be in accordance with the *formal* criterion, viz. the free development of each as a condition for the free development of all, articulated in §2 and §7? On the argument of §2 one requires only that the process be *progressive* (or minimally regressive), which is obviously an issue for debate. Moreover, the non-actualist, non-historicist substantive theory will situate only *possibilities* for advance towards (or halting regress from) the desired direction.

In this book I have been articulating what is the ontology of absence. This is our starting point. It is not anthropic because absence is, I have argued, a necessary feature of the natural world, and one which, moreover, has ontological priority over presence (cf. C2.1 and C3.5). Nevertheless, in the ethical domain, which is (see §1) social-relation dependent, it is essential to commence from experienced or experiencable absences, which are unfulfilled needs, lacks, wants or, in the setting of primary polyadization, elemental desire (so that difference is ontologically prior to identity). Desire entails referential detachment, whence we proceed through causality and classification to ontological stratification and alethic truth. From absence also springs constraint qua contradiction, and via the contradictions within and between differentiated and stratified entities, we proceed to emergence and thence to totality inwardized as the reflexivity shown in agency. But reflexive agency is capable of judgement and so is subject to the dialectical universalizability of the judgement form. Sociality necessarily implies solidarity, with or in self-emancipation and an orientation to the totalizing depth praxis to universal human emancipation which will usher in the good society, oriented to concretely singularized universal human autonomy. This is the dialectic of desire from freedom, which we could nominate (1) the *dialectic of agency*, set off by the absence or lack implicit in desire.

Now in §7 I argued for the transition from fact to value and theory to practice, presaging the transition from fiduciary form to naturalistic content (and the dialectical perspectival switches from, for instance, the figure of capital to the ground of labour or from the media star to the dole queue, or from the centre of the Pentagon or the Tokyo Stock Exchange to the periphery of Somalia or the New York homeless) in two ways: (α) through the process of *explanatory critique*, which is familiar from my previous writings so I will not pursue it further here, and (β) through the *theoretico-practical duality* of the judgement form

developed in §2. We can, however, proceed even more directly from
(γ) the axiological commitment implicit in the expressive veracious
judgement, whether in the domain of theoretical or practical (or other
kinds of) reasoning, straight to the ethical tetrapolity I outlined in §7,
and to the goal of universal human autonomy, without making the
detour through the explicitly moral realm, viz. as follows:

> [I] [axiological commitment in the expressively veracious judgement
> (e.g. an assertoric utterance)] → (1) concretely singularized
> fiduciariness (→ solidarity) → (2) explanatory critical theory plus
> concrete utopianism plus theory of transition (in a
> theory−practice helix based on participatory research) ↔ (3)
> totalizing depth praxis, including, of course, the politics of
> transition → (4) universal human autonomy, (a) subject to the
> constraints imposed by (i) the needs and rights of future
> generations and other species (ii) and ecological limits and (iii) the
> principle of balance or the dialectical mean and the meta-ethical
> virtue of phronesis or practical wisdom; and (b) grounded in a
> conception of the open-ended moral evolution of the species,
> ideological struggle and the material dynamics of change.

The resulting normative order will be based on the multiple
generalization of the TMSA, including the traditionally feminist
virtues of care, sensitivity to the suffering of others (for to suffer is, as
Marx remarked, what it is to be), solidarity and *trust*. It is worth
mentioning here that it is the trustworthiness of the primary polyad
which endows the infant with the existential security that at once
silences its scream, nurtures its self-esteem and lays the basis for the
amour de soi which underpins solidarity and altruism alike. The
reality of the social bond, based on the primary existential of trust,
both quenches desire and, in the process of development, transforms
its object, in (2) *the dialectic of education of desire* to wants and only
collectively attainable needs by the axiological necessities which
comprise the reality principle, understood as the alethic truths of
four-planar contemporary society.* The logic of desire and of
interest point in the same direction.

The transition from form to content — and the context — of the
eudaimonistic society — is implicit in every desire, assertoric remark
or successful action. Let us look at some of the other ways at which

---

* Those with a taste for alliteration will note that it is a sixth T, trustworthiness, that
underpins the dialectic of 7 E's in §7 and that I added before totalizing to the other 5 T's
of transformist transitional politics. See Figure 2.13 on p. 121 above.

we can arrive at the same result. We can resume with (3) the *dialectic of malaise*. A malaise is an ill and a constraint. Insofar as it is unwanted and unneeded, we are rationally impelled, ceteris paribus (a qualification which is always necessary in open systems, but which it would be tedious to repeat), to a commitment to absent it, and thus to an absenting practice. And thence into absenting all dialectically similar ills, and thus to absent all the *causes* of such constraints, including oppressive power$_2$ formations, and from there to absent all ills or constraints, and hence their explanatory critically identified causes, precisely insofar as, *in constituting ills or constraints, they are dialectically similar*. And from here it is, in theory, but a short hop to the free society, which satisfies or approximates or approaches the formal criterion of the free flourishing of each and all, as substantiated by a four-planar theory of human nature in society.

Second, from (4) the *dialectic of cognition*, we can begin from frustrated desire or the pathology of everyday life (see §3). Agents N desire x and are constrained from achieving it. They wish to remove this constraint. They therefore seek out its causes and acquire the practical knowledge to get rid of them. Again, by the logic of dialectical universalizability, they are committed to getting rid of all dialectically similar structures and hence to their causes and to the acquisition of the knowledge to absent them. Thence they are rationally committed to getting rid of all dialectically similar situations which act as constraints qua constraints. And thence once more to the flourishing society. Next from (5) the *dialectic of equity*. The principle of sufficient practical reason states that there must be a ground for differences. If there is no such ground then we are rationally impelled to remove them. This will almost inevitably initiate a drive to overthrow the totality of master−slave relations, and implant in their place a society based on a core equality between human beings by virtue of their shared species nature with differentiations justified by the concrete specificities and singularities, needs and powers* of the particular individual. The dialectic of equity can also be used to develop and generalize Gewirth's argument for the recognition of freedom and wellbeing as universalizably necessary conditions for successful action,[38] say ϕ under a description, to an argument for the *realization* of the *potential* of all agents to perform dialectically similar acts; and from there to an argument for the *development* of all dialectically similar potentials; and from there it is but a short step to

---

* The speculation that such matters are not subject to rational investigation is refuted by the work of Len Doyle and Ian Gough,[37] Maureen Ramsey and a flourishing research industry.

argue for the development of all *potentials qua potentials* and we are at Marx's definition of a socialist society as one 'in which the free development of each is the condition of the free development of all', i.e. the eudaimonistic society, which may be regarded as an extended explication of the principle of equity. Gewirth, for his part, does not see how far the logic of universalizability must take him. Next (6) the *dialectic of de-alienation*. Insofar as a person is separated from something essential to their needs, nature or healthy human functioning, no one who is not prepared to see themselves so alienated can fail to be committed to its restoration, insofar as they do not infringe the reciprocally recognized rights of others. This is a prima facie case for *socialism*, insofar as it rationally portends the sublation of the generative separation of the immediate producers from the means and materials of production and *their* rational regulation of their use.

The dialectic of de-alienation can be broadened, as anticipated in §5, into a (7) generic *dialectic of desire*. If the dialectic of desire involves the desire to be desired and this involves the desire to be recognized, then, again through the logic of dialectical universalizability insofar as this involves the capacity to enjoy rights and liberties, it entails the *real enjoyment* of equal and universally reciprocally recognized rights and liberties, including the right to de-alienation and the enjoyment of health, education, access to resources and other liberties. And by an extension and deepening of the argument it entails the right of all subjects$_2$ to be free of, and thus to the abolition of, the totality of master−slave relations, including internalized and intra-psychic ones, globally and inter-/intra-generationally and with due respect to the needs and rights of other species in the context of developing four-planar human nature. This dialectic rationally demands the satisfaction of the cognitive and empowering conditions for universal human autonomy, so that, in the first instance, if agents are so disposed, it must be included within level (4) of freedom, but then, in the next place, upon their coming to see their real interests, under the description of the free development of the concrete singularity of every other individual as a condition for their own free development. This takes us into (8) the *dialectics of transition*, and the two-way traffic between truth and freedom, form and content, on which I will comment immediately below. The generic dialectic of desire ([7] above) can be motivated in part by (9) the *dialectic of desire for freedom*. This turns on the consideration that *human beings, by and large, want to be free, under some* (sets of) *description(s)*. And the logic of dialectical universalizability will rationally motivate them to accept freedom for *all* in dialectically similar circumstances, and then ultimately freedom as such (as dialectically valued) irrespective of circumstance. This will clearly depend not only upon immanent critique as part of counter-hegemonic struggle but also upon the possibility of mutually reinforcing virtuous spirals and spreads among freedoms — powers and needs — such as might be involved in extending participation in democracy, generalizing and safeguarding universally recognized rights, implementing equities (implicit in dialectical universal-izability), abolishing oppressive power$_2$, and ultimately the totality of such (again by the logic of universalizability), relations, radically concretely singularized local, regional, and necessarily global (see §7) autonomies (implicit in absolute reason — dr$_a$' in dϕ) and socializing the market without the compulsion or lack of opportunity to work subject to the recognition of the duty to care implied by the right to flourish. Let us now consider (10) the *dialectic of universalizability* itself. The T/P consistent fiduciary remark implies solidarity, ranging from moral and material support through empowerment, in its aspect of freedom, to participation in the depth totalizing practice concerned. This may be implicated in a dialectic of social science from neutrality to explanatory critical rationality to emancipatory axiology to dialectic per se (the subject of the sequel to this book) and by transition from descriptive morality through immanent critique to redescriptive morality to formal omissive metacritique through counter-hegemonic struggle to explanatory critical morality and metacritique (MC$_2$, dg', dr$_p$') through the totalizing depth praxis to emancipatory axiology.

One could add to these dialectics indefinitely. There is (11) a *generic dialectic of interests*. It is in N's real interest to ϕ, since it contributes to her flourishing or wellbeing or develops her potentialities. She is constrained from ϕ-ing by x. She seeks to absent x, and to unearth the causes of x, say an oppressive power$_2$ relation R, structuring an institutional complex. She is driven to solidarize with others oppressed by R, and logically to all oppressed by R. They engage in the totalizing depth inquiry and praxis necessary to overthrow R. The reality principle will probably show R to be systematically buttressed by, or interconnected with, a network of such relations and institutions. This will underpin the conatus to dialectical universalizability. The reality principle will also see to it that the transition between perceived interests and wants and perceptions (by agents) of their real interests, at the minimum, of wanted needs, occurs. From seeking to absent the causes of x, she will seek to absent the causes of all similar x's, i.e. frustrations on human flourishing for herself, and for everyone else so frustrated. From viewing the constraints on ϕ-ing as wrong, and as seeking to absent them, she will

view all dialectically (transfactual, actionable, concretized) similar
constraints as wrong and seek to absent them. And then she will
processually orient herself against constraints qua constraints, that is,
constraints as such, and to absenting the absence of a society based
on the principle of concretely singularized universal human
autonomy subject to the relational condition of totality, that it be a
mediated unity predicated on diversity.

In principle, the logic of dialectical universalizability takes two
forms — one (α) corresponding to the level of critical reason and the
other (β) corresponding to the level of (totalizing depth) explanatory
critical reason. But the first without the second is inefficacious and so
considerations from the lowest level of reason, instrumental reason,
will drive agents from (α) to (β). Their respective logics are as follows:

In case (α):   to absent an ill
to absent all (dialectically) similar ills
to absent all ills as such.

In case (β):   to absent an ill
to seek out the causes for the ill.

Then either (i): to absent it/them
to absent the causes of all (dialectically) similar ills
to absent all ill-producing causes as such
to absent all ill-producing causes seen as
    constraints
to absent the absence of universal human
    emancipation.

And/or (ii)   to seek out the causes of all (dialectically) similar ills
to seek out the causes of all ills, seen as constraints$_2$
    as such, and
to absent them, i.e. set out on the path to the
    eudaimonistic society.

It is worth going into this in a bit more detail. Tautologically, people
act in accordance with their perceived interests, and if their perceived
interests are their real interests, instrumental reason alone will entail
the passage from explanatory to (ultimately, totalizing depth)
explanatory critical reason. It would seem that through what I will call
the (12) *dialectic of material interests* agents will discover that altruism is
in their purely egoistic interests. In §7 I argued the case for the
rational necessity of the eudaimonistic society from the side of post-
Fordist production, let us now approach it from the point of view of
consumption in the age of consumer capitalism. To get from wants,
which are frustrated, to wanted needs is to get from perceived to real

interests, and from individual to collective agency (and thence to that totalizing agency prefiguring a unity-in-diversity). Agents only have to grasp the causal connection between a referentially detached frustration and a referentially detached systemic power$_2$ relation. This is the education that the reality of the social bond, both of social bondage and of the social solidarity between subjects$_2$, i.e. the reality principle, will impose on their own self-interests. (See Figure 3.10 below.) Failure to discover the alethia of the contours of their four-planar social circumstances will lead to the continued frustration of their own desires, while failure to act on it will lead at least to cognitive dissonance, T/P inconsistencies and *pathologies of praxis*. The reality principle will secure a dialectic from instrumental rationality via explanatory critical rationality to the eudaimonistic society. In this way it nicely complements the dialectic from consciousness via self-consciousness to reason articulated from the standpoint of production in §7. The naturalistic vision that wo/men as such are free, vastly extended from Hegel's conception of liberty, but that to win their freedom they must absent the constraints$_2$ on it, will inform the moral realism of all who are or side with subjects$_2$. The dialectic desire → wants → interests → knowledge → real interests → desired (wanted) needs → collective → totalizing agency is entailed by the most self-centred interest. But what of the possibility of the oppressors 'buying off' individuals? This cannot be generalized of course — the roulette wheel always wins. But it may work in particular cases. Are such agents to be written off as lost souls? They have sacrificed their rational autonomy, and perhaps lost their self-esteem. But they remain in essence free. And this is where the unity of immanent critique and dialectical universalizability in the dialectic of self and solidarity must balance sensitivity to concrete singularity and transfactuality with sensitivity to absence and actionability. This,

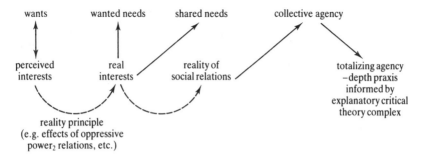

Figure 3.10 The Dialectic of Material Interests

too, is just one of the reasons why the dialectic of desire to freedom cannot predict, but only inform, the future.

The dialectic of desire to freedom is essentially a *dialectic of content from truth to freedom via wisdom*. In principle and in practice this is a two-way process. Freedom is as much a condition of truth as vice versa, and in the learning process which is the dialectic of theory and practice each mutually informs the other. But, for any degree of freedom, given only a commitment to moral realism, one augments it in a dialectic, initiated by desire through referential detachment to truth conceived as an axiological need, and alethically as expressing both the grounds (truth) of one's grounds and the requirements of the reality principle. In practical reason this last must always be supplemented by the *actionability* (or feasibility) principle. A social bond may be real, but if subjects can be persuaded neither, as Habermas would put it, by 'the force of the better argument', nor by the causal impact of that bond on what they take their real interests to be, directional action based on consciousness of that bond is impractical.

Suppose it is suggested that I have smuggled morality into the fiduciary nature of the expressively veracious remark. This does not matter a jot. Through the naturalistic, descriptive and evidential components of the judgement form, and the requirement that differences, changes and unchanges (i.e. the status quo) be grounded in a substantial theory of four-planar and concretely singularized developing human nature, the *form* of the moral judgement is explicated by the *content* of the explanatory critical† (= explanatory critical plus concrete utopian plus transitional) theory. Theoretical reason merely says that the world is so and entails a commitment to act on it. Practical reason says how we are to change the world in accordance with naturalistically grounded theory. The moral truth or moral alethia, the good, is universal human flourishing, and it, subject to the principles of prefiguration and actionability, absents or deconstrains all the constraints in its way. The logic of my argument entails that both needs (the negative generalization) and resources and opportunities for the development of potentialities (the positive generalization) are rights, subject to reciprocal and universal recognition and democratically adjudicated global constraints. But what of rational agency itself? It is in a person's real interest to flourish, and to come to acquire the disposition, knowledge and power to do so. And it is in a person's interest simpliciter to come to know what their real interests are, unless over-riding circumstances prevail. Why the exit clause? From the standpoint of concrete singularity implicit in my moral realism an agent has to treat herself as an emergent totality. A different principle applies to emergent totalities, including internally related collectivities of agents, from their constituent moments, aspects or parts. The world is an open system in process, in which in particular circumstances, all sorts of contingencies may arise and, in certain circumstances, justify backsliding. A principle for emergent totalities could justify this, and indeed argue that a virtuous existence *requires* the breaking of actualistically formulated or geo-historically specific rules. (The same position could be arrived at by the application of the principle of actionability.) This can be generalized. Totalities are not aggregates. So we can apply, at any place-time-context, *a principle of fold-back*, which is at once a recognition of the character of a non-centrist-expressivist-triumphalist-endist process, and an application of the principle of actionability* and of the doctrine of the Aristotelian mean (which I have already invoked in §7), specifying only optimal progress (which may be negative) in the direction to which the logic of dialectical universalizability flows, putting a constraint on the constraining of constraints, which may on occasion be a necessary condition for any moral or social progress at all.**

The same principle for emergent totalities should make it explicit that morality is not exhaustive — it is only part of the art of 'living well' — with space — literally, a room of one's own; time — literally again (cf. Marx on the shortening of necessary labour time, i.e. of the working day, as a prerequisite for the realm of freedom) — for the cultivation and enjoyment of aesthetic, more generally hedonistic, private and public pleasures. Conceptions of the good society have almost always over-socialized man (sic). As the logic of dialectical universalizability has the causal efficacy of a normative conatus — a tendential drive — it is important to recognize the constraints placed on it by the principle of actionability, which will reflexively incorporate principles of prefigurationality. Moral realism and axiological and spatio-temporal constraints will see to it that the ungrounded discriminations shown in love, friendship, particular

---

* This is perhaps the place to stress the non-actualist character of actionability. Actionability implies that a thing can be done, not that it will. It is also worth pointing out that the moral realism I am articulating, entailing the irreducibility of 'ought' to 'is', is in no way hypostatizing. For moral truth, as social-relation dependent, is of course constellationally contained within being.

** This may be in a dialectic of constellational progress → transition → entrenchment, on which one could bring to bear the dialectic of nodal/switch/connector (totalizing) points and measure relations. However, even for successful entrenchment, it may be necessary to constantly counterpose to the presence of the past a vision of a more *pleasurable* future, to sociological individualism, the transfactuality of global intra-dependence, etc. etc.

concerns, are not undermined. Neither will the phenomenon of 'moral distance'. But it is this very same phenomenon, conceived as *moral distanciation* or the stretching of the moral imagination that the logic of dialectical universalizability requires, that enables its extension to include the rights of unborn generations, other species, the ecosphere and possibilities such as the violation of life, or even possibilities of life, elsewhere in the cosmos by space travel.

Freedom, like truth, satisfies all the moments of dialectical critical realism. It is stratified at 1M (in being composed of levels and degrees, informed by ontologically stratified alethic truth); a geo-historical process of absenting constraints, especially constraints$_2$ on the absenting of ills or the presencing of possibilities at 2E (thus the moment of concrete utopianism, which identifies 'the positive in the negative', must always be grounded in real possibilities-in-process); inexorably totalizing at 3L in virtue of its form and content and in the transition from form to content (including the excluded, empowering the powerless, rendering visible the unseen and explanatorily critiquing the conditions of injustice, animating at both margins of inquiry in every intra-action, fundamentally constitutive power$_2$ relations included); and irreducibly agentive at 4D, neither disembodying nor de-agentifying (reifying) concretely singular human beings and oriented to the totalizing collective self-absenting of their ills. This last remark raises two issues. First, the dialectic of self and solidarity foreshadowed by the assertoric and fiduciary components of the imperatival moment of the judgement form. The slave who knows her slavery must come to know and articulate and achieve her humanity before she can become free. The eudaimonistic society must satisfy the criteria for rational agency, subject to the principle for emergent totalities, for universal human autonomy to be effective. But the greater danger is surely not that of unwanted solidarity in the individualism of consumer capitalism. Although I have argued that the reality principle will tend to undermine this individualism, it is here in particular that immanent critique must be remorselessly practised arm in arm with the logic of universal-izability. However, in a world at once increasingly homogeneous and increasingly inequitous, transformative tendencies will become exponentially radicalized (i.e. radically negative) and activity become increasingly intra-activity. Eudaimonia, necessarily universalizing, will prove even more impossible in one country than socialism was.

In this section we have been tracing through the implications of the theoretico-practical duality of the judgement form, and/or that of the explanatory critical† grounds entailed by the practical fiduciary remark (which, by a valid perspectival switch, applies equally to every expressively veracious assertoric sentence). Both can be derived, via the chain from the absence implicit in elemental desire through referential detachment and acknowledgement of the reality principle to ontological stratification and alethic truth. And both point, via the logic of dialectical universalizability, to the eudaimonistic society. The dialectic

[II] absence (2E) − primal scream − desire − referential detachment (1M) − alethic truth − assertoric judgement − dialectical univer-salizability (3L) − universal human emancipation (4D) − eudai-monistic society-in-process

is concordant with Marx's goal of a (in my terms, concretely singularized) 'association in which the free development of each is the condition for the free development of all'. But how consistent is it with the other basic principles — as distinct from actually existing practices — of socialism? In §7 I have already partially answered this question, suggesting distributive principles along the lines of 'from each according to their concretely singularized wants, abilities and needs and, at a minimum threshold, from what they would expect to receive from others ceteris paribus, i.e. unless exceptional circumstances prevail', where this is to be understood as the right to be subject to universally reciprocated and recognized rights and, 'to each according to their essential needs, wanted possibilities and social virtues (e.g. creative enterprise, willingness to participate in necessary but undesirable or arduous tasks) and, at a minimum threshold, what makes it unnecessary to sell their labour-power'. This would certainly satisfy Marx's distinction between the realm of necessity and the realm of freedom, in which the development of human energy became 'an end-in-itself' including the possibility of a state of affairs in which labour became 'life's prime want' provided labour is taken in the generalized sense of C2.9. Before commenting further on this I want to make some elementary points about a eudaimonistic society.

First, autonomy leaves the world axiologically underdetermined. There must be a field of unconstrained choice, save by respect for global constraints and universal rights. Second, such a society would be an open process. Geo-history would not have come to an end (nor does it make much sense to say that it would start then). Contradictions would exist, of necessity. Difficult decisions would have to be taken, democratically — at a plurality of spatial and organizational levels and spheres of interest — by sometimes circuitous decision-making routes. There would be competing conceptions of the details of the eudaimonistic society, grounded in competing theories of four-planar social being, almost inevitably represented by competing parties. Diversity and pluralism would flourish. Under such conditions one can invert and transform the Hegelian triad as follows:

(α) *Universal civic duty* — unless exceptional circumstances prevent an agent from performing any such duty, conceived precisely as the right to be subject to universal rights and participate in globalized democracy.

(β) *Social virtue* — in which innovation, initiative, enterprise, participation in (participatory, representative, syndicalist and other forms of) democracy, and/or in a socialized market, would be rewarded. It is to be hoped that increasingly these rewards would be internal to the practices concerned, but if this proved not to be the case, then the rewards would be material ones.

(γ) *Individual self-realization* — not (at least, not necessarily) in the family but exactly how the socialized, singularized individual pleases — the domain of unquestioned choice.

The importance of the second realm of social virtue (corresponding to Hegel's 'civil society') is, in part, that it provides a forum for the *expressive* and *agonistic* aspects of human behaviour (cf. C2.9) and the *tacit knowledge* of the immediate producers (as distinct from the bureaucratic knowledge of corporations and planning bodies). It cannot be gleaned from Marx's writings whether he appreciated the need for a mediating realm, but it seems unlikely that he did. Ironically, most indebted to the oppositional realm of Essence epistemologically, he paid scant regard to it programmatically. Is this because he underestimated the presence of the past in humanity — of dead labour in living labour? The presence of the past would also receive its due in the shape of the commitment to *constitutionality*, seen precisely as a resource for the future. (γ) corresponds, of course, to the domain of what I have been calling life politics. A balanced life would be a unity-in-diversity, in which (γ) could not be appropriately captured by the concept of 'leisure'. Universal civic duty, (α), would be coordinated around maximum possible free choice of activity in partial totalities based on a normative order informed by the values of trust, solidarity, sensitivity to suffering, nurturing and care. Each of these realms would be in the interest of all. Thus, at (β), everyone would benefit from a greater efficiency of resource use in which currently external (dis)economies were internalized. A final point to stress here. Such a society would still be in transition: emancipatory/

transformist, as well as movement, politics would carry on, with the evolution of the moral consciousness of the species as open as the arts, sciences and technologies. (Cf. Figure 3.11.)

I have been arguing for a combination of moral realism and ethical naturalism. Moral realism is manifest in the fiduciary aspect of the logic of dialectical universalizability and is grounded in the fact that I cannot help but take a position in an already moralized world. This position will comprise a relational dialectic. Ethical naturalism is manifest in the alethic aspect of the logic of dialectical universalizability and is grounded negatively in the aporiai of other positions (e.g. the endless regress of decisionism, where values must inevitably be grounded in facts, as they will be so explained) and positively in the fact that I have shown how moral propositions (e.g. · 'lack of access to educational resources is wrong' or 'capitalism is based on a categorial error' or 'the inter- and intra-national distribution of resources is characterized by growth in inequities') can be known, i.e. true and adequately justified. Substantially the position developed here is a consequentialism (with universal human autonomy oriented to concrete singularity as perhaps a Fichtean task only ever asymptoptically approachable) — with, at the deontological level of the ethical circle I described in §7, a hugely expanded conception of universally recognized and concretely singularized rights to include, inter alia, needs and potentialities for development, on the basis of a positive generalization of the concept of freedom, subject only to 'trumping' by a catastrophe clause; and, at the level of virtue theory, a radically transformed table of virtues, grounded in solidarity, reflecting the reality of social intradependence, and nurtured by care and sensitivity to sufferings, enjoyments and needs of others and nature (so that the ecological would be among the virtues). In the eudaimonistic society every concretely singular individual would be true to, of, in and for herself and every other.

One final comment. There is a difference between emancipatory and emancipated action, as there is a difference between the liberation of oneself and the removal of a constraint from the outside (this is not to denigrate the value of the latter, merely to remind the reader that the former task still remains). The concrete utopian imagination is not a prescription for the future. The eudaimonistic society would be an open one in which it would be up to the totality of concretely singularized individuals to decide what to do with their freedoms. Dialectic is the process of absenting constraints on absenting absences (ills, constraints, untruths, etc.). It is not in the business of telling people, in commandist (Stalinist) or elitist (Social Democratic) fashion what to do. Rather it is better conceived as an

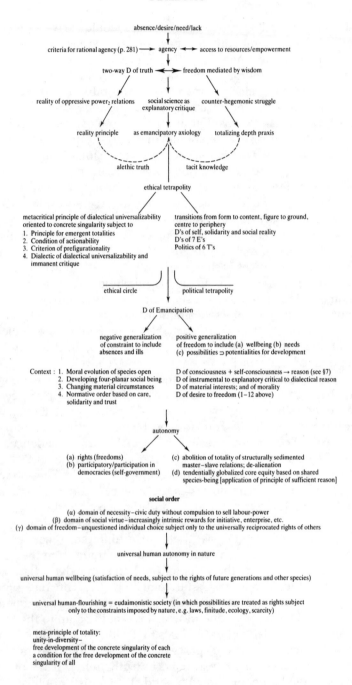

Figure 3.11 Implications of the Dialectic of Freedom

inner urge that flows universally from the logic of elemental absence (lack, need, want or desire). It manifests itself wherever power$_2$ relations hold sway. It is the heartbeat of a positively generalized concept of freedom as flourishing and as autonomy and as reason. It is irrepressible.

§ 11 Dialectical Critical Realism and the Dialectics of Critical Realism

The foundational moment of critical realism was a Copernican/ Darwinian revolution which stood the world back on its feet again, critiqued the *epistemic fallacy* and situated epistemology constellation-ally within ontology. It enabled the critique of anthroporealism, especially in its dominant empirical realist form, and irrealism in philosophy, monism and deductivism in the philosophy of science, positivism and hermeneutics in the philosophy of social science, and anti-realist ideologies masquerading as sciences. The system of dialectical critical realism constitutes a second wave of critical realism, structured around the critique of *ontological monovalence* and pivoting on the ontological primacy of the category of *absence*. The result is a regional extension on to the terrain of dialectics, a topical enrichment, e.g. into the philosophy of space and time and into ethics, a theoretical deepening, through its 1M−4D analyses, and a historical generalization, via the metacritical dialectics of a wider species of irrealist philosophies than that of pre-existing critical realism. It takes time for a new system to gain ground. But dialectical critical realism will stand the test of time. And sooner or later concepts such as referential detachment, alethic truth, existentially constitutive process and intradependence, multiply emergent distanciated spatio-temporalities, the irreducibility of tensed spatializing process, rhythmics, concrete singularity, negative being, contextual action, Tina formations and constellationality will take hold, as, say, intransitivity and transfactual efficacy have done.

The ontological realism that dialectical critical realism sustains is *alethic* (1M) (structured and transfactual), *polyvalent* (2E) (spatio-temporal and A-serial processual), *holistic* (3L) (emergentist, mediated and concrete), *agentive* and *moral* (4D). If absence is the crucial missing category (rendering a system vulnerable to omissive critique), its effect is inherently detotalizing (resulting in liability to dialectical sublation). The effects of the categorial errors (formed, say, as a product of illicit fusions or fissions) manifest in aporiai, antinomies, etc. are T/P inconsistency, detotalization (including alienation and splits), reification or dichotomous dualism, irrationalism (as expressed in the fact/value divide), repression (Diderot's Syndrome), Tina compromise formation, grafting, supplementarity, equivocation, duplicity and ideological plasticity, along with perhaps implicit or even overt complicity with the powers that be. Dialectical critical realism claims that it avoids these consequences, and in C4.2 I will give an indication of how both the textbook problems of philosophy and more esoteric genres can be rationally resolved. But they will not disappear as a result of metacritique alone. For they are sustained by the material circumstances of our being, which can be transformed only by depth praxis of a totalizing kind. Historically the fact that there is such a thing as *the* problem of knowledge stems from the monistically presumed and/or solipsistically pursued quest for an incorrigible, unhypothetical initiating point, in mimesis with God, which inevitably splits reality into two (viz. that which conforms to its criterion and that which does not), generating the first great problem of philosophy, viz. the problem of opposites, or negation, or the one and the other — and this in its wake generates a second great problem, namely of how the one can account for the many, most obvious in the problems of natural kinds and natural necessity, that is, of universals in respect of classificatory/taxonomic knowledge and induction for the causal/explanatory sort.

Dialectical critical realism claims to derive the rational directionality of geo-history, but it is deeply contingent and dependent upon that totalizing depth praxis, in a multiply fractured world, to which I have frequently referred in this chapter, whether this is the path humanity will tread or not. Moreover, it is incumbent upon a retotalizing inquiry of the kind undertaken here to reflexively situate itself. What are the conditions of possibility of dialectical critical realism? The eclipse of philosophical reason in the post-Hegelian *Götterdämmerung* and the demise of the Humean Viceregency in the form of orthodox philosophy of science coincided with the end of the post-war boom, more than a whiff of revolt and even revolution and the rebirth of a free Marxist current in the new eclecticism of a still malaised social science. The multi-tiered stratification of the natural sciences was a palpable reality and slogans of the type 'If you can split/spray it/them, it/they exist/s' abounded. Relativity theory, quantum mechanics, the liberation of the colonies, the threat of a nuclear holocaust and looming ecological crisis rendered conventional assumptions obsolete. The time was ripe for ontology; and as the seventies made way for the eighties and the events of 1989, for a new account of *change*, especially in the context of the collapse of communism, the poverty of most materialist dialectical philosophy and the monstrous inequities of the strife-torn, crisis-ridden chaotic new world order that Bush, Benetton and Hayek were in the process of ushering in. It is in this milieu that dialectical critical realism came into being. And it claims not only to build on critical realism, but also to sublate previous dialectics in one that, as far as I know, uniquely sustains an adequate account of *negativity*, the essence of all dialectics.

Since at least Derrida we know that all philosophies have their priorities. Dialectical critical realism prioritizes difference over identity, negativity over positivity, absence over presence, totality over its aspects, relations over their relata, structure over agency. At the same time it is characteristic for dialectic systems to produce their own paradoxical reversals. Dialectical critical realism is not short of these. Thus we move from anti-anthropomism at 1M to humanism at 4D, from anti-centrism with respect of knowledge, language and politics to the recentrification of subjects$_2$, at 1M itself from attention to difference to the recognition of *underlying identity*, at 3L from dialectical universalizability to concrete particularity and to diversity as a necessary condition for unity; and in the dialectic of freedom arguably from the most naturalistic premises to the only moral solution to the problems that beset humanity, and from primal scream to the perfect life. Some other features of dialectical critical realism should be noted here. *Referential detachment* necessitates ontology; *alethic truth* resolves the textbook problems of philosophy; *concrete singularity* is the key to the realm of freedom. Systematically I am arguing in ethics for a moral realism which highlights what is normally taken to be the objection to it, namely its first-person (singular or plural/collective) action-guiding character, in combination with a naturalism which treats the capacity to transcend its so-called fallacy as its greatest virtue, in the transition from fact to value, theory to practice, form to content, figure to ground. At the same time I combine a strongly non-anthropocentric account of spatio-temporality with a commitment to an equally non-anthropocentric account of the irreducibility and the reality of A-serial tense which, when it is defended at all, is normally defended on the grounds that it is necessary for the intelligibility of human experience and action but not for anything else.

In C2.10 I argued that there is no one way of ordinating dialectical critical realism. I stand by that, but there is, nevertheless, a particularly natural way to present it, which is, in a sense, the way I have presented its fine structure in this chapter. We start from the 'ontological arguments' (a concept I have already justified in C2.6) of the type given in §§1 and 3. Beginning with *absence*, taking the form of desire (in the context of primary polyadization up to the level of global intra-dependence), we establish in one step, as Figure 3.12 makes clear, referential detachment, the horizon of those axiological necessities which comprise the reality principle, the case for ontology and the concept of existential intransitivity, and the necessity for differentiation (implied, of course, in the self-identification of the other memebrs of the polyad) as a condition for scientific classification and explanation. The second leap is therefore to stratification, entailing both transfactuality and alethic truth. Change is already implicit on the primordial act of referential detachment or even occurrence of the onset of desire. But we make this explicit from the metatheorem that to change is to cause is to negate and, if determinate, to absent; and that to contradict is to negate, and we can develop the full range of 2E categories here, from constraint through dialectical contradiction and overt conflict to non-antagonistic argumentation. We are now in the realm of space, time and tensed process; and, together with stratification and contradiction, this leads us onto the plane of emergence and, with it, multiple control, mediation, internal relationality and thence directly into the 3L sphere of totality, which encompasses the multiple quadruplicity of the concrete universal ↔ singular and the phenomena of holistic causality. Reflexivity is the inwardized form of totality and manifests itself in the agency of stratified selves over distanciated space-time. Agency, on the one hand, leads us back to our starting point from anything from speech action, cooking a meal to experimental praxis. Lack, on the other hand, as suffering from constraints or ills, takes us into that absenting absentive agency intrinsic to the dialectic of the desire to freedom, through any of the routes I rehearsed in the last section and into the totalizing depth praxis of explanatory axiology through a transformed transformative trustworthy totalizing transformist transitional dialectic of life, movement, representative and emancipatory politics embedded in the dialectics of centre and periphery, process and product, present and past, and intra-dependent counter-hegemonic struggles over oppressive power$_2$ relations to the eudaimonistic society of universal human autonomy and flourishing. In this process the transition from fact to value passes over into the transition from form to content, ultimately naturalistically grounded in a theory of the possibilities of a four-planar developing social being-in-nature. The whole process involves just seven steps, as shown in Figure 3.12.

It could be said that the dialectic of freedom depends not just upon the logic of the judgement form but also, viz. in its reference to four-planar human nature, upon the whole scaffolding of dialectical critical naturalism as set out in C2.9. It is true that this follows from the

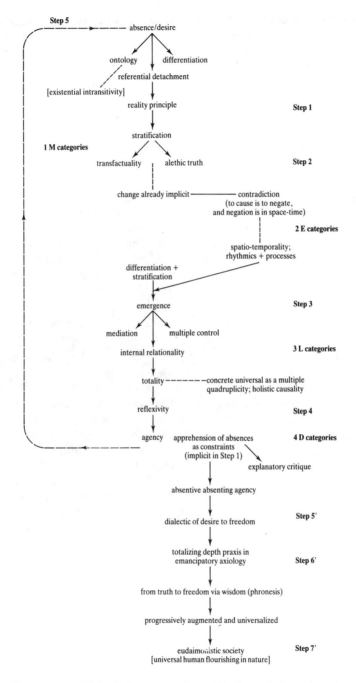

Figure 3.12 Dialectical Presentation of Dialectical Critical Realism

TMSA but that and the dislocated dialectic and duality of structure and agency and the four-planar theory which it entails (though not of course the precise specifications of the substantive social scientific theory) all flow from the conditions of possibility of intentional embodied agency. If it is contended that the existence of discursively moralized oppressive power$_2$ relations is merely a contingent fact about contemporary human society then the dialectic of freedom can — all the better — be presented as sound, transfactual and potentially counterfactual.

The transcendental argument for absence in C2.1, showing that any world containing human agency must change, is, of course, complemented by others, so there is nothing anthropomorphic about the dialectic presented here, although naturally, insofar as we know, 4D intentional embodied agency, and thus the parameters of the dialectic of freedom, only applies in the human realm. That argument can, however, also be generalized to any argument for the impossibility of ontological monovalence in any world which *changes*. And we saw the thorough permeation of the four levels of *causality* — 1M transfactuality, 2E spatio-temporal process, 3L holistic causality and 4D intentional agency with *negativity* (cf. §5 above). It is worth remembering that as dialectical critical realism develops we move in a *diagonal* from real to transformative to radical (totalizing) negation until it can be presented in something approximating a linear form. However, this does not make it autogenetic; it is a contingent fact that these phenomena exist. Note also that absence plays a crucial role quite independently of the generation of the categories of each degree or level of critical realism and in the critiques apposite to them. At 1M absence is present in the form of existential intransitivity and alterity, including non-anthropocity, absence from consciousness and actuality in the critique of subject–object identity theory which automatically entails a supplementary dualism, as we have seen, and so an absence from self, split or detotalization. At 2E the connection is obvious. But it is just worth repeating the two most relevant metatheoretical equations here:

[1] to reason = to cause = to negate = to absent = to contradict = to (negatively) constrain

[2] absences = constraints = ills = falsehoods = untruths to human nature

so as to generate:

[3] moral truth (alethia) = the good = universal human freedom, i.e. the realization of the concrete singularity of each, as a condition, in the realm of totality (where diversity is a condition for unity), of the realization of the concrete singularity of all

and our definition of dialectic as

[4] absenting constraints (including constraints$_2$ and other inequities) on absenting absences (more generally ills, which function as constraints).

At 2E, of course, we often have the phenomenon of constitutive absence (in the geo-historical process, of the past and the exterior) and may extend it to 3L in the form of intra-activity (the constitutive efficacy of another not itself, which only dubiously counts as absence). Absence is, however, already explicit in 3L. First, macroscopically, in the form of the partial totality (the only plausible form), which is not only disconnected from other parts of reality but is also shot through with external as well as internal connections and level-specific or absolute voids. Second, it appears immediately in the form of a detotalization, alienation or split(-off). Finally, at 4D, embodied intentional agency typically expresses itself in the form of transformative negating praxis (absenting absentive agency) and is informed by wants, or (in principle) rationally assessable causally efficacious beliefs, but most elementally as desire — that is, in either case mediated by absences.

It is not difficult to penetrate through the ideological jungle and identify the characteristic effects of the irrealist philosophies, which are also the source of the philosophical and extra-philosophical problems they generate. At 1M, irrealism destratifies, undermining science, and resonates a punctualist conception of the self with atomistic conceptions of society. As a condition of the possibility of identity or equivalence theories they typically reify and naturalize knowledge, chiming with the logic of commodification, and cutting the ground from under critique. At 2E, irrealist philosophies denegate change, undermining geo-historicity and resonate with ego-ethno-anthropo-conceptions of (social) being; in general functioning, as I have argued that the 'analytic problematic', founded on the denial of dialectic and negativity, does, as an ontology of stasis and an axiology of repression. At best, they normalize past and local changes, ideologies and freedoms. The source of the aporiai they generate stems just from their positivity or monovalence. As at 2E irrealist philosophies deny change, so at 3L they deny inter/intra-action. Their watchword here is: disconnect. They detotalize, divide and rule. Ontological extensionalism is made for empire-builders, manipulators and the masters of subjects$_2$ who want to distract their eyes from the top of the power$_2$ relations on which they sit. Detotalization is, as might be expected, the source of philosophical aporiai here. At 4D, irrealist philosophies tend to deny either embodiment or agency, nowadays more usually the latter; but they are for the most part forced back into denying embodiment in the intrinsic aspect (the first-person case) and agency in the extrinsic aspect (when they can view the world as an object and there is no axiological imperative upon them to act). Thus they end up denying both embodiment and agency. As they permeate down from the rarified stratosphere of philosophy, irrealist ideologies act to disempower and fragment the agent. And the absence of a concept of agentive agency is the rock on which post-Kantian philosophy founders.

What are the dialectics *of* dialectical critical realism? 1M dialectics tend to be of stratification, superstructuration and emergence, but also of inversion, mediatization and virtualization. As dialectics of non-identity relations they constellationally contain the ideological reflections of the logic of identity and simple, expressive, undifferentiated unity. There are also dialectics within and between different levels of critical realism. And an inversion, duplicity (dual) or complement will immediately enforce a T/P inconsistency, detotalization or compartmentalizing split-off and axiological indeterminacy (at 2E−4D), as well as resulting in some Tina compromise. The dialectics of real and actual, essence and existence, figure and ground, alterity, heterology, metaphor and metonymy, analogical grammar and trace fall within the former group. 2E dialectics tend to be dialectics of node and transition, boundary/frontier, process and change but also of contradictions in a ground, hermeneutic and other forms of struggle and of differential spatio-temporal rhythmics; ideologically they incorporate a sundered world of oppositions, and bipolarities. If the first ideological reflection, viz. of simple expressive undifferentiated unity, corresponds to the erstwhile Soviet state, the second approximates the state of international relations in the cold war or, of course, the generative separation that is the condition of possibility of global commodificaiton, reification and fetishism. 3L dialectics are typically dialectics of inter- or intra-activity, totalization and detotalization, alienation, compartmentalization, perspectival switch, constellationality, interiorization and exteriorization, centre and periphery. They admit of various forms. Thus a split-off may be recognized as such, or repressed and appear in some other guise, or it may be tacitly presupposed as a complement or be subjected to duplicative projection or introjective identification, or a compromise formation may result. There is an interplay between dr/da, d + /d −, dt/d − t and dconcept- or society-dependent or dnot. This swings us into the dialectics of 4D through mediating notions such as de/re-centrification and (ir)reflexivity. Here we are on the terrain of dialectics of democracy, enlightenment, emancipation, concrete utopianism and explanatory critique, of the dialectical argument which is dialectical critical realism's dialectic of freedom. But also dialectics of disempowerment, ideological mystification and alienation, of the fragmentation of the personality and the enervation of the self.

There are many other ways of coordinating dialectic, e.g. as epistemological, ontological, relational, metacritical, ethical, axiological, aesthetic, etc. Most of these will be readily susceptible to treatment within the contours of dialectical critical realism. And there are many other ways in which one can diffract dialectic. But it is not difficult to situate the dialectics of geo-historical individuals within the dialectical critical realist grid. Thus Hegel's dialectic is clearly of a 3L kind, as is Lukács's. Gramsci's is 2E/4D. Colletti's, which mystified him, is of a 1M character, as is Marcuse's, which he fully understood. Adorno's, with its heavy emphasis on non-identity, is clearly a vehicle of 1M. But a rounded emphasis on reality must make room for both structure and difference, contradiction and change, totality and reflexivity, desire and eudaimonia. We must remember that philosophical dialectics may be a Nietzschean gadfly on the neck of the authorities and that their primary function is to act as an underlabourer for irreducibly heteronomous and a fortiori dialogical social sciences (cf. §7 above), together with other practices, both scientific and non-scientific, of a putatively emancipatory kind.

4

Metacritical Dialectics: Irrealism and Its Consequences

§ 1 Irrealism

Generally philosophy has been irrealist. In fact I think Hegel would not have been wrong if he had described the history of philosophy as that of explicit idealism and implicit realism.[1] In any event, as I have already claimed that realism is inexorable, and in this chapter I am going to argue that philosophy has the aspect of a socially conditioned causally efficacious relational dialectic, philosophical irrealism constitutes a prima facie paradox.

Normally to be a realist in philosophy is to be committed to the existence of some disputed kind of being (e.g. material objects, universals, causal laws; propositions, numbers, probabilites; efficacious reasons, social structures, moral facts). In this work I have championed descriptive, explanatatory and taxonomic realism in the natural and social world alike, and in particular extended the existing critical realist commitment along the 1M–4D line, through non-anthropism, stratification, differentiation and change; negativity, contradiction, space-time, tense and open process; totality, reflexivity, agency, morality, truth and freedom. In each case I have argued that irrealism, or realism of a false or inappropriate kind, leads to theory – practice inconsistency, susceptibility to dialectical comment, detotalization, Tina compromise and ideological plasticity. Hence the well-known phenomenon of the pre-prandial philosophical irrealist and/or sceptic turning into a post-prandial realist.

We should be wrong to assume from its irrealist timbre — where the crucial questions are the character and form of its axiologically necessitated realist compromises — that philosophy's role has invariably been reactionary. Although it would not be incorrect to see it in general as the aporetic, unconscious and pliable retrospective normalization of the status quo ante, one must remember that the status quo ante has comprised beginnings (of the new geometry, of

308

secularized individualism, of the rising bourgeoisie, of non-anthropic physics) as well as continuities and endings; that philosophers have participated notably in the sciences (normally) and politics (sometimes) progressively as well as nostalgically (a few names will suffice: Aristotle, Descartes, Hobbes, Leibniz, Kant); and that, at critical historical turning points, its role has typically been *Janus-faced*. Think, for instance, of the *philosophes* of the Enlightenment, with an ideologically saturated account of the form of the new science, committed to the spread of its content and that of the freedoms upon which it ultimately depended.

How did philosophy become irrealist? Much as I hate to concur with the conventional wisdom, the story must begin with great-grandfather Parmenides, upon whose quest for an unhypothetical starting point, ultimate responsibility for both the *epistemic fallacy* and *ontological monovalence* (and the consequent detotalizations and reifications [cf. 1M−4D]) must be placed. But we know Parmenides still only relatively opaquely and a story with firmer historiographic credentials can be told from Plato on. Two great problems have dominated philosophy: (α) *the problem of the one and the other*, of *diremption* from an assumed original unity, of negation and of change — the dialectical problem par excellence; and its analytical counterpart, (β) *the problem of the one and the many*, of order and its opposition, the problem of *chaos*. The immediate origin of both for us lies in the Platonic response to worrying change and diversity — the problem of *relativism*, bounding the tradition. The analysis of negation in terms of difference and the establishment of a (potentially) dialectically accessible hierarchy among the Forms, aligned under the primacy of the Form of the Good, provides, as Whitehead correctly appreciated, the base-line for all subsequent philosophy. Dialectic justified foundationalism and eidetic foundationalism justified the practice of dialectic. The Aristotelian critique of Platonic transcendence, vital though it was (pinpointing the homologous character of Plato's 'explanations' of the sensate world), coupled with Aristotle's underestimation of the possibilities of dialectic as a potential alternative to intellectual intuition, led to what I have called *'primal squeeze'*, the elimination of the middle term of natural necessity — if only as a place holder for an eventual alethic realism — the original fault-line, around which the irrealist tradition has played.

From this point on (β) generated aporiai of taxonomic and explanatory knowledge, the best known of which are the problems of universals and induction, to which Aristotelian nous, Christian faith, Cartesian certainty, Humean custom, Kantian synthetic a priori, Fichtean intellectual intuition, Hegelian autogenetics (hyperintuition) or Strawsonian dissolution cannot provide an answer. Indeed, once dialectic, in its Platonic or Aristotelian declensions, failed, the Aristotelian critique must inevitably lead to the generation of a *new transcendent*, God or social convention constituting the normal alternatives (to Wittgenstein and the present day) to the absent concept of *ontological stratification*.

Moreover, there is in Aristotle, as in Plato, a unity between the two great problems. As the other in the problem of the one and the other became the formless, the flux (β), it reappeared as the lack of a coherent principle of differentiation, to delineate the many as ones (for, were they to be knowable, there should be a form or essence for them). The absence responsible for this is, of course, that of the transfactuality of relatively enduring causal structures and generative mechanisms in open systems. I have given, through Hegel, this irrational other of philosophy, the worm in the heart of the tradition, the recalcitrant surd of non-being, the status of the 'demi-', the 'demi-actual' as the weak actualism of a constellationally closed open system and the 'demi-present' as the (spatialized) future in the constellational closure of an open totality. As it is, the *other* other, the absented concept of absence, was stoically forgotten (Plato), sceptically denied (Aristotle) and placed on one side (viz. the past) in the unhappy consciousness of a Hegel. The repressed returned in early twentieth-century physics and Bolshevism to shatter the complacency of what one commentator has called the 'arch of knowledge tradition'[2] held in place by a monistic theory of scientific development and a deductivist theory of scientific structure. By the seventies they had crumbled. But it requires not just transcendental realism to make sense of structure and accommodate the constellational identity of judgemental rationality (in the intrinsic aspect) within epistemic relativity (in the transitive dimension) within ontological realism (in the intransitive dimension), but dialectical critical realism to place absence and absenting at the heart of a non-monovalent ontology, and so avoid the detotalizations and reifications that would otherwise result.

None of this is to imply that no progress has been made in the history of philosophy. On the contrary, in my forthcoming *Plato Etcetera* I will tell its story as a succession of *Achilles' Heel critiques*, of the metacritique of Platonic forms, Aristotelian substance, Cartesian certainty, Humean scepticism, Kantian freedom, Hegelian historicity, Marxian communism, etc. Moreover, in the irrealist tradition, the parameters of which I shall shortly outline, any adequate metacritical history will have to see, for instance, Descartes's role in subjectivizing and inwardizing rationalist criteriology (and so ensuring the eventual victory of empiricism) as a condition for both the new physics and secularizing Christianity for the politics to come in which it would be appreciated, to use Hegelian terms, that wo/men as such were free — a principle without which the dialectic of freedom I sketched in C3.10 would collapse. Moreover, we will have to see Hegel's impact precisely as bringing about a reductiones ad absurdissimum, just as J.S. Mill thought, of transcendent metaphysics in coming so close to achieving the goals of traditional philosophy, inherited from Parmenides, Plato and Aristotle (although heavily mediated by Spinoza, Fichte and Schelling) within an immanent metaphysics of experience (the legacy of Kant). The tension is apparent in the younger Hegel between (α) a radical atheist historicist this-worldly humanist and (β) a rationalist logico-spiritual absolutist (which presages the expressivist-centrism, cognitivist-triumphalism and con-stellational endism of whom in C2.3 I dubbed Hegel Mark II). Hegel sees his own fate in the late 1790s mirroring that of Jesus, a beautiful soul ensnared by the positivity of the people he would teach and, as such, alienated from them. So he adopts a *Geist*-centred standpoint, underpinning (β), and deploys dialectic as a technique for transfiguring a purely empirical reality with a conceptual realist gloss. This is his achievement. But, in reinventing dialectic with the sting of the analytic reinstatement in its tail, he accepts the (α/β) split of the unhappy consciousness, with the impotence of theory, non-immanence of the future, etc. as the price to be paid for escaping Jesus's fate. His system marks the heat-death of the traditional goals of philosophy. Insofar as they are still accepted it is at the cost of the unhappy consciousness of those who know the tides of geo-history are rolling over them.

To those who ask 'why did (Hegelian/irrealist) dialectics fail?', one must give a double answer. In the first place it failed because it accepted analytical criteria — monovalence, analytical reinstatement in dialectical connection, the epistemo-logicization of reality, eidetic actualism, empirical realism, etc. In the second place, because the problem of diremption cannot be consistently stated within the structures of irrealism as a really contemporaneously existing fact. It can be acknowledged only ex post after it has already been overcome. 'Geo-history', absence, split, gulf, is always placed in the past (or elsewhere), and freedom in another world, or, insofar as it is in this world, as what concrete subjects$_2$ have managed triumphantly to obtain. Dialectics will always be dominated by analytics within the irrealist problematic.

In Figure 4.1 I represent in broad outline terms the structures of the irrealist *traditions*. One must remember here that irrealism is

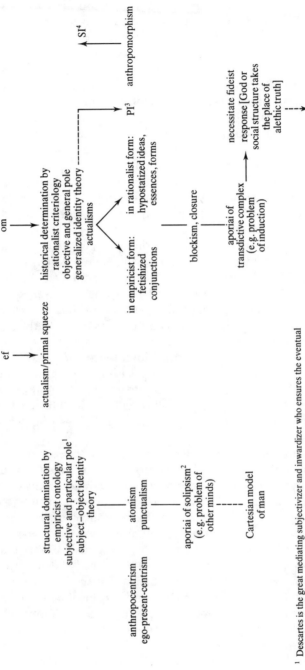

Figure 4.1 The Structure of Irrealism

1 Descartes is the great mediating subjectivizer and inwardizer who ensures the eventual victory of empiricism.
2 The aporiai of solipsism no less than those of the transdictive complex necessitate a fideist response. In fact, as indicated in §2, they can themselves be situated within the transdictive network.
3 PI = positivistic illusion (reduction of theory to experience).
4 SI = speculative illusion (reduction of theory to philosophy).

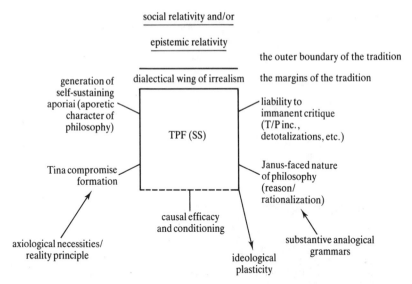

Figure 4.2 The Tradition in Its Context — a Standard Theory Problem-Field Solution Set

constituted by multiple problematics both over and at any one time, and that each problematic is compatible with a wholy array of positions. Characteristically philosophies come as packages — as what I will call theory problem-field solution sets — which are related dialectically to extra-philosophical reality as Figure 4.2 indicates, where the marginality of dialectic and the bounding character of epistemic and/or general social relativity are displayed. I earlier differentiated the *internal* duplicity of subject−object theory and its generalized form, actualism, which must equivocate over the existence of material objects or the efficacy of laws in open systems, from the *external* duplicity occasioned by, say, the problems of solipsism or of the transdictive complex, such as induction, which can be 'remedied' by resort to fideistic grafting. A third figure is the *tacit* duplicity of dialectical antagonistis, such as subjective empiricism and objective idealism (cf. C2.5) or of empirical realism and conceptual realism. For, epistemologically, what are the ideas of conceptual realism but brute facts, established results, while, ontologically, what are facts but hypostatized ideas? This third case includes the dialectical wing of the irrealist tradition, which is displayed in Figure 4.3. In the first case we have dialectics of repression and compromise formation; in the second case of inconsistent complex formation; in the third case the mock or sham battle of tacit complementarity.

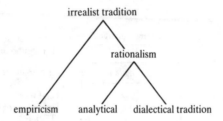

Figure 4.3 Dialectical Stream of Irrealism

These may be combined and/or substituted in various ways. If the arch aporia of the subjective, empiricist and particular pole of the tradition is that of solipsism, which is resolved by seeing social relations as the condition of possibility of subjectivity, the arch aporia of the objective, rationalist or empiricist and general pole is that of the transdictive complex, which is resolved by seeing natural necessity as a condition of social relations or, more simply, just of general knowledge (including the epistemic validity — when it is — of induction). As it is, the fideist response to these aporiai, generating the new transcendent, as a detotalizing alienating split-off, interiorizes a dualism or pluralism within the monistic theory, so inserting internal within external duplicity, resulting in a necessary repression, compromise and theory/practice inconsistency anyway. Dualism, split and heterology are at the heart of the irrealist tradition, whether it is made explicit (as in Plato or Kant) or not (as in Aristotle, Hume or Hegel). As we are dealing with a theory problem-field solution set the very distinction between internal and external duplicity collapses and any grafting, etc. appears as equivocation and compromise. Underpinning the subject—object identity theory to which the irrealist traditions aspire is the unholy trinity, diagnosed in C2.5, of the epistemic fallacy, ontological monovalence and the primal squeeze on natural necessity (resulting in the seeming options of the positivistic or speculative illusions — which it was Kant's greatness to try to bypass *but* in the medium of philosophy, not science, and without ontology, so no *natural* [non-anthropic] *necessity* was possible). Any position in this ensemble results in theory/practice inconsistency, Tina formations, alienations, split-offs and the de-agentifying reification and fetishism depicted in Figure 4.4. These are meta-critically identifiable results. But, of course, irrealist theory problem-field solution sets will result in more apparent antinomies, dilemmas and contradictions, such as the return of non-being necessitated by the actualistically inspired drive to closure, resulting in surds such as

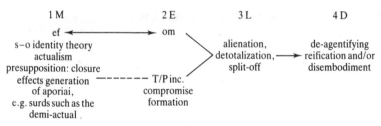

Figure 4.4   1M−4D Logic of Irrealism

irrational existents (the demi-actual), etc. It is to the consideration of these that I now turn.

§ 2 The Problems of Philosophy and Their Resolution

There is, when one thinks about it, something odd about the assumptions normally informing discussions of the 'problems of philosophy': (a) there are the assumptions, recently questioned by Kripke,[3] that philosophical problems cannot be real, that there must be something 'artificial' about them and, furthermore, that they cannot possess real, multiple and possibly contradictory geo-historical grounds and conditions; and (b) there are the assumptions that there is something uniquely philosophical about them, where philosophy is understood as the referent of a tradition and/or a disciplinary matrix. There is something profoundly detotalizing about both (a) and (b). If you ask a Cretan for directions on holiday and in the course of his reply he ventures the observation that all Cretans are liars, you would do well to reconsult the guidebook before accepting his advice. Of course, this is not the way the problem is normally put. But, as usually expressed, it lends itself readily to dialectical critical realist resolution. The Cretan's statement may be transfactually true but, on this occasion, counterfactual, i.e. actually false. Disposi-tionally, Cretans may be liars but this does not militate against an occasional outburst of truth. The bulk of this section will consist in a rational resolution of textbook and more esoteric genera of 'problems of philosophy', conceived in 1M−4D terms. But I shall want to insist on the *critical, symptomatic* and, at the limit, *dialectical* reality of the 'problems of philosophy'. Critical — because a crisis point might be defined as one in which scepticism (say about the social or moral order) becomes real. Symptomatic — because, for example, the late medieval proliferation of quiddities reflected the collapse of ontological stratification that I have labelled 'primal squeeze'.

Dialectical — because there are points at which one needs to talk of the being of non-being, or open totality, which provoke a genuine and an initially contradictory distanciation of our conceptual field.

For the most part, however, I shall be treating paradox as the surface form of categorial error, betraying the fact that something is conceptually amiss, as a prelude to the metacritical dialectics to come. The basic trouble at 1M problems of philosophy* lies in the *destratification of reality*, the absence of de re necessity, more generally actualism and the failure to sustain non-identity relations. The source of the chief real problems here are at least superficially precisely the same as those which underlie the irrealist tradition, including anthropism, especially in its ego-present-centric form. But if we look a little deeper we will find the logic of commodification. Moreover, it, and the fetishism (a real categorial problem and hence one suitable for philosophy, if ever there was one) to which it gives rise, turns on a typical 1M category mistake — the reduction of powers to their exercise (labour-power to labour). The key malaise at 2E is the *positivization of reality*, the absence of de re negativity, more generally ontological monovalence. The main real problem here is that of epistemic (and more generally, ontological, including, of course, social-relational) relativity, diversity and change. The fount of problems at 3L is the *detotalization of reality*, ontological extensionalism. It includes the absence of de re thought; and is manifest in the real problem of *alienation* as an index of the detotalizations and other effects of the contradictions and splits in the world of late/ postmodernity. The source of the aporiai at 4D is the *de-agentification of reality* (the lack of a concept of an emergent powers materialist, putatively rational, causal agentive agency); and it is reflected in (or rather a reflection of) the world historical problem of agency, of the apparent absence of the deep totalizing conveyors of the dialectic of freedom sketched in C3. It should be noted that the principal source of the traditional problems of philosophy that I am now about to work through is in each case an *ontological absence*, and it is, of course, the absence of the concept of absence in ontology that it is dialectical critical realism's intention to remedy.

The index problems at 1M — the home of the problem of the one and the many, as 2E is the abode of the one and the ('its') other (including the problem of opposites) — are the problems of induction (the aporiai of explanatory knowledge) and the problems of universals (the aporiai of taxonomic knowledge), which dialectical

---

* At this point I want to re-emphasize that it cannot be assumed that problems, any more than other phenomena generated in open systems, possess a single source.

critical realism will resolve by reference to the concepts of a posteriori knowable natural necessity and natural kinds, in which the concept of alethic truth will play a vital role. But it includes a vast array of problems, encompassing the self-referential and self-predicative paradoxes, the paradoxes of implication and of open systems, all those problems which are generated as the result of the transdictive generalization of the problem of induction, its analogues, metaphoric and metonymic displacements and condensations, and all those problems which the textbook categorizes under the heading 'scepticism'. But let us start with an easy one — the problem of free will and determinism. Determinism flows from the reduction of the necessary to the actual and free will will seem nugatory because of the reduction of the possible to the actual. A consequence is that if we take a dialectical claim to the effect that women desire freedom, in the sense of self-determination or autonomy, so that what they do is not predetermined before they do it, we seem to be talking nonsense. But both reductions to the actual are faulty. It certainly makes sense to say of an agent x that she is freer than y if x has a greater range of kinds of actions — that is, more possibilities — open to her. And it makes sense to say that her actions are autonomous provided we remember to see her as stratified and constraints such as the laws of nature as setting limits but not predetermining what she does.

Let us turn to the arch-problem. Why cannot a Member of Parliament suddenly start to bear prunes? It is physically impossible, in virtue of his genetic constitution, for an MP, while retaining his essential structure as a human being, to sprout prunes — even on a Saturday afternoon. In the same way strontium must, while retaining its electronic configuration, burn with a red flame. It cannot start on 29 February 1996 AD to manifest a yellow hue and still remain strontium, i.e. constitute an element composed of the same sub-atomic structure. So both the old and new (Goodman's) problems of induction are rationally resolved by reference to *ontological stratification*. At the same time (the transductive generalization), strontium can easily *look* blue (at the domain of the empirical) to someone wearing appropriately coloured spectacles. The problem of induction is naturally linked not only to Goodman's paradox, but also — as I have shown in detail elsewhere[4] — to Hempel's paradox (a sudden burst of the sun on a British Bank Holiday is irrelevant to the colour of ravens), the problem of subjunctive conditionals (metals will still conduct electricity, in virtue of their possession of free electrons, even if not actually exposed to it) and the problem of distinguishing a necessary from an accidental sequence of events (even if there is a perfect correlation between the Swedish birth rate and the import of bananas into Poland or a visit by Madonna to Hawaii there is *no connection* between them) and the corresponding problems on the normic open-systemic side.[5] Quine's problem of the indeterminacy of explanation is a straightforward consequence of the principle that there is a general — and infinite — number of ways of describing the development of a system over any finite region of space-time. I have already described in C3 the aporetic splitting of the actual that must occur in open systems. There is no reason why the problem of induction cannot be generalized to incorporate non-cognitive components of actions generally, or to bring out the presuppositions of social conformity implicit in the actualist problematic, or be extended to take in the Hobbesian problem of order. Wittgenstein's 'private language argument' can be seen as a variant of it, as weak resemblance theory can be seen as a perspectival switch to it on the taxonomic front. Feyerabend's 'anything goes' can be viewed as metaphoric Dadaist and Winchian 'rule-uniformity' as metonymic hermeneutic displacements of the problem of induction.[6] Scepticism about particular knowledge, and, more generally, solipsistic, as well as transdictive, aporiai, can be pulled under its canvas, as any particular claim is susceptible to a potential infinity of verifications from a potential infinity of observers and agents, etc. This is, of course, a consequence of the universalizability of the judgement form. It is easy to see how the other pair of the Quinean trio — translation and reference — fall vulnerable to the same transdictive problem-field. But so too, by the same token, scepticism about any external world, other minds, my own body and my past states and therefore myself and any thought I have now, and therefore anything at all, are trapped into and rationally resolved once we sublate the solipsistic-fideistic theory problem-field solution set. One consequence of this is that the poles of the irrealist tradition depicted in Figure 4.1 are internally related to each other, in such a way that if one pole collapses, the other must inevitably succumb.

It will be remembered from C1.9 that I showed how the Platonic self-predicative paradoxes were located squarely in the same problem-field solution set. Plato tries to explain an instantiation of 'blueness' in terms of its participation in the form of 'Blue', instead of appealing to a deeper level of structure, say its manifesting light of a certain wavelength.* This reflects the *homology* characteristic of the 1M problem-field. In fact, in the case of all the aporiai we shall be

---

* Again it should be reiterated that I am not condemning Plato for what he could not know, merely exploring how a certain problem-field, for which our contemporaries have no excuse, came about.

investigating, whether reducible to homology (or vicious regress), contradiction, irrelevance or reductio ad absurdum, the general mark of failure is the 'absence of progressive import', whether or not mediated by axiological indeterminacy (or the absence of sufficient grounds for action). This homologous pattern reappears in the twentieth-century self-referential, heap, ω paradoxes and the paradoxes of material implication. Thus we avoid the triviality of Tarskian schema and point the way to an alethic explanation if, instead of writing

[1] 'grass is green is true' if and only if grass is green,

we substitute

[2] ' "grass is green" is true' is assertable insofar as there is [level of objective truth], or we have good reason to believe that we may be able to come to [level of subjective certainty], a scientific [or causal] explanation of it.

Such an explanation is the *alethia of* or real dialectical reason (or dr') for the greenness of grass.

The heap or ω and set-theoretic paradoxes (such as the paradox of the preface) arise only because we insist in characterizing totalities in the same way as we characterize their units, elements or parts. We regard them as aggregates rather than *emergent structures* with sui generis causal powers. I have already stressed that we can have genuine 2E occurrences of the problem of induction, when we are forced to think the constellational identity, or, perhaps better, co-incidence, of identity and non-identity (within a changing structuratum). So, given my diagnosis of 1M paradoxes, at least in their principal incarnations, as turning on homology, how do I avoid Grelling's paradox: 'is "heterological" heterological?' By seeing the question, insofar as it posits an identity relation, as itself exemplifying homology, and so *ungrounded* in a dialectical critical realist framework. However, insofar as it posits a non-identity relation between the two tokens of heterology, the set-characterizing token must be supplied with an emergent principle of structure and the instance-designating token with a corresponding principle of differentiation, in rather the same way as, in order to evade the need for erasure, I appealed to the concept of a 'meta-reflexively totalizing situation'. In this case it would be natural to say that the set, insofar as it can come to stand for an emergent principle of structure, is not an instance of itself — any more than a person is an instance of (rather than partially explained and defined by) their genetic constitution. At the limits of new problematics we must always be ready with a non-valent-Socratic response.

Finally, we have to deal with the paradoxes of material implications. These are really a reductio of irrealism. The paradoxes are, in their simplest form, that a false proposition materially implies everything and a true proposition is materially implied by anything. Nowhere is the absence not only of relevance but also of necessary connection more palpable. Dialectical critical realism can, however, trump this paradox too, because the one case in which the principle is not immediately intuitively false is the one in which an antecedent is true and a consequent false. Yet, if given an actualist interpretation, that is the condition of structures that must act in open systems and the logical form of all the laws known to science.[7]

At 2E, dialectical critical realism insists on the reality of non-being (absence), and the concomitant contingency of existential, alongside essential (cf. 1M), questions, contradictions and processes. It is 1M stratification that helps us to think the constellational identity of judgemental rationality (in the intrinsic aspect) within epistemic relativity (in the transitive dimension) within ontological realism (in the intransitive dimension) which allows us to internalize the consequences of the twentieth-century revenge of the repressed fact of change. But to think absence we need the critique of monovalence and to think absenting the concept of tensed rhythmic process. We have to unify ontology in a general theory of being including non-being, and causality as absenting process. The result of the failure to think negativity has been a judgemental irrationalism and eclecticism, amounting to the kenosis of reason, theory/practice inconsistency, Tina compromise, metaphysical λ's, splits and ideological plasticity. Despire this, the transmutation along the transitive dimension, from positivism to postmodernism, has at least alerted philosophers to the phenomenality of diversity and change. To think coherently absence and negativity, philosophy needs to sustain the existential intransitivity of ontology, dynamize causality, processualize being, and reflexively situate critique, in a dialectic which will take it from concern over phlogiston's non-existence to that of concern over sub-Saharan malnutrition.

A preoccupation with the archetypal problem of opposites is a natural symptom of a class and multiple $power_2$ relationally divided world. In fact it is as a problem of opposites — mind and body, reason and cause, the forms and the flux, universals and particulars, social v. natural science, hermeneutics v. positivism, analytic and synthetic — that the problems of philosophy are most typically posed. And the struggle has characteristically been between dualism and reduction-ism, between the Gods and the Giants, the Friends of the Forms and the Friends of the Earth. At first glance, reductionistic positivism has won, but I have noted the tacit presupposition of necessary dualistic residues (to avoid the detotalization of the reductionist) in C3.9 and philosophy's heavy anthropic emphasis. It is here that, above all, we need a dialectical critical naturalism grounded in an emergent powers materialism (both figures of constellational identity) that sees reasons as encompassed within the category of causes, subjectivity within society within nature, etc. Where the answer is not an emergent powers orientation, it is almost always, as in the case of the analytic/synthetic problem, in an absent mediating term (in this case, once more, natural necessity).

Detotalization at 3L is symptomatic of an alienated world. Its sign is split, and is clearly connected, as cause and effect, to 2E opposition. Thus: the hypostatization of thought, whether in Platonic, Cartesian or Kantian forms; the divide between fact and value — or, at a metacritically identifiable level, the generation of surds, such as the demi-actual (in Hegel), individual responsibility for everything (in Kant) or backgammon as a response to the problem of induction (in Hume). In a way retotalization within a differentiated, stratified, negativized and re-agentified unity can be put forward as an umbrella response to the problems of philosophy. Thus the problem of akrasia arises only because we assume that will is, could or should be the only componential spring of action; that is, from implicitly detotalizing desire, sentiment, self-esteem, etc. The most important thing for an explicitly totalizing philosophy not to detotalize is itself, which is why I have placed such great emphasis on reflexivity and the capacity of dialectical critical realism to situate itself in C3. In fact the detotalization of philosophy is its endemic crime.

De-agentification and reification at 4D are two paradoxical results of an anthropic irrealism. Here it is important to distinguish purely philosophical from broader problems. For philosophy de-agentifies the concept of agency and even denegates it. Yet agents still act, although perhaps more impotently than would otherwise have been the case. But the reification of human beings as labour-power and their accounting in terms of abstract units of homogenized commodified time possesses a different dimension of reality. Here the conatus that would carry us from desire to freedom must convey us from philosophy into substantive social science — as explanatory critique and emancipatory axiology — lest we face that ultimate detotalization, emasculation and unhappy consciousness that philosophy's 'ivory towers' always threaten to close in on us.

I now begin an excursus into the passage in the metacritical history of western philosophy from Kant to Marx, mainly to explain how dialectical philosophy got into its present (pre-critical realist) impasse. We will here have a concrete opportunity of seeing how 'the problems of philosophy' arise in the systematic unity and tensions of the thought of particular thinkers.

§ 3 Contradictions of the Critical Philosophy

> Reason would overstep all its limits if it took upon itself *to explain how* pure reason can be possible. This would be identical to the task of explaining *how freedom is possible.*
>
> K A N T

It was Kant's desire to show how Newtonian science was compatible with Pietist morality. But to make his system work he ended up having to *duplicate* Laplacean determinism within the *noumenal* world following an original choice (moreover, of the whole of everything) outside time. Nothing better illustrates the contradictions, inconsistencies, alienations and splits into which the critical philosophy falls. To structure my argument I am going to set up three Achilles' Heel critiques, corresponding to Kant's three 'Critiques'. But my intention is also partially reconstructive — to show how *had* Kant pursued different options theoretically available to him, Fichte, Schelling and Hegel might have inherited a materialist framework, instead of transcendental idealism, for the germination of modern dialectic.

The Achilles' Heel of the First Critique is Kant's incapacity to sustain the concept of a discursive intellect. Prima facie, he can sustain discursivity (the intransitivity of phenomena) or intellection (the knowability of the intellect), but not both — the only ways he can overcome this dilemma are (i) by conceding that we can after all *know*, rather than merely *think*, the Leibnizian transcendent realm that underpins the Humean empirical manifold, or (ii) by granting that we have direct intellectual encounter, or *Anschauung*, with the mind-in-itself, and a fortiori with the synthetic a priori propositions of critical philosophy. We cannot be banished on *two* sides from intransitive reality. Aside from this, in an adjacent point, Kant's actualism, spelled out clearly in the 'Postulates of Empirical Thought', leaves him unable to sustain either (a) the conditions of the possibility of experience in science, which are given by the contingency of the alignment of the domains of the real, the actual and the empirical

($d_r \geq d_a \geq d_e$); or (b) the role of causal agency — we are unable to affect the source of the given, whereas this is the whole point of experimental praxis in science and, on Gibsonian ecological perception theory, reflects an antiquated view of perception (for perception is precisely a search for things to change). In any case, the centrepiece of the transcendental deduction — the derivation of the three analogies — in the form of principles of substance, causality and interconnection (totality) — are too undifferentiated, undynamic and closed for an empirical science to work with.

How might Kant have repaired this situation? He might have distinguished (α) transcendental arguments, as species of retroductive-explanatory arguments, without any substantive (anthropic, absolutist, idealist, cognitivist; Newtonian-Euclidean-Aristotelian) epistemological commitments from (β) general conceptual schemes (what I have elsewhere called 'metaphysics$_b$'[8]) or the hard-core of research programmes and both from (γ) transcendental idealism, his doctrine that man constructs the world he knows. He could then have used transcendental arguments to establish, on the subjective side, the reality of the noumenal self as an embodied judging person, conceptualizing the world, as a causal agent intervening in it, experimentally, morally, spatio-temporally, and as the seat of geo-historically relativized synthetic a priori principles sui generis; and, correspondingly on the objective side, the reality of the 'transcendental object', now reconstructed to encompass the independent existence and transfactual efficacy of explanatory significant structures in a differentiated world and, had he been daring, a changing world in (objectively) contradiction-riven open spatializing tensed process, in which emergent agents absent the repressive given in a quest for this-worldly human autonomy. The truth of the after-life would then have been the possibility of finite freedom. As it is his uneasy balancing act has remained a permanent saddle point for subsequent thought, graphically expressed in Pierre Duhem's 'Physics of a Believer'.[9]

The Achilles' Heel of the Second Critique is Kant's incapacity to sustain the concept of freedom, or even causal agency. But it is important to appreciate that what makes freedom (morality and agency) impossible is the nature of Kant's resolution of the third antinomy, i.e. his conception of an actualist-determinist-Laplacean realm conforming to the three analogies, which necessitates placing 'free man' outside it. That is to say, it is his phenomenal (Humean) empirical realism which necessitates his noumenal (Leibnizian) transcendent realism. There is asymmetry in the tacit duplicity of dialectical counterparts. Kant's concept of a *Willkür*, or the executive

DIALECTIC

aspect of practical reason, combined with his thoroughgoing determinism, makes each individual responsible for anything that ever has or will happen — a doctrine that is surely the *Liebestod* of morality and, pace Weber, a recipe for inactivism, the displacement of geo-history onto a heavenly *Jenseits*, where a benevolent god will dispense happiness in accordance with virtue. But on the basis of what principles? For if we are all responsible for everything, we must all be equally so. Morality thus loses its agent-directing power, along with its rationale. There is no time to rehearse the other well-known objections to Kantian ethics: for instance, the split in man* between duty and desire, which so affected Hegel's generation; or Hegel's own charge that Kant cannot be 'serious' about Kantian morality, for the truly holy will would render it redundant.

Can we attempt a dialectical critical naturalist transformation of Kant? Jettisoning his empirical realism would allow causal agency to be included in the system in which human beings act. And we would be without the centuries of false dichotomies or pseudo-syntheses between the positivistic sciences of nature and the conceptualized, linguistified or moralized sciences of society. Society could be seen as conceptual-dependent, but not -exhausted; and concepts as potentially masking, screening or distorting social reality. Moral realism, as involving an objective relation to the system of social (and other) relations, could have deployed the Kantian golden rules, while recognizing the necessary transfactuality, processuality, concrete singularity and agent-specificity, and consequent 'communitarian' diversity, of the situations in which the criterion of universalizability applies. Concepts of moral distance and imagination could have usefully been invoked in the context of a moral consequentialism, grounded in a naturalistic conception of human nature (among other species) in socialized nature and justifying a vast extension of reciprocally recognized rights. Concrete utopianism in this life would replace the after-life and human solidarity 'rational faith'.

The Achilles' Heel of the Third Critique is Kant's tacit recourse to a theologically motivated teleological reason or an 'as if' to attempt to remedy the primary problems left unresolved by the first two critiques. Take the problem of induction. The second analogy cannot resolve it any more than Aristotelian nous or Humean backgammon. Only with ontological stratification, dialectical reason and an alethic concept of reason will we have good grounds for believing that the world will 'carry on' — and then *transfactually*, not actually — under the descriptions under which we know it *or not* as the case may be.

---

* It must be recorded that Kant on woman is loathsome.

Kant's achievement here is to have seen the importance of reflective, as distinct from determinate, judgement, but he gives this only a regulative role in organizing the results of science. Retroduction, and the identification it may presage, is at best an organon of, not an algorithm for, science. Or take the case of scepticism in its narrower aspect. If the potential achievement of the First Critique is to show that the condition of possibility of subjectivity is a knowledge of objects, and vice versa, i.e. the transcendental unity of consciousness — which, we should now recognize, is an *achievement* not a presupposition — is a condition of the possibility of our knowledge of an objective world,* what guarantee do we in fact have that the phenomena we apprehend in *Anschauung* are in accord with the transcendental object, let alone the 'thing-in-itself'? Kant is therefore constantly tempted in *The Critique of Judgement* to make nature mind-like to effect the required correspondence, just as in the first case, i.e. in respect of the problem of induction, God is invoked as a surrogate for structure.

Collingwood has described the resulting situation and the splitting of 'egos' that occurs well:

> As Kant's critical philosophy develops, it seems to contradict itself at least twice. In the first critique ... where Kant is enquiring into the metaphysical foundations of physical science or our knowledge of nature,** his doctrine is that we can know only a phenomenal world which we make in the act of knowing it. In the second critique ... where he is enquiring into the metaphysical foundations of moral experience, his doctrine is that in moral experience we know our own mind as things in themselves. In the third ... his doctrine is that the thing in itself which constitutes the phenomena of nature has the character of mind; so that what we know in our practical and moral experience is of the same kind as what we think, but cannot know, in our theoretical experience as students of natural science.[11]

Without the missing term of natural necessity or alethic truth, Kant could not conceive the possibility of an explanatory critique, and with it the critique of ontological monovalence, and a radically negativized concept of causality, that is, of an emancipatory axiology, capable of

---

* There is a multiple ambiguity in the term 'objective' as it appears in Kantian and associated studies. It can mean (a) existentially independent of human beings (i.e. an object), (b) intersubjectively constituted (i.e. a reproduct/transform such as a fact), (c) (quasi-)phenomenally constituted, (d) impersonal, (e) abstract, (f) the intentional object of our sensory awareness or (g) just the antonym of any sense of 'subjective'.

** At this point it must be interposed that in Kant's later writings on the metaphysics of nature per se, mediations between phenomena and noumena — or, if you like, phenomenal and/or noumenal splitting — abound.[10]

addressing our critical question par excellence, which is: *how is the emancipation of embodied beings in space and time possible?* The divisions, dichotomies and dualisms of Kant's philosophy perfectly prefigure the dirempt world bursting into being at the dawn of modernity. Hegel's generation yearned for a lost totality. They experienced Kant's teaching that this quest is dialectical illusion as meaning that a self-divided society was here to stay. Hegel stood out from his contemporaries by eventually seeing that to rationally entwine its description with roses *was* to restore the lost totality — as a unity-in-diversity. In this way he remained true to the quiescence, subjectivism and actualism of Kantian thought. Hegel is popularly conceived as an over-achiever but I am going to show that his dialectical idealism remained firmly anchored in, and shackled to, transcendental idealism. Before I can show this, however, there is a story to be told.

§ 4 Dilemmas of the Beautiful Soul and the Unhappy Consciousness

The story that I am about to unfold in the next three sections pivots around a thinker who wanted (α) to satisfy the traditional objectives of philosophy within an immanent metaphysics of experience, that is, who wanted to realize idealism, but from the standpoint of transcendental subjectivity, i.e. without sacrificing Kantian gains; (β) to find identity-in-difference, unity-in-diversity, harmony-in-conflict — more precisely to work out a way, as Schiller and the Scottish enlightenment had already prefigured, of returning to a state of Greek-like absolute ethical life (*Sittlichkeit*), as Schelling came close to doing, but without foregoing the complexity and autonomy (cf. Fichte) characteristic of the present; and (γ) to develop a technique of transfiguration which would overcome the contradictions, splits and divisions of the contemporary world, of which the Unhappy Consciousness of the Kantian philosophy was the index, while avoiding the fate of the Beautiful Soul. This technique — of redescription — was 'Hegelian' dialectic. The Beautiful Soul was not just a 'character' — one of which the *Phenomenology* is full — but the very prototype of the alienation of spirit around which Hegel was to weave his tale. And the Unhappy Consciousness marked the acceptance of the positivity, or fate (uncomprehended necessity) as opposed to freedom, implicit in the failure to understand the self-dirempt world of modernity. (α)–(γ) will become, respectively, the principles of *realized idealism, spiritual (constellational) monism* and the *immanent teleology* of the dialectic to its conceptual realist transfigurative end, which I have called *analytical* (empirical realist) *reinstatement in dialectical connection*. What I want to do now is to show how Hegel, in attempting to overcome his own personal self-diagnosed 'hypochondria', comes eventually to *accept* an Unhappy Consciousness in order to avoid Jesus's fate — the original of the Beautiful Soul.

From the time when Hegel left Tübingen (and his friends Hölderlin and Schelling) in 1793 to his reunion with Schelling in Jena in 1800, Hegel's writings belong mainly to the genre of 'civil theology'. In his early fragments, there is a moving dialectic of love which is, on the one hand, his first attempt at a critique of the philosophy of the understanding and, on the other, an anticipation of a dominant thematic of the *Phenomenology*, the desire for mutual recognition, reconciliation and forgiveness. Suppose he had maintained his interest in a dialectic of love. An anomaly in the *Phenomenology* could have been avoided. This occurs at the beginning of the chapter on 'Self-consciousness' after his frightful transition from Understanding, which it is worth dwelling on for a moment. 'It is manifest that behind the so-called curtain, which is to hide the inner world, there is nothing to be seen unless we ourselves go behind it, both in order that we may thereby see, and that there may be something behind there which can be seen.'[12] Nothing better illustrates Hegel's failure to transcend a Kantian standpoint, his anthropic subjectivism and actualism. This is re-affirmed in Stoicism, Reason and Absolute Knowledge.* The anomaly. Desiring self-consciousness is on the stage. It is easy to construct an argument for another observing self-consciousness, e.g. for the capacity of the first to be recognized (or desired) as one of its kind. But Hegel does not give it. His second self-consciousness just appears out of the blue — for the life-and-death struggle to ensue. Had Hegel had the feminist insight to note that social self-consciousness presupposes social relations of trust, nurture and care, a dyadic (gendered) structure would have been built into the alienation of self-consciousness of necessity, and he might have seen in it a dialectic, if not of love, one of care/sympathy/solidarity, at least equal and complementary to and presupposed by the dialectic of mutual recognition. And Marxists might then have far sooner not presumed but investigated the reproduction of labour-power.

In Hegel's early writings Jesus is presented as an archetypal

---

* 'What is rational has no truth; what is conceptually comprehended, *is* not. When reason thus speaks of some *other* than itself, it in fact speaks merely of itself; it does not therein go beyond itself.'

Kantian. Jesus's basic dilemma is clearly expressed in 'The Positivity of the Christian Religion' (1795–96). In order to avoid the fate of the Beautiful Soul, isolated from his community, Jesus is forced to assume the mantle of the Messiah, an after-life (*Jenseits*) is posited and his teachings are accepted, not on the basis of reason, but on that of authority, so heavily 'positivized' are the Jewish people, and later the Roman slaves, among whom his disciples spread his teaching. This is the origin of the unhappy consciousness; and of Hegel's interpretation of the positivity of Christian consciousness that both Kant and Fichte had mercilessly attacked. But in 'The Spirit of Christianity and Its Fate' (1798–99) Hegel breaks from Kant, inveighing against the split between duty and desire, resuming his earlier dialectic of love, seeing it as a mediator, ultimately *agape* or divine grace. Here we have the first manifestations of the themes that morality is tolerance or mutual forgiveness (*Verzeihung*), and that opposition and difference are essential to life. There is no doubt that his reading of Steuart, in the context of the socio-political backwardness of Germany, was a secondary influence here, resonating with the thematics of what I earlier (in C1.6 and C2.5) called Schillerian dialectic in which his generation was well steeped. At the same time he was growing increasingly impatient of purely negative criticism, seeking to shift from his erstwhile this-worldy, atheistic, humanism (Mark I) to a position which would discern the inherent rationality in the actually existing order of things, to find 'the rose in the cross of the present', to reconcile himself to the world as it was, no longer as it could be or might have been (Mark II).

His chosen medium for his turn was philosophy and on his arrival at Jena in 1800 he wrote papers that endorsed Schelling's — five years his junior and already a famous figure — criticism of Fichte's subjectivism and moralism (Fichte, Hegel opined, 'is stuck fast on an ought'). By 1802 he was developing his own system, independently of Schelling, showing, outside the philosophy of nature, a far more complex engagement with detail than Schelling, especially in the spheres of logic and *Sittlichkeit*, whose absolute, intuitively attained in a 'point of indifference' (rather than in the medium of thought), he would later liken to 'a cow in the night'. All this, however, was at a heavy philosophical price. For his move to an actualist *Geist*-centred perspective introduced a this-worldly/other-worldly split into his own philosophy. He was forced, like his earlier Jesus, to accept religion and the whole letter of orthodox Christianity, as a *Vorstellung*, to mimic God's creation of the world both in the radical autogenetics of his *Logics* and in the transition from Logic to Nature, and to tell his *Geistodyssey* as a history of self-estranging spirit now fully rationally comprehended. However, for the absolute to be realized, it must be comprehended, and so his constellational closure entailed his actualism. As idealism was realized, the contradictions of life were pressed, fully developed and overcome in thought. However, in so doing they remained, but as deified — 'entwined with roses' — in life. Compelled to accept conventional ways of speaking, his dialectic merely embellished them in the dynamic architectonics of the absolute idea. There arose an avalanche of recrudescent surds. I consider here only three of the most important. First, there is the problem posed by Krug's pen or the number of species of parrot. This is surely ontologically, objectively quite determinate. Yet it is evidently, admittedly not epistemically, subjectively or Hegel-rationally, so. This certainly seems to open up a subject — object gap, or to be an unknowable thing-in-itself, or to be sheer but knowable accident, or to belong to the province of an untransfigured empirical science. That is to say, absolute idealism would need to incorporate heteronomy, intransitivity, natural necessity and open totality. Second, if philosophy is a child of its time, and only appears on the scene ex post facto, then absolute idealism must be relativized lest it loses its claim to be fully developed. A philosophy that is invulnerable to change would have to reflexively incorporate principles of self-development and so sustain a genuine concept of absence.* Third, if geo-history is not at an end, then the one thing one cannot do in the hot historicized societies of modernity, in which transformative praxis is the negation of the given, is to reproduce the status quo ante. His own philosophy would have to accommodate a notion of transformative praxis that was capable of bringing about (and sustaining the description of) changes in the categories it took upon itself to describe — as, of course, the categories from causality (no transfactuality in Hegel) to class (no proletariat, albeit a problem of poverty, in Hegel) have changed from Hegel's time. Hegel escapes the fate of the beautiful soul and nearly achieves the traditional objectives of metaphysics only to be stuck fast with an unhappy consciousness (manifest in the split between left- and right-wing Hegelianism) and to suffer the recrudescence of surds that have plagued absolutist anthropic actualist monovalent philosophy. In particular the detotalizations that result from any attempt at an absolutist closure account for the split noted in C2.3 between Hegel Mark I and Hegel Mark II.

---

* Hegel's genuine fear of change — a product of the rejection of his youthful hopes — is not well known. Thus, in reaction to student riots in Berlin, he writes, 'I had hoped that these fears and hopes would be over.'[13]

§ 5 Master and Slave: From Dialectics of Reconciliation to Dialectics of Liberation

The chapter on 'Self-consciousness' is certainly one of the most impressive in Hegel's oeuvre. Contrary to popular misconceptions, it does not seem to have particularly influenced Marx, but it has palpably influenced subsequent Marxist and non-Marxist readers alike. In the preceding section we observed the aweful transition from Consciousness to Self-consciousness and the anomalous appearance of a second self-consciousness. The basic drive of self-consciousness, and the rest of the *Phenomenology* which takes place in accordance with the principle of preservative sublation — so to speak, within it — is to abolish the distinction between subject and object, so that self-consciousness becomes its own object; and, through the mediating notion of autonomy, which embraces forms of knowing or truth and modes of acting or freedom, reflecting the duality of absolute and objective spirit in Hegel, the *Phenomenology* is at once an epistemological and an ethical work. Self-consciousness first attempts to preserve the external character of the world by taking hold of it in desire. But this fails. One desire begets another and the subject remains dependent on the external world. The two self-consciousnesses now engage in a life-and-death struggle,* fuelled by two contrary goals — (a) to negate the other, and (b) to achieve recognition from it. One wins and becomes master, the trembling other his slave. But who really wins? At first blush it seems the master achieves recognition and freedom, while the slave experiences only work and discipline. But Hegel argues that the slave wins, since in work he recognizes himself in the object of his labour and so removes its external character. Note that Hegel's argument is not that the master becomes dependent on the slave.

This paves the way for the transition to Stoicism. Unlike the moments of Consciousness — sense-certainty, perception and understanding — the Stoic is engaged in pure thought (*Denken*) — for concepts are the products, not just the objects, of consciousness. His material position is a matter of indifference to the Stoic. Thus the slave Epictetus becomes the intellectual master of the emperor Marcus Aurelius. This is a position from which Hegel never departs. There is a direct line from Stoicism to Absolute Knowledge and the

---

* This is a motif that appears over and over again — in, for instance, the dialectics of nobility and war, and it is present in the dialectic of wealth and elsewhere. It is also implicit in the fundamental dialectic of determinate being or *Dasein* — the dual mechanism of incandescent effervescence and eidetic eternity. Hegel's essential idea seems to be that fear for one's life is a necessary condition for full self-consciousness.

hyperintuitionism of the Logic and the subsequent transition to nature, in heterocosmic affinity with the creation of the world by God (who remains, however, a mere picture image or *Vorstellung*). There is a sub-plot to the story, too. For it is the culminating part of Absolute Knowledge, where the alienation of spirit is overcome, which inspires the young Marx. Marx substitutes labour for spirit, distinguishes objectification and alienation and corrects Hegel's confinement of labour to abstract mental labour with a materialist emphasis on practical transformation.

But the main show must go on. The Stoic falls short of Absolute Knowledge just insofar as he is not able to make the transition from form to content. He produces the forms of thought but remains heteronomously dependent, in the style of a Kant, on the external world for their content. What the Stoic ignores, viz. the reality of the world, the Sceptic attempts to deny. Of scepticism, which continues to play such a prominent role in the theory problem-field solution sets of philosophy, Kojève has aptly remarked that its real basis is private property. Only these who need not sell their labour-power can afford to be sceptics. But the Sceptic, who makes explicit what is implicit in Stoicism (cf. dc′), is guilty of theory/practice inconsistency and heterology. His deeds belie his words. He leaves his study by the entrance to the building rather than the second-floor window. The Unhappy Consciousness is aware of the duplicitous contradiction in scepticism. But he maintains the aims of Self-consciousness and still seeks to negate the world by taking refuge in asceticism or in projective other-worldliness, displacing his aspirations onto a *Jenseits*, a beyond or after-life, where happiness will be in accord with virtue, as in Kant.

And there Self-consciousness ends. We enter the domain of Reason, characterized, Hegel says, by its idealism and in practice by a soaring self-confidence in the rational accessibility of the world. Hegel never resolves the contradictions of the unhappy consciousness, most obviously manifest in the split between the this-worldly Hegel Mark I and the *Geist*-centred Hegel Mark II. What about the contradiction between master and slave? Hegel's duality is explicit in his two resolutions. When assuming the mantle of absolute spirit it is in the transition route from Stoicism all the way to Absolute Knowledge. But, under the aspect of objective spirit, its resolution comes in the mutual recognition, reconciliation and forgiveness shown in the ethical life (*Sittlichkeit*) of a nation quite late on in the *Phenomenology*. It would, however, be historiographically and hermeneutically wrong to seek its resolution in the *Phenomenology of Mind* alone. Instead we must see it in the context of Hegel's work as a whole, and in particular both in the system he was elaborating in Jena prior to the *Phenomenology of Mind* and in his subsequent systematic *Philosophy of Spirit* and *Philosophy of Right*, each containing themes resuming the chapter on 'Self-consciousness' in the *Phenomenology*. Here the contradiction is firmly resolved in the domain of objective spirit, in the third member of the triad populated by the family (the realm of particular altrusim), civil society (of particular egoism) and the state (universal altruism), in the reciprocal recognition of rights and duties in a constitutional liberal proto-democratic state.

But what about our generalized concept of master−slave or discursively moralized power$_2$ relations? Hegel had already seen in the *Jena Realphilosophie* that the economy (civil society) operates in a 'blind and elemental' manner and had called there in effect for state intervention. But the state he identified in his later writings did not even find a place for the working class as a class, so overlain was it with feudal residues. And in §195 of *The Philosophy of Right* he candidly admits that he can find no resolution to the problem of poverty which so 'agitates society',[14] identifies the juxtaposition of extravagance and waste as a 'wrong' and speculates proleptically on the economy being forced 'despite an excess of wealth'[15] to mitigate pauperization and economic poverty by seeking colonies abroad, in a manner which strikingly anticipated Marx's reflections in the *Grundrisse*,[16] using the world market as an outlet for over-production. While praising Hegel for his candour and insight, we must indict him for an analysis of society which failed to see generalized commodity production as based on the illicit fission implicit in the exchange of non-equivalents which is foundational of the wage-labour/capital contract, spawning an ideology presented in the so-called rational state which represented partisan sectional interests as universal (most notably through the mediation of the bureaucratic class), while drawing back from generalizing his concept of master−slave relations to include the inequities and illicit fusions stemming from the non-parity of equivalents he so painstakingly analysed − a form of intellectual shortfall which can be subsumed under the real negational categories of omissive critique and metacritique.

Hegel's resolution fails. Does Marx's succeed? Marx fails to fulfil his programme (his famous six brochures) and subsequent Marxists, with notable exceptions, have only just begun to complete, and update, his 'unfinished business'. He presents his system in a similarly linear and autogenetic fashion to Hegel, although it is interspersed with fascinating and detailed historical commentary, but his autogenetics is based on an unquestionably transformationalist and impeccably empirically controlled approach, and his starting point is unquestionable. But he does not engage, except in occasional writings, in the globalization of capitalist production and remains fixated on the wage-labour/capital relation at the expense of the totality of master—slave relations (most obviously those of nationality, ethnicity, gender, religious affiliation, sexual orientation, age, health and bodily disabilities generally). Meanwhile the ex-Soviet Union, at least from Stalin on, forgetful of the presence of the past and the outside, attempts to build socialism in one country, eventually sinking back into a simple undifferentiated unity (reflecting the most primitive logic of Hegel's Being) with a bureaucractic elite presiding over a commandist state, one set of power$_2$ relation-holders having replaced another, acting on the basis of an impoverished concept and practice of freedom which did justice neither to constitutionality nor to civic and human rights nor to the dispositional (including agonistic and expressive) aspects of rational autonomy in a world of increasing global intradependence and technological change demanding incentive, innovation and decentralization (reflecting the Essence Logic of capitalism). In this world various slaves produce and fight for competing masters, while masters compete against each other and actively seek to exploit the differences between slaves. In this New World Disorder the contradictions analysed by Hegel and Marx, gross inequity and endemic waste, retain all their former force but are accentuated by the dialectics of centre and periphery of commodification, and of figure and ground of late/postmodernity, the massive presences of the past and the intrinsic outside and the alienations resulting from subjugation$_2$ in a partial totality. The unhappy consciousness retains all its relevance as a figure in which to think the fragmented, decentred, disconnected periphery in chronic ill-being or communal violence while an equally enervated centre soaps up the mediatization of a punctualist virtualized hyperreality. The logic of this is presented in Figure 4.5.

The two themes of master—slave relations and the unhappy consciousness have to be (1) extended, continued and retotalized, e.g. to take into account the changing spatialization of the tensed processes of global commodification and the massive resulting inequities; (2) generalized, e.g. to take into account not only Marx's dialectic of de-alienation but also the totality of master—slave relations in four-planar social being (including internalized, intrapsychic, e.g. libidinal, ones) on the basis of the generalized and dialecticized perspectives set out in C2.9 and C3.10 in a conception of a holistically causally efficacious open totality in nature, grounded in a naturalistic ethics of care and solidarity and a conception of the

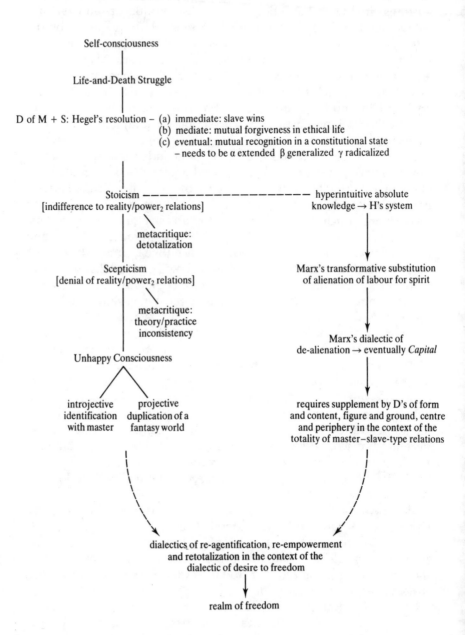

Figure 4.5 Dialectic of Master and Slave

moral consciousness of the species as open, in which the recognition of differences-in-identity (non-uniformity) provides the ground for the recognition of identities-in-difference, generating a unity-in-diversity engaged in explanatory critical/concrete utopian/transitional prefigurative depth totalizing counter-hegemonic struggle; and (3) radicalized, e.g. with a much richer and deeper conception of freedom, democracy, rights, education, health and wellbeing (in which in particular the concept of freedom is radicalized, to include both needs and possibilities for development) in a remoralized world in the context of a synthetic fusion of life (singular), movement (rhythmic), representative (mediated) and emancipatory (dialectically universal) politics. This thoroughgoing extension, generalization and radicalization of the dialectic of freedom is, of course, mandatory at the power/discursive/normative intersect of ideology.

Let us sum up the strictly philosophical significance of this. Modern philosophy starts with the Cartesian ego. Kant shows this to be an impossibility, and argues that an objective manifold is a condition of the possibility of the subjective transcendental unity of apperception which reciprocally allows us to synthesize the empirical manifold presented by a world unknowable-in-itself. Hegel sees the transcendental unity of self-consciousness as a social achievement which is ultimately grounded in a public world of moral order, enshrined in the constitutional structures of his rational state. Let it be said that this is a tremendous advance on Kant. But Marx identifies the real basis of the Hegelian state in civil society (later, modes of production) founded on the alienation and exploitation of labour-power, and in his systematic dialectics shows capitalism as a geo-historical product, destined to make way for one in which labour becomes 'life's prime want'. Dialectical critical realism argues that the Marxian goal in which 'the free development of each is a condition of the free development of all' can be achieved only by an extension, generalization and radicalization of Marx's dialectic of de-alienation into a dialectic of liberation from the totality of master—slave relations, and that this moral goal of universal human autonomy is a presupposition of the most elemental desire, the first initiating act of referential detachment, induced by negativity in the guise of absence. There is a conative drive to freedom linking Descartes to Kant to Hegel to Marx to dialectical critical realism. And each successive position may be seen as engaging in a metacritique, that is, isolating an omission in the preceding one.

§ 6 The Metacritique of the Hegelian Dialectic

> When the absolute stands on one side, and limited positive
> reality on the other, and the positive must all the same be
> preserved, then this positive becomes the medium through
> which the absolute light shines, the absolute breaks into a
> fabulous play of colours; and the finite, the positive [sic] points to
> something other than itself.
>
> MARX

In §5 I portrayed Hegel as a Stoic, and in §4 as a figure of Unhappy
Consciousness. Given that the Unhappy Consciousness explicates
the logic implicit in Stoicism, there is no incompatibility in these
depictions. Indeed, on either and both, Hegel himself falls prey to the
T/P inconsistency characteristic of the mediating figure of the Sceptic,
i.e. is subject to a metacritical dialectical comment (dc'), which this
section provides, and to the denomination of his system, in the terms
of C2.7, as a Tina compromise.

I am going to ordinate my critique along two dimensions, which I
will represent respectively by Roman and Greek letters. Hegel's
dialectic is supposed to satisfy criteria of (a) rationality and seriousness
(the lack of which is the gravamen of his own critique of Kant), (b)
totality and (c) clarity. Hegel's system is often thought to be protected
by the post festum paradox, viz. that to criticize it is to show that one
does not understand it. But I am going to use his criterion of
seriousness to generate an immanent critique. Then again it is sometimes
claimed by critics that Hegel is liable to the charge of attempted over-
achievement, that his system is 'too full'. Here I use his criterion of
totality to generate what I will nominate an omissive critique, showing
that, contrary to the customary charge, his system is too empty,
replete with absences, voids and vanishing mediators. Finally I will
employ his criterion of clarity to establish an antinomial critique.

My second dimension of ordination aligns the three motivations for
his Bildung that I gave in §4, viz. (α) his ambition to realize the
traditional goals of philosophy within an immanent metaphysics of
experience, (β) his quest for a differentiated totality or a unity in
diversity and (γ) his desire to avoid the fate of the Beautiful Soul
without an Unhappy Consciousness, to the three keys to his dialectic
which I fashioned in C1.6 and my colligation and interpretation in
C2.5 of the three branches of materialist criticism of Hegel which can
be traced back to Marx. Let me briefly summarize these as (α')
realized idealism (Hegel's principle of identity), to which I
counterposed Marx's epistemological materialism and proleptic

critique of the epistemic fallacy, centrism-expressivism and Hegel's failure to sustain the autonomy of nature; (β') constellational spiritual monism (Hegel's 'logical mysticism'), to which I counterposed Marx's ontological materialism and critique of the speculative illusion (the form of the 'primal squeeze' in the 'unholy trinity'), triumphalism and cognitivism; and (γ') preservative dialectical sublation (Hegel's immanent teleology), against which I affirmed Marx's practical materialism, my critique of ontological monovalence, Hegel's endism and his inability to sustain the geo-historicity of social forms.

(a) and (α) may be loosely aligned, but as the dimensions of criticism overlap, further systematization would be arbitrary. One can, however, say at the outset that in virtue of (α') *intransitivity* is lost and we have a series of *illicit fusions* or conflations between natural and conceptual necessity, negation and dialectic; in virtue of (β') *transfactuality* disappears and we have a whole group of problems stemming from Hegel's (expressivist-kinetic-eidetic) actualism and constellational monism, opening up a series of fissions; and finally that on account of (γ) *transformative praxis* is lost and there arise aporiai generated by Hegel's denegation of incompleteness and change, again producing recalcitrant surds and splits.

(a) I shall start my immanent critique, which I shall interpret in the broad spirit allowed by the Hegelian maxim that the truth is the whole, and more especially the conformity of an object to its notion, by making a number of fairly simple points. First, against the post festum paradox, it is obvious that Hegel's system may be criticized on the grounds that many of its nodal transitions are faulty, arbitrary, unclear and/or circular in the sense that they presuppose what they have to prove. One could cite here especially the (1) transition from understanding to self-consciousness in the *Phenomenology* (discussed in §4); (2) that from determinate finite to infinite being, which underpins and necessitates the subsequent transition (3) from the sphere of essence to that of the notion in the *Logics*; and (4) that from logic to nature in the System expounded in the *Encyclopaedia*. But the transitions from (5) the unhappy consciousness to reason; (6) nature to mind; (7) civil society to the state; and (8) objective to absolute spirit are equally pivotal in their own spheres and equally faulty. Second, one could take Hegel's cardinal transition, the argument from *Dasein* or determinate being that determines the static evanescence of Hegel's system, and is the archetype for the conceptual realist gloss with which Hegel coats his empirical realism, the mechanism of the analytic reinstatement in dialectical connection. What does Hegel accomplish? In immanentizing transcendent reality, Hegel collapses the intransitive, structured, transfactual and at least ontologically bivalent reality of scientific investigation to actuality; while in transcendentizing actuality, Hegel eternalizes it, transmuting it sub specie aeternitatis. The effect of this double substitution (i) of the logical present for a tensed geo-history and (ii) of spirit for structure is to undermine the possibility of science and change alike (and of course, inter alia, the social sciences). Third, we could look at Hegel's own self-understanding of his method. If it is (x) transformationalist, which is the most reasonable interpretation of it, then Hegel does not succeed in generating content out of form alone and should both withdraw his strictures against Kant and be explicitly heteronomous, making clear his whole empirical manifold. If, on the other hand, it is indeed (y) hyperintuitive, then Marx's and Trendlenburg's critiques of his method must be accepted: unreflected empirical criteria are tacitly absorbed and projected onto the play of the parthenogenetic process, betraying a contradiction between Hegel's gnoseological theory and his dialectical practice. If, finally, it is (z) purely phenomenological (descriptive), then, aside from the fact that this is a plausible interpretation only of the *Phenomenology* and possibly the *Histories*, Hegel is vulnerable to a charge that, for each dc' there will be a multiplicity of possible dr's, so that he has justified neither the uniqueness nor the unilinearity of his results. In each case, an auto-subversive 'lack of seriousness' is indicated.

Let us follow up what I am calling the simple critique by looking at Hegel in 'Essence'. From the perspective of the experimental natural sciences, or even that of the category of determinate absence (a huge void in Hegel's thought) establishing, as we saw in C3, the case for referential detachment, thought applies to, but is not intrinsically constitutive of, being (as distinct from our discourse about being).* Existence becomes intransitive; there exist realities, such as many of those described in 'Essence', which are not essentially dependent on thought; it becomes crucial to distinguish natural from conceptual and from social (which is not conceptual, but conceptualized) dialectics; and there cannot be a global dialectics of nature (qua being), where some dialectical categories like negation will, while others like reflexivity will not, apply to it. The transfactuality of laws and the occurrence of open systems entails that we must have the categories of non-apparent essence and non-actual essentialities; and similarly multiply determined events, conjunctures, compounds,

---

* Hegel is guilty of the most jejune fallacy when he says that the 'principles of the ancient or modern philosophies, water [does he mean signified or referent? — he lacks a distinction between sense and reference which is just as important as that between reference and referent], or matter, or atoms are *thoughts*; universals . . . not things'.[17] The concept man cannot eat — a point over which Feuerbach was equally confused.

contingencies and accidents — all of which, in his reinforced 'weak actualism' (to use a distinction I have previously developed[18]), he must put down as demi-actualities (my term). Thus we have the recrudescence of the Kantian unknowable thing-in-itself (although it is really the same aporia that generates Aristotelian accident [or non-being]). Suppose it is pointed out that Hegel's monism is of a constellational kind. The demi-actualities are there for the sake of *Geist*. This now involves the recurrence of a Fichtean endless task (of eliminating their irrationality in the vain search for closure), with the absolute postponed to a Beyond (*Jenseits*), or at least seen with the obscurity of a Schellingian point of indifference. Here we have linked up with the omissive and antinomial critiques. Hegel's totality is empty of non-actualized essence, as it is of essence not intrinsically related to transcendental subjectivity, indicating his failure to transcend transcendental idealism in respect of science. In effect Hegel's conceptual necessity is Kant's transcendental necessity without Kant's restricting condition, so that Hegel spiritualistically ontologically trans-substantiates the Kantian phenomenal world, without Kantian discursivity (ectypal heteronomy). Just as Hegel does not advance beyond transcendental idealism in terms of scientific explanation, he systematically subordinates causality to teleology, drawing out the esoteric message of the *Critique of Judgement*. This in turn lays the basis for Marx's functionalist proclivities. At the same time Hegel is subject to interpretive antinomies; which push his position back to that of a Kant, Fichte or Schelling. Parallel considerations could be adduced by looking at almost any other sphere of Hegelian philosophy. Take the philosophy of history. Is the philosophical *Nachdenken* really consolation for the 'slaughter-bench' of history? If it is, then it is being administered to the wrong subjects and deserves the fate of Hegelian 'punishment'. For this is injustice on the level of Hobbesian 'moral absurdity'.

Hegel's commitment to identity theory generates, at the point of identity, a point of duplicity, which, with a licensed constellationality and an unlicensed axiological indeterminacy, becomes a point of complete ideological plasticity. At the level of understanding, Hegel remains, and says he remains, firmly committed to empirical realism. His dialectical connection merely masks an analytic reinstatement. There is no method/system contrast of the sort that the left Hegelians imagined. For the fact that he never developed categories of real determinate non-being and the way the negation of the negation transports determinate being to spiritual infinity exactly matches the way in which logical negativity is undone as logical contradiction cancels itself. His logicization/spiritualization of being, constellational

closure and preservative dialectical sublation ensure the victory of
Hegel Mark II and that the only authentic Hegelians are right-wing
ones. In so doing, Hegel is untrue to his theory of truth which would
vindicate the unity of theory and practice in practice, that is, in
transformation of (socialized) reality to comport it to a rationally
grounded notion of it. Instead we have the split between theory and
practice (only notionally reconciled in the absolute idea) manifest in
the theorem that those who make history do not understand it and
those who understand it do not make it. Hegelian freedom is the fate
of the Stoic; his logicism that of positivity; his reason that of
rationalization of the actually existing order of things. His greatness
lies neither in his method nor his system, but in his philosophical
acuity in his judgement of his predecessors and peers and the depth
and detail of his analysis in the spheres of objective and absolute
spirit. It is true that I have credited him for his epistemological
dialectic but, in the end, this is eristic, because it terminates in an
allegedly closed consistency.

This leads me on to (b) — the omissive critique. At 1M painting a
picture that flatters as it comforts humanity, he fails to sustain non-
anthropic objectivity, to vindicate sheer alterity, existential
intransitivity, referential detachment, non-spiritualized (that is,
natural) necessity, especially in the forms of ontological stratification,
transfactual efficacy and an alethic concept of truth. At 2E he is
unable to sustain ontological bivalence (or, better, polyvalence),
simple determinate absence, transformative negation, rhythmic
tensed spatializing process, unsublated and dialectical, but non-
logical, contradiction and negativity generally. At 3L his failings
include the lack of open totality, full autonomy and the reflexivity of
critique. At 4D he is unable to sustain essential transformability,
(transformed) transformative (trustworthy) totalizing transformist
transitional praxis, a non-sociologically reductionist ethics, dialectical
rationality or absolute reason. One could also take a different
perspective on the omissive critique by setting it in the $(\alpha)-(\gamma)$
dimensionality outlined earlier. The most relevant signposts here are
at (α) the absence of intransitivity and of the autonomy of nature,
which Hegel sees under the aspect of petrified mind; at (β) the
absence of natural necessity (and transfactual efficacy) and of activity
irreducible to mind (in Marx's terms, of labour other than abstract
mental labour); and at (γ) the absence of the category of absence and
of the irreducible geo-historicity of social forms. But important here
also are his inability to uphold the critical distinctions between (i)
causality and teleology (the latter, where applicable — viz. in the
realm of intentional human agency — is constellationally contained

within [i.e. a form of] but over-reached by the former) manifest, for example, in the dominance of ex post epistemologically illegitimate teleological pull over ex ante teleonomic push in his dialectical transitions; and (ii) objectification and alienation, thus rationally transfiguring the status quo. In general one can align 1M- and 3L-oriented critiques under (β) and 2E- and 4D-oriented ones under (γ). Another perspective on the omissive critique is to consider the critical lacunae in the various stadia of Hegel's philosophy. Thus we have already noticed the absence of essential transfactuality in the sphere of Essence and of essential transformability in Objective Spirit, where globally hot geo-historicized societies with butterfly effects may reproduce tomorrow in Leicester a transformation today in Tokyo. More basically the existential facts of finitude and scarcity and the character of human praxis as transformative agency mean that, in making, we cannot simply replicate the conditions of our making, we must negate or absent, that is to say, change them. Even the announcement of the closure of geo-history undoes it. More generally it should be noted that the whole Hegelian edifice is axiologically inconsistent with the transformative potential implicit in the praxis necessary to reproduce the plateau-structure and so continue the life of *Geist*. There are a whole galaxy of aporiai associated with Hegel's Plateau-nic theory of spirit; and we could add to the omissive critique here Hegel's failure to generalize, extend and radicalize the transcendental deduction we discussed in §5. Again, on this third line, it could be argued that opacity (and hence lack of rationality) is essential to certain human activities, including perhaps art. But before we turn to the antinomial critique, it is perhaps worth pressing Hess's challenge to Hegel and ask how he could rationally combine the constellational closure of geo-history, essential to his system (for the owl of Minerva flies only at dusk), with his refusal to speculate about the future. Here is another *prise de position* which may have had deleterious effects on Marx and Marxists.

(c) The antinomial critique. We have already noticed the in-built duplicity and pliability of Hegelian dialectics in virtue of his (allegedly) realized idealism at (α). A materialist dialectic of *determinate* (transfactual or actual, positive or negative, intractive or otherwise, agentive or not) *finite being*, with a strong concept of dialectical contradiction such as I developed in C2.3, would see its negation as real and potentially transformative, viz. into a changed determinate being (either the same or not, and if not the same, of the same or a different kind), and *its* transformative negation as matching the formula earlier given for the negation of the negation as the geo-historical transformation of geo-historical (process-in-)products, rather than Hegelian transportation to infinity and reinstatement of the same.* The collapse of intransitivity (and transfactuality) inescapably leads to the collapse of change.

I shall focus my remarks here mainly on the principle of constellational spiritual monism (β) and preservative dialectical sublation (γ). What we will be dealing with are structures of interrelated antinomies, reflecting real ambivalences, indeterminances, splits, absences and detotalizations in the Hegelian system. At (β) we have the key problem of monism (and dualism) itself, which incorporates the problem of opposites, the transition to nature, the deduction of Krug's pen (touched on in §4) and the aporiai of the demi-actual (just discussed); the problem of matter, of necessity and of contingency, of actuality and of rationality, of teleology, of sense-experience, the autonomy of philosophy; of Hegelian subjectivity and the Hegelian absolute. At (γ) we have the archetypal problems of incompleteness and of change. As we have seen, the malaise at (β) is Hegel's failure to achieve an *absolute absolute*, which divides reality into two — the half that Hegel can account for and the half that he cannot. The normal Hegelian reply that the various species of parrot, or contingency, or matter or the irrational are there precisely for the sake of categorial completion would do were it not for the claim that Hegel makes for his (autogenetic) method and his strictures against other philosophers for their dualisms and/or shortfalls. For left with the irrational half of reality, Hegel is no better off than a Kant, Fichte or Schelling. Supposing the irrational half is consigned to the domain of the empirical sciences. Hegel is now faced with the question of what guarantee he can possibly have that work here will not seep back *essentially* on to his system and dialectic, as the harbingers or actual purveyors of categorial change. This is what I will call endosmotic refutation. So we have in respect of the problem group structured around (β) a triple-pronged scenario: (i) the recrudescence of a surd, (ii) the opening up of a Kantian unknowable thing-in-itself, a Fichtean endless task or a Schellingian obscurity,** and (iii) the possibility of endosmotic refutation. This is the measure of Hegel's failure to achieve the traditional goals of philosophy and/or, alternatively, of his methodological self-delusion.

This problem group is closely associated with the figure of constellationality. This is really a figure of identity-in-difference or

---

* Philosophy's 'same' is the same 'same' as in Aristotle (as instances of species), in Hume (as constant conjunctions), in Fichte (as the endless task), in Nietzsche (as eternal recurrence), in Wittgenstein (the rule of resemblance — but in resemblance what explains the difference?).

** This list is illustrative, not exhaustive.

unity-in-diversity. Used metacritically, as I have tried to employ it, it is, as such, unobjectionable. Thus the emergence of thought from being may be said to instantiate the constitutional identity of thought within being, consisting in the over-reaching of thought by being as well as its constituting an aspect of being. But, besides failing to distinguish identity and unity, almost always Hegel gets the terms, where their meanings are comparable, the wrong way round. It is here that talk of a materialist inversion of Hegel makes some, albeit limited, sense. Thus we have the identity of identity and difference within identity, not difference, which is the condition and constituter of identity relations (cf. 1M non-identity); the identity of thought and being (conceived as matter) within thought, not being, etc. There arise here the problems of whether the minor (materialist) term is compatible with its idealist over-reaching; what degree of torque, or, if you like, independence, it is allowed to enjoy; and that of the unpalatable teleology of their relationship (the contingent is there for the sake of necessity, etc.).

The figure of constellationality is also heavily implicated in the Hegelian response to problem group (γ), where it is used to effect a *dynamic spatio-temporal*, as distinct from synchronic (quasi-causal, actually teleological), *closure*. The paradoxes here turn around precisely the fact that Hegel cannot rule out real essential incompleteness in his knowledge or change in nature and social life (including philosophy) either immediately or endosomatically, affecting categorical change, so undermining the plausibility or completeness (and hence truth) of his system. Hegel is caught in this dilemma: either world history is indeed at its goal, as he modestly says it seems to be, at the end of his lectures of *The History of Philosophy*, or the work which he admits needs to be done in his lectures on *The Philosophy of History* 'belonging to the empirical side' will have fallibilistic implications for absolute idealism. The other key figure here is that of preservative determinate sublation. Given everything is preserved (as 'negative presence') in a cumulative memory store, then the question Hegel has to answer is by what criteria are some but not other attributes positively retained in a transition or sphere? Again in the absolute idea or absolute spirit Hegel would seem to have to resort to the device of constellationality to hold erstwhile contraries in a hierarchical unity.

It will be remembered in C1.7 that I argued that $dr^0 \geq dr^\dagger \geq dr' \geq dr'' \geq dr''' \geq dr''''$ where dr^0 is a result, $dr^\dagger$ is a resolution of a contradiction, dr' its rational resolution, dr'' conforming to radical preservative determinate negation, dr''' effecting our reconciliation to life and dr'''' mutual recognition in a free society. It is obvious that neither scientific explanations nor geo-historical transitions generally conform to dr″. Transformative sublations, or sublations containing transformative negations, are far more frequent than the preservative *Aufhebung*. But other possibilities abound, including the preservative reproduction of the opposition; the occurrence of vicious degenerative, dissipative, fragmentary, chaotic, detotalizing (externalizing), generally inverse-sublatory spirals and spreads; the mutual ruin or non-preservative undoing of the contraries; the preservative undoing of their opposition accompanied by hierarchical inversion and chiasmus with or without erasure (associated with Derrida); the simple non-dialectical separation or distanciation of the poles; the absorption of one by another, with or without an internalization of their opposition; the grafting of the opposition onto another element or opposition producing a more complex, displaced and/or condensed form, and/or the simple indeterminacy, ineliminability or differential interpretation of the outcome. It would be foolish to suppose that Hegel did not consider some of these alternatives. But his epistemological triumphalism, relentless teleology and constellational closure inevitably inclined him to the preservative *Aufhebung*. In the at least as contradictory, but more sombre, world of the late twentieth century we cannot afford not to see this as only one possible figure of change.

§ 7 Marxian Dialectic I: The Rational Kernel in the Mystical Shell

We witnessed and explained Marx's account of the mystical shell of Hegelian dialectic in C2.6. What was its rational kernel? Were remnants of the shell involuted and buried deep inside it? And what effects may that have had on Marx's work and on Marxism? Let it be said straight away that although there is no one rational kernel in the Hegelian corpus (any more than there is a single mystical shell) the rational kernel for Marx was above all Hegel's *epistemological dialectic*, entailing both (quasi-)ontological stratification (superstructuration) and the principle of (immanent) metacritique. And that the most important effect of this was that he was able to theorize the dialectical explanation of capitalism in terms of contradictory forces stemming from an (itself dialectically contradictory) common causal ground (dg′). The mystical elements within Marx's own positive dialectic, which I will describe in the next section, are more complicated. They consist partly (a) in what he took over from Hegel in direct or displaced form, and partly (b) in an excessive over-reaction to Hegel or a neglect of valid Hegelian principles, procedures or insights. To give an example of the former, actualist residues combined with ethical sociological reductionism to render him (and the majority of subsequent Marxists) impervious to the need for a William Morris-type moment of positive concrete utopianism to stand alongside Marx's negative explanatory critique. As an illustration of the latter one might take the way in which a substitution of transformative for preservative dialectical sublation led him (and future Marxists) to underestimate the massive presence of the past.

Marx had two moments of great heterocosmic affinity with Hegel. The first, in 1844, was when he was fired by the *Phenomenology* and especially its final section on 'Absolute Knowledge'. For the 'alienation of spirit' read the 'alienation of labour' with the necessary amendments to Hegel's concept of labour and a differentiation of objectification as such from geo-historically specific forms of alienation. The second, in 1857, was when he was inspired by the *Science of Logic*, and extracted from it the lesson that the capitalist mode of production had to be grasped as a pan-concrete totality of its moments in motion and dynamic intra-action. One other determination is worth recording — the way in which Hegelian dialectic, and, in particular, motifs from the second book of the *Logic* ('Essence'), with its regional logic of opposition between or differentiation of hierarchicized pairs, acted as a surrogate for the scientific realism that was, in a context imbued with vulgar positivism, the almost inevitably absent methodological fulcrum of his work.

It is important to my argument that Marx became by the time of *Capital* a scientific realist committed to the view that explanatory structures, or (in Marx's favoured terminology) essential relations, are (a) distinct from, (b) often, and even normally, out of phase with (that is to say, disjoint from) and (c) perhaps in opposition to the phenomena (or phenomenal forms) they generate. Thus Marx remarks that 'all science would be superflouous if the outward appearances and essences of things directly coincided'[19] and comments 'that in their appearances things often represent themselves in inverted form is pretty well known in every science except political economy'.[20] But Marx never satisfactorily theorized his scientific, as distinct from simple material object, realism, which, together with four other asymmetries in his intellectual formation, helped to account for the 'overloading' of the concept of dialectic in Marxist thought. These other imbalances were under-development of the critique of empiricism, as distinct from idealism; of the intransitive dimension and the theme of objectivity in contrast to the transitive dimension and the theme of labour; of normativity in comparison to historicity; and of the research programme of historical materialism as against that of the critique of political economy.

In contrast to the founders of dialectical materialism and western Marxism, Engels and Lukács, whose own dialectical emphases were primarily ontological and relational respectively, Marx's own self-understanding was epistemological. Indeed he often uses 'dialectical' as a synonym for 'scientific' (following Hegel). Thus in the famous 'Afterword' to the second edition of *Capital* he quotes the St Petersburg reviewer's (albeit incorrect positivistic) description of his method to say 'when the writer describes so aptly the method I have actually used, what else is he describing but the dialectical method'. But, as I have just argued, Marx's method, although materialistic and empirically grounded, is realist, and as such, it commits him to a subject-specific ontological and a conditional relational dialectic as well. In a letter to J.B. Schweitzer Marx lets out that 'the secret of scientific dialectics' depends upon comprehending 'economic categories as the theoretical expression of historical relations of production, corresponding to a particular stage of development of material production'.[21] Marx understood his dialectic as *scientific* because, through the critique of political economy and the socio-economic categories it reflected, his dialectic set out to explain the contradictions in thought and the crises in socio-economic life in terms of the specific contradictory essential relations generating them; as (geo-)historically *relational*, because it was both rooted in, and (conditionally) an agent of, the changes in the very relations and circumstances it described; as *critical*, because, taking the metacritical form of a dialectical argument (see C2.6), it demonstrated the geo-historical conditions of applicability and the limits of adequacy of the categories, doctrines and practices it explained; and as *systematic*, because it sought to trace the various geo-historical tendencies and contradictions of capitalism back to certain structurally constitutive contradictions of its mode of production.*

We may distinguish wider senses of critical (which I shall call critical†) and systematic (systematic†) dialectics corresponding to Marx's distinction between his empirically controlled (and immanently critical) mode of inquiry and his quasi-deductive mode of exposition, which corresponds to the Lockian/Leibnizian or alethic moment in science. Marx's systematic† dialectics, which we may also call his presentational dialectics, consists, as we have it, of an ex ante

---

* The most important of these are the contradictions between the use value and value of the commodity and between the concrete useful and abstract social aspects of the labour it embodies.

unilinear Hegelianesque dialectic, intermingled with all manner of fascinating geo-historical exemplifications and sociographic asides, of the form that social production takes under capitalism, beginning, in *Capital*, Vol. 1, C1, with the dialectics of the commodity and culminating in *Theories of Surplus Value* with the critical history of political economy and, a fortiori, reflexively of itself. It is an unfinished pan-concrete totality (in the sense of C2.7) — which should be properly understood as a partial totality, albeit as Marx thought the ultimately determinate (explanatorily most important) sector of social life. We must inscribe Marx's presentational dialectics within his overall critical project, very far from finished, which was also of course a causal intervention in social life. His critical dialectics strictu sensu takes the form of a triple explanatory critique — of economic theories, agents' categories and schemata and the generative structures and essential relations which underlie them. It may best be regarded as an empirically heteronomous, open-ended, materially conditioned and geo-historically circumscribed materialist dialectical phenomenology.

It is not primarily Marx's dialectical definitions and derivations, but the dialectical explanations and critiques on which they are based, that are distinctive of Marxian dialectics. These are, to repeat, an explanation of opposing forces, tendencies and principles, in terms of a common causal ground (cf. C2.3) and critiques of false or otherwise inadequate theories, phenomena and circumstances of working and living in terms of their socio-economic conditions of being. Marx's critique of political economy aspires to 'save' most of the phenomena explained by pre-existing political economy and so approximates a preservative sublation, although it is arguable whether he is successful in this. But in attempting to save the phenomena theoretically, Marx radically transforms their descriptions, and in situating the phenomena in a new explanatory-critical context, he contributes to a process of their non-preservative transformative negation — Marx's *practical* dialectics.

So Marx is indebted to Hegel for (a) his epistemological dialectics in the absence of scientific realism, (b) two moments of heterocosmic affinity, incorporating transformed concepts of alienation and labour and totality in process, (c) utterly transformed concepts of negativity, contradiction, praxis and dialectical reason (although this is not to say that Marx was entirely clear about the first two) and (d) the exoteric procedural form of his presentational dialectics. This is the diffracted materialist rational kernel of Hegel's dialectic for Marx. Now is there a mystical shell within, besides or despite the rational kernel? The answer is, unfortunately, an emphatic *yes*.

§ 8 Marxian Dialectic II: The Mystical Shell in the Rational Kernel

We have to consider [A1] direct inheritances, [A2] displaced legacies, [B1] excessive over-reactions and [B2] neglect. In investigating [A1]–[B1], and to some extent [B2], I will once again use the (α) = realized idealism, (β) = spiritual monism and (γ) = preservative sublation grid, and their implications, as my principal points of reference. Whether the charge pressed against Marx be actualism, monism or post-dated endism, the issue of determinism, be it of a class or economic reductionist kind, is bound to arise, so it would be as well to tackle it head on at the beginning. I have already critiqued determinism as a general position in C2 and C3. In a Marxist context the issues have revolved around the questions of whether outcomes, such as the demise of capitalism, are (a) inevitable, (b) predictable and (c) fated (in the sense of being bound to transpire whatever people do). In respect of (a) we have to distinguish the case of (i) a *conjunctive multiplicity* from (ii) a *disjunctive plurality* of causes — both characteristic of open systems. In each case Marx is pulled in opposite directions. At (i) he wants to maintain determinism only tendentially, but without falling into eclecticism. At (ii) he wants to trace a clear line of development, but leave open the possibility of mutations. Thus at (i) he repeatedly acknowledges the manifold of determinations operating on geo-historical outcomes: 'an economic base which in its principal characteristics is the same [may manifest] infinite variations and gradations, owing to the effect of innumerable external circumstances, climatic and geographical influences, historical influences from the outside, etc.'[22] At the same time: 'in all forms of society it is a determinate production and its relations which assigns every other production and its relations their rank and influence. It is a general illumination in which all other colours are plunged and which modifies their specific tonalities. It is a special aether which defines the specific gravity of everything found within it.'[23] Just as Marx talks of influences, Engels writes in a well-known letter to Bloch of 'an endless host of *accidents* [my italics] [amidst which] the economic movement finally asserts itself as necessary'.[24] The question is are these *just* accidents, or do they not belong to as thoroughly institutionalized and complex spheres as the economy, and are they not internally related to and dialectically necessary for (and perhaps, for example, conjunctually contradictory to) the economy? If so, any analysis which excludes them is going to be detotalizing.

Since Althusser and Poulantzas, Marxists have become aware of the need to theorize other levels of the social totality, and since feminism and the black movement, other dimensions of social oppression (of course Engels was no slouch on this). But should not multi-sectoral analysis and polydimensionality have been *situated* ab initio? Did not perhaps Marx after all displace *Geist* onto labour — and a specific kind of labour — albeit operating with an entirely different kind of methodology, as he displaced Hegel's cognitive triumphalism onto practical Prometheanism and his endism into Communism? And was not this a source of the neglect of the sheer weight of national, ethnic and religious, as opposed to class, differentiations that burst the Second International asunder in 1914? These questions become particularly pressing when one considers Marx's analysis of ideology and the components of the social cube and more generally four-planar social being. There is a neglect of the normative/moral — an effect of Hegel's sociological reductionism of ethics — and discourse/communicative dimensions, as distinct from the power dimension, of ideology. Further, employing an undifferentiated concept of ideology, some Marxists have just assigned ideas to the 'superstructure' forgetting at once Marx's analysis of commodity fetishism and the role of scientific and technological ideas in constantly revolutionizing the forces of production. Closely related to this is a peculiar individualism in Marx's work which just because, unlike Hegel, he never constructed a system (rather initiating a research programme), bypasses what a Sartre would call certain necessary mediations: (i) the stratification of the personality and the concrete singularity of the individual; (ii) the plane of inter-subjectivity, positing an unmediated relation between the individual and society; (iii) directly related to this, the realm of what I called in C3.10 'social virtue', corresponding to Hegel's civil society, including a domain of innovation, initiative and enterprise necessary to a dynamic, pluralistic socialist society; (iv) the depth of the sedimented institutionalization of structures, on the plane of social relations, other than the economy; and (v) the mediations, e.g. of a constitutional kind, that indicate a failure to take seriously either what Hegel would call the 'internal teleology' of practices or the concrete universal conceived as a multiple quadruplicity.

Closely connected to these issues are Marx's concept of the dialectic of de-alienation and freedom. The dispositional aspect of rational autonomy, which relates directly to the role of motivation and incentives and thus to the vexed question of the market under socialism, is neglected. Despite his Prometheanism and recognition of the way in which capitalism was changing humanity, there is no real dialectic of subjectivity, of a changing four-planar human nature, which would have to incorporate a dialectic of morality and a conception of the moral evolution of the species as unfinished. Marx, for all his distinction between the stages of socialism, fails to give any indication of what I called in C3.7 substantive in addition to merely formal criteria of a better species of society. This is linked, of course, to his reductionism in ethics and negativism in politics, in which explanatory critique is not complemented by a concretely utopian vision of an alternative society. This is also reflected in the absence of a prefigurative moment in his thought, despite his emphasis on the educative aspects of increasingly socialized labour. And both are connected to his failure, already remarked, to come to terms with the material, in comparison with the ideational, presence of the past (and, to a degree, of the intrinsic outside).

To some extent, with the benefit of hindsight, I have been visiting Marx with the sins of his successors, but there is an original for them. In the context of global intradependence and the presence of past, the voluntaristic attempt to build socialism in one country, on the basis of a supposedly omniscient commandist party state, informed with an unmediated conception of four-planar social being and an unsituated and dedispositionalized conception of freedom, with scant regard for constitutionality and neglect of civic and human (as distinct from socio-economic) rights, leading to the sinking of the USSR into an undifferentiated expressive unity (resonating with the most primitive Hegelian logical realm of Being), can be given Marxian credentials, however much Marx would have loathed the outcome.*

It is not the unilinear character of Marx's presentational dialectics, but their actualist, monistic, demoralized and utopian (in the pejorative sense of not naturalistically grounded in a fully four-planar analysis of human being) nature that I am complaining about. They constitute the mystical skeleton rattling around in the cupboard of geo-historical materialism. I will directly address the question of levels of analysis (the vertical, rather than horizontal, aspect of non-actualism) shortly, but for the moment we can conclude only that the neglected periphery of social science was left in the same boat as the Hegelian demi-actual. The best that can — and probably must — be said for Marx was that he was committed to the development of an integrative (asymmetrically structured) pluralism, driven by the logic of commodification and reification.

---

* The three Hegelian logical realms of being, essence and notion, which I am using as place-holders in this chapter in a relatively uncritical, provisional way, may be situated metacritically by their coordination to the respective principles of realized idealism, constellational spiritual monism and immanent teleology, and, more macroscopically, to the spheres of the understanding, the dialectical moment proper and speculative reason as articulated in C1.

Turning now to the issue of the plurality of causes, Marx is once again pulled in contrary directions. For in the Preface to the first edition of *Capital* (1867) he remarks that 'the country which is more developed industrially only shows, to the less developed, the image of its own future', clearly suggesting a unilinear view of geo-history. (From which spread the functionalist and evolutionary, developmentally unfolding models characteristic of Marxism for most of this century.) Ten years later, he roundly denounces, in his letter to Mikhailovsky (November 1877), those who would convert his 'historical sketch of the genesis of capitalism in western Europe into a historico-philosophical theory of the general path every people is fated to tread, whatever the circumstances in which it finds itself', and many passages in the *Grundrisse* (1857–58) similarly suggest a multi-linear view of history.

It is easy to acquit Marx of the charges of historicism and fatalism.[25] Despite this, Gramsci saw fit to describe 1917 as 'the revolution against Karl Marx's *Capital*'. There is an obvious tension here between Marx's critique of political economy, which was highly developed by him, and the research programme and transformational praxis of geo-historical materialism, which were not. Connected to this issue is the old conundrum of free will and determinism, which I have already brusquely resolved in §2 above. More interesting perhaps is Marx's juxtaposition of two concepts of freedom in *Capital*, Vol. 3, C48 — the first consisting in the rational regulation and minimization of necessary labour, the second in the 'development of human energy' as 'an end in itself'. The first invites the question 'who regulates the regulators?' As for the second, it is unclear whether Marx conceived such free creative activity, in communism, as totally unconstrained by social forms, political mediations, geo-historical circumstances and natural limits, about the last of which ecologically minded socialists would obviously wish to have something to say.

Many more questions could be asked about Marx's epistemology — either by employing 1M–4D componential analysis or by utilizing the $(\alpha)-(\gamma)$ grid, but rather than pursuing these here I want to say something about the question of levels of abstraction. It is obvious that Marx sees class society as a particular form of human society and capitalism as a particular form of class society. Capitalism may itself be broken down into stages, following, for example, the Japanese school of Uno and his colleagues or the periodization of Mandel. Adopting the former approach and characterizing contemporary capitalism in terms of the coordinates of consumerism and post-Fordism, to get a grip on its exact causal-spatio-temporal dynamic one would have to build into it: multiple determination by many regional

institutions (nation states, superveillance techniques, social movements, information technologies), relations and dimensions of
oppression (power$_2$ relations), modes of sanction and discourse,
including of course their various ideological intersects, demographic
flows, and a host of other phenomena. In addition one would have to
take into account internal relations, mediations, contradictions and
conflicts between these various entities in the way I indicated in C2.
In the explanation of any concretely singular conjuncture, further
elements would be involved. These would have to include not only
the precise specification of particular instantiations of four-planar
social being, but also the effects of extraneous structures and
generative mechanisms, as well as all kinds of contingencies, which in
no way lie within the province of a developed geo-historical
materialism. Figure 4.6 depicts a spectrum of levels from the relatively
abstract to the relatively concrete.[26]

I have described the subsequent fate of the Marxist dialectic, and
Marxist philosophy generally, elsewhere.[27] Whether in dialectical
materialism or in the dialectical (e.g. Lukácsian, Sartrian) or materialist
(e.g. Della Volpean, Althusserian) wings of western Marxism, Marx's
dialectic typically assumed an idealist and Marx's materialism an
empiricist form. This is not to disparage all the work that was done in
this period (a personal reaction is that from within this canvas the
work of Adorno will stand out). But for Marxism to progress now as a
research tradition it is faced with a clear methodological choice
between the neo-positivism of analytical Marxism, the neo-
Kantianism of Habermasian communicative action theory, the neo-
Nietzscheanism of post-Marxism or dialectical critical realism. (This
quartet in fact parallels the options outside Marxism as well.)

If it be thought that in this section I have been unduly harsh on
Marx, then one should bear in mind the following quote from the
Phenomenology:

> Our epoch is a birth-time, and a period of transition. The spirit of man has
> broken with the old order of things hitherto prevailing, and with the old
> ways of thinking . . . this gradual crumbling to pieces, which did not alter
> the general look and aspect of the whole, is interrupted by the sunrise,
> which in a flash and at a single stroke, brings into view the form and
> structure of the new world. But this new world is perfectly realized just as
> little as a new-born child . . . a building is not finished when its foundation
> is laid . . . science, the crowning glory of the spiritual world, is not found
> complete in its initial stages.[28]

Then one should take to heart this quotation from Marx's 'Eighteenth

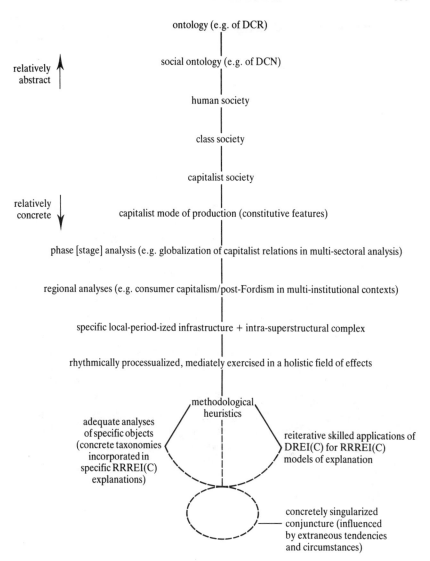

Figure 4.6 Levels of Analysis in Marxism

Brumaire of Louis Bonaparte':

The tradition of all the dead generations weighs like a nightmare on the brain of the living. And just when they seem engaged in revolutionizing themselves and things, in creating something that has not yet existed,

precisely in such periods of revolutionary crisis they amazingly conjure up
the spirits of the past to their service and borrow from them names, battle
cries and costumes in order to prevent the new scene of world-history in
this time-honoured disguise and this borrowed language.[29]

§ 9 Metacritical Dialectics: Philosophical Ideologies — Their Sublation and Explanation

A *metacritique*$_1$ (MC$_1$) isolates a relevant *absence* in a text, theory or
practice, indicating an incompleteness, T/P inconsistency, detotalization, split or reification of some kind. A *metacritique*$_2$ (MC$_2$) constitutes
or contains an *explanation* of it, and in general depends upon a prior or
concomitant *metacritique*$_1$ or sublation of the entity under analysis. In
a way this whole book, and in particular C3 and §2 of this chapter, is a
sublation (ds') of irrealism, in its analytical and dialectical, empiricist
and rationalist, critical and non-critical forms. So in this section I will
concentrate on metacritical$_2$ dialectics for the most part, undertaking
only a contribution to the explanation of philosophical ideologies that
I intend to address elsewhere,* employing a mixture of diachronic
and synchronic analysis. I shall take 'philosophy' to refer to a
tradition, a professionalized institution and a theory problem-field
solution set, reproduced in its particular dominant declensions
largely in virtue of its ideological effects and transformed at geo-
historical nodal or turning points under the auspices of particular
agencies. But philosophy is a great condenser and its discontinuities
can be as easily exaggerated as missed.

Thus the history of western philosophy can be largely seen as a
quest for an unhypothetical starting point, something unconditioned
and one. Parmenidean monism generated the two great problems of
philosophy — of negation, opposition and, at the limit, reflexivity and
change; and of multiplicity, order and, at the limit, chaos and flux —
the one entraining the dialectical, the other fostering the analytical
genre. That is why it is so important to insist on sheer *alterity*,
existential intransitivity and the critique of the epistemic fallacy and
anthropism implicit in the Eleatic one. This is also why I have been
able largely to tell my story as one of the search for subject−object
identity. Of course, not all philosophers claim to have achieved or
found it. To Aristotle one can counterpose Plato, to Hegel, Fichte, to
Mach, arguably Popper. To this theme — of the *transcendental*

---

* I have given a prototype of this in SRHE, C3.

*impossibility of monism** — I will return. The first great problem of philosophy was 'dissolved' by Plato in his analysis, really mystification and repression, of negation and change in terms of difference. Against this I have set the critique of ontological monovalence, and the vindication of hitherto sequestered *absence*. The second great problem was first 'resolved' by Aristotle's immanent theory of knowledge, but this only sets the scene for *the generation of a new transcendent*, most usually God or social convention. For nous cannot do the job that I have tailored *alethia* to do.

The primordial mistake of philosophy can be looked at in two ways. First as the epistemic fallacy. For it is this which powers the drive to subject—object identity theory. For, on subject—object identity (or equivalence) theory, *knowledge becomes a surrogate for being*. This inevitably stems from Parmenidean monism, but it is the single defining characteristic of the irrealist tradition. Monism and subject—object identity theory eliminate *alterity* and diversity, and *absence* and change alike. Hence it is the epistemic fallacy that necessitates the doctrine of ontological monovalence, on this way of looking at things. The absence of the concept of absence in turn necessitates actualism which, in its role as generalized identity theory, reduces the possible (cf. ethical descriptivism) and the necessary (cf. epistemological descriptivism) to the actual and accounts for the 'primal squeeze' and the third great absence, of *alethic truth*, in the unholy trinity. The direction of explanatory connection therefore looks like as in Figure 4.7. Once established, these connections are reciprocal. Thus actualism makes change impossible, necessitating a monism at its token/type level, generating the new transcendent, only fideistically warranted in the absence of alethic truth. This inevitably detotalizes reality, splitting it into two; and means that philosophy must be explicitly or implicitly dualistic, whatever its monist-reductionist-actualist aspirations. Meanwhile the Parmenidean-Platonic-Aristotelian quest for an unhypothetical starting point was curiously repeated by Descartes in his search for incorrigibility, esoterically generating a monism too — a solipsism

---

* Primary polyadization is necessary for individuation, and hence self-identity. It generates immediately transcendental refutations of any monism (or solipsism) or dialectics of a generalized Schillerian type. This last has, as in Hegel's case, always been connected to assumptions of an original monism, prior to the moment of self-diremption or -alienation. Understanding individuation as a polyadic achievement and foregoing the assumption of a unitary origin allows us to save the contours of the Schillerian schema but only if the dialectic is conceived as local and tensed, in which event it has a minimum five-term structure and is open at beginning and end. In this neck of the philosophical woods, fundamentalism, monism and irrealist dialectic connive.

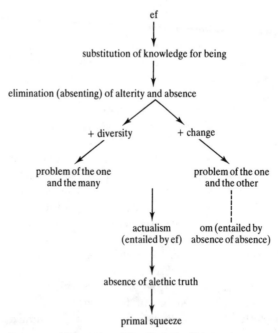

Figure 4.7 The Unholy Trinity

from which modern philosophy has only just escaped. As seen in §2, to (and constellationally contained within) the aporiai of the transdictive complex at the level of general knowledge stemming from actualism, we now have aporiai of solipsism at the level of particular knowledge, once again necessitating a fideistic response, and a detotalization of reality. These problems (α) of the one and the other are symptomatic of a class-divided and sundered society, and they act to stall the possibility of change; while (β) those of the one and the many are metaphoric of diversity and relativity and metonymic of the totality of master−slave relations. They can be represented as in Figure 4.8. In Hegelian dialectical terms the three levels represent the three logics of being, essence and the notion respectively.

It should be added that the explanatory primacy of the epistemic fallacy, on this way of regarding things, does not undermine my earlier arguments for the conceptual primacy of absence. It is implicit in every act of referential detachment and explicit in any act at all, including the primordial Eleatic *statement* of monism (a tradition-creating act) just as it is implicit in the coming into being of the monist itself. This leads us naturally to the second way of looking at the primordial failing of philosophy.

This is to recognize that a monistic starting point conceptually prevents, insofar as the monism is complete, i.e. truly monistic, change, including a beginning or enunciation, of itself (which would be a performative contradiction) — just as it is reciprocally entailed by the absence of change. On this account the doctrine of ontological monovalence moves to the fore. It immediately entails actualism and the elimination of alterity and thus the epistemic fallacy on which knowledge *is* being (there is no other). The presence of another generates the possibility of a plurality. There is no doubt that this is the more elegant presentation, especially when it is appreciated that only a monism can satisfy the demand for the unconditioned, the starting point which is the ending point, the circle of an eternally closed totality. (See Figure 4.9.)

But whichever tack we take it is important to see that there are two mutually reinforcing category mistakes — ontological monovalence and the epistemic fallacy — the latter generating ontological actualism and primal squeeze, and that while ontological monovalence immediately generates the problem of the other, identity theory inevitably generates a new transcendent, explicitly or implicitly, an other, resulting in an alienating detotalization or split (at 3L) which extrudes the theorist who, if (s)he is to reflexively situate herself, must be placed in one or other of the realms. This typically entails de-agentification in the form of either disembodiment or reification or both (at 4D). To the problems that identity theory bring there can only be a fideistic response, whether it be subjectively or objectively formulated. But fideism collapses when monovalence is rejected. Agency, or emergence, or structural change, undermines the course of nature which would otherwise have prevailed. Causally efficacious absenting spoils actualism at a stroke and any fideistic solution which

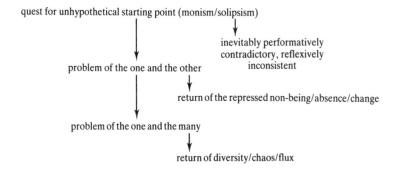

Figure 4.8

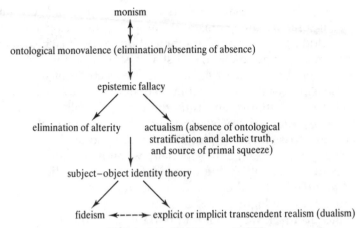

Figure 4.9 Fideism or DCR?

seeks to underpin our present knowledge is immediately rendered void. Any feasible story must incorporate ontological change explicitly. There seem to be three alternatives here: to allow for the reality of tense, becoming and transformative change, in accordance with norms of judgemental rationality, as dialectical critical realism does; to end fideistically fundamentally, as Hegel does, or deposit an endless regressive task, as Fichte, equally fundamentalistically, does; or to eclipse reason altogether, as neo-Nietzscheans do — to palimpsest rationality or see it as an extension of or pretension to something other than itself, such as caprice, 'western democracy' or the 'will-to-power'. Neither ego → ethno → anthropism nor fideism will, I am submitting in this book, do. Indeed the former violates norms of discursive argumentation and must collapse into a spontaneist fideism. So it is dialectical critical realism and the new enlightenment (for which I have pleaded elsewhere[30]) or reliance on faith or fate, Hegelian 'positivity'.

Philosophy is often straightforwardly presented as a battle between the Gods and the Giants, the Friends of the Forms and the Friends of the Earth, with Kant often shuttled in as an arch-compromiser. But the ultimate victory of empiricism was secured by Descartes's subjectivization and inwardization of rationalist criteria of knowledge. This opened the way for Lockian scepticism about essences, Berkeleian scepticism about matter and Humean scepticism about everything. In fact Hume cannot be simply portrayed as *only* a sceptic. For, as I have tried to stress, the history of philosophy is multiplex, as convex as it is concave. His interpretive antinomies are at least as remarkable as Hegel's. He is (a) the *arch-positivist*, providing the *hard-core* of most significant subsequent philosophy — from Kant, Hegel, Nietzsche to postmodernism, from Mill and Mach to Russell and *both* Wittgensteins, to Dummett, Davidson, Rorty and Quine; (b) the all purpose *sceptic*, inimitably exemplifying the aporetic-dogmatic character of philosophy as a theory problem-field solution set (*TPF(SS)*); (c) the first great modern *irrationalist* who accepts the unhappy consciousness of a deductivist analysis of inductively unknowable causal laws; (d) the *ironist* whose quest for literary fame remained unsatisfied; (e) the *fideist* who stood by common sense and played backgammon despite his uncertainties about an external world, other minds, the uniformity of nature, the existence of the past and of his own self; and (f) finally the *conventionalist* conformist who upholds law, order, private property and the prevailing order of things, epistemic and social alike. And the list could be continued. Kant *involuted* structure, but the synthetic a priori could not do anything to discriminate between the transfinity of possible causal laws consistent with the empirical data. Hegel Mark I historicized the Humean hard-core, but, like Kant, Mark II had to be explicitly dualist to sustain identity theory. Nietzsche deconstructed knowledge but left Humean ontology intact. The late Wittgenstein could only duplicate the problem of induction but to the question of how we know the rules of the language game we are playing will carry on under the de/prescriptions we think we know them, he could give only a fideist-conventionalist response. When the crises of twentieth-century thought and life struck home, philosophy could only follow the transmutation route from the absolute foundationalism of logical positivism through conventionalism, pragmatism and a variety of other positions to the overt irrationalism and judgemental relativism which is the inexorable outcome of its primordial quest.

In the light of this trajectory I do not apologize for taking positivism to elucidate certain metacritical themes. For the transformed transformative practice of philosophy — as dialectical underlabourer for emancipatory social science — which I am motivating, philosophy has to be thoroughly ex-Humed. Before this let me discuss some voids — first (a) in orthodox terms, then (b) along 1M−4D lines. (a) The absent ontology secured by the epistemic fallacy is, from a metacritical perspective, constituted by reified facts and closed systems; the absent sociology masked by methodological individualism admits, in addition to substantive individualism in the domain of civil society, commandist (Stalinist), elitist (social democratic), authoritarian (neo-liberal) or organicist (right conservative) states;* the critique of metaphysics, entailing the absence of metacritics, means that the hard-core of philosophy lacks a concept of itself, detotalizing itself, resulting in a lack of reflexivity and performative contradiction; finally, absent axiology means that philosophy lacks a concept of agentive agency, while the ethical scepticism, implicit in Humean Viceregency and explicit in the post-Hegelian *Götterdämmerung* which replicated it, implies the lack of any real grounding for ethics (the impossibility of any transition from 'is' to 'ought') and the concomitant proliferation of emotivist characters — the manager, the therapist, the aesthete — with which Alasdair MacIntyre has furnished us.[31] To these we could add the expert, the bureaucrat, the fixer, the media star, the soap persona, Vietnam or Essex Man. Let us turn to the sequence of 1M−4D absences characteristic of the hard-core or deep structure of post-Humean philosophy. The 1M absence of structure normalizes or mystifies science and encourages a shallow depthless account of society, while the absence of differentiation uniformalizes or stereotypes social identities. The 2E absence of absence, as I have already suggested, rationalizes past change and liberties at the expense of the possibility of present and future ones; but it also deprocessualizes ontology generally and screens social conflict and contradiction and, to a degree, the existence of social inequities and ills. But probably its most important effect is to sequester existential questions generally. The 3L absence of totality and reflexivity hides splits, inconsistencies, divisions such as those of class, gender, ethnicity, etc. and alienation — the estrangement of part or whole of one's essence from one's self — generally. The 4D absence of agentive agency encourages the fragmentation and enervation of the personality and a disempowering/impotent sense of self, while underpinning all manner of projective or introjective identifications, that is, of unhappy consciousness.

Whilst on the topic of the metacritical voids let me deal with the effect of some of the more obvious presences. The wretched alliance of *ontological actualism* (more of the superficial same, the McDonaldization of surface reality), *epistemological reductionism* — the squeezing of the middle terms of natural necessity, experimentally controlled scientific theory and the alethic truth of things — and *logical extensionalism*, which converts the love of wisdom into the fetishism of technique, results, as we have seen in §1, in mutually inconsistent theories. Punctualism, in its ego-present-centric (exclusive

---

* Thus we have here the formula empiricist ontology ↔ individualist sociology ↔ collectivist state.

disjunctive) form denies history and downplays spatiality; only the present (here) exists. Blockism, which posits an opposite inclusive conjunctive totality of all (space-)times, denies the openness of the future, thus complementing the indexicalist denial of the past. Actualism scouts possibility and hope, while atomism, displaced onto the social plane, reinforces the bias against collective agency and cooperative associationalist enterprises.

But it is time to get to the heart of the irrealist problematic. Scepticism, and the aporiai on which philosophy as a *disciplinary matrix* feeds, [1] acting in the context of a TPF(SS), poses the questions that *subject − object identity theory* [2] equivocally answers. Here we have a series of what I am going to call *anthroporealist exchanges*, depicted in Figure 4.10. At the same time, just to take the most obvious example, subject − object identity theory generalized as actualism is both (i) unjustifiable (cf. the problem of induction) and (ii) falsified in open systems, where constant conjunctions do not obtain (the problem of transduction). Hence it presupposes two things. First a realist complement, which will function as a surrogate transcendent, so we have the *irrealist ensemble*:

$$[1] \rightarrow [2] + [3].$$

But, to operate in a world which is in fact dialectical critical realist, it requires in addition a *Tina defence mechanism* to act both as a metaphysical λ or escape clause in its irrealist guise [4a] and surreptitiously to allow it to operate transfactually when the situation demands [4b]. The resulting system is a *Tina compromise formation* (see Figure 4.11). Formally, and in practice, the resulting system produces

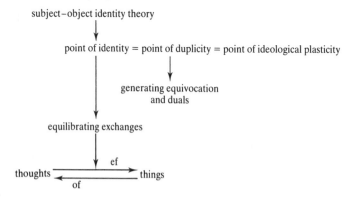

subject−object identity theory

point of identity = point of duplicity = point of ideological plasticity

generating equivocation
and duals

equilibrating exchanges

thoughts ⟷ things
of   ef

Figure 4.10 The Anthroporealist Exchanges

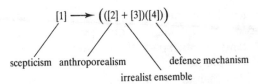

Figure 4.11   The Structure of a Tina Compromise Form

all manner of inversions, T/P inconsistencies, splits, detotalizations and recalcitrant surds. But it allows reification to co-exist with voluntarism, extensionalism to operate by a tacit recourse to the non-extensionalist concept of the same (i.e. to invoke a signified formally elided in the direct connection postulated between signifier and referent), personalism to sit side by side with emotivism, self-referential paradox to be avoided by a tacit hypostatizing self-alienation. In a nutshell, it generates the ideological effects which reproduce the irrealist problematic.

It will be noted that the illicit fusion in [2] can be put in the form of the non-exchange of equivalents which parallels the logic of commodification; and the fetishism which results from the closure of open systems parallels the effects of commodity fetishism, which also functions to represent sectional interests as universal. (The resulting Tina compromise is, of course, the source of diverse fissions.) There is thus a double fetishism involved, together with a double alienation in science. If we regard the ideological complex as underpinned by the primal generative separation of capitalism and as incorporating the effects of other master–slave relations, then we can see the famous trio of Stoicism, Scepticism and the Unhappy Consciousness as operating as ideologies of bondage and legitimation at once in a duplex fashion. Stoicism purports indifference to reality and power$_2$ relations while Scepticism attempts to deny them. At the same time the Unhappy Consciousness duplicates reality in explicitly (e.g. Leibnizian) or implicitly (e.g. Kantian) transcendent form and/or involutes it, as is typical of post-Kantian philosophy. But the Unhappy Consciousness which introjects the master's ideology or projects one for slaves is a leitmotif for *philosophy generally*, revealing the *alienation from reality* that haunts *irrealist philosophy*, whether of foundationalist or irrationalist timbre. And this is one reason why Hegel is such a good diagnostic clue to philosophy. *The erstwhile beautiful soul must make a Tina compromise with axiological necessity*, the reality principle or alethic truth.

In a full treatment of the metacritical dialectics of irrealism many other topics would be considered. Some of these we have already broached. Internal duplicity results in repression, dysyntonic symptoms in the form of aporiai, antinomies or componentialized or externalized split-offs. External duplicity, such as we have seen to be inherent in [3], in the transcendent complement to anthroporealism, incorporating both anthropocentric and anthropomorphic forms, typically necessitates the grafting of a defence mechanism such as [4]. The tacit duplicity of dialectical counterparts results in the respective mutual presupposition of the contraries, i.e. the inconsistent interiorization of the counterpart (at the intensive margin of inquiry and vice versa at the extensive). It is therefore in effect a complex system of *internal duplicity*, the multiply mediated compounding of categorial error upon error. The anthropism which is characteristic of irrealism means that in seeking its substantive 'analogical grammar' the underlying model of man (sic) will inevitably play a major part. His name is Crusoe, abstracted from the past and the outside, intradependence (except as Friday), social relations in the strict sense and inevitably a master. This is bourgeois man. But alongside this, the classical conception of action by continuous contiguous contact, a strictly speaking incoherent corpuscularianism (see C2.1) and the assumption of closure all play a part. I have already explained the dependency of dialectics, at least in its Hegelian form, upon the analytical problematic. A transformationalist reading of Hegel must be accepted. His aim is to transfigure the facts, be they of philosophy or society (or nature), as he understands them, in a context defined by a Humean-Kantian hard-core, so as to reconcile himself to actuality and to comfort and flatter his contemporaries by showing them to be the vehicle of realized absolute spirit, accomplished geo-history. His dialectic identifies contradictions, mainly as a result of some incompleteness in the self-realization of spirit, which he remedies by expanding the universe of discourse so as to remove the contradiction between the erstwhile contraries. As for the materialist dialectic of Marxist philosophy after Marx (and setting on one side substantive works of Marxian social scientific theory), this could be said to be defined as the unhappy consciousness of the split between the objectivist processual empiricism of dialectical materialism and the characteristically subjectivist totalizing idealism of western Marxism.

An iconic representation of one system of relations within the irrealist problematic is depicted in Figure 4.12, while the core structure of the Tina compromise is represented in Figure 4.13. The first step in putting matters right is to understand the constellational identity of judgemental rationality (in the intrinsic aspect) within epistemic relativity (in the transitive dimension) within ontological

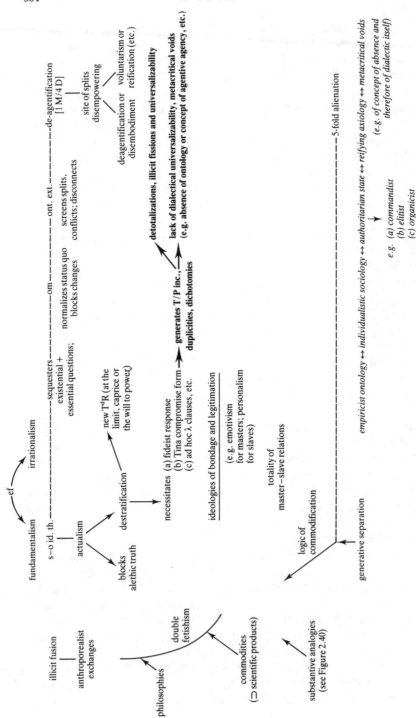

Figure 4.12 The Metacritical Ideo-logic of Irrealism

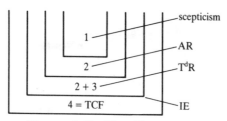

Figure 4.13 Tina Formation

realism (in the intransitive dimension), incorporating alterity, absence and alethia, stratification, tensed process and negativity generally, totality, reflexivity and agency, oriented to the alethic *explanatory critique* of particular philosophical ideologies. For irrealism is ultimately not only a *repressive* but also a *causally efficacious* ideology; not only in social science but in social life too, as I shall now proceed to show.

§ 10 The Consequences of Irrealism

The most obvious consequences of irrealism are for philosophy itself. Irrealist philosophy is *autosubversive*. In particular it is chronically prone to immanent critique, T/P inconsistency, dc', performative contradiction, heterology and lack of universalizability; to commissive as well as omissive critique, that is, absences, detotalizations, reifications and splits; to repression, grafting and Tina compromise. Historically, the irrealist tradition can be subjected to a sequence of *Achilles' Heel* critiques. Thus Parmenides cannot sustain the concept of the one. Plato cannot sustain the morality of Socratic reasoning without recourse to the *Forms*. But the Forms cannot be upheld without self-referential paradox and tacit recourse to the transient sensate world; moreover, the transience of this world cannot be undermined by the Platonic *act* of the analysis of change in terms of difference. Aristotle mires himself in the aporiai of substance and cannot without an appeal to a transcendent God account for the intelligibility of his own scientific practice. Descartes cannot sustain the cogito and must yield to an antinomy between doubt and himself. An Achilles' Heel critique seeks to show that it is precisely where a position seems strongest that it is actually most weak. Thus Kant cannot sustain an intelligible concept of freedom, or Hegel of historicity. Post-Nietzschean philosophy cannot account for the concepts of undoing or erasure, nor have Marxian socialists produced a plausible vision of flourishing under socialism. A Feyerabend or Rorty, and sometimes a Davidson or Quine, refuse to talk about the causal efficacy that they admit goes on 'out there' (and ultimately accounts for everything) with the consequence that they cannot repeat or explain themselves. (For what is it that they cannot repeat but an intransitive existent, a real [social] worldly object?) The new fundamentalism is as dogmatic as the old, and the new relativism, except when constellationally embedded in ontological realism, as irrationalist. *Irrealist philosophy lacks.* It lacks the concept of non-anthropism, ontology, intransitivity, stratification, transfactuality, absence, contradiction, totality, reflexivity and agentive agency. It lacks the concept of a social-relation-dependent, naturalistically grounded moral truth; of a non-anthropic tensed spatializing process or rhythmic, just as it lacks the concept of alethic realism, of the truth of things and states of affairs, as distinct from propositions and systems of them. It lacks the concept of the presence of the past and the openness of the future, of systematic intra-activity and the contingency of being. Above all, it lacks the concept of irrealism, of metacritique, and of philosophy as a field of effects. (The biggest lie is that philosophy leaves everything as it is.) It even lacks the concept of lack.

However, in this section I want to concentrate on the consequences of irrealism not for philosophy per se, but for society. Irrealism may function as a general ideology either (α) directly or (β) mediately, through the generation of specifically philosophical ideological effects. Thus I argued in C2.10 that the analytic problematic, an ontologically actualist monovalent and extensionalist theory problem-field solution set, functions as a *repressive ideology* unconsciously and aporetically normalizing and freezing past changes and liberties, prohibiting the possibility of present and future ones. Emotivism is the moral ideology of those who do not need to work, decisionism is the ethics of the slaves of masters who are themselves masters of slaves, personalism is the philosophy of slaves who accept that description. An unmediated, deprocessualized ethics, personalism takes hold of the concrete singular, denudes him or her of their concreteness, tells them that ought implies that they can and must, quite irrespective of their abilities, needs and wants. It then blames them, and, if the misdemeanour is great enough, punishes them. It is part of the same conceptualized machinery that augments the growth of, and gives the state an (often uneasy grip on the) monopoly of, the means of violence and decides when it is legitimate to kill, while ontological monovalence, the absence of the concept of absence, conveniently hides existential questions. It is unsurprising that Hegel invoked the cunning with which reason had waited for him (and, presumably, in the twentieth century, Fukuyama*) to justify the 'slaughter-bench of history'. We are 'thrown' into a world of multiple and contradictory ideologies of bondage and legitimation, underpinned by irrealist category mistakes, and *locked* into a position–practice system, with its duties and responsibilities — be they of superveillance or of office cleaner — *pre-legitimated* for us.

In §8 we looked at the Hegelian residues (and, to a degree, the lack of them) in Marx. It is not difficult to see in these (α) practical expressionism and centrism, (β) tendential monism (unidimensionality), quasi-actualism and Prometheanism, and (γ) post-dated endism. There is a failure to complement explanatory critique with concrete utopianism, based on the moral irrealism implicit in his sociological reductionism of ethics. This is in part consciously derived from Hegel and in part an unconscious inheritance of Hegel's constellational closure of geo-history. (This, insofar as it involves the denial of an open future, may well make Hegel vulnerable to Popper's critique of historicism after all — although not in the

---

* At this point it is necessary to say a word about Fukuyama.[32] First, it is not generally recognized that he owes as much to Nietzsche as to Hegel. Second, nor is it normally appreciated that, brilliant though his Hegelian mentor, Kojève, was Kojève's atheistic, humanistic reading of Hegel truncates Hegel's system by two-thirds. *The Philosophy of Nature* is explicitly repudiated. But no sense can be made of the *Logics* without the *Vorstellung* or picture-imagery which functions both to initiate them and to terminate them in the transition to nature. This is a minor point. More important, metaphysics cannot be immanentized and the traditional goals of philosophy realized, unless actuality is transcendentized, which it is in spiritual-logical, not natural, necessity. Without this the *Logics* are incoherent. You cannot pick and choose with one for whom the truth is the whole. Third, the drive from the dialectic from master–slave to mutual recognition is, as we have seen in §5, a *radically incomplete one*. There is no reason intrinsic to the *Phenomenology* why this drive should not stop at mutual forgiveness, rather than the reciprocal recognition of rights. But if we grant Hegel the latter position (as I have argued we should) then rights must logically be extended to include such phenomena as de-alienation and the abolition of the totality of discursively moralized oppressive power$_2$ relations. There is no reason, for instance, to believe that the hereditary monarchy is either the *telos* or *finis* or summit of concrete singularity. Fourth, Fukuyama ignores the link between the new information-based technologies and new modes of socialized self-awareness; and indeed, positively, has nothing distinctive to say about the *social sciences* and what I have argued is their necessary emancipatory role (entailed by their explanatory function). Fifth, his master concept *thymos* (Platonic 'spirit', characteristic of the warrior-guardian caste) is not in fact used by Hegel to initiate the drive towards mutual recognition which begins instead with *desire*, as Kojève correctly emphasizes, and in the *Phenomenology* itself the emphasis is, as I have already remarked, on reconciliation and mutual forgiveness (consistent with the persistence of an oppressive power$_2$ relation) rather than recognition of the rights associated with democracy, or, indeed, liberalism as such. Finally, the irony of Fukuyama's book is that *thymos*, which is first wheeled in to explain the success of *liberal democracy*, as distinct from plain capitalism, is, at the end, used to account for the *economic success* of the non-individualist and undemocratic regimes of South East and East Asia. *Thymos*, in other words, is an instrument of capitalism, not democracy. And Fukuyama's argument is a *non sequitur*.

way Popper thought.) The result of this is that we still lack plausible models of what a socialist economy, democracy or world-order might look like. *Global intradependence* and the unconcealed *presence of the past* and *the constitutive intrinsic outside* made the inevitable comparison between the East and the West in respect of both production and consumption all the more poignant. The command economies of the all-knowing Laplacean homuncular party states of the erstwhile actually existing socialist societies ignored (a) the tacit knowledge of the immediate producers; (b) the dispositional aspects of rational freedom, including the expressive and agonistic aspects of human behaviour; (c) the need for multiple mediations, in the realm of civil society, including socialized markets, between the individual and the party state. There has been a neglect of transitional politics and complex pluralistic and mediated formations, in which socialist virtues could triumph both technologically and ideologically over their capitalist rivals. Politically, there has been no understanding of *self*-emancipation (and the difference between solidarity and substitutionism); or of the criterion of concrete singularity alongside the multiplicity of mediations necessary in the civic sphere. There has been little emphasis on constitutionality and the recognition of democratic and human rights; and, until very recently, of the need to take into account the totality of discursively moralized oppressive power$_2$ relations. Actually existing socialism failed in part because it did not deign to consider that the immediate producers and consumers, rather than the party managers, might know best how to tackle, both collectively and through socialized markets, questions of technological innovation, incentive, production, distribution and exchange under socialism.[33] The result of the communist societies' fallback into a simple expressive unity, increasingly incapable of integrating innovative change into their economies and weighed down by the costs of the Cold War, overlain with a (literally) incredible ideology, was a state apparatus without legitimacy and a populace denied basic human rights. The fact that the commandist party states were characterized by immense theory/practice inconsistency, with an ideology of organic unity, decentralized democracy and rights and a positivistic practice of the manipulative use of instrumental reason in a reifying social mechanics, should have suggested what happened on philosophical grounds alone, if the dialectical thread of this book is correct. The ensuing kenosis and collapse of the actually existing socialist societies took none so much by surprise as the international relations 'realists' by name. But these so-called 'realists' cannot see social intra-activity for national boundaries, dimensions of sociality other than power, and levels of reality other than the most superficial. Before we leave the topic we must comment on Marx's failure to thematize the questions of levels of abstraction broached in §8, a function of his programmatic collapse of the categories of mediation (of Essence in Hegelian terms), any necessary condition for the achievement of a true unity in diversity. Dialectical materialism, cast in the mould of a destratified processual objective empiricism, after a brief debate between Deborin and Bukharin in the late twenties, and subjected to the sort of Zhdanovite discipline that gave Soviet biology Lysenko, had nothing constructive to say about this state of affairs. The issue between Menshevism and Bolshevism was never properly debated, primarily due to the defaulting of the orthodox side to their own 'national interests' in 1914, a classic instance of the delusionary representation of sectional interests as universalistic ones. Nor did western Marxism, for the most part of an (again) destratified but this time totalizing subjective idealist character, have very much to offer except bemoan the world-historical problem of agency, i.e. the fragmentation, global dispersal and apparent bourgeoisification of sections of the proletariat.

Meanwhile, in the West, social democracy flourished in particular regions for long stretches of time, and in the so-called 'third world' Marxism-Leninism became a leading ideology of national liberation. However, in the heartlands of capitalism, when social democracy captured government, its style was *elitist* as distinct from commandist, but it here again operated manipulatively, using instrumental rather than explanatory critical reason, in a social engineering rather than agent-empowering state, once more ignoring the tacit knowledge of the immediate producers and their separation from control of the means of production alike. Moreover, it was generally anti-Soviet in character, thus increasing the pressure on the beleaguered East. At the same time when the ex-colonies became formally independent some combination of local national bourgeoisie, multi-national corporations and local militia normally took control. And, where they did not, as in Cuba or Nicaragua, Angola or Mozambique, the erstwhile resistance movements were subjected to horrendous pressure by the USA or US-backed regimes.[34] Instead of a complex differentiated society, oriented to the free flourishing of the concrete singularity of all, representing a genuine pluralistic unity in diversity, attaining and transcending the Hegelian logic of the notion, what lay before radicals was the sunken mass of the decentred communist party states or regimes in the West whose socialism was elitist and shallow. Small wonder that there is a crisis of socialism. But the dialectic of desire to freedom, which I

outlined in C3.10 (cf. §5 above), is not dead, nor even resting, by
whatever name it chooses to call itself. Its pulse is insistent, though it
is highly contingent and dependent upon all of us whether progress
in its direction will be positive or negative.

The logic of my argument in C3.7 was that the social sciences have a
crucial role to play here. Some progress has taken place in the last
third of this century. Theory is no longer uniformly frowned upon,
forms of research other than number-crunching (which has its proper
place too) go on. A critical realist current exists. But a generally
dichotomous character persists. Issues which should have been long
settled still split the human, and, to an extent, the natural, sciences:
between realism and irrealism, positivism and hermeneutics,
individualism and collectivism, structuralism and historicism,
between qualitative and quantitative and large-scale and micro
research (this last in physics as much as in sociology); and the fact/
value and theory/practice shibboleths remain for the most part
entrenched. Irrealist positions have their own repercussions. Thus
positivism inevitably generates in its wake interactionist and/or
reductionist regresses. Hermeneutics splits into neo-Kantian
(Weberian) or dichotomized (Habermasian) and pure (Gadamerian
and/or Winchian) wings. And so on. In *Dialectical Social Theory*, the
sequel to this study, I shall give some indication of what a truly
dialectical critical realist social science would look like; and of how it
may come to ground naturalistically generated substantive criteria for
a feasible society oriented to the concrete singularity of each as a
condition for the realization of the concrete singularity of all.

§ 11 Diffracted and Retotalized Dialectics

In this book we have diffracted the concept of dialectic and *retotalized*
it under the sign of *absence*. In C2.5 we liberated this concept, whose
lineage was initially traced in C1.6, from its Hegelian moorings. In
this section I will explore some of the implications of the diffracting
critique, as well as considering the nature of the diffraction itself.
Hegelian dialectic was critiqued from a materialist standpoint, taking
our cue from Marx, for its realized idealism, spiritual monism and
immanent teleology which we correlated respectively with our
critique of the epistemic fallacy, 'primal squeeze' (the lack of a
concept of natural necessity) and ontological monovalence, which
were jointly dubbed the unholy trinity.

To the epistemic fallacy I have opposed the constellational identity
of knowledge within being and an achieved, but fallible and partial,

subject — object non-identity theory; to primal squeeze, ontological stratification and alethic truth; and to ontological monovalence, ontological polyvalence, with the recognition of the fourfold polysemy of absence, bearing witness to the dynamic character of being. In the unholy trinity of the epistemic fallacy, (which entails ontological destratification and thus:) primal squeeze and ontological monovalence, the last must be regarded as most basic. Absence is ontologically prior to presence, and it is essential to the ontology of causality, spatio-temporarily, totality, agency and morality. Thus no purely positive world could exist. And absence immediately implies alterity (at 1M), and denial of it produces detotalization or alienation (at 3L) and reification of the denier (at 4D). Moreover, its denial would itself be an absenting (real negating) act, resulting in performative contradiction. For the logical primitives of asserting and denying, $(\sqrt{})$ and (x), are, as intentional, more or less causally efficacious acts, and, in any event, real, i.e. constellationally contained within, as instances of, the ontological primitives of being and non-being, (e) and $(-e)$ (see C2.1). Any world containing change (e.g. any one containing agency) must contain absenting. Let us go through some of the consequences of this. First, for the unholy trinity. Denial of ontological polyvalence (including non-valence) implies actualism, the generalized form of subject — object identity theory. This is powered by the epistemic fallacy, on which knowledge either just *is* or acts as a surrogate for being, prohibiting criticism and critique. It is simply refuted by any speech action (what did you say again?) or the most elemental absence expressed as desire, both of which presuppose referential detachment (detachment of the referent from the act of reference), the stratified form of which is alethic truth, that is to say, the truth of things, not propositions. This not only resolves the standard textbook problems of philosophy (see §2), but also sets us on the road to the dialectic of freedom. Before this, there are theorems to record. To reason can be to cause. This is to change, transform or to absent or to negate transfactually efficaciously (at 1M), rhythmically or tensed (spatializingly) processually (at 2E), possibly holistically (at 3L) and, in the human world, perhaps in virtue of our embodied intentional agentive agency (at 4D). Transformative negation may be more or less radical, a condition for dialectical contradiction, which also presupposes dialectical connection or totality, the inwardized form of which is reflexivity manifest in, for example, agency. An agent may be frustrated by a constraint, and seek to absent the constraint (which may take the form of discursively moralized power$_2$ relations), and hence to identify and absent its causes. In virtue of the judgement form, by the logic of dialectical universalizability, she is bound to seek to absent (and so engage in the depth totalizing practice for the absenting of) all dialectically similar constraints, and then, by a further step, all constraints as such. The concept of constraint can be negatively generalized to include absences such as unwanted and remediable ills, which act as constraints. And the concept of freedom may be positively generalized to include concretely singularized needs and possibilities (potentialities for self-development or self-realization) as rights. And we arrive at the eudaimonistic society, on which the development of the concrete singularity of each is a condition of the realization of the concrete singularity of all, underpinned by the transitions from fact to value, form to content and figure to ground, involving the abolition of the totality of master–slave-type relations. This goal, which explicates the rational directionality of geo-history, can be seen, by the merest transcendental perspectival switch, to be implicit in every assertorically fiduciary remark, or, at a stretch, every intentional action. *To act is to absent is to presuppose universal human emancipation.*

In this chapter I have shown how Hegel's commitment to subject–object identity theory, constellational monism and the constellational closure of geo-history inexorably generates recalcitrant surds, such as the demi-actual (irrational existents), detotalizing reality, or the injunctive paradox involved in his plateau theory that we are to reproduce the status quo in what can only be transformative praxis, negating the given! Hegel is, moreover, susceptible to the very own omissive metacritique, which is his most enduring contribution to dialectic. Hegel did not over-achieve, as custom has continually complained:* his system is too empty, not too full — at 1M, of a robust concept of alterity; at 2E of the dialectical concept par excellence, absence itself; at 4D of post-Hegelian (Mark II) transformative praxis. Only at 3L in the realm of totality, in the sphere of the notion and of spirit does his system really bite. And here it is in the interests of a transfigurative reconciliation with actuality, to paint 'a rose in the cross of the present'. Moreover, he by no means sustains his critique of analytical reasoning. His contradictions are logical, not dialectical, classes which by no means inevitably intersect (as I showed in an examination of Marx's dialectics); and he achieves only an analytic reinstatement transfigured in dialectical connection. Moreover, his totality is vitiated by closure, both systematically and

---

* CF. J.S. Mill: '[Hegel] has fairly earned the honour which will probably be awarded him by posterity of having logically extinguished transcendental metaphysics by a series of reductiones ad absurdissimum.'[35]

spatio-temporally, in virtue of which we can fairly accuse him of being untrue to his theory of truth (as we saw in C1.7).

Unfortunately the story does not end there. For Marx, seizing on two moments of heterocosmic affinity — in the alienation of labour and in capital as a totality in motion — and using Hegel's epistemological dialectics, with its principles of immanent critique and superstructuration (conceptual stratification) as a surrogate for an absent scientific realism which is the true methodological fulcrum of his work, takes over mystical skeletons in Hegel's rational cupboard — residues of actualism, monism and endism — which go on to have their own historical effect, including a historical incidental, a relatively fruitless opposition between different currents of Marxist philosophy, none of which succeeds in breaking with the epistemic fallacy, primal squeeze and ontological monovalence.

In looking at some of the implications of the materialist diffraction, we can observe first of all that certain disputes fade into insignificance: for instance, the 'great debate' over whether there can be a dialectics of nature. I have argued that there is nothing anthropomorphic about the concept of absence. On the other hand, the dialectic of freedom I have outlined clearly could not apply in an entirely inorganic world. In between, the usefulness of categories like dialectical contradiction will depend (a) transitively, upon the disciplinary tradition in which one is working, and (b) intransitively, upon the empirical question of whether there are relatively fast auto-subversive tendencies in structures deriving from the structure itself or some other common dialectical ground (dg'). As for the issue of whether contradiction simpliciter is necessary for change, apart from the use of contradiction as a synonym for constraint, it seems clear that the 'inner complicity argument' of C2.3, cashed out in terms of intrinsic liabilities to change, must be adjudged correct: so that contradiction per se is indeed essential to change. Another old conundrum should be put to rest. There is no necessary conflict between formal logic and dialectics. Arrays of dialectics do not breach the law of non-contradiction. At the same time this principle is dialectically dependent. And so I prefer to talk, in the case of, say, epistemological dialectics, of the *dialectic of analytical and dialectical reasoning*, with analytical reasoning an invaluable moment in the process of scientific thought. But it takes two to make a quarrel. And the analytic problematic has typically used a duplicitous combination of epistemic and ontic fallacies to generate, through the ontological transposition of the normative epistemic principles of identity and non-contradiction, what, following Adorno, I have called 'identity-thinking'. This in turn generates an ideological onto-logic of stasis and, insofar as change is necessary for freedom, a normative climate of oppression. So the analytic problematic is not the anodyne entity it appeared to be, and is very far indeed from being neutral in its effects. Another canard that must be laid to rest is that dialectic necessarily involves opposition, antagonism or strife. It does not.

It is worth re-emphasizing at this point the sheer variety of dialectics. The dialectic is a flexible instrument, but it is built around a hard core: the logic of freedom.[36] There are good and bad dialectics, from an evaluative point of view. But the dialectic is neither good nor bad in itself, except insofar as it empowers us in our understanding and transformation of reality. In this study we have looked at the genealogy of the concept of dialectic; and the interplay between dialectic and the fundamentalism, reductionism and monism that I have systematically attacked. We have seen that it was Hegel's claim to have realized these traditional goals of philosophy within an immanent metaphysics of experience, purchasing an Unhappy Consciousness (which may stand as a metaphor for philosophy as a whole) in order to avoid the fate of Jesus, of the Beautiful Soul, that produced a watershed in the eclipse of reason. We have explored Aristotelian dialectic — this is dialectic *as* argument, as distinct from the dialectical arguments we investigated in C2.6 which are characterized by the fact that they entail false, or at least partial, limited or incomplete, necessities. We, however, saw that Aristotelian dialectic failed because of its incapacity to save the epistemological detachment of the consequent. We have examined Kantian dialectic, and the pros and cons of Kantian dialectical limit versus Hegelian dialectical totality. Although Kantian philosophy is dichotomous and detotalizing in the extreme, we observed that if Kant was pushed in a materialist direction it would not be easy to come to a decision between them, particularly as the world is characterized by decentred non-expressivist partial totalities. In fact the three great philosophical systems — those founded by Aristotle, Kant and Hegel — all find a niche in the dialectic of freedom advanced in C3. We have taken a more rapid glance at more recent and contemporary exponents of pro- or anti-dialectical philosophy. In particular I have criticized the practice of Nietzschean forgetting and Heideggerian erasure as unnecessary consequences of an insufficiently stratified and laminated conception of the self and an insufficiently differentiated and distanciated concept of space-time. For all the achievements of post-Nietzschean philosophy, without the development of a new non-anthropic ontology of the sort this book purports to provide, for reasons I have explained, contemporary philosophy follows, with the recognition of the reality of epistemological relativism, a transmutation route from positivism through conventionalism and pragmatism to a superidealist, voluntaristic hyper-irrationalism.

I would like to have had more time to deal with specifically conceptual dialectics. At least five genres must be distinguished. (1) There is the linguistified discursive dialectics, characteristic of Waismann if not Wittgenstein and of Foucault in his middle period. This falls to the aporia that it cannot sustain the concept of intentional embodied causal agents — it rather disembodies or de-agentifies (or both) the person involved. (2) There is conversational dialectics which harks back to the Greek archetype. This is surely the method of civilized discussion and debate, weighing the force of the considerations and arguments in favour of or against a particular proposition until a consensus prevails. However, as a useful antidote to this as a plausible description of, say, science as it is (rather than as it ought to be), one might re-read Hegel's discussion in the *Phenomenology* of the 'Kingdom of the Beasts'. (3) Then there is hermeneutical dialectics. This is a fascinating topic, but a rough dissection will have, for the moment, to suffice. On the one hand, we have sociological reductionists, into which camp one must arguably place Gadamer and certain neo-Wittgensteinians such as the contemporary Harré,[37] who take the same line as Winch, that society is not only dependent upon, but also exhausted by, its conceptual reality. This is clearly untenable, as I have urged in detail elsewhere. On the other hand, stand the neo-Kantians, who synthesize hermeneutics with a still essentially unreconstructed empirical realism. Their most prominent contemporary representative is Jürgen Habermas, who still scathingly attacks ontology (for which, in this book, I hope to have made a watertight case) while the rationality of his whole project points to the need to thematize it as a social science which, like Chomsky's, is reconstructive and, as such, should be explicitly realist and, qua emancipatory, critical alike.

(4) Next there is methodological or heuristic dialectics. This will figure prominently in the sequel to this study, which will offer new bases for geo-historical-sociological reasoning. As it is, at the level of generality at which *Dialectic* is inevitably pitched, only very general maxims can be derived: 'seek out contradictions in essential structures rather than, or at least in addition to, empirical regularities' — this is the way you will identify endogenous sources of change; 'reconnect apparently unrelated phenomena at both intensive and extensive margins of inquiry' — to discover whether holistic causality is in fact at work; 'treat geo-historical process and intra-activity as existentially constitutive'. This is how one identifies the presence of the past or outside and of totality. Treat events as conjunctures;

ideologies as both knowledge – discourse/power/normative intersects and compromise formations with reality (and spot categorial errors within them); fully understand why referent must be detached from referential acts and you will be on your way to ontological stratification and alethic truth; regard agents as tacitly empowered practical knowers and see subjects$_2$ as at once 'thrown' and engaged in counter-hegemonic struggles.

(5) Finally, there is specifically philosophical dialectics. Metacritically, we can see the theory problem-field solution sets and antagonisms, such as empiricism v. rationalism, fideism v. enlightenment, analytic v. (irrealist) dialectic, as constituted by, or as examples of, the tacit complicity of dialectical counterparts. A general formula can be given for this: anthroporealism and the new transcendent that it inevitably generates comprise an irrealist ensemble and yield a Tina complex, as a compromise with the axiological necessities that compose what I have called the reality principle. This ineluctably generates in its wake T/P inconsistency, detotalization, duplicity, equivocation and great pliability for ideological use. All this lies within the field of *metacritical dialectics*, and we can trace connections between these philosophical consequences and the logics of generative separation, alienation, commodification, reification and fetishism and more general ideologies which serve to legitimate the plurality of discursively moralized power$_2$ or master – slave-type relations. But before metacritical explication comes immanent critique and problem resolution. I have shown in §2 how the problems of philosophy are generally susceptible to diagnosis and resolution along the lines of the 1M – 4D constitution of critical realist dialectic, composed by the moments of non-identity, negativity, totality and transformative praxis respectively. The faults indexing the aporiai and antinomies of philosophy are typically destratification (ontological actualism), positivization (ontological monovalence), detotalization (ontological extensionalism) and de-agentification (disembodiment and/or reification) at 1M – 4D respectively. This is not to imply that each problem has a single source, nor that philosophical problems cannot be real. Arising out of the vast array of problems of philosophy, the quest for an unhypothetical, unconditioned and/or incorrigible starting point generates two mega-problems: the problem of the one and its 'other' (e.g. opposite), crucial for the irrealist dialectical tradition, and the problem of the one and the 'many' (as manifest in the problems of universals and induction), antinomic for the analytical mainstream. I have shown how both mega-problems can be rationally resolved and critically

explained. In particular one must reject both the Platonic analysis of change in terms of difference, and the dialectical temptation to deny alterity (sheer determinate other-being) by analysing difference in terms of change.

The materialist diffraction of dialectic makes possible distinctions between ontological, epistemological, relational, metacritical, conceptual, practical, ethical, etc. dialectics. There is no space to rehearse my account of these here; save to make two points. First, I have constructed my epistemological dialectic by using a critical realist sieve on Hegelian dialectics, but, of course, for dialectical critical realism epistemological dialectics is constellationally contained within and over-reached by ontological dialectics; that is to say, there is a hiatus between transitive and intransitive dimensions, marking the necessity for a concept of existential intransitivity. Second, my ethical dialectics implies the radical extension, generalization and deepening of Hegel's dialectic of freedom, and Marx's own radicalization of Hegel's dialectic of reconciliation, mutual recognition or forgiveness into a dialectic of de-alienation — from, as I have just reprised, elemental desire to universal human autonomy oriented to the needs and possibilities of the concretely singularized individual in the context of what I have called four-planar developing social being or 'human nature' in the light of a conception of the moral evolution of the species as open.

It is time to retotalize the dialectic. Whether one conceives dialectic as argument, change or freedom (and each rationally presupposes its predecessor), the critique of ontological monovalence, that is, of a purely positive account of being, holds the clue. For the point of argument is to absent mistakes, the point of change to absent states of affairs, structures, totalities, etc. and the point of freedom to absent constraints, or more generally ills which can always be conceived as absences or constraints. Hence we arrive at the real definition of dialectic as the axiology of freedom — or as *absenting absences*, or, applied recursively, as *absenting constraints on absenting absences*. Hence my multiple proofs of the necessity for negative being — in static and dynamic modes — and my stress on the tri-unity of cause, space and time and on irreducibly tensed A-serial (spatializing) process. My prioritization of negativity is in accord with the dialectical tradition. Hence it is just worth emphasizing the need for the concepts of transfactuality, totality and transformative praxis — with the famous 'negation of the negation', conceived metacritically, as the (in general multiple and contradictory) geo-historical transformation of geo-historical products. As for absolute reason or dialectical rationality, this is best conceived as the *coherence* of theory and practice in practice, rather than as their unity simpliciter — for unities can be of many (e.g. antagonistic) types.

§ 12 Dialectic as the Pulse of Freedom

This book is coordinated around five main axes: (a) an orientation to social science and cognate practices of their kind, proffered in C3.7, for which I continue to conceive myself to be a mere underlabourer; (b) the dialectical enrichment of critical realism; (c) necessarily, given the duality of theory and critique, the extension of the existing critique of irrealism; (d) the non-preservative sublation of Hegelian dialectic; but (e), above all, the development of a novel, and, as I have just summarized, retotalized account of dialectic based on an adequate account of negativity, on which all dialectics hinge, the critiques of ontological monovalence and extensionalism (that is, of respectively purely positive and detotalizing accounts of reality) alongside critiques of ontological actualism and de-agentification to link to the critique of the anthropocentric epistemic fallacy in a four-dimensional dialectic and an explication of the logic of dialectical universalizability which pursues to the full the radical implications of the vindication of negativity, and a fortiori dialectic. Dialectic is the absenting of constraints on the absenting of absences (ills, and causally lower-order constraints) and, since constraints, negatively generalized, are just the absence of freedoms, *dialectic* is equally *the axiology of freedom*, the implications of the positive generalization of which I have only just begun to tap. Dialectic is the yearning for freedom and the transformative negation of constraints on it. It depends upon the positive identification of the existentially intransitive existence of absences and their transfactually efficacious, A-serial rhythmic, totalizing, agentive elimination in a praxis from desire via truth to freedom, practically mediated by wisdom. *The strength of its presence is the measure of the pulse of freedom* — of its health, or transformative power.

   I am not going to comment on (a) directly in this concluding section, since this is the subject of the sequel to this study. Nor am I going to elaborate any further on (d) (partly because an extended treatment, *Hume, Kant, Hegel, Marx*, is in the offing), except to say that I hope in my critique to have done justice to what is of enduring significance in Hegel's epistemological dialectic. A logical (or other) contradiction is not something to fear and/or to seek to disguise, cover up or isolate.

Rather it should be taken as a sign that the existing conceptual field is incomplete in some relevant respect. And in the σ and τ transforms that I discussed in C1 it generates the Gödelian dialectic:

[1] radical incompleteness − contradiction − greater totality,

which is of immense significance in science.

The development of critical realism in this book is, for the most part, preservative. Hitherto existing or prime moment — 1M — realism is grounded on categories of non-identity: non-anthropocentric ontology (and the contingency of human being it entails), existential intransitivity, transfactuality, the distinction between the domains of the real, the actual and the empirical and so on. In *Dialectic* I have, however, added to the existing repertoire of critical realism at several levels. In the first place, I have added radical analyses of reference, meaning and truth, especially in the notion of *referential detachment* and in a many-layered explication of truth entailing a level of *alethic truth* or the truth of, or reason for, things or phenomena, rather than propositions, together with an exegesis of the *judgement form* with very extensive and prima facie surprising implications. I have also shown how it is possible to derive transcendental realism from premises which do not essentially involve natural science, and made extensive use of the new figure of constellationality, exemplified by emergence which it would be cumbersome to rehearse here. A not unimportant result of the work is the demonstration that non-identities, and the categories with which 1M realism has been concerned such as (positive) existence and causality, presuppose absence and the second edge — 2E — categories of negativity.

At 2E *Dialectic* argues for the ontological priority of the negative over the positive, on the grounds, inter alia, that a material object world without absences is physically impossible, while the converse is not the case; and that any world including change, and thus our world, including those material changes which are the consequences of embodied intentional causal agency, must be ontologically bivalent (and, I have further argued, polyvalent and non-valent). The development of 2E realism involves an elucidation of the different modalities of contradiction, in which it is important to distinguish Marxian dialectical from Hegelian logical contradiction (which may intersect), and from Kantian *Realrepugnanz* or non-contradictory equilibria of opposing forces of independent grounds. Moreover, it implies an extension of critical realism's 1M concerns with existence and causality to a co-equal concern with *spatio-temporality* (conceived as sui generis causally efficacious) and from a pre-occupation with structure and difference, through the concept of a rhythmic as an *irreducibly tensed spatializing process*, to the phenomena of emergent, disjoint, overlapping, intersecting spatio-temporalities and to the theme of the existentially constitutive presence of the past and the outside. Further, 2E realism, in its codification of real > transformative > radical > linear negation, deconstructs an exclusive distinction between process and product and sees social beings as paradigmatically constituting geo-historical processes-in-product(being)-in-ongoing-processes.

Third level — or 3L — realism also presupposes 2E — now in the form of detotalization, alienation, split or split-off, which may take a number of different forms, from repression through compromise formation to projective identification. Among the categories of totality are internal relationality; *intra-activity*, which includes the existential presence of one entity in another; concrete universality, conceived as a *multiple quadruplicity*; holistic causality; mediation; and reflexivity. Not only is the phenomenon of the existential constitution or permeation of one entity or category by another essential to the intelligibility of many passages in Hegel and Marx (of the 'production is also consumption' kind), it is solidly grounded scientifically in the phenomenon of *primary polyadization* which also entails the epigram *ex nihilo nihil fit*. It also entails the impossibility of any monism and/or solipsism, the essentiality of contradiction to change, where contradiction is conceived as constraint or as what I called in C2.3 'inner complicity' and the refutation of the classical conceptions of corpuscularian (atomic) matter and action by contact. Moreover, we begin to appreciate dialectic as that great loosener which breaks down exclusive dichotomies — between present and past, process and product, one being and another; and which allows for constellational, dispositional and rhythmic identities and for the non-valent co-incidence of identity and difference and identity and change (which are not the same). And we begin to recognize that logic, for all its indispensability in the dialectic of analytical and dialectical reasoning, neither constitutes (though, of course, it is contained within) nor determines ontology, but merely defines how the world must be if we are to successfully apply certain techniques.

Fourth dimension — or 4D — realism also explicitly presupposes 2E. *Agency* is paradigmatically nothing but transformative praxis or the absenting of the given by more or less informed desire, want, lack or need. But the categories of agency, which include a stratified conception of the self, defined ultimately by its dispositional identity with its changing causal powers, must be embedded in a dialecticized critical naturalism, situating a dislocated dialectics of structure and agency, in the context of the development of a four-planar conception of social life — defined by the components of the stratification of persons, material transactions with nature, inter-/intra-subjective relations and social relations. The last two comprise the social cube. At the intersection of the knowledge−discourse/communicative, power$_2$ (master−slave-type relations of exploitation, domination and control) and normative/moral dimensions of the social cube flow lies ideology. In a strong, but not necessary, sense this embodies categorial error. Connecting discursively moralized power$_2$ to master−slave relations we can see the figure of Stoicism embodying indifference, Scepticism denegating power$_2$ relations and the Unhappy Consciousness as introjectively identifying with the master or projectively duplicating a hyperreal world where slaves become masters or media stars.

In the realm of agency I elaborate a *moral realism*, which exploits the first-person action-guiding character of morality to distinguish descriptive, redescriptive and explanatory critical morality from actually existing moralities, while arguing that moral propositions and a fortiori moral truth or the good can be known via a *naturalistic ethics* which can ground the transitions from 'is' to 'ought' (fact to value) and thence from theory to practice and form to content in a variety of ways. Finessing the logic of dialectical universalizability I argue that the ultimate moral truth is nothing but freedom in the form of the *eudaimonistic society*, in the sense of universal human autonomy and flourishing. The dialectic of freedom, which goes all the way from primal scream, initiated by absence, to universal human emancipation and the perfect life, does not predict the future course of events, only the *rational directionality* of geo-historicity. It does, however, constitute a complete dialectical argument which progressively extends, deepens, generalizes and radicalizes the Kantian, Hegelian and Marxian transcendental deductions (as I show in §5). For instance it entails the abolition of the totality of (including internalized) master−slave-type relations in orientation to concrete singularity as a condition for a genuine unity-in-diversity. The argument implies that the moral evolution of the species be regarded as open. The dialectic of freedom goes as follows. We start from absence in the context of primary polyadization manifesting itself as desire. This entails referential detachment and we are soon into classification and causality and thence onto the plane of ontological stratification and alethic truth. Absence has already been presupposed (and in the dialectical circle of C3.11 Figure 3.12 agency entails it), and in the context of the contradictions within and between differentiated and stratified entities, emergence and thence totalities result. The inner form of totality is reflexivity which implies a stratified self capable of making assertoric judgements. The fiduciariness or trustworthiness of the expressively veracious judgement, which is dialectically universalizable along all four components, implies both solidarity and that the grounds be themselves grounded by a combination of explanatory critique, concrete utopianism and a theory of transition yielded by the totalizing depth praxis that the judgement entails. And then by a multiplicity of routes (mapped out in C3.10) the logic of dialectical universalizability takes us to the eudaimonistic society, the goal of which is concretely singularized universal human flourishing. I have spelled out some of the implications of this in C3 but it is at any rate formally consistent with the goal of an 'association in which the free development of each is a condition for the free development of all' — 'the condition' because unity presupposes a diversity, and totality difference. Dialectic, then, to re-emphasize, is absenting constraints on absenting ills (constraints, absences, oppressive power$_2$ relations, inequities, structures) inimical to concretely singularized human needs and possibilities. It is implicit in the most rudimentary desire and it implies a society in which each is true to, of, in and for themselves and every other (including future generations and other species) subject to the constraints imposed by nature. It is absolute reason, and in this book I have given some grounds for hope (and the praxis hope inspires) that humanity might progress towards it.

But *Dialectic* is still not quite through. For we have as yet to consider the other extension of critical realism that agency entails: metacritical dialectics. In §2 I showed how dialectical critical realism can resolve both orthodox and heterodox problems of philosophy — a task *Plato Etcetera* will expand on. But a dialectical critical realist needs to know not only how but why — the object of metacritique. The first step in the metacritique of irrealism — which incorporates dialectical as well as analytical wings and encompasses the irrationalist response to the twentieth-century collapse of Aristotelian-Cartesian-Lockian-Kantian-Hegelian-Nietzschean (who never doubted actualism) verities — is to identify the dual forms of anthroporealism: anthropocentrism corresponding to the subjective and particular pole, anthropomorphism to the objective and universal pole. The historical source of the epistemic — ultimately anthropic (cf. C3.1) — fallacy which underlies anthroporealism is located in the mists of Eleatic doctrine (as is the dogma of ontological monovalence) but it has more obvious social effects. To keep the explanation both simple and at a necessary level of generality, we need deal here only with the basic concepts of existence, causality, space and time. I have claimed that irrealism has been historically determined by rationalist epistemological criteria, which were subjectivized and inwardized by Descartes, to lay the way open for the structural domination of solipsistic empiricist ontology, essentially laid down by Hume, but involuted and modified by Kant. Here atomism and actualism have co-existed with punctualism and blockism, presupposing the reification of facts and the fetishism of closed systems respectively. These concepts are all readily vulnerable to critique. The atomist must find a place for absence (voids), punctualism must give way to a distanciated concept of space-time, reification to a conception of the social production of facts (as distinct from non-social things), actualism must admit to the reality of a multiply determined and contradictory world, blockism must bow to an open totality, and the fetishism of closed systems to an adequate notion of experimental activity.

However, anthroporealism inevitably generates in its wake a range of (in its own terms) insoluble problems, the best known of which are, at the atomist pole, those of solipsism, and, at the actualist pole, those of what I have called the transdictive complex, the most notorious of which is the problem of induction. Predictably these have, in the absence of concepts of primary polyadization and alethic truth, necessitated a fideistic recourse to a new transcendent — with God, spirit, social structure, convention or rules taking the place of (intransitive) ontological stratification in the case of the transdictive complex and taking the place of the ontological priority of the (transitive) social world into which the epistemic neophyte is 'thrown' in the solipsistic case. (Latterly, however, a spontaneist, voluntarist, mutation, whose most prominent apostles are Rorty and Feyerabend,[38] has come into vogue.) This combination,

[2] $AR + T^dR = IE,$

is the irrealist ensemble, an inconsistent combination of subject−object identity theory and dualism. It cannot be over-emphasized that it is actualism which necessitates particular subject−object identity theory, just as the solipsistic aporiai, traditionally accorded a fideist response (whether immediately, as in Descartes, or mediately, as in the later Wittgenstein) are locatable within the transdictive complex. Second, ontological monovalence not only entails actualism and the epistemic fallacy, but a solipsistic (all-pervasive token) monism and idealism. For any monist must be capable of differentiating herself from within the whole and so possess the concepts of alterity and absence alike; while if the whole was undifferentiatedly material it could not know itself. This is the ultimate fount of philosophy's irrealism.

To be causally efficacious in the world, the irrealist ensemble must make a compromise with axiological necessities or the reality principle in what I have called a Tina complex or formation: viz.

[3] $IE = (AR + T^dR) \rightarrow TF$

This multiply contradictory complex readily generates 2E T/P inconsistency, leading to a 3L detotalization or split and at 4D either disembodiment (the revenge of the Cartesian-Kantian repressed in discourse or two-language theory) or de-agentification (physicalistic reductionism which cannot sustain itself without reflexive inconsistency or performative contradiction) or both — in any event, generating a contradiction or a split between embodiment and intentionality. Thus we have

[4] TF at 1M $\rightarrow$ T/P inconsistency at 2E $\rightarrow$ detotalization at 3L $\rightarrow$ disembodiment/de-agentification at 4D.

The resultant vector generates through the anthoporealist exchanges equivocation and duplicity, through the new transcendent ad hoc metaphysical λ clauses, grafting or supplementarity, and through the Tina compromise heterology, aporiai, antinomies and great ideological plasticity. Underlying these are substantive analogical grammars and the whole infra-/superstructural complex from the dynamic of global commodification (where critical dialectics of figure and ground and centre and periphery may have vital counter-hegemonic roles to play) to ideologies legitimating existing power$_2$ relations. What are the most characteristic ideological effects of this complex? At 1M the transitivization and destratification of being ('there is no depth'); at 2E the normalization of past and local changes and freedoms and the denial of present or future possible ones ('history is in the past'); at 3L the detotalization of reality and the hypostatization of thought ('disconnect — divide and rule'); and at 4D the denial of agentive agency, the disempowerment of empty or fragmented selves ('you're a robot' — 'no, I'm just hyperreal').

In short, irrealist philosophy, insofar as it is causally efficacious, is disemancipatory; and thus, for this reason if no other, undialectical in its effect. This point is not a digression but is rather central to the book. For a dialectical argument to be complete, it must show or at least sketch the *necessity* of the *falsity* it submits to immanent, omissive and Achilles' Heel critiques (cf. C2.6). The argument for a transformed transformative practice in philosophy will, however, meet with little success unless it joins hands with the totalizing depth praxis that dialectical rationality demands.

Let me sum up the argument of the book. Negative is a condition for positive being, and being a condition for knowledge; alethia is a condition of fiduciary, adequating or expressive truth (and there can be no language use without referential detachment or closure of the epistemological circle — in totality — without transcendental detachment); natural possibility is a condition for natural necessity, which is a condition for natural actuality, whether contingent or otherwise. In the bipolarity of absence, absenting has ontological priority over the absent and the absent has epistemic primacy in our world. Alethic truth, as optimally grounding reason, can be the rational cause of transformative negating agency in absenting constraints on self-emancipation, that is, on the liberation of our causal powers to flourish. For to exist is to be able to become, which is to possess the capacity for self-development, a capacity that can be fully realized only in a society founded on the principle of universal concretely singularized human autonomy in nature. This process is dialectic; and it is the pulse of freedom.

Notes

1. Introduction

1. Letter to Engels, 14 January 1858.
2. PON2, p. 169.
3. See SRHE, p. 25.
4. RTS2, pp. 36ff.
5. RR, p. 181.
6. Cf. J. McCarney, 'The True Realm of Freedom', *New Left Review*, 189 (1991).
7. Cf. A. Sayer, *Method in Social Science: A Realist Approach*, London 1984, p. 82.
8. PIF, p. 126.
9. *Being and Nothingness*, New York 1966, Part 1, C1, Section 4.
10. From *A Contemporary Critique of Historical Materialism*, London 1991, pp. 4–5 on.
11. See SHRE, p. 4.
12. *Enquiry Concerning Human Understanding*, Indianapolis 1955, p. 85.
13. Cf. SRHE, C3.
14. *Of Grammatology*, Baltimore 1976, especially Part 2, C2.
15. L. Althusser and E. Balibar, *Reading Capital*, London 1968, pp. 96–7 and passim.
16. Cf. B. Ollman, *Alienation*, Cambridge 1971, Part 1, C1.
17. *The Social Production of Space*, Oxford 1991, C5.
18. *The Philosophical Discourse of Modernity*, Cambridge 1987.
19. Cf. PON2, p. 64 and RR, p. 182.
20. G. Buchdahl, *Metaphysics and the Philosophy of Science*, Oxford 1969, p. 3.
21. Cf. J. Evans, *Aristotle's Concept of Dialectic*, Cambridge 1977.
22. See, e.g., *Topics* 1.2.101e.3b.
23. *Hegel*, Cambridge 1975, C1 and passim.
24. *Kant on History*, ed. L.W. Beck, New York 1963, p. 3.
25. Ibid.
26. *Die Vernunft in oder Geschichte*, ed. J. Hofmeister, Hamburg 1933, pp. 77–88.
27. *The Philosophy of Right*, Oxford 1952, p. 12.
28. *Science of Logic*, London 1969, p. 56.
29. RTS2, p. 123.
30. See M. Rosen, *Hegel's Dialectic and Its Criticism*, Cambridge 1982, pp. 73ff.
31. See especially *Introduction to the Reading of Hegel*, New York 1969.
32. To borrow a phrase from S. Žižek, *For They Know Not What They Do*, London 1992.
33. J.N. Findlay, *Hegel: A Re-examination*, London 1958, p. 77.
34. See M. Kosok, 'The Formalization of Hegel's Dialectical Logic', in A. MacIntyre, ed., *Hegel*, New York 1972.
35. Cf. ibid, p. 255.
36. See RTS2, C3.

37. SRHE, p. 30.

38. S. Kripke, 'Wittgenstein on Rules and Private Language', in I. Bloch, ed., *Perspectives on the Philosophy of Wittgenstein*, Oxford 1981.

2. Dialectic

1. Cf. RR, p. 32.

2. See R. Hare, 'Meaning and Speech Acts', *Philosophical Review* (1970), pp. 19ff.

3. Cf. RTS2, p. 87.

4. Cf. A. Lovejoy, *The Great Chain of Being*, Cambridge, Mass. 1936.

5. Cf. J. Shotter, *Knowing of the Third Kind*, Utrecht 1990.

6. Cf. F. Pirani, 'Cosmology in Crisis', *New Left Review*, 191 (1992).

7. *Hegel*, Cambridge 1975, CIII.

8. Cf. M. Bunge, *Method, Model and Matter*, Dordrecht 1973, C9.

9. See *Scientific Realism and Social Thought*, Hemel Hempstead 1989.

10. See ibid.

11. G. Della Volpe, *Logic as a Positive Science*, London 1980.

12. D. Dennett, *Consciousness Explained*, Harmondsworth 1991.

13. Cf. RTS2, C2.5, PON2, C3.3, and SRHE, C3.1.

14. Cf. RTS2, p. 107.

15. Cf. my entry on 'Materialism', in *Dictionary of Twentieth-Century Social Thought*, eds W. Outhwaite and T. Bottomore, Oxford 1992, and PIF Part 2 respectively.

16. From which Nancy Cartwright's *How the Laws of Physics Lie*, Oxford 1983, derives its actualist title.

17. Cf. RTS2, C1.3.

18. For a similar point, see B. Ollmann, *Dialectical Investigations*, London 1993, C1.

19. For a specific social interpretation of what I am treating as a generic phenomenon, see Arno J. Mayer, *The Persistence of the Old Regime*, London 1981.

20. Cf. M. Davis, *City of Quartz*, London 1991, and E. Soja, *Postmodern Geographies*, London 1989, C8-9.

21. Cf. M. Polanyi, *The Tacit Dimension*, London 1967.

22. Cf. J.J. Gibson, *The Senses Considered as Perceptual Systems*, London 1966.

23. PON2, p. 92 applies.

24. Cf. SRHE, pp. 26 and passim.

25. PON2, p. 42.

26. SRHE, p. 110.

27. Cf. M. Godelier, 'System, Structure and Contradiction in *Capital*', in R. Blackburn, ed., *Ideology in Social Science*, Glasgow 1972.

28. Cf. in this connection the important work of R. Kanth, *Capitalism and Social Theory*, New York 1992, R. Albritton, *A Japanese Approach to Political Economy* (forthcoming) and A. Shamsavari, *Dialectic and Social Theory*, London 1991.

29. *The Poverty of Philosophy*, Collected Works, Vol. IV, London 1976, p. 192.

30. *Contingency, Irony and Solidarity*, Cambridge 1989.

31. SRHE, p. 185.

32. *Critique of Pure Reason*, trans. N. Kemp Smith, London 1967, b. 329-36/a. 273-80.

33. SRHE, p. 113.

34. 'Marxism and the Dialectic', *New Left Review*, 93 (1975).

35. Cf. RTS2, p. 181.

36. Cf. also on the impossibility of backwards causation generally, D.H. Mellor, *Real Time*, Cambridge 1981, esp. C10.

37. S. Rosen, *Hegel: An Introduction to the Science of Wisdom*, London 1977, p. 273.

38. I owe this expression to Rosen, *Hegel's Dialectic and Its Criticism*.

39. C.I. Lakatos, 'Falsification and the Methodology of Scientific Research Programmes', in *Philosophical Papers. Vol. I*, Cambridge 1979.

40. *Nicomachean Ethics*, Book 1.1094, p. 25.

41. Cf. M. Dummett, *The Game of Tarot*, London 1990.

42. Cf. R. Pirsig, *Zen and the Art of Motorcycle Maintenance*, London 1976.

43. L. Wittgenstein, *Lectures and Conversations*, ed. C.J. Barrett, Oxford 1966, pp. 15–16.

44. Cf. B. Winocott, *The Child, the Family and the Outside World*, Harmondsworth 1964, or E. Erikson, *Childhood and Society*, Harmondsworth 1965, and M. Rustin, *The Good Society and the Inner World*, London 1991.

45. *Entailment*, Princeton 1975.

46. Marx to Kugelmann, 6 March 1865.

47. Marx to Engels, 14 January 1858.

48. *The Science of Logic*, London 1969, pp. 154–5.

49. For a more detailed exposition see SRHE, C3.

50. End of third manuscript of *Economic and Philosophical Manuscripts*.

51. Cf. RR, C7, and PIF, Appendix 2.

52. *Capital, Vol. 1*, C1, Section 2.

53. Marx to Lasalle, 16 January 1864.

54. Cf. S. Haack, *Philosophy of Logics*, Cambridge 1978, and D. Bloor, *Wittgenstein*, London 1983.

55. Cf. my entry on 'Models', in *Dictionary of the History of Science*, eds B. Bynum and R. Porter, London 1981.

56. Cf. P. Anderson, 'The Affinities of Norberto Bobbio', in *A Zone of Engagement*, London 1992.

57. PON2, p. 5, SRHE, p. 13.

58. Cf. RTS2, p. 37.

59. G. Kortian, *Metacritique*, Cambridge 1980, p. 37.

60. Cf. RR, C7.II.

61. See RTS2, pp. 29ff. and W. Outhwaite, *New Philosophies of Social Science*, London 1977, C3.

62. See RTS2, C3.3.

63. On private property as a second-order mediation, see C.J. Arthur, *Dialectics of Labour*, Oxford 1984, and I. Mészáros, *Marx's Theory of Alienation*, London 1970.

64. Cf. RTS2, pp. 76–7.

65. Cf. SRHE, p. 274.

66. RTS2, C2.4.

67. Cf. my entry on 'Tacit Knowledge', *Dictionary of the History of Science*, eds B. Bynum and R. Porter, London 1981.

68. Cf. W.H. Walsh, 'Subjective and Objective Idealism', in D. Heinrich, ed., *Kant oder Hegel?* Stuttgart 1983.

69. Cf. W.H. Walsh, *Hegelian Ethics*, London 1969.

70. See R. Gasché, *The Tain of the Mirror*, Cambridge, Mass. 1986. A good introduction to supplementarity is contained in C. Norris, *Derrida*, Harmondsworth 1987. See also J. Llewelyn, *Derrida on the Threshold of Sense*, London 1987, and G. Spivak's 'Introduction' to *Of Grammatology*, where the concept of supplementarity is most systematically developed in regard to Rousseau's writings on 'Writing'.

71. See, for example, *After Virtue*, London 1981.

72. See D. Will, 'Psychoanalysis as a Human Science', *British Journal of Medical Psychology*, 93 (1980).

73. See for an exposition I. Soll, *Hegel's Metaphysics*, Chicago 1964, C4.

74. For an excellent exposition, see C. Taylor, *Hegel*, Cambridge 1975, CXIV.

75. SRHE, C2.2.

76. See my review of Terry Eagleton's *Ideology: An Introduction*, London 1991, in *Philosophical Books*, 33 (1), 1992.

77. Cf. N. Geras, 'Marx and the Critique of Political Economy', in R. Blackburn, ed., *Ideology in Social Science*, Glasgow 1972.

78. For expository convenience I consider only pure reason, but its extension to practical and aesthetic reason is simple. Cf. C4.3.

79. Cf. especially G. Webster, 'The Relation of Natural Forms', in M.-W. and P. Saunders, eds, *Beyond Neo-Darwinism*, London 1984, and B. Goodwin et al., eds, *Dynamic Structures in Biology*, Edinburgh 1989.

80. For a more detailed account, see RTS2, C3.

81. RTS2, p. 83.

82. I owe this term to T. Smith, *The Logic of Marx's Capital*, New York 1991.

83. *A History and Philosophy of the Social Sciences*, Oxford 1987, p. 10. He himself attributes the term to Maurice Mandelbaum.

84. Cf. PON2, C4.5.

85. *Dialectics*, Albany, New York 1977.

86. Cf. S. Körner, *Experience and Theory*, London 1966, and J. Ziman, *Reliable Knowledge*, Cambridge 1978.

87. *Dialectics*, p. 12.

88. RTS2, pp. 14, 97ff. and passim.

89. Cf. I. Copi, 'Essence and Accident', in J. Moravesik, ed., *Aristotle*, London 1967.

90. Cf. PON2, C4.5.

91. Žižek, *For They Know Not What They Do*.

92. An excellent introduction to Habermas's still developing oeuvre is contained in W. Outhwaite, *Habermas*, Cambridge 1993. Habermas's most relevant work in respect of the antinomy I am discussing here is *The Philosophical Discourse of Modernity*, Cambridge 1987. The so-called 'exchange' between Searle and Derrida was published in *Glyph*, Baltimore 1977.

93. Cf. A. Danto, 'Basic Acts', *American Philosophical Quarterly*, 2 (1965).

94. Cf. H. Patomäki, 'Concepts of "Action", "Structure" and "Power" in "Critical Social Realism" ', *Journal for the Theory of Social Behaviour*, 21 (2) (1991).

95. PON2; SRHE, C2.2; RR, C5–6.

96. Cf. PON2, pp. 186ff.

97. See T. Benton, 'Marx and Natural Limits', *New Left Review*, 178 (1990).

98. See *Troubled Pleasures*, London 1990, and many of the contributions to E. Frazer, J. Hornsby and S. Lovibond, eds, *Ethics: A Feminist Reader*, Oxford 1992.

99. Cf. for the respective concepts A. Giddens, *The Consequences of Modernity*, Cambridge 1990, and F. Jameson, *Postmodernism, or, The Cultural Logic of Late Capitalism*, London 1991.

100. SRHE, p. 126, and RR, p. 99.

101. *Introducing the Morphogenetic Approach* (forthcoming).

102. Cf. SRHE, pp. 217ff.

103. Cf. P. Auerbach on the relative neglect of the role of education in 'The Fall of Education', *New Left Review*, 192 (1992).

104. RTS2, p. 77.

105. Cf. PON2, C2.6 and Appendix; SRHE, C2.5–2.7; RR, C6; PIF, Appendix 1.

106. Cf. G. Arrighi, 'The Rich and the Poor', *New Left Review*, 189 (1991), and P. Singer, *Practical Ethics*, Cambridge 1975, C8.

107. Cf. RTS2, C2.4.

108. London 1991.

109. New York 1993, p. 10.

3. Dialectical Critical Realism and the Dialectic of Freedom

1. 'Pragmatism Without Method', in P. Kurtz, ed., *Sidney Hook: Philosopher of Democracy and Humanism*, Buffalo, New York 1983, p. 263.

2. PIF, Part 2.

3. *Being and Time*, Oxford 1963, p. 249 (originally published 1927).

4. 'On Vagueness', *Australian Journal of Psychology and Philosophy*, 1 (1923).

5. SRHE, pp. 161–2.
6. *Of Grammatology* p. 168.
7. Cf. SRHE, C3.6.
8. Letter to Engels, 27 June 1867.
9. For more detail on Marxian theories of truth, see my entry on 'Truth' in *A Dictionary of Marxist Thought*, eds T. Bottomore et al., 2nd edn, Oxford 1992.
10. *Popular Scientific Lectures*, Chicago 1894, p. 192.
11. W. Outhwaite, 'Laws and Explanations in Sociology', in J. Hughes et al., eds, *Classical Disputes in Sociology*, London 1989.
12. See, e.g., A. Donegan, 'The Popper–Hempel Theory Reconsidered', *Philosophical Analysis in History*, New York 1966.
13. Cf. PON2, p. 87.
14. Ibid., pp. 91–2.
15. See R. Bhaskar, ed., *Harré and His Critics*, Oxford 1990.
16. Eds K. Baynes, J. Bohman and T. McCarthy, Cambridge, Mass. 1987.
17. 'Overcoming Epistemology', ibid., p. 477.
18. Cf. SRHE, C3.4.
19. Cf. Postscript to the RTS2.
20. See I. Mészáros, 'Negation', in *A Dictionary of Marxist Thought*, eds T. Bottomore et al., 2nd edn, Oxford 1992.
21. Quoted in S. Timpanaro, *On Materialism*, London 1975, p. 92n.
22. *The Logic of Marx's Capital*, New York 1992.
23. Cf. M. Fisk, 'Logic', in *A Dictionary of Marxist Thought*, eds T. Bottomore et al., Oxford 1983.
24. Cf. *Hegel's Phenomenology — An Introduction*, Brighton 1977.
25. On which see T. Benton, *Natural Relations*, London 1993.
26. Cf. SRHE, C2.1.
27. RTS2, pp. 121–2.
28. See my entry on 'Naturalism', in *Dictionary of Twentieth-Century Social Thought*, eds W. Outhwaite and T. Bottomore, Oxford 1992.
29. But cf. PON2, C2.6, and PIF, Appendix 2.
30. PIF, pp. 154–5.
31. Cf. SRHE, C2.5–7.
32. Cf. D. Elson, 'Market Socialism or Socialization of the Market?', *New Left Review*, 182 (1989).
33. Cf. PON2, pp. 411–14.
34. PON2, p. 153.
35. Plato, *Meno, Dialogues*, Oxford 1953, 80d.
36. Cf. E. Wolfe, 'Irrationality', in T. Mischel, ed., *The Self*, Oxford 1977, and G. Guignon and D. Riley, 'Biting the Bullet', in A. Malachowski, ed., *Reading Rorty*, Oxford 1990.
37. *A Theory of Human Needs*, London 1991.
38. See A. Gewirth, *Reason as Morality*, Chicago 1979. For a clear exposition and defence of Gewirth's argument, see D. Beyleveld, *The Dialectical Necessity of Morality*, Chicago 1991.

4. Metacritical Dialectics

1. Cf. *The Science of Logic*, London 1969, pp. 154–5.
2. D. Oldroyd, *The Arch of Knowledge*, London 1986.
3. 'Outline of a Theory of Truth', *Journal of Philosophy*, 72 (1975).
4. RTS2, C3.6.
5. Ibid., pp. 225–6.
6. Cf. RR, C3, and PON2, C4.4 respectively.
7. Cf. RTS, p. 166.

8. SRHE, C1.3.

9. *The Aim and Structure of Physical Theory*, New York 1962.

10. Cf. J.N. Findlay, *Kant and the Transcendental Object*, Oxford 1981, CVIII.

11. *The Idea of Nature*, Oxford 1946, p. 119.

12. *The Phenomenology of Mind*, London 1949, end of chapter on 'Force and Understanding'.

13. Hegel to Creuzer, 30 October 1817.

14. *The Philosophy of Right*, Oxford 1952, p. 279.

15. Ibid., p. 150.

16. Harmondsworth, 1973, pp. 277–8.

17. *The Science of Logic*, CV, 'Final Remark'.

18. RTS2, C2.4.

19. *Capital*, Vol. 3, C48.

20. *Capital*, Vol. 1, C19. For more on Marx as a realist, see my entry on 'Realism' in *A Dictionary of Marxist Thought*, 2nd edn, eds T. Bottomore et al., Oxford 1992.

21. 24 January 1863.

22. *Capital*, Vol. 3, C47, Section 2.

23. *Grundrisse*, Introduction.

24. 21 September 1890.

25. See my entry on 'Determinism', in *A Dictionary of Marxist Thought*, eds T. Bottomore et al., Oxford 1992.

26. In composing this figure I am indebted in different ways to the discussions on this topic of Roger Albritton, John Allen, Bertell Ollman and Andrew Sayer.

27. See especially RR, C7, and PIF, Appendix 2.

28. *The Phenomenology of Mind*, Preface, pp. 75–6.

29. *Selected Works*, London 1969, p. 97.

30. See RR, C1.

31. Cf. *After Virtue*.

32. See *The End of History and the Last Man*, London 1992.

33. Cf. R. Blackburn, 'Fin de Siècle', in R. Blackburn, ed., *After the Fall*, London 1992, and H. Wainwright, *Arguments for a New Left*, Oxford 1993, for stimulating reflections on these matters.

34. Cf. N. Chomsky, *Year 501*, London 1993, and *Rethinking Camelot*, London 1993, for devastating documentation.

35. *An Examination of Sir William Hamilton's Philosophy*, 6th edn, London 1989, p. 60.

36. Cf. D. Forbes, 'Introduction' to *Hegel's Lectures on the Philosophy of World History*, Cambridge 1975, p. xxiii.

37. See R. Bhaskar, ed., *Harré and His Critics*, Oxford 1990.

38. For critiques, see PIF and RR, C3 respectively.

Glossary

1M = Prime (first) moment. Characterized by non-identity relations, such as those involved in the critique of the epistemic and anthropic fallacies, of identity theory and actualism. Unified by the concept of alterity, it emphasizes existential intransitivity, referential detachment, the reality principle and ontology which it necessitates. More concretely, it fastens on to the transcendentally necessary stratification and differentiation of the world, entailing concepts of causal powers and generative mechanisms, alethic truth and transfactuality, natural necessity and natural kinds. Its dialectics are characteristically of stratification and ground, but also of inversion and virtualization. Its metacritics turn on the isolation of the error of destratification.

2E = Second edge. Unified by the category of absence, from which the whole circuit of 1M – 4D links and relations can be derived, its critical cutting edge is aimed at the Parmenidean doctrine of ontological monovalence (q.v.), the Platonic analysis of negation and change in terms of difference and the Kantian analysis of negative into positive predicates. It spans the gamut of categories of negativity, contradiction and critique. It emphasizes the tri-unity of causality, space and time in tensed rhythmic spatializing process, thematizing the presence of the past and existentially constitutive process. Its dialectics are typically of process, transition, frontier and node, but also generally of opposition including reversal. Its metacritics pivot on the isolation of the error of positivization and the oppositional aporiai to which it inevitably gives rise.

3L = Third level. Unified by the category of totality, it pinpoints the error of ontological extensionalism, including the hypostatization of thought. It encompasses such categories and themes as reflexivity, emergence, constellationality, holistic causality, internal relationality and intra-activity, but also detotalization, alienation, split and split-off, illicit fusion and fission. Its dialectics are of centre and periphery, form and content, figure and ground, generative separation and de-alienation, retotalization in a unity-in-diversity. Its metacritics pivot on the identification of detotalization. There is a special affinity with 1M, since totality is a structure.

4D = Fourth dimension. Unified by the category of transformative praxis or agency. In the human sphere it is implicit in the other three. Metacritically, it pinpoints two complementary kinds of ontological de-agentification — (dualistic) disembodiment, typical of (e.g. discourse in) the intrinsic aspect (q.v.), and (reductionist) reification, characteristic of the extrinsic aspect. There is a special affinity with 2E, since agency is (intentional) causality, which is absenting. Agency is sustained philosophically by an emergent powers materialist orientation and substantively by the concept of four-planar social being in nature with the moral evolution of the species, like the future generally, open. Its dialectics are at the site of ideological and material struggles, but also of absolute reason and it incorporates dialectical critical realism's dialectic of desire to freedom (see C3.10).

A-series. The ordination of events by the explicitly tensed past, present and future as distinct from the B-serial earlier, simultaneous and later or the spatio-temporally indefinite C-series (see C3.5).

Absence. Understood to include non-existence anywhere anywhen. It is systematically bipolar, designating absenting (distanciating and/or trans-forming) process as well as simple absence in a more or less determinate level-/context-specific region of space-time; and in fact reveals a fourfold polysemy: product, process, process-in-product and product-in-process — which may be recursively embedded and systematically intermingled. It includes, but is far from exhausted by, the past and outside. It is the central category of dialectic, whether conceived as argument, change or the augmentation of (or aspiration to) freedom, which depend upon the identification and elimination of mistakes, states of affairs and constraints, or more generally ills — argued to be absences alike.

Absolute reason (or dialectical rationality). The unity — or better, coherence — of theory and practice in practice.

Actualism. The reduction of the necessary and the possible, constitutive of the domain of the real, to the actual. Actualism is inherently dilemmatic since these reductions cannot be consistently carried out. This is readily witnessed in open systems, where actualism can be saved only by the forfeit of knowledge (i.e. philosophy sustained at the price of science) or, as in the case of the Hegelian demi-actual, by according the non-actual a lower ontological status as irrational existents (a form of weak actualism [see RTS, C2.4]). In general $D_r > D_a > D_s$, whether D_s is empirical or conceptual.

Agency. Intentional transformative praxis caused by real, even if routinized, unconscious, multiple, anterior (including long prior) and/or contradictory reasons; which issues in a state of affairs that, unless it was overdetermined (as in a firing squad), would not have occurred otherwise.

Alethic truth. The truth of, or real reason(s) for, or dialectical ground of, *things*, as distinct from *propositions*, possible in virtue of the ontological stratification of the world and attainable in virtue of the dynamic character of science.

Alienation. The condition of being estranged or separated from what is constitutive of, or essential to, one's nature, causal powers or wellbeing. Its origin is in the Hegelian Beautiful Soul, alienated from her community, which eventually becomes the self-alienation of absolute spirit. In Marx it signifies generative separation or the alienation of the immediate producers from (a) their labour, (b) their product, (c) the means and materials of their production, (d) each other, and the nexus of social relations within which their production takes place, and (e) ultimately themselves. It is the sign of detotalization and split.

Alterity. Sheer determinate other-being, irreducible, contrary to the irrealist dialectical tradition, to a unitary origin or a common denominator.

Analytic problematic. Constituted by the illicit ontological contra-position of the logical norms of identity and non-contradiction, and underpinned by the mutually endorsing epistemic and ontic fallacies, it entails 'identity-thinking' and, inter alia, 'fixism', i.e. the presupposition of fixed subjects, generating an ideology of stasis and repression (see C2.10 and C3.5).

Anthropism. Incorporates, subjectively, anthropocentrism — literally, taking man as the centre or goal of the cosmos — and, objectively, projective anthropomorphism — painting or interpreting the cosmos in the image of man. The anthropic fallacy is the analysis or definition of being in terms of human being. As such, it underpins anthroporealism in its various guises — empirical, conceptual, Nietzschean (will-to-power) realism. Anthroporealism is implicit in subject – object identity or equivalent theory, where it involves a tacit exchange of epistemic and ontic fallacies.

Aristotelian propaedeutics. The continual circulation of discourse in and out of the sphere of formal reasoning, in which meanings and truth values remain stable, typical of everyday life, but also necessary for the dialectic of dialectical and analytical reasoning essential to science.

Atomism. Literally meaning without interior space. Argued in C2.1 to be conceptually incoherent. But associated, as corpuscularianism, with the Cartesian paradigm of action-by-contiguous-contact, and the achievement of Newtonian locally celestial closure, it provides a source of philosophy's analogical grammar. It is complicit with and provides a model for bourgeois individualism. It is entailed by empiricist justificationism, the dominant twentieth-century form of the quest for incorrigibility or search for an unhypothetical starting point. As such, it implies the reductionist demand for an autonomized or empty mind.

Autonomy. Self-determination. Rational autonomy entails the capacity (hence the knowledge, power and opportunity) and disposition to act in one's real interests. A theoretico-practical bridge concept linking truth to freedom mediated by wisdom in a two-way dialectic.

Beautiful Soul — See Alienation.

Blockism. The postulation of a simultaneous conjunctive totality of all events.

Cause/Causation. A cause is typically either an antecedent condition or a generative mechanism. The causal chain in *Dialectic* characteristically consists in the transfactual efficacy of the generative mechanisms of a structure, the rhythmic (spatio-temporal) exercise of their causal powers, possibly multiply mediated by holistic causality, and, in the human sphere, dependent upon intentional human agency, codetermining a conjuncture.

Concrete. (a) Co-relative to abstract; (b) well-rounded. The concrete universal is a multiple quadruplicity constituted by structures, particular mediations and singularities, rhythmically processualized. The concrete singularity of an individual human being consists in a core species-being, particular mediations and rhythmics, uniquely individuating her or him as in effect a natural kind sui generis. Concrete utopianism consists in the exercise of constructing models of alternative ways of living on the basis of some assumed set of resources, counterbalancing actualism and informing hope.

Conjuncture. Events in open systems are multiply determined, hence conjunctures, and things are correspondingly compounds.

Consistency/Inconsistency. No general formula for developmental consistency can be given other than progressive import, which is necessarily dependent upon judgement intrinsic to the [description of the] process concerned. Theory/practice consistency in a praxis in a process should be practical, directional and universalizably accountable such that it is transfactual, concrete, actionable and transformative. Theory/practice inconsistency leads to pathologies of action, from repression through compromise formation to ad hoc grafting.

Constellationality. A figure of containment within an over-reaching term (e.g. epistemology within ontology, reasons within causes), from which the over-reached term may be diachronically or synchronically emergent. It may take the form of identity, unity, fluidity, etc. In Hegel it is invariably teleological and a sign of closure.

Constraint. An absolute or relative prohibition, whether natural or social and remediable or not. The concept may be negatively generalized in the social sphere to include any kind of ill.

Contradiction. This concept ranges from constraints to conflicts. External should be distinguished from internal contradictions, which include the 'inner complicity' arguably necessary for change; and dialectical from logical contradictions, which intersect (when grounded in a common mistake) but are not coterminous. Dialectical contradictions are mutually exclusive internally related oppositions, conveying tendencies to change. (See C2.3.) Most, but not all, dialectics are consistent with the formal logical norm of non-contradiction.

Critique. Paradigmatically distinguished from criticism in that it isolates the source or ground of the imputed error. As such an explanatory critique may license a negative evaluation on the causes of the error concerned. An immanent critique isolates a theory/practice inconsistency; a metacritique$_1$ an absence or incompleteness in the theory of the practice which a metacritique$_2$ additionally explains. An Achilles' Heel critique pinpoints the blindspot in a theory, characteristically at what appears to be its strongest point, and a series of Achilles' Heel critiques constitutes a dialectical phenomenology.

De-agentification. This may take the philosophical forms of (dualistic) disembodiment or (reductionist) reification, manifesting itself sociologically in the enervation or fragmentation of agents or groups, impotent empty selves, fissiparousness and alienating retrojective, introjective, projective, etc. modes of identification (e.g. in a fantasy world).

Detotalization. A split, e.g. a dualistic dichotomy or split-off, which may manifest itself in a projected exteriorization or some other guise. Detotalization may be induced by an absence, separation, illicit fission or gulf.

Dialectic. Anything from any relation between differential elements to the absenting of constraints on the absenting of absences, or ills. This concept is diffracted both intensionally and extensionally from its Hegelian moorings in C2.5 and retotalized under the auspices of the concept of absence throughout the book. Dialectical detachment consists in the jettisoning of refuted conclusions.

Dialectical argument. A form of transcendental argument in which the ontological necessity of false (or limited) premises, categories or results is established. (See C2.6.)

Dialectical critical realism. The system of categories and configurations presented in this book, as a 1M—4D network. There is no single sequence of presentation, although a particularly natural way, starting from the absence implicit in desire, is suggested in C3.11, but others are articulated, e.g. in C2.10. Its aim is to provide a framework, especially through the differentiated unification of critical realist dialectic by 1M—4D relations and *their* unification by the 2E category of absence or real negation, for understanding real geo-historical dialectical processes, which constellationally contain 'analytic' or morphostatic ones.

Dialectical universalizability. All four aspects of the judgement form are universalizable although in different ways (see C3.2). Action and its groundings should both be universalizable, in the sense of transfactual, concrete, actionable (i.e. agent-specific) and transformatively directional.

Duality. Necessary co-relatives, such as theoretical and practical reasoning, so that typically, but not always, one may be seen under the aspect of the other. In dialectical critical realism dualities are punctuated by a hiatus, which stops a reductionist collapse and signifies a difference in orientation or spatio-temporal lag.

Ego-present-centrism. See Indexicalism.

Emancipation. Characteristically the transition from an unwanted, unnecessary and oppressive situation to a wanted and/or needed and empowering or more flourishing situation.

Emergence. A relationship between two terms such that one term diachronically or perhaps synchronically arises out of the other, but is capable of reacting back on the first and is in any event causally and taxonomically irreducible to it.

Epistemic fallacy. The analysis or definition of statements about being in terms of statements about our knowledge (of being). In subject—object identity or equivalent theory it entails the converse ontic fallacy, viz. the definition or assumption of the compulsive determination of knowledge by being. It nowadays most usually takes the form of the linguistic fallacy, and underpinning it lies the deep-rooted anthropic fallacy.

Ethical tetrapolity [expressive veracity → axiological commitment] → (1) fiduciariness → (2) content of the explanatory critical theory complex [= explanatory critique + concrete utopianism + theory of transition] ↔ (3) totalizing depth praxis of emancipatory axiology → (4) freedom qua universal human emancipation.

Existentially constitutive process. The constitution of a thing by its geo-history. This is one of the four moments in which the presence of the past and of the outside manifest themselves (cf. C2.8).

Explanation. Theoretical explanation consists in description, retroduction, elimination, identification and correction: DREI(C). Applied explanation in resolution, redescription, retrodiction, elimination, identification and correction: RRREI(C). Practical problem resolution in diagnosis, explanation and action: DEA. Normative change in description, explanation and transformation: DET.

[Ontological] extensionalism. The division of a totality into discrete, separable, externally related parts, manifest as in, for example, the extrusion of thought, or contradiction, or morality, from reality — for instance, in the fact/value divide.

Fideism. At the level of the aporiai of the transdictive complex (q.v.), the absence of a concept of ontological stratification, natural necessity or alethic truth (manifest in primal squeeze) necessitates reliance on a surrogate such as God, social convention or custom which cannot be rationally justified. Similarly the absence of a concept of primary polyadization (and the dialectic of individuation it implies), or of the necessary pre-existence of social relations, necessitates a fideistic escape from solipsism. The aporiai of the solipsistic complex can ultimately be situated within those of the transdictive complex. Fideism inevitably generates a dualism within monism or more generally subject – object identity theory.

Four-planar social being. Defined by the planes of (a) material transactions with nature, (b) inter-/intra-subjective relations, e.g. along the power, communicative and moral sub-dimensions of the social cube, (c) social relations sui generis, defining the level of social institutions, and (d) the stratification of the personality. The moral evolution of the species is to be regarded as unfinished.

Freedom. Degrees of freedom consist of agentive freedom, formal legal freedom, negative freedom from, positive freedom to, emancipation from specific constraints, autonomy, rational autonomy, universal human autonomy, wellbeing, flourishing, progressively dependent on the positive generalization of the concept of freedom to include needs and possibilities for development as rights. (See C3.10.)

Heterology. Either (a) not true of, or applicable to, itself (contrary: autology); (b) not the same as itself (contrary: homology); and/or (c) not true for and/or to itself (contrary: autonomy which, if it includes de-alienation, entails true in itself also).

Holistic causality. May be said to operate when a complex coheres in such a way that (a) the totality, i.e. the form or structure of the combination, causally codetermines the elements; and (b) the form and structure of the elements causally codetermine each other, and so causally codetermine the whole.

Identities. Constellational identity is the containment or co-inclusion of one thing within or by another. Dispositional identity is the identity of a thing with its changing causal powers. Rhythmic identity is the identity of a thing with the exercise of its changing causal powers. These identities constitute three kinds of ultimata.

Identity theory. Parmenidean monism, Aristotelian hylomorphism, Humean positivist phenomenalism, Hegelian phenomenology are examples of subject−object identity theories but the drive to subject−object identity or equivalent theory is established by the epistemic fallacy, and in modern times by the post-Humean/Kantian denegation of ontology. Without a transcendental realist ontology, philosophy is driven to identity theory, and in particular by its generalized form, actualism, and thence to the paradoxical and dehumanizing reification of facts and their conjunctions. In C2.10 and C3.5 subject−object identity theory is connected to other identity theories especially identity thinking and fixism, and their effects. Dialectical critical realism involves a partial, fallible, achieved knowledge subject−object non-identity theory, buttressed by the distinction between the transitive and intransitive dimensions and the recognition of the constellational containment of epistemology within ontology.

Ideology. $Power_2$/discursive or communicative/normative or moral intersects of the social cube — in a strong sense embodying categorial error.

Indexicalism. The assumption that only the present (and by extension, the here) exists. It inevitably leads to irrealism about causality and existence, and thence to a punctualist solipsistic ego-present-centrism.

Internal relationality. An element A is internally related to B if B is a necessary condition for the existence of A, whether this relation is reciprocal/symmetrical or not.

Intra-action. Occurs among internally related elements in three basic modes: (1) existential constitution, in which one element is essential and intrinsic to another; (2) permeation, in which one element contains another; and (3) connection, in which one element is merely causally efficacious on the other.

Intransitive/transitive dimensions. The intransitive dimension is initially the domain of the objects of scientific knowledge: but the concept can be extended to take in anything existentially intransitive, whether known, knowable or not. The transfactuality of laws and socialization into science imply the distinction between the intransitive or ontological and the transitive or epistemological dimensions of science. This latter must logically be extended to include the whole material and cultural infrastructure of society.

Intrinsic/extrinsic aspect. The intrinsic aspect is the normative aspect of science, or more generally, the intentional aspect of agency. It is constellationally contained, in the case of science, within the transitive dimension; more macroscopically, within the extrinsic or causal aspect of agency. Therefore the category of causality, for instance, constellationally includes, but is not exhausted by, that of rationality.

Judgement form. This has four aspects — expressive veracious; fiduciary; descriptive; and evidential — all of which are universalizable (see C3.2), and has a theoretico-practical duality built into it.

[Metaphysical] λ clause. An escape clause that every axiologically, transcendentally and/or dialectically refutable metaphysical system requires as a safety net, reflecting the posture of weak actualism (Cf. RTS C2.4 and SRHE C3.5).

Levels. A key concept for distinguishing strata of ontological depth, levels of discursive analysis (e.g. talking about from talking within), layers of emergence and superstructuration. The avoidance of homology, intimated by Hegelian dialectic (cf. C1.9), and refined by critical realist alethic truth (cf. C3.2), is the key to the resolution of most of the textbook problems of philosophy (cf. C4.2).

Materialism. Epistemological materialism asserts the independent existence and transfactual activity of at least some of the objects of scientific thought. That is to say it is equivalent to transcendental realism. Ontological materialism asserts the unilateral dependence of social upon biological (and more generally physical) being and the emergence of the former from the latter. It is thus consistent with the emergent powers materialist orientation defended here, which is in turn consistent with the possibility of dual and multiple control. Practical materialism asserts the constitutive role of human transformative agency in the reproduction and transformation of social forms. This makes it congruent with the transformational model of social activity — providing we understand both in the negatively generalized way of C2.9.

Mediation. If A achieves C via B then B may be said to mediate their relation.

Monism. See Primary polyadization.

[Ontological] monovalence. A purely positive account of reality. Fatally flawed by the transcendental deduction of the necessity for real negation or absence (see C1.3 and C2.1), it acts ideologically to screen the epistemological and ontological contingency of being and to sequester existential questions generally, as ontological actualism sequesters 'essential' ones. The result is the doubly dogmatically reinforced positivization of knowledge, and eternalization of the status quo. In opposition to ontological monovalence I argue for ontological bivalence — or better, polyvalence — plus the possibility of a non-valent response to problematic axiological choice situations as a propaedeutic to the Socratic strategy of problematizing the question (see C2.4).

Negation. Has a process/product homonomy and a fourfold polysemy (see Absence). Real negation is consistent with distanciation without transformation; transformative negation is consistent with exogenous sources of change; and radical negation is consistent with multiple determination within a totality. Therefore we have the theorem: real negation $\geq$ transformative negation $\geq$ radical negation $\geq$ linear negation. I argue that negative is a condition for positive being and hence knowledge. Unlike most philosophers my paradigm of real negation is determinate non-being, not nothingness.

Negativity. Conveys better than negation simpliciter the processual aspect of absence. It also incorporates the other primary sense of negativity in dialectic besides absent being: ill-being. These are united in the dialectic of desire to freedom (see C3.10).

Open systems. Systems in which constant conjunctions of events do not occur, so laws cannot be regarded as empirical regularities or actual qua universal-and-necessarily-certain generalizations of instances. If the openness of systems entails the falsity of actualism, the openness of the future entails the falsity of endism, blockism and historicism (in Popper's sense); while the depth openness of nature entails the falsity of cognitive triumphalism.

Perspectival switch. The switch from one transcendentally or dialectically necessary condition or aspect of a phenomenon, thing or totality to another which is also transcendentally or dialectically necessary for it.

Phronesis. Practical wisdom, necessary for dialectical rationality, and, as the supreme meta-ethical virtue, for the two-way dialectic of truth and freedom. Phronesis almost always requires a degree of *sophrosyne* or balance, thus tying in with the themes of totality, wholeness and health.

Politics. Emancipatory/transformative, representative, movement and life politics constitute four types, in all of which participation in/participatory democracy may play a greater or lesser role. Transformed transformative trustworthy (fiduciary) totalizing transformist transitional politics is the praxis of emancipatory politics.

Power$_1$–Power$_2$. Power$_1$ is the transformative capacity intrinsic to the concept of action as such, whereas power$_2$ is the capacity to get one's way against either the overt wishes and/or the real interests of others in virtue of structures of exploitation, domination, subjugation and control, i.e. generalized master–slave-type relations. Around such relations hermeneutic and other more material (but still conceptualized) hegemonic/counter-hegemonic struggles may be waged.

Primal squeeze. The squeeze between the domains of metaphysics (cf. the speculative illusion) and the a priori, and those of experience (cf. the positivistic illusion) and the a posteriori, ruling out empirically controlled scientific theory and natural necessity alike.

Primary polyadization. Necessary for individuation, and hence self-identity. It operates as transcendental refutations of any monism, including solipsism, and of straightforward dialectics of a Schillerian type, presupposing a unitary origin prior to the moment of diremption and self-alienation.

Punctualism. An atomistic concept of space-time, refuted by the distanciated spatio-temporailty necessary for time-consciousness and more generally any non-contiguous (or even contiguous) causality.

Realism/Irrealism. Realism in philosophy asserts the existence of some disputed entity; irrealism denies it. Thus one can be a realist about causal laws and an irrealist about God. Generally in *Dialectic* irrealism is taken to include anthropism, actualism, monovalence, extensionalism, de-agentification and alethic, spatio-temporal and moral irrealism. Most hitherto existing dialectics, like analytics, have been irrealist (under the dominance of analytic irrealism). I argue that realism, like ontology, is inexorable.

Reductionism. May be ontological and/or epistemological, ethical, agentive, etc. Thus reductionism in epistemology has often taken the form of reducing theory to experience (the positivistic illusion) or to philosophy (the speculative illusion). Here what are required are the mediating terms of empirically controlled scientific theory and natural necessity. Metaphysically, reductionism has often been opposed to dualism. Thus we have the familiar alternatives of disembodiment or reification in relation to human agency. Here the solution normally involves an emergent powers orientation and figures such as constellationality and duality-with-a-hiatus.

Referential detachment. The detachment of the act of reference from that to which it refers. This establishes at once its existential intransitivity and the possibility of another reference to it, a condition of any intelligible discourse at all. Referential detachment is implicit in all language-use and conceptualized praxis, e.g. playing football. There are no a priori limits on what can be referred to — this is the generalized concept of reference and referent.

Reflexivity. The inwardized form of totality. It is necessary for accountability and the monitoring of intentional causal agency. The concept of a meta-reflexively totalizing situation (see C2.8 and C3.8) can explain how knowledge is possible without erasure.

Reification. To be turned into a thing, as in the commodification of labour-power, closely connected with fetishism, to be invested with magical powers, as in the animation of the commodity, especially in the form of money. In philosophy, it occurs in physicalistic reductionism, where it is often accompanied by — in the tacit complicity of contraries — dualistic disembodiment (e.g. in discourse theory, denaturalized hermeneutics). In epistemology the reification of facts, accompanied by the fetishism of conjunctions, implies and is implied by the hypostatization of ideas (cf. C2.5).

Relativism. Epistemic, like spatio-temporal, relativity must be accepted and foundationalism rejected. It is quite consistent with judgemental rationalism in the intrinsic aspect and ontological realism in the intransitive dimension of science. Epistemic relativism must be distinguished from judgemental relativism, into which non-foundationalist irrealism tends to fall.

Rhythmic. Tensed spatializing process consisting in the exercise of the causal efficacy of a structure or a thing; which, as such, may have supervenient causal powers of its own. Symbolic of the tri-unity of space, time and causality in dialectics.

Scepticism. In Hegel, the denial or denegation of reality, including, as I generalize it, $power_2$ relations. Its real basis is alienation or generative separation. It is the archetypal figure for theory/practice inconsistency — e.g. in Hegel's case between those who make and those who understand history. Generally philosophy is inherently aporetic and, as a disciplinary matrix, typically takes the form of a theory problem-field solution set.

Social cube. Highlights the differentiation and dislocation within four-planar social being.

Spatio-temporality. Spatio-temporality has a fivefold character as (a) a referential grid, (b) a measure, (c) a set of prima facie mutual exclusion relations, (d) a potentially emergent property, perhaps with causal powers of its own, and (e) a generally entropic process. Spatio-temporalities may be emergent either as new relata of an existing system of material things or as relata of a new system of material things. Spatio-temporalities may be multiple, elongated, disjoint, intersecting, overlapping, contradictory, etc. As a process, causality is typically intrinsically both spatialized and tensed. But both the disembedding and emergence of space from time and vice versa are possible and instantiated in our world.

Stoicism. In Hegel, indifference to reality, including, as generalized here, $power_2$ relations. The book argues that there is a direct line from Stoicism to absolute knowledge to autogenetic hyper-intuitionism, and that Hegel never departs from the attitude of the Stoic.

Structure. Science reveals levels of structure which are knowable in the dialectic described in C3.2. Its essential movement is given by that from manifest phenomena to generative explanatory structure, which may eventually be empirically identified or otherwise detected, e.g. via its causal powers to effect perceivable phenomena. The structure of a thing is constituted by its causal powers, which, when exercised, manifest themselves as tendencies. A structure will typically be instantiated in a multiplicity of structurata. A concretely singularized individual can be understood as a uniquely laminated structuratum.

Sublation. In its Hegelian sense it has the threefold meaning of to cancel, preserve and transcend. But most rational resolutions are transformative in part, and a distinction seems necessary between essential and/or valuable and other features. Furthermore, it cannot be assumed that in real geo-history results are invariably or even necessarily normally rational resolutions (cf. C1.7 and C4.6).

Superstructuration. The characteristic movement of the Hegelian dialectic. *Dialectic* argues that the Marxian notion of a superstructure may be usefully combined with the concept of an intrastructure, where the base provides merely the conditions of possibility or framework conditions of the intrastructure.

Tendency. In open systems laws must be analysed as tendencies, which may be possessed without being exercised, and exercised without being actualized. Corresponding to the distinction between intrinsic and extrinsic and between stimulus and releasing conditions, a variety of different concepts of tendency can be built up. And the same exercise can be repeated in respect of the other moments of the causal chain (q.v.). (Cf. C2.4.)

Tina formation. Theories and practices which violate axiological necessities require defence mechanisms, including λ escape clauses, supporting connections which may function as Derridean supplements, and assume the form of a compromise — a Tina formation — as a necessary accommodation to reality.

Totality. Totalities are systems of internal relations (q.v.), which may assume various forms of intra-activity (q.v.) and operate via holistic causality. Sub-totalities are separated by blocks, but most totalities of concern to science, at least macroscopically, are *partial* as well, displaying external in addition to internal and contingent besides necessary connections. Absenting an essential element or component of a thing effects detotalization. Self-referential paradox, performative contradiction, reflexive and/or theory/practice inconsistency all result in detotalization, yielding liability to immanent critique in the context of conceptualized (hermeneutic and material), hegemonic/counter-hegemonic struggles over discursively moralized power$_2$ (or generalized master−slave-type) relations.

Transcendental. Transcendental realism asserts the independent existence and transfactual efficacy of structures and efficacious things. Transcendental arguments are species of retroductive-explanatory arguments (familiar to science), in which the premises embody some categorical necessity. Transcendental detachment is from the premises of a transcendental argument to a focus on the implications of its conclusion(s), or, dialectically, of its metacritical presuppositions.

Transdiction/Transdictive complex. Transdiction is inference from the observed to the unobserved. It includes induction and transduction, retroduction and retrodiction. The aporiai of the transdictive complex are generated by the absence of a concept of natural necessity and, more especially, that of alethic truth. The aporiai of the solipsistic problem-field (those of particular knowledge) can be set and resolved in a transdictive context. (Cf. C4.2.)

Transfactuality. The exercise of the causal powers of structure, that is, the working of a generative mechanism, e.g. as manifest in the operation of all the natural laws known to science, must be interpreted as applying transfactually, that is to say in closed and open systems alike. Other critical realists have used concepts such as transphenomenality and trans-situationality to highlight this necessity. The result of not interpreting laws transfactually is that the normic statements with which they are expressed are immediately falsified in open systems, and practical science is left without any epistemic credentials.

Transformational model of social activity (TMSA). Articulates relationships between social structure and human agency (cf. PON, C2, SRHE, C2.2 and RR, C5−6). Dialectic requires its negative generalization so that structures can persist in virtue of our present inaction, having been generated in virtue of the practices of the dead. This is another instance of the presence of the past. Process here appears as the mediator between structure and agency. The generalization of TMSA situates the tensed dislocated dialectics of structure and agency, as well as correcting a one-sided emphasis on particular kinds of transformation/work/care/forbearance, while still avoiding the errors of reification and voluntarism (cf. C2.9).

[σ, τ, etc.] transforms. The conceptual work done in the identification (σ) and repair (τ) of an inconsistency, leading in general to the expansion of the conceptual field, that drives the Hegelian (and, finessed, the epistemological) dialectic on. The ρ and υ transforms signify the extra-scientific inputs and outputs respectively in this process.

Trust. Fiduciariness is one of the four components of the judgement form, the truth tetrapolity and the ethical tetrapolity; it is a constituent of transformist politics and underpins the triadic relationship between self- and mutual esteem and existential security. A good case can be made for considering it the primary existential. In C3.8 I argue that there are four kinds of trust: abstract, mediated, concrete and personalized.

Truth tetrapolity. Constituted by normative-fiduciary, adequating, expressive-referential and alethic truth. See C3.2.

Unhappy Consciousness. Scepticism, or theory/practice inconsistency, or more generally categorial error, aware of itself, seeking refuge in the case of reality in asceticism or other-worldliness and in respect of power$_2$ relations in, for example, introjective identification with the master's ideology or projective absorption in a fantasy world made for slaves. If Stoicism typically corresponds to 1M, and Scepticism to 2E, the Unhappy Consciousness reflects detotalization at 3L, and may further manifest itself in dualistic disembodiment and/or reductionist reification at 4D. In this book philosophy is argued to be a veritable citadel of the Unhappy Consciousness.

Unholy trinity. The trio constituted by the epistemic fallacy, ontological monovalence and primal squeeze. As the epistemic fallacy, mediated by actualism, determines primal squeeze, the trinity can be seen as a function of a couple. Moreover as ontological monovalence, taken literally, entails the exclusion of alterity (primaeval monism) as a perspectival switch on absence, it must be regarded as the primordial failing of western philosophy.

Unity-in-diversity. For a human totality to be genuine it must represent the concrete singularity, and particular differentiations of each individual. The ultimate basis of unity is given by our shared species-being or common humanity and social relationality; and in practice, by our subjugation to the effects of the same or similar sets of oppressive power$_2$ relations.

Name Index

Subject Index

indeterminacy, axiological 57−9, 72, 80, 119, 157, 281, 319, 339
indexicalism 130, 210, 231, 232, 252−5, 257, 316, 360−1, *399*
indifference 8, 18, 154, 184
individual *see* singularity, concrete
individualism and atomism 91, 159, 233, 294
individuation 125, 131, 230, 355n.
induction 16, 111−12, 119, 138, 324−5; in critical realism 300, 317−19; and identity theory 232, 312, 359, 361; and prime moment 35−6, 75, 131, 236, 316−18; and second edge 36, 75, 81, 183, 244, 319, 321, *see also* intuition; transdiction
injunctive paradox 119, 210, 372
intentionality 50−3, 95, 127−8, 144−5, 153, 155−7, 164, 172, 209
interdependence: existential 6, 115, 302
interests: dialectics of material 290−1, **291**; sectional/universal 168, 180, 275, 332, 362, 369
intra-activity 58, 123, 223, 245, 294, 305−6, 368, 380, *399*; and inner relationality 79, 97, 123−5; of totality 53, 100, 125−6, 200, 209, 240
intra-constitution 123, 125, 199
intra-relationality 160, 174, 183, 190, 199, 209
intra-subjectivity 161, 172, 178
intradependence 299, 302, 333, 350, 368
intransitivity, existential 79, 91, 114, 149, 164, 299, 354; in critical realism 304, 379; in Hegel 337, 338, 340, 342; and ontology 45, 212, 230, 302, 320, 377; *see also* detachment, referential
intrastructure 53, 97, 127, 198, 404
intuition 16, 25, 111−12, 138, 181−2, 309
inversion: in Hegel 87, 89, 93−5, 343; and prime moment 306, 392
irrationalism 112, 231, 233−4, 251, 300, 320, 359, 382; *see also* detotalization
irrealism 206, 227, 308−14, **313**, 378, 382−4; analytical 100, 194, 311; and argument 105, 111; consequences 365−70; dialectic 100, 139, 195, 272, 311−12, **315**, 355n., 376; of Hegel 88, 92, 96, 99, 130; logic of 195, **196**, **315**, **364**; and ontology 47, 48, 78, 184−6, 192−3, 205−6, 233, 305−6, 357; and spatio-temporality 253−4; sublation 204−307, 314−22, 354, *see also* absence; actualism; causality; dualism; epistemic fallacy; identity theory; monovalence, ontological; philosophy, problems of; realism; squeeze, primal

judgement form 200, 265, 282, 325, 379, *400*; descriptive 178, 221, 262; evidential 178, 221, 262; expressive veracious 177, 178−80, 200, 221−2, 262, 274, 286, 292, 382; fiduciary 177−9, 221−2, 262−3, 294, 382; universalizability 171, 177−8, 179−80, 211, 220−1, 263, 285, 318, 371−2, 382

kinds: natural 124, 317, 392

knowledge 180, 191, 228, 236, 269; absolute 330−1, 404; explanatory 36, 124, 237, 309; positivization 43, 111−12, 184−6, 392; taxonomic 36, 124, 237, 300, 309, 316; types 231−2, 267, 296, *see also* epistemic fallacy; epistemology; ontic fallacy; power

3L (third level) 9−10, 12−13, 14, *392−3*; and absence 42−3, 52−3, 106, 183, 202, 248, 305, 360, 371; and contradiction 63, 75, *see also* detotalization; emergence; extensionalism, ontological; reflexivity; split; totality
λ-clause 115, 117−18, 157, 184, 361, 384, *400*
language: and truth 218, 223, **271**
levels 131−4, 151, 206, *400*
limit: dialectical (dl′) 104, 121−2, 134, 175, 200, 268, 374
linguistic fallacy 112, 206, 397
loco-periodization 54, 141, 144, 251, 257
logic 84−5, 136, 193−4; and being 72, 79, 191; and dialectics 67, *68*, 99, 199, 373, 380, *see also* contradiction, logical

1M (prime moment) 8−13, 14, 23, 131, 316, 392; and absence 42−3, 48, 105, 183, 248, 304, 360, 371; and actualism 206, 234−7; and freedom 294; and induction 35−6, 75, 131, 236, 316−18; and natural necessity 47, 340; and stratification 202, 218, 234, 236, 262, 306, 320, 340, 384; and tendency 191; and truth 218−19, 237, 340, *see also* contradiction; emergence; epistemology; non-identity; ontology; transfactuality
master-slave relations 175, 187, 197, 330−5, 381; abolition 180, 267, 284, 287−8, 372, 381; in Hegel 60, 90, 154; struggles against 62, 66, 120, 335
material implication paradox 236, 317, 319, 320
materialism *400*; contemplative 107, 246; dialectical 97, 217, 300, 352, 363, 369; emergent powers 32, 51, 172, 198, 209−10, 246, 316; epistemological 87, 91−4, 96, 337; ğeo-ĥistorical 87, 94, 350−1; ontological 87, 93−4, 337; practical 87, 94, 337; reductionist 51−2, 151, *see also* diffraction
meaning 191, 215, 222−3, **223**, 385
mechanisms: generative 36, 155, 226, 240
mediation 113−14, 115, 126, 130, 137, 172, 380, *400*; in Marx 349−50, 369; multiple 144−5, 160, 302, 368; and process 114, 133, 155; vanishing mediators 27, 139, 142, 336
memory, cumulative 31, 62, 138−9, 245, 343
metacritique 91, 289, 300, 310, 332, 335, 382; MC_1 265, 354, 396; MC_2 226, 354−65, 396; and absence 184, 244, 360; immanent 195, 344
monism: critique of 45, 47n., 173, 180, 192, 233, 312, 320, 354−7, 374, 380; in Hegel 18, 87, 92, 95, 245, 250, 337−9, 342, 348, 372; in science 224−5, 310; spiritual 92, 327, 337, 342, 348, 370; tendential 367; token 44−5, 77, 107, 183, 248, 383; transcendental

causal 51–2, 280–1; critical 261–2, 290; depth explanatory critical 261; dialectical (dr') 46, 99, 101, 136, 163, 199, and argument 103–4, 109, critique 189–95, 198, 201, 272, and Hegel 11, 17, 23–4, 28, 29–30, and science 35–6, 80, 237, 261–2, and truth 219, 222; explanatory critical 261–2, 289, 291, 369; instrumental 210, 261–2, 274, 290–1, 368; moral 260–1; practical 65, 66–9, 79, 133, 180, 222–4, 247, 260, 262, 264, 292, 324; sufficient 178, 181, 221, 235, 287; theoretical 65, 66–9, 79, 133, 175–7, 180, 221, 247, 264, 292; totalizing depth explanatory critical 261, 290
reductionism 47n., 180, 198, 235–6, 248, 374, 402; and dualism 181, 198, 246, 321; and emergence 50, 51–2; epistemological 193, 232, 360; ethical 340, 345, 349–50, 367; sociological 265, 345, 349, 367, 375
reference: and existence 40, 233–4; and referent 40–1, 130, 222–3, see also detachment, referential
reflexivity 21, 91, 285, 307, 403; meta-reflexivity 148–50, 209, 273, 319; and third level 9, 134, 183, 202, 209, 273–4, 340, 360, 380; and totality 272–3, 302, 371, 382
regress, vicious 119, 132–3, 157, 212, 318
reification 258, 274–5, 277, 300, 306, 371, 403; and absence 44, 184, 239; of fact 4, 47, 194, 205, 207, 209, 233, 359, 383; and irrealism 321, 357, 362; reductionist 393, 406
reinstatement, analytic 62, 73, 78, 90, 270, 311, 337–8; and dialectical connection 74, 113, 119, 198, 238, 327, 339, 372
relationality, internal 10, 58, 69, 100, 124, 209, 302, 380, 399, see also dialectic, relational; intra-activity; totality
relations: dialectical 56–72; discursive 90, 153, 161–2; non-identity 316, 319; normative 153, 161; social 54–6, 114, 153–6, 163–4, 168, 172, 209, 273, 349, 363, 381, see also master-slave relations; power
relativism 122, 309, 403; epistemic 9n., 112, 211, 218, 231, 245, 275, 310, 316, 320, 363, 374; judgemental 359, 403; perspectival 169–70
remark, dialectical (drkç) 118, 134–5, 175, 200
repression 176, 208, 250, 257, 274, 300, 305, 380; in irrealism 237, 312, 365, 366
retotalization 12, 98, 128, 321, 370–8
retrodiction 133, 158, 224, 232
retroduction 26, 109, 158, 232, 325
rhythmics 251, 299, 403; and causality 52, 53–5, 77, 106, 114; and co-presence 54, 140, 143–5; and social being 96, 160, 163–4, 167, 201; and tense 252–3, 257, 380, see also process
rights and freedom 284, 288–9, 292, 295, 297, 324, 350, 372

scepticism 8, 17, 18, 184, 231, 325, 360, 403; and irrealism 233, 244, 317–18, 358–9, 361–2, see also Consciousness, Unhappy
science: and argument 104, 107–12, 199, 226,

227–8; and contradiction 80, 83–5, 229; and critical realism 4, 14–15, 26, 189, 211; and dialectic 80, 83–4, 108–10, 115, 136, 236–7; and differentiation 302; in Hegel 34–8, 90–1, 138–9, 338–9, 342; in Marx 93–5, 345–6; philosophy of 224–7, 231, 300; pure/applied 34, 224, 226; and real negation 5, 83; and reasoning 52–6, see also dialectic, epistemological; dimension, transitive; efficacy; negation, transformative; ontology; social science; totality; truth
self see personality
self-consciousness 270, 326–9, 330–1, 335, 337
self-determination see autonomy
self-emancipation 2, 6, 101, 171, 179, 278, 282, 285, 368, 385
self-predicative paradox 131, 236, 318–19
self-realization 106, 176, 282, 296, 363, 372
self-referential paradox 44, 236, 274–5, 319, 365
separation, generative 48, 102, 113, 128–30, 187, 248, 263, see also alienation
singularity, concrete 169–71, 178, 202, 266–7, 268, 299, 349, 368; and concrete universal 114, 129–31, 133, 171, 178–9, 199, 209, 222, 385; and judgement 178–9, 200, 382; and morality 221, 264, 273, 292–3, 324, 381, see also freedom
social science: critical realist 2, 370, 378; as evaluative 259, 261–2, 289, 370; as explanatory critique 2, 157–8, 169, 172–3, 203, 208, 259, 261–4, 321; as science 155, 156–8, 258, see also axiology, emancipatory
socialism: crisis 2, 48, 193, 203, 300, 367–9; and freedom 288, 294–5, 366
sociology 93–4, 144, 146, 193; individualist 193–4, 233, 359
solidarity 179, 180–1, 221–2, 259, 261, 285, 289, 294, 382
solipsism 181, 186, 194, 232, 318, 355–6, 383
sophrosune see balance
Soul, Beautiful 71, 74, 167–8, 197, 279, 311, 326–9, 362, 374, see also alienation
spatio-temporality 155–6, 198, 403–4; and absence 257, 371; and causality 44–5, 53–4, 77, 83n., 114, 141, 145–6, 198, 210, 232, 377, 379–80; and change 53, 83, 257; closure 129–30, 252, 373; and concrete universal 129–30; disembedding 49, 251, 257; emergent 39, 53–4, 83n., 125, 198, 201–2, 251, 257–8, 273, 299; as five-fold 251, 403; as irreducible 210, 256, 299, 301; and negativity 239, 243; reality of 210, 252–3, 255, see also distanciation; irrealism; tense
spirit, absolute 18, 113, 118, 331, 337, 343, 363
split 17, 257, 277, 304–5, 312; and actualism 181–2, 237; and third level 42, 118, 321, 357, 380, 384
split-off 146, 201, 237, 274; and third level 42, 53, 184, 208, 305–7, 380
squeeze, primal 337, 402; and irrealism 111, 115, 121, 181, 184–5, 194, 199, 309,